AF352693

*Conservative Thought and American
Constitutionalism since the New Deal*

Conservative Thought and American Constitutionalism since the New Deal

Johnathan O'Neill

Johns Hopkins University Press
Baltimore

Johns Hopkins University Press
2715 North Charles Street
Baltimore, Maryland 21218
www.press.jhu.edu

Library of Congress Cataloging-in-Publication Data is available.

ISBN 978-1-4214-4462-8 (hardcover)
ISBN 978-1-4214-4463-5 (ebook)

A catalog record for this book is available from the British Library.

*Special discounts are available for bulk purchases of this book. For more information,
please contact Special Sales at specialsales@jh.edu.*

CONTENTS

ACKNOWLEDGMENTS

This book examines how various types of conservative thinkers assessed the American constitutional order in the second half of the twentieth century. The analysis traces major ideas and schools of thought that both criticized and adapted to the developments that surrounded them. It is offered with the hope that vigorous debate about the need for constitutional change and the requirement of constitutional preservation will remain an abiding component of American political thought.

This study matured over several years, prolonged by the velvet bonds of domesticity and a too-long stint as department chair. Along the way portions of it were presented at a conference at the University of Texas at Austin School of Law at the kind invitation of Professor Sanford V. Levinson; and at the Rothermere American Institute, University of Oxford, England, at the kind invitation of Professor Paul Kerry during his fellowship there. Material support came from the Earhart Foundation and the Georgia Southern University Faculty Development fund. The University System of Georgia's GIL Express system, connecting all of the state's university libraries, was an indispensable and reliable resource, as was the friendly staff at the Zach S. Henderson Library on my home campus. I am grateful to Laura Davulis at Johns Hopkins University Press for her interest in the project and her professionalism throughout the process of publication. I also thank Steven Baker for the expert copyediting that improved the clarity of the book.

Two friends and fine scholars, Paul D. Moreno and Joseph Postell, kindly read the final manuscript and provided insights and corrections that improved it. For encouragement and support over the years I thank them and Alan Levine, Vincent Phillip Muñoz, James R. Stoner Jr., and Keith E. Whittington. My thinking about constitutionalism continues to be influenced by Herman Belz, the teacher who set the example in so many ways. I am grateful to my brother, the political theorist Daniel I. O'Neill, for understanding me as only a brother can, for innumerable heartening conversations, and for the now-only-occasional rollicking good time.

My greatest debt is to my family, whose love and forbearance sustained my efforts. As we move into our third decade of marriage, I remain both fortunate and thankful to have found Rebecca all those years ago in Maryland. This book was written as we watched our little girls grow into strong and versatile young women. For Annie and Maggie, know that your love and your talents too helped ensure that it was completed.

I gratefully acknowledge permissions granted by the following publishers to adapt and use material from earlier essays: "Constitutional Conservatism and American Conservatism," in *NOMOS LVI: American Conservatism*, edited by Sanford V. Levinson, Joel Parker, and Melissa S. Williams (New York University Press, 2016), 292–335; "Traditionalist Conservatism and the Administrative State: The Diagnosis of a New Social Form," *Political Science Reviewer* 42, no. 2 (December 2018): 398–430; "The South and American Constitutionalism after the Civil War," in *The Political Thought of the Civil War*, edited by Alan Levine, Thomas W. Merrill, and James R. Stoner Jr., published by the University Press of Kansas, © 2018, used by permission of publisher; "Straussian Constitutional History and the Straussian Political Project," *Rethinking History: The Journal of Theory and Practice* 13, no. 4 (December 2009): 459–78, used by permission of the publisher, Taylor & Francis Ltd., http://www.tandfonline .com; "The First Conservatives: The Constitutional Challenge to Progressivism," www.heritage.org, July 5, 2011.

*Conservative Thought and American
Constitutionalism since the New Deal*

Introduction

Varieties of American Conservatism after the New Deal

American conservative thinkers varied in their responses to the transformation of constitutional institutions wrought by the New Deal in the 1930s and elaborated by the Great Society in the 1960s. This book argues that different kinds of conservatives deployed their respective core principles to criticize the new order and to defend those aspects of American constitutionalism they most valued. While continually disagreeing with one another and sometimes with aspects of the Constitution, they agreed that defending it was better than abandoning it—even as they necessarily adjusted and accommodated themselves to the post–New Deal reality. Conservative thought shaped conceptions of constitutional propriety and possibility, instigated lines of argument that eventuated in concrete political actions, and bounded what could be considered the legitimate reach of the modern American state. This book is the first to explain the full scope and complexity of this important feature of American political thought.

As an intellectual history this study takes ideas seriously and strives to understand thinkers as they understood themselves. Conservative constitutional thought existed in a broader political and social context, to be sure, but ideas are not explained in terms of subpolitical urges or by reducing them to their environment. Nor is there direct concern here with the formation of conservative identities as a matter of political sociology.[1] Instead the focus is on how conservative thinkers understood the institutional arrangements of the New Deal order. Consequently, the criteria for selecting the figures analyzed are that they saw themselves as conservative in some sense—not as progressive liberals—and that from their differing perspectives they assessed the changes in the structure, relationship, and role of constitutional institutions.

At the end of the past century, much-noted calls for historians to give more attention to American conservatism prompted an outpouring of scholarship on nearly every aspect of the subject.[2] Excellent studies were published on suburban grassroots activism, the shape of Republican party building and electoral successes in the South, the influence of evangelicals, the role of racism and affirmative action—and the list goes on. This rich literature makes it clear that conservatism in some form has always been woven into American history—no longer can it be simply dismissed as a reactionary atavism or a mere "backlash" against inevitable liberal "progress." Yet constitutional issues and institutions on which conservatives focused have been mostly ignored, especially since the New Deal. Historians have been preoccupied with social and cultural modes of analysis and have mostly ceded constitutional questions to political scientists and law professors. Although this book does repeatedly cite authors from those disciplines as both scholarly interpreters and subjects of analysis, another of its major goals is to retrieve the neglected subject of constitutional history and combine it with the examination of distinctly conservative ideas.

This study is rooted in the premise that, in a constitutional regime, intellectual-political debate about the legitimacy and authority of institutions gradually shapes and limits the options available in everyday politics. Topics such as the populist far right, religious identity, or single-issue interest groups are treated only incidentally in what follows. These developments typically had more particularized or immediate concerns that were part of the context of the broader discourse I focus on but rarely involved sustained consideration of the nature and tendency of American constitutionalism as a form of political order. This is not to say they were unimportant or inconsequential but rather that in my interpretation these developments occurred within the parameters of what intellectual-political discourse made possible or acceptable for conservatives in the New Deal order.

The New Deal sets this book's point of departure: it was the fundamental turning point in twentieth-century constitutional history that realized in practice many Progressive conceptions of political science, jurisprudence, and constitutional change from the preceding few decades.[3] This basic claim is uncontroversial and is affirmed by scholars writing in several different fields and from a variety of perspectives.[4] One need not look far for judgments that the New Deal was a constitutional "revolution," or the creation of a new "system" or "order," or perhaps even a "refounding." The realization of Progressivism in the New Deal displaced the old model of dual federalism, along with a Congress that was locally rooted and relatively strong in comparison to the executive. The Supreme Court endorsed the centralized, interventionist, and bureaucratic governance of the modern regulatory welfare state, and with it the Progressive conception of the Constitution as a "living" document that must change with the times—often via the president's tutelary leadership of public opinion. American constitutionalism was thus fundamentally reordered. As shown in the introductory overviews to parts I through IV of this book, a new administrative state was created, federalism was severely eroded, and more powerful modern forms of the presidency and judicial review emerged. Most aspects of the New Deal order were further advanced as the century went on, and occasionally pared back at the margins, but its basic form remained.

Constitutions change, but they do not turn on a dime. The New Deal did not wholly erase the inherited understanding of the US Constitution as a written fundamental law made for a federal polity, a law whose forms and procedures bound all institutions and officers according to the underlying theory of natural rights and government by consent. That older view was more overwhelmed by the New Deal than killed off. The new dispensation was laid over its predecessor without fully undoing the reality or the memory of what was defeated. This perspective accords in a general way with the understanding of the relationship among political order, institutions, and change developed in the subfield of American political development. It proposes that politics be studied as the interaction of different political "orders," which typically form at different times and with differing logics of authority whose manifestation in institutions persists over time. Political orders and their constituent institutions overlap and contest one another. Political actors vary in their orientations toward them, accepting and using the logic and authority of some while resisting that of others. The result is not a smoothly integrated "system" with a mainspring that brings lesser parts into full coherence or equilibrium until replaced by another system but is instead a far less distinct intermingling of order and change. A chief feature is that "the passage of time is filled with contentious interactions among different ordering arrangements."[5] Accordingly, this book frequently refers to the New Deal as an "order" (or sometimes more loosely as a "system"), insofar as the political and institutional changes of that period endured thereafter, marking a substantial alteration in the aims, methods, and authority of

American government. But again, these changes did not completely destroy what came before, nor did they wholly determine what came after, in the realms of either institutional development or intellectual-political debate. Conservatives recalled and defended elements of the old order, combined and deployed them with their own core principles, and continually criticized and contested the New Deal order as they discerned their places within it.

This conceptual frame helps further delimit this book's primary subject. In analyzing the ideas and arguments that conservatives used to assess the institutional and political patterns installed by the New Deal, the book considers specialized legal and jurisprudential topics only secondarily. Much of the recent scholarship on constitutional conservatism has focused on jurisprudence, legal argument, and litigation (including my own earlier book on originalism).[6] Valuable as they are, such works analyze mostly lawyerly arguments and the institutional infrastructure and organizational strategies that conservatives used to advance their agendas before the Supreme Court, often on very particular sets of issues. The creation of new organizations to propagate conservative jurisprudence and to win lawsuits was certainly an aspect of the overall conservative response to modern judicial review, as such scholarship helps us to see. Yet the legal-jurisprudential issues that have received so much recent attention were surrounded and nurtured by a broader conservative constitutional discourse about the authority and reach of the New Deal order. This book explicates how this criticism's deep and variegated roots provided the conceptual grammar, perspective, and audience not only for originalism, the Federalist Society, and issue-oriented litigation campaigns but also for consequential developments in numerous other areas beyond law and jurisprudence. It is hoped that this expanded scope will enrich our understanding of the interaction and cross-pollination of conservative thought with more discrete and technical legal-jurisprudential developments.

The Varieties of American Conservative Thought: Core Principles

The central tenets and fundamental cleavages among the schools of American conservatism have been the subject of definition and differentiation for some time. Previous scholarship enables the presentation of a compressed overview of these schools' primary features. The following is a synopsis and not an exhaustive portrait, one geared toward an explication of the ideas most relevant to conservatives' assessment of post–New Deal constitutionalism. It is also a composite statement designed to orient the subsequent analysis; not every figure in each category would necessarily accede to all aspects of these descriptions.[7]

Traditionalists

Traditionalist conservatism valorizes the cultural and local realm of life apart from the public and political, which are secondary. Traditionalists say that a worthwhile and truly human existence is rooted in family, community, culture, and, often but not always, religion. A constitution emerges to protect and facilitate a society's understanding of the good and virtuous life as experienced on an authentically human scale. Sometimes this view is announced by saying that the written constitution of governmental forms and procedures expresses, and is ultimately subservient to, the unwritten constitution of culture and custom. Many traditionalists are deeply indebted to Edmund Burke. They typically emphasize the English and Christian roots of American civilization, as well as its ties to the natural law tradition of the West. Burkean conservatism was central to Russell Kirk's influential *The Conservative Mind* and subsequently was applied more specifically to American constitutionalism in a book he subtitled *Reflections on Our Conservative Constitution*.[8] In addition, Southern Agrarianism (which Kirk admired) is properly understood as a form of traditionalist conservatism. Originally a pre–New Deal literary and cultural defense of southern distinctiveness, it continued to have at least some influence in constitutional politics into the 1980s and 1990s. In those decades some traditionalists also adopted the label "paleoconservative" to distinguish themselves from neoconservatives (discussed below).[9]

Despite the American Revolution, traditionalists often emphasized the continuities between colonial America and the newly independent nation.[10] The rebellious colonists fought to continue their practice of local self-government and to defend the traditional, common law rights of Englishmen from a distant but meddling empire. Indeed, following Burke, traditionalists insisted that 1776 was "a revolution not made, but prevented." Both the Declaration of Independence and the Constitution were outgrowths and articulations of a long-established understanding of politics and government. The founding of America was thus a conservative act and by no means a revolutionary upheaval. While not wholly denying the relevance of John Locke, natural rights, and social contract theory, traditionalists downplayed their significance and subsumed them into their larger narrative of continuity. The Declaration especially was read against the background of the common law and natural law traditions, diminishing the innovation and universality that other conservatives associated with it.[11] The result, often quite explicit, was rejection of the claim that natural rights and human equality were the definitive American ends that the Constitution was meant to secure. That account of the American founding was said to be historically inaccurate and, especially since Abraham Lincoln, to have unleashed a messianic, ideological politics of individualism and egalitarianism that had all but effaced the proper understanding of American constitutionalism.[12]

The traditionalist vision of the constitutional order thus held that its aims were less modern and more circumspect than what became of it. Originally constitutionalism was structural and procedural, establishing only the methods by which a religious and republican people deliberated and governed itself under God. To distinguish this view from the mistaken one that elevated the Declaration, figures such as Willmoore Kendall and George Carey and M. E. Bradford employed Michael Oakeshott's distinction between "nomocratic" and "teleocratic" political orders.[13] A nomocratic order established modes of operation for conducting official business in accord with the established customs of society, while a teleocratic order sought the ever fuller realization of an abstract end or goal. The Constitution originally had been nomocratic—encouraging moderation and deliberation about common concerns according to set procedures and limits—but it had become increasingly teleocratic, transformed by the crusade for greater equality and more rights, often in the name of the Declaration.[14] The move from a nomocratic to a teleocratic regime was the fundamental "derailment" of the American tradition that traditionalists regarded as the source of the nation's constitutional and political ills. A debasing, incomplete modern politics of rights and equality had become sovereign over what was once a Christian humanist culture, necessarily miscasting the original purpose of American constitutionalism and skewing its subsequent development. Traditionalists argued that American constitutionalism, at least originally, was not fundamentally modern and liberal, and not the first instantiation of a new universalism of natural rights and equality.[15] Rather, it was the humble attempt of a people to sustain their established mode of deliberative and consensual self-government, under the ultimate judgment of their God.[16]

Thus it has been well said that the traditionalist brand of conservatism (sometimes also called "old Right" conservatism) had no positive political program other than " 'containing liberalism' [or] 'boxing in' liberal justice."[17] What traditionalists have most wanted from American constitutionalism is what they insisted the founding had achieved: a limited federal government that intruded only minimally into state and local affairs, so that families, churches, and communities could foster the good life according to inherited conceptions of morality, virtue, and justice.[18] After the New Deal, traditionalists became increasingly pessimistic that any such constitutional project was still viable.

Libertarians

Libertarians aimed always to maximize individual liberty and support the un-coerced "spontaneous order" of society rather than state control.[19] The latter idea, derived most directly from the Scottish Enlightenment, held that as individuals pursue their own ends and interact with one another, a coordinated and evolving order arises—one that is patterned without being designed or directed. The market is the essential spontaneous order in the libertarian worldview. It efficiently coordinates production and distribution through mutually beneficial, voluntary exchanges that reflect individual self-interest as pursued in light of the information contained in the price mechanism. It is a key tenet of libertarianism, as developed especially in the work of Ludwig von Mises and Friedrich A. Hayek, that a centrally planned (socialist) economy is impossible: no single entity can process the widely dispersed knowledge necessary for economic efficiency.

In nearly all situations, libertarians privilege human freedom and reject coercion by the state. This dedication to individual liberty was sometimes rooted forthrightly in the theory of natural rights, especially as articulated by John Locke and the Declaration of Independence, which he so influenced. Sometimes liberty was treated in a utilitarian and consequentialist fashion, as a social construction or inherited custom that has proven attractive and efficient over time. Liberty and the market as a spontaneous order reinforced each other because the latter was based on freely chosen exchanges among individuals who competitively pursued their own interests. Another hallmark of libertarianism was tolerance of others' self-regarding and "victimless" activities or associations, most saliently in the realms of drug use and sexuality. Likewise, libertarians favored a foreign policy based on the proposition that free trade brings prosperity and peace, and they opposed mercantilism, colonial conquest, and most armed intervention not directly related to self-defense.

In its moderate form, libertarianism advocated the minimal state and the large sphere of individual liberty broadly characteristic of the nineteenth-century American polity. The term "libertarian" is now often used interchangeably with "classical liberal": both emerged in contradistinction to the larger and more interventionist state of twentieth-century "progressive liberalism" and social democracy.[20] Moderate libertarians accepted a small range of "public goods" as legitimate subjects of state provision or regulation. More radical or pure libertarians denied the very concept. Radical libertarianism tended toward anarchism, or perhaps "anarcho-capitalism." On this view, market exchanges can satisfy all or nearly all human needs, and to the extent that government existed, it was responsible for enforcing property rights and the principles of tort and contract. Some radical libertarians even suggested that roadways, policing, and national defense could be contracted to private corporations.

Whether moderate or extreme, libertarians were confident that they knew the truth about political things, and they had a very certain positive program. Politics was always about "liberty versus power" and "man versus the state." The libertarian goal was simply to defend the first from the inevitable depredations of the second. This understanding distanced early forms of libertarianism from American constitutionalism, as in the case of Albert Jay Nock (1870–1945), a journalist and author who remained a foundational figure for the libertarian movement. The state was in essence a criminal enterprise, the "political means" for expropriation from honest folk who made their living by productive "economic means." This was as true in the United States as anywhere else, and Nock did not think much of the Constitution or any claim of a principled politics in defense of it.[21] Nock inspired Murray Rothbard, an influential postwar libertarian who was always willing to advance his views by alliances of convenience with everyone from anti-Vietnam hippies to Patrick Buchanan. But his libertarianism-cum-anarchism also pronounced the Constitution a failure. Perhaps unsurprisingly, in his self-described "extremist" vision, the New Deal would go. But so too would the Federal Reserve and Internal Revenue Service. Rothbard would "not stop until we repealed the Federal Judiciary Act of 1789, and maybe even think the unthinkable and restore the good old Articles of Confederation."[22]

Such deep antistatism continued to lead some notable post–New Deal libertarians to extremist rejection of American constitutionalism, but that stance gradually diminished. An influential early example of greater rapprochement was Hayek's admiration for the original American Constitution. He admired its protection of liberty through the rule of law: it compelled government to act according to previously announced, general principles that could not be suspended by those in power. This crucial fact was what gave Americans "a constitution of liberty, a constitution that would protect the individual against all arbitrary coercion." Consequently, Americans had "been able to defend freedom by defending their Constitution."[23] Although Hayek developed doubts about the long-term prospects of the American project, he did not think it had originated as just another corrupt act of statist pilfering. In this regard it is notable that Randy E. Barnett, a leading libertarian who is treated in several of the following chapters, seemingly took a cue from Hayek's praise of both the Ninth

Amendment and the Privileges or Immunities Clause of the Fourteenth Amendment by featuring them in his own constitutional theory. Reconsidered in the right way, then, the Constitution could be squared with foundational elements of libertarianism.[24]

Straussians

Leo Strauss (1899–1973) was a German Jewish émigré scholar of the history of political thought and a central figure in post–World War II conservative intellectual history. He led a return to the "Great Books" of Western civilization to reencounter their teachings about reason, nature, God, and morality.[25] Strauss said this reconsideration was urgent because Western civilization was in crisis. It had come to doubt or disbelieve its own claims of justice and right. No longer did revealed religion set the moral standard of society. Enlightenment rationalism had not only failed to bring universal prosperity, freedom, and justice but was no longer sure what was right by nature or whether there was a human nature apart from historical circumstance. The modern crisis was the inability to "know what is good and bad, what is right and wrong."[26] Moderns had become convinced that neither reason nor revelation could answer the fundamental human question of Socrates: "What is the best way of life?" Strauss's most famous work addressed the problem by considering the conflict between the idea of natural right and historicism, and between natural right and a modern social science based on the fact-value distinction.[27]

Strauss traced the crisis of the West to "three waves of modernity," the trend in political thought that had displaced ancient political philosophy and biblical morality with historicism, positivism, and nihilism.[28] From Machiavelli to Hobbes and Locke, on through Rousseau, and finally to Nietzsche and Heidegger, Western thought had steadily abandoned its traditional attempt to discern universal truths and then to live by them. Instead it had endorsed materialism, appetite, and the claim that all standards were time and culture bound, and hence meaningless. Finally, modern thought had arrived at the conscious construction of "values" to govern one's self and perhaps others—self-creation and the will to power. In this way modern rationalism had self-destructed. There was now a grave danger in the absence of standards by which to condemn, say, the Nazis. There was also an opportunity, which Strauss pursued: a way out of the crisis via recovery of the confrontation between the conceptions of morality and human excellence found in the Bible and the ancient idea of natural right. This project, in turn, required the conservation of modern regimes that permitted such a recovery, such as the United States. As a refugee from the Nazis, Strauss keenly appreciated this point, though he remained a friendly critic of American shortcomings as he understood them.[29] Indeed, he stated more emphatically than was typical of him that an education in the great ideas of Western civilization, particularly after communism and fascism, taught that "wisdom cannot be separated from moderation" and hence that "wisdom requires unhesitating loyalty to a decent constitution and even to the cause of constitutionalism."[30]

Strauss did not study the United States directly, but this teaching enabled his students to take seriously the political theory of the nation's founding and its constitution. But in doing so they faced a problem. As one recent study put it, for Strauss modernity was "bad" because it was low. Basing politics on passions-cum-rights, modern regimes built on and perpetuated an impoverished vision of humanity. And America was modern. It was derived most fundamentally from Locke's theories of rights, consent, and social contract. The United States as a regime had not attempted to cultivate virtue or to defer to the rule of the wise. Moreover, it had proven susceptible to successive destructive waves of modernity, thus endangering its once stable, though flawed or incomplete, foundation. Yet Strauss's students, who saw the critique of America inherent in his teaching, still wanted to affirm that America was "good" and that its constitutionalism was worthy of defense and preservation.[31] The solution to this problem, recently described by James W. Ceaser as "the core of 'Straussianism' insofar as it has become a project of American political thought," was "to restore the possibility of the idea of natural right" but "in a way that takes into account the shortcomings of the modern doctrine of natural rights and that seeks to modify or correct it."[32]

Approaches differed on how best to do so. But, in general, Straussians considered the origin, development, and current tendency of American politics and constitutionalism from the perspectives of Platonic political philosophy and Aristotelian political science. The ancients could help to "modify" or "correct" America in light of the older, better understanding of human beings, philosophy, and politics. These efforts produced protracted and occasionally vehement disagreements among those who differently elaborated the apparently conflicting aspects of Strauss's designedly veiled and ambiguous teaching. The full substance of these debates cannot be engaged here, though appreciating their basic contours clarifies the differing versions of the Straussian approach to American constitutionalism.

"West Coast" Straussians, led by Harry V. Jaffa (1918–2015), defended the philosophy of natural rights and social contract as America's definitive political basis but did so in a way that sought to exempt or insulate it from the ensuing destructive waves of modernity. This move depended on the contestable claim that the founders understood only Locke's surface teaching, supposedly compatible with Aristotle and Christianity, or else that Locke's true teaching was in fact so (despite Strauss's apparent view that Locke's doctrine of rights and consent rested on the Hobbesian ground of materialism and atheism). Jaffa and his students held that "nature and nature's God," as announced in the Declaration and further explicated by Lincoln, grounded human equality and natural rights. "All men are created equal" in that they are above mere animals but beneath perfection or god. Human equality was thus an abstract truth applicable in all times and places, though it could be described in either Aristotelian or Christian terms. Either description generated the duty to respect other people as expressed in the language of rights, which in turn justified limited government based on consent.[33] On this view, Lincoln had recalled America to the Aristotelian politics and Christian morality embodied in the proper understanding of its founding principles—the philosophical truth of its political tradition. He had not needed to "refound" the nation to correct its modern errors. Therefore, the way to combat modern decline was with "a straightforward and patriotic return to the founders" and to Lincoln's unsurpassed defense of their achievement.[34] This understanding of natural rights and limited government was the basis for and the original purpose of American constitutionalism. Evaluating subsequent constitutional developments by this standard, West Coast Straussians aimed to resist and contain various manifestations of the second and third waves of modernity.

"East Coast" Straussians, once led by Allan Bloom, were more intransigently Platonic in doubting that any appeal to nature in politics ultimately could be justified by reason. Consequently, this group intervened less directly in political affairs. Indeed, some East Coasters inclined toward a detached philosophical contemplation that quietly accepted its tension with all claims of moral virtue or political right.[35] Likewise, the East characteristically held that since Strauss's basic negative judgment on modernity clearly applied to the United States, it always needed modification and elevation by principles from outside modern natural right.[36] One result of that view was an emphasis on education, in particular an inquiry into the great contest of ideas in Western civilization and consideration of where America stands in light of them. Such an education could produce "a renewed, thoughtful, and therefore undogmatic or reasonably qualified appreciation for the strength and validity of the principles underlying our Constitution."[37] Nevertheless, another important finding of this inquiry was that the American founders' emphasis on individual rights and institutional architecture slighted the education of citizens. They must be taught the virtues and morals proper to republican self-government if it was to endure.[38] In a similar vein, East Coast Straussians frequently drew on the Aristotelianism of Alexis de Tocqueville's *Democracy in America*. It offered the best statement of the premodern elements in the United States that fostered the virtues and morals necessary to sustain it against mass democracy's individualism and relativism—especially the ethic of moral self-restraint derived from Christianity and sustained in local government and civic association.[39]

Another eastern approach, exemplified by Harvey C. Mansfield Jr., was to argue that American constitutionalism contains opportunities within itself to be better than its modern elements. Virtue was "called forth" without ensuring the practice of it, and likewise the Constitution fostered reasoned deliberation about the public good without guaranteeing it would happen. The presidency was a prime example of an office that creates only the opportunity, but not the certainty, that its occupant will act virtuously or reasonably. Mansfield similarly argued that representation, federalism, and the separation of powers provided opportunities to moderate and elevate public opinion toward reason and the common good. This "constitutional space" between popular will and government action facilitated (again, without guaranteeing) deliberative and informed self-government.[40]

Straussians were thus conservative defenders of American constitutionalism who nevertheless thought it had weaknesses or blind spots that must be actively addressed. They echoed and elaborated Strauss's own statement, itself an application of ancient political science, that "we are not permitted to be flatterers of democracy precisely because we are friends and allies of democracy."[41] Moreover, despite the differences captured in the "East versus West" labels, as Ceaser has concluded, Straussians "agree on the need for a political foundation in America based on a regulating idea of natural right that combines the substance of modern rights with the appreciation of certain classical virtues."[42] Prepared by Strauss to consider America anew in light of the ancients, Straussians aimed to preserve, supplement, and improve American constitutionalism as the best possible regime under modern conditions.

Neoconservatives

Neoconservatism swirled around the periphery of these more established and recognizable forms of conservatism. Often described as an intellectual-political "tendency" or "persuasion," it has remained notoriously difficult to define. In large measure this was because neoconservatives began as liberals and endured as a small but diverse lot that often incorporated the principles of other conservatives without following precisely any single doctrine.[43]

Neoconservatism originated among anticommunist liberals (previously some had been socialists or Trotskyists) who accepted the central regulatory-welfare tenets of the New Deal. In the 1960s neoconservatives grew disappointed by the results of Great Society reformism and alarmed at the destructive hedonism and anti-Americanism of the New Left and the counterculture. Led by Irving Kristol at *The Public Interest* and Norman Podhoretz at *Commentary*, the characteristic neoconservative critique of Great Society reforms was that centrally administered social engineering by the federal government often foundered on the realities of human nature, culture, and local circumstance. Modern American government was overloaded with quasi-utopian tasks it could not perform, having grown overconfident in the ability of social science and expertise to cure social ills and create a fully egalitarian society.

A central component of the neoconservative critique was the idea of the "new class." This social stratum, said neoconservatives, was made up of highly educated professionals, managers, consultants, many university faculty, government bureaucracies, the media, and the burgeoning public interest litigation and legal aid sectors. The new class both advocated and benefited from interventionist government. Neoconservatives undertook to battle the new class, arguing instead for more private social ordering, market competition, and traditional values that emphasized family, community, individual self-restraint, and equal opportunity. These themes did indeed echo other types of conservatism. Yet neoconservatives found the older, traditionalist conservatism of custom and prescription to be hidebound and unavailing in the modern age of technological innovation, commerce, and mass communication. Likewise, libertarianism often seemed too close to the libertine self-indulgence and bacchanalian nihilism of the 1960s, and therefore incapable of sustaining the old-style liberal bourgeois society neoconservatives supported. Neoconservatives usually did not engage constitutional issues as directly or elaborately as the other schools of conservatism. However, they existed for decades alongside the others and staked out important positions that merit attention amid the broader constitutional debate.

Another basic element of neoconservatism was support for an activist foreign policy and opposition to the post-Vietnam drift into "détente" and "coexistence" with communism. Once the Cold War concluded, neoconservatives continued to advocate an interventionist foreign policy and soon crashed into the center of public attention after the terrorist attacks of September 11, 2001. The fraught question of this development's relation to the thought of Leo Strauss is addressed in chapter 7.

Of course, conservative thinkers often interacted with their confrères and with those of differing principles, engaging in debates, disagreements, alliances, and occasionally in outright intellectual feuds. Individuals rarely shifted from one school to another, though they sometimes accepted or adapted the arguments of others. Likewise, individuals were occasionally "purged" beyond the realm of respectable opinion by erstwhile companions. It would overly disrupt the exposition in the following chapters to justify the categorization of every thinker in every instance. In general I have sorted writers by their self-described orientation, their intellectual lineage and associations, and their basic approach to the topics under discussion. Various compendia have likewise been consulted.[44] Inevitably some categorical placements are more tenuous than others, and some intellectual connections weaker than others, but no claims about influence or affiliation have been made baselessly or pejoratively.

As for conservatives' principled disagreements, feuds, and purges, they are well documented and well explicated in the now substantial scholarly literature. Perhaps the paradigmatic instance was *National Review*'s banishment from its environs of some radical libertarians and far-Right extremists. Also well known among scholars was Harry Jaffa's series of attacks on anyone (traditionalists most often) he deemed insufficiently grounded in the Declaration of Independence and the statesmanship of Abraham Lincoln. These intellectual debates and overt clashes, some very public and by now rather familiar, typically turned on the philosophical differences sketched above, often by disputing the first principles of the American founding and the meaning of the Civil War and Reconstruction. This book does not reconstruct each of these conflicts or debates, in part because it has been done so well by others and in part because these episodes rarely pertained directly to the ways American conservatives assessed the specifically constitutional-institutional problems of the post–New Deal era. Their more abstract battles over philosophical first principles and historical meaning are accounted for when they impinged demonstrably on conservatives' constitutional analysis.[45]

Structure of the Book

Parts I through IV open with a definition and synthetic historical overview of each of the basic institutional transformations that made up the post–New Deal constitutional order: the rise of the administrative state, the erosion of federalism, the ascendance of the modern presidency, and the development of modern judicial review. These compressed summaries of what judges, lawyers, executive branch officials, and politicians were doing chart the basic shape of American constitutionalism in the modern era. Chapters in each part then consider how different conservatives responded. The subjects of parts I and II lend themselves to the same order of presentation (traditionalists, neoconservatives, libertarians, Straussians), while parts III and IV deviate somewhat from this sequence in order to better represent the temporal dynamics of the arguments they treat. Relatedly, the rise of the "unitary executive" as a defense and elaboration of modern presidential power was not derived directly from any of the established schools of conservatism, but all of them contended with it to some extent. This theory is treated in relation to the administrative state in chapter 2 and in relation to foreign policy in chapter 6. Similarly, modern judicial review induced all conservatives except neoconservatives to take up litigation as a way to defend and advance their principles. This development is analyzed briefly at the end of chapter 10. The conclusion considers how the varieties of conservatism (again excepting neoconservatism) approached Congress, the institution they most frequently slighted or maligned, yet the one with the most authority to address the numerous problems of post–New Deal constitutionalism that so concerned them.

Looking at American conservatism through the particular lens of constitutional thought underscores that the New Deal altered the basic template of the nation's politics and institutions in ways that conservatives simply could not undo. Whatever their deepest political principles, conservatives' orientation toward the preservation of constitutional fundamentals could never be truly counterrevolutionary. Instead they had to adapt and find their way within the new order, though often they did so reluctantly and inconsistently. Likewise, because distinctive forms of conservatism often conflicted with one another, and sometimes with the Constitution itself irrespective of the New Deal transformation, constitutional discourse could cohere or rally conservatives only to a limited extent. It did so up to a point because conservatives wanted both to advance their respective views amid the realities of the new order and to affirm the Constitution as much as possible. But underlying principled disagreements inhibited a more integrated view that might have made conservatives more unified and therefore more consequential in concrete and politically programmatic ways. This limitation puts conservatives' too frequent neglect (and sometimes outright hostility) toward Congress in a more troubling light. That approach now appears shortsighted and dangerous in ways that conservative constitutionalists might have paid more attention to, and still could amid today's pressing concerns about polarization, incivility, and the nearly dead art of compromise.

PART ONE

THE ADMINISTRATIVE STATE

An Overview

In the late nineteenth century, Congress began creating institutions to regulate specific industries or sectors of the economy based on social scientific expertise and a generally Progressive conception of the public good. These regulatory bureaucracies expanded into numerous areas over the course of the twentieth century. This growth was a complex process of legal and institutional evolution that, though usually opaque to everyday people, gradually produced rules and regulations that keenly affected their lives. Liberal reformist political opinion came to identify this development with "progress" itself. Consequently, regulatory bureaucracies were central to the New Deal order and were again invigorated from the mid-1960s through the mid-1970s. A blow-by-blow narration of these shifts and their accompanying doctrinal bases need not be delineated here. What had become abundantly clear by the middle of the twentieth century was that the "administrative state," through its bureaus and agencies, had legal governing authority, delegated by Congress, over the liberty, property, and myriad social interactions of nearly all citizens and businesses.[1]

Attempts to accommodate bureaucratized regulatory practices placed significant strain on the constitutional system. From one angle the administrative state was successfully "constitutionalized" insofar as American bureaucracies achieved neither wholly unified and concentrated power nor the command-

and-control authority characteristic of a European-style state. Rather, regulatory bureaucracy was compelled to adapt to America's pluralistic political culture, with its penchant for limiting, diffusing, and checking official power through the forms and processes of the separation of powers and the rule of law.[2] Progressive and New Deal state builders were limited, sometimes despite their deepest wishes, by constitutional imperatives and existing institutional patterns. At all stages of its growth, the administrative state was subject to legal proceduralism, congressional oversight and revision, judicial review, and interest group political bargaining—all of which helped it become both more deeply entrenched, yet less overtly threatening.[3]

The administrative state is now a seemingly permanent and legitimate feature of the constitutional system, but Americans have never rested easy with it. It has challenged the nation's established preference for private ordering, individual choice, representative and accountable governance, and local control.[4] As nearly any serious study of the topic acknowledges, much of the concern has been about the "uncertain fit" of the administrative state within the Constitution's tripartite separation of powers.[5] Accordingly, a major feature of its history has been the ongoing battle for control between Congress and the executive as each branch has alternately sought to command or condemn it. This conflict occurred variously through the budgeting process, the reorganization and staffing of agencies, congressional oversight hearings about their actions, or some form of legislative veto or extra approval for major agency rules—all amid an intricate and confusing body of Supreme Court jurisprudence that waxed and waned in the amount of oversight and deference accorded to the agencies, Congress, and the president.[6] A related issue, which preceded the administrative state and intensified during its development, concerned just who in the government had the constitutional authority to remove administrative officials and for what reasons.[7] Accordingly, a defining feature of public administration as a field of scholarly inquiry has been the ongoing attempt to justify and constrain the power of government bureaucrats in light of the basic principles of the constitutional order.[8]

Concerns emerged early about the dubious constitutional legitimacy and methods of the administrative state. For decades it has been described in terms of extremity and crisis.[9] Consider its characteristic institution: a bureaucratic agency staffed by unelected subject-matter experts who have legal authority to regulate. Congress delegates some of its legislative authority to them. Typically the delegation describes the agency's remit in vague terms—in essence pointing it at a complex policy area and giving it vast discretion to govern based on its expertise. Under the terms of their organic statutes, plus the Administrative Procedure Act (1946), agencies issue rules and resolve disputes brought by entities affected in some way by those rules, often acting as negotiator, prosecutor, and judge. Under the *Chevron* decision (1984), the US Supreme Court will "defer" to an agency's reasonable interpretation of ambiguity in the statute that created it—thereby giving it considerable discretionary latitude.[10]

Not only are these officials unelected, but they are also difficult to displace. Cabinet heads serve at the pleasure of the president, but lesser officials typically can be removed only for causes that Congress has delineated. Since the famous case of *Humphrey's Executor v. United States* (1935), officials in independent agencies are not subject to at-will removal by the president. Accordingly, officials not readily accountable to the public nevertheless exercise—often in the same institution—legislative, executive, and judicial powers in pursuit of policy goals so vaguely stated as to require, despite their supposed basis in expertise, fundamentally political decisions. Thus the separation of powers and the rule of law are severely strained, if not wholly violated. A leading text on administrative law concludes that "the constitutional framers would roll over in their graves" if they knew the situation today.[11] Numerous, ongoing attempts at the regularization and restraint of administrative power have not overcome the basic problems of legitimacy and accountability.[12]

The administrative state was a product of Progressive liberalism. Having its beginning in Progressivism as a political reform movement and its dramatic success in the New Deal, its central aim was provision of social security through forms of government regulation and direction that truncated popular rule and private ordering. Consigned to the antediluvian past was the congressionally dominated, decentralized, and unruly party system, with its traditional suspicion of the federal government and especially the presidency. These were anachronisms that obstructed progress toward a more interventionist, centralized, and service-delivering state. The old way lost to the bureaucratic and executive-centered administration of regulatory and welfare programs, understood as new-style positive rights, which were themselves underwritten politically not by the party system but by mass popular acclaim for their articulation in presidential rhetoric. This was the aim of Franklin Roosevelt's call for an "economic declaration of rights" to be delivered by means of the new administrative state. "The day of enlightened administration has come," he declared. This shift to what is sometimes called "programmatic liberalism" fundamentally reshaped the party system, the presidency, and the power and reach of the federal government. The purposes and forms of once popular but limited government changed, as described in the pathbreaking work of Sidney M. Milkis. "Programs or benefits were presented as 'rights.' With the advent of the economic constitutional order, a commitment to limited government gave way to support for programmatic rights, for programs intended to guarantee the social and economic welfare of the individual. The tendency to view programs such as social security as 'entitlements' created a veritable 'administrative constitution' in which government programs were viewed as tantamount to rights, and thus worthy of protection from the vagaries of party politics and elections."[13]

This template was expanded in the new wave of regulation that began in the wake of the New Left politics of the 1960s. Encouraged by the enlivened discourse of rights, courts were drawn deeper into the governing dynamic along with administrative agencies, congressional subcommittees, and "public interest" groups. This process, and courts' role in it, took on even greater significance in the post-1968 period of partisan dealignment and divided government, especially after the Vietnam War and the presidency of Richard Nixon suggested that the executive branch might not always be a dependable ally of programmatic liberalism.[14] The administrative state marched on. Major government institutions and numerous private-interest groups likewise continued their contest for its direction and for its benefits, but its constitutional legitimacy remained suspect.

American conservatives thus confronted in the administrative state a controversial but well-established alteration of the constitutional system. They made sense of this change in relation to their understanding of that system and their own fundamental principles. As they regrouped after the New Deal and eventually became more intellectually and politically consequential, conservative critiques of the administrative state proceeded from several angles. These critiques were theoretical, considering the progressive liberal regulatory-bureaucratic state as a form of social and political order; historical, assessing how and why that order managed to displace much of the old constitutionalism; and legal, attempting to legitimate, constrain, and direct it within the terms of post–New Deal constitutional law and jurisprudence. In the last-named category was the theory of the "unitary executive," which emerged in the 1980s and 1990s. It was a more thoroughgoing defense of the presidency than had been typical of conservatism in earlier periods of American history, and was sustained in part by the jurisprudence of Supreme Court justice Antonin Scalia. Still, despite some chastening of liberal ambitions in the wake of the Great Society, and some pointed confrontations during the presidency of Ronald Reagan, by the end of the twentieth century, conservatives had little altered the basic course of the administrative state. But their explication and criticism continued and intensified. Today the administrative state is an object of growing concern for conservative scholars, politicians, jurists, and others interested in the nature and tendency of American constitutionalism.

CHAPTER ONE

Traditionalists, Neoconservatives, Libertarians, and the Administrative State

Traditionalists identified the administrative state as part of a deeper social transformation that challenged constitutionalism. They saw modern mass democracy as inducing a new elitist and managerial social form in which centralized government bureaucracies crowded out or subsumed private order and civil society. All of social life was supposedly coming under the sway of a "new class" of technocratic and managerial experts. The old constitutional system obstructed this change and thus was an obstacle to be overcome. Traditionalists' broad-gauge perspective meant that their analyses were usually rather abstract and general, more often in the vein of social theory and history than of law and jurisprudence.

Neoconservative skepticism about interventionist social policies led naturally to criticism of the administrative state and attacks on the "new class." Neoconservatives, too, generally eschewed legal and jurisprudential analysis and instead focused on the limited capacity of bureaucracy and social science expertise to effectuate sound policy. They had no designs on dismantling the modern state but argued that it could not deliver on many of its aims and therefore should be curtailed.

Libertarians built on the work of two towering thinkers, Friedrich A. Hayek and Ludwig von Mises, who diagnosed bureaucracy as a central manifestation of the modern state's challenge to individual liberty and the rule of law. Their influence fed into the rapid development of "public choice" criticism of bureaucracy in the second half of the twentieth century. This kind of analysis affirmed the basic libertarian desire for limited government, yet went further by doubting the very concept of the public good. Influenced by these ideas, more specifically constitutional libertarian commentary regarded the administrative state as plainly and profoundly incompatible with the Constitution as it had been originally understood.

Early Traditionalists

Scholars have rarely remarked on Russell Kirk's attention to what we now call the administrative state in *The Conservative Mind* (1953), his seminal statement of the traditionalist perspective.[1] Likely this is because of Kirk's larger emphasis on Edmund Burke and moral and cultural decay. Nevertheless, the characteristic traditionalist concern with locality, community, and civil society attuned Kirk to the looming threat of the "planned society" and the " 'cult of the strong remedial state' " run by a "super-bureaucracy" whose members were the "planners of the new order."[2] Kirk forecasted that "resistance to the idea of a planned society" would preoccupy twentieth-century conservatives. The "New Society" clearly aimed at "equality of condition" but augured even worse. It tended toward social control and the "destruction of all ancient political institutions in the interest of the new dominant elites."[3] Nor was the "central direction" of "social planners" likely to spare religion, the family, or private property in the name of such "progress."[4]

Kirk thus identified the administrative state with more clarity than he is usually credited. American constitutional democracy remained a source of political wisdom and hope that must be defended as a "system generally more friendly to liberty than any other in our age." The Constitution was a "sagacious conservative document" whose "balance of interests and powers" could thwart "centralization."[5]

Kirk called on Alexis de Tocqueville in seeking to understand the administrative state, as various kinds of conservatives did for the rest of the twentieth century. The dawning of the new order appeared to be "what Tocqueville predicted long ago as 'democratic despotism.' "[6] He quoted at length Tocqueville's now well-known description of the petty, anomic, yet comfortable lives of democratic citizens who are supervised by a centralized and tutelary state. Over several pages Kirk offered what one scholar has described as a "generally fair and judicious account" of Tocqueville's warning about how democracy and administrative centralization could combine into a new type of mild but degrading tyranny.[7] Kirk concurred with "Tocqueville's loathing for an existence like this," the ugly and terrifying "ideal of twentieth-century social planners."[8]

Robert A. Nisbet, a historical sociologist, social theorist, and traditionalist also was much influenced by Tocqueville, and Kirk had lauded Nisbet's *Quest for Community* (1953).[9] Nisbet's fundamental claim was that the rootlessness and hunger for community characteristic of contemporary life resulted from the modern democratic state's displacement of traditional groups and social forms in the name of equality. The rise of the centralized nation-state, especially once it allied with democratic equality, gradually dissolved or subsumed any form of community that lay between the individual and the state. Intermediary associations decayed as the state's centrally and bureaucratically administered policies took command of an ever greater number of spheres of life.[10] Nisbet called bureaucracy the "new despotism," a "fourth branch of government" that was "suffocating more and more of the freedoms and rights the Constitution was framed to protect."[11]

Nisbet (drawing on Tocqueville) said this change also produced "loose" or rootless individuals who then sought community, order, and security in the very state power that was destroying it. "To feel alone—does this not breed a desire for association in Leviathan?" The natural human quest for community, despite itself, fostered the growth of the interventionist democratic-bureaucratic state.[12] In the United States, the idea of a national community expressed in the state derived from the modern liberal project of Progressivism and the New Deal, which had installed "the gods of political centralization, collectivism, central planning, and devotion to national state over traditional society."[13] The older orientation of liberalism toward limited government was abandoned as the centralized state became the locus of "social rehabilitation."[14] Moreover, liberalism had come to understand this process as "progress"—the inevitable direction of history. The humanitarian amelioration of suffering and the provision of security, once found in traditional civil society, would now demand more centralized and bureaucratically administered government policies and programs.[15] Nor had the supposed conservative revival of the 1980s reversed this trend. Americans had seemingly gotten used to the "liberal provider-state" and the bureaucracy as "the bearer of goodies." Americans' response to bureaucracy and state centralization was to "curse it, deride it, abhor it, all the while they are beckoning it to them with one hand."[16]

The challenge of the administrative state informed Nisbet's understanding of conservatism as such. He pointedly defined "the sole object of the conservative tradition" as "the protection of the social order and its constitutive groups from the enveloping bureaucracy of the national state."[17] Conservative freedom was the "freedom of community and of association as well as of the individual. The problem of freedom is to protect the social ties intermediate to the individual and the state as buffers against the spreading power of governmental bureaucracy."[18] Conservatism thus understood was apparent in the structure of the Constitution, which protected individual and communal liberty by limiting, dividing, checking, and balancing the power of the central government. Individual and communal liberties "existed, as it were, in the interstices of the Constitution." It is notable that Nisbet approved Alexander Hamilton's resistance to a bill of rights, favoring instead older, more corporate and local conceptions of liberty.[19] Deemphasizing rights, contract, and legality, Nisbet articulated the characteristically traditionalist view that in protecting civil society and local custom, the Constitution was more ancient and medieval than modern. But he doubted that the postwar conservative renaissance had much chance of displacing the new order.[20]

Both Kirk and Nisbet saw the administrative state as part of a new social form sustained by a "new class" of intellectual-technocratic "managers"—a new elite with a vested interest in statist expansion. The basic idea of a new class had a long history, emerging initially from the concern in Marxist political discourse that bureaucracy was taking on interests of its own that opposed the scheduled takeover of the proletariat.[21] James Burnham developed this claim in *The Managerial Revolution* (1941), and both Kirk and Nisbet were influenced by him.[22] Burnham had a complicated intellectual genealogy. A former Trotskyist whose mature thought elaborated his understanding of Machiavelli's views on power and elites, he became a leading anticommunist and a major figure at *National Review*. Burnham is properly categorized as a traditionalist insofar as he held that social and political order depended on nonrational factors such as myth or tradition. Although he approved of the "social utility" of tradition rather than any specific content, and thus remained in tension with mainstream traditionalists, his arguments about the "managerial revolution" were crucial for the traditionalist assessment of the administrative state.[23]

Burnham drifted from his youthful Marxism without wholly jettisoning its structuralism and determinism. His initial aim was to explain why capitalism had not collapsed and why socialism in Stalin's Soviet Union had not moved smoothly into its predicted final phase. The "managerial revolution" had separated ownership from day-to-day control as part of the shift form entrepreneurial to corporate capitalism. Now this change was being elaborated and extended across all sectors of modern society, argued Burnham. Modern corporations, government, and major organizations required technically skilled managers to plan, coordinate, and execute their vast activities. The managers and their bureaucracies, in both corporations and government, had more to gain by integrating and directing the complexity of modern social interactions than by fundamentally disrupting them. Thus, managers in bureaucratized institutions the world over were becoming a new ruling class with an identity and interests of its own, fusing the economy with the state. Managers would plan, regulate, and distribute society's resources through the coercive power of the central government. And the New Deal was the American version of the managerial revolution. In America, as elsewhere, a new class ascended by wedding itself to statist growth and control, successfully displacing the old bourgeois entrepreneurial elite that had been satisfied with minimal and decentralized government.[24]

Burnham developed this argument in *Congress and the American Tradition* (1959).[25] The managerial revolution marked the victory of modern liberal tenets: the unlimited potential of human nature; government's capacity to solve most or all social problems; use of rational science and bureaucratic expertise to direct private economic enterprise. Liberals also typically favored plebiscitary or mass democracy ("democratism") as opposed to conservative moderation or mediation of the popular will. They had come to see the president as spokesman for the masses, rather than the deliberated and compromised policies issuing from the locally based Congress. These liberal principles had been adumbrated in Progressivism and then secured in the New Deal. From then on, Congress, along with the intermediary institutions of civil society, was subordinated to both the plebiscitary version of democracy expressed through the presidency and the managerial bureaucracy of the administrative state.

Burnham called this development "Caesarist" in its attributes—"democratist, plebiscitary, bureaucratic, centralist." Its "typical political form link[ed] a huge, pervasive governmental bureaucracy with a Caesarism-tending political leadership sanctioned by mass plebiscites" and functioned "primarily through administrative decree while using an assembly as a recording device and sounding board."[26] The fall of Congress in the face of the modern presidency and the bureaucratic new class likely spelled the end of American constitutionalism's ability to limit and balance power for the sake of human liberty. (Burnham's consideration of Congress is addressed in this book's conclusion.)

These early traditionalists' attention to the new managerial class and the progressive liberal goals of the administrative state were mostly displaced by the subsequent focus of Russell Kirk and his followers on cultural and moral decay.

Nevertheless, the idea echoed through the analyses of important traditionalists. For example, Robert Nisbet employed the concept in the 1970s and 1980s, arguing that liberalism had become "little less today than a vast celebration of bureaucracy, or at least of the governmental interventions in society which automatically bring with them a network of bureaucrats."[27] This "clerisy" was the governing class in the "new absolutism" that had resulted from what Burnham had identified as the "managerial revolution."[28] It was bent on "progress" toward state-enforced egalitarianism in every form.[29]

The Traditionalist Critique Elaborated

Samuel Francis, author of a monograph on Burnham, argued that traditionalists were "beautiful losers" who had "failed" against the administrative state. Despite having long set the moral and cultural tone of the nation, traditionalists had not yet fully grasped that the managerial revolution had displaced the old bourgeois elite they represented.[30] Gone were traditionalist or "old" Right commitments to "constitutionally limited central government, largely independent local and state government," and its characteristic entrepreneurialism and ethic of "restrained" individualism.[31] The new managerial regime, now often labeled "progressivism" or "liberalism," had triumphed. Francis distilled its attributes with more penetrating concision than even Burnham himself. Starting from the modern presumption that human beings were malleable and perfectible products of their environment, the managerial regime would improve them under the direction of "a scientifically trained elite with power to redesign the environment." At its core this approach was collectivized, centralized, and "largely unrestrained by traditional legal, constitutional, and political barriers. It rejected or regarded as backward, repressive, or obsolete the institutions and values of traditional and bourgeois society." People were to be emancipated and remade as "cosmopolitan participant[s] in the mass state-economy of the managerial system."[32]

This was the "revolution" the New Deal had made as the state subsumed and directed society.[33] Francis insisted that the traditionalist old Right associated with *National Review*, Burnham excepted, had been too intellectualized and backward looking to adequately resist the change. Instead, most traditionalists simply accommodated themselves to the new order while thinking that they were still conserving their place in the establishment. But "the revolution had already occurred" and the old bourgeois elite had lost. There was nothing left of their class to conserve. As a class "it had been dethroned and [now] a counter-revolutionary mission, not 'conserving,' was its mission, its proper strategy."[34]

Like Kirk, Burnham, and Nisbet, Francis addressed the administrative state at the level of social theory. Emphasizing the structuralist aspects of Burnham's thought more than they had, Francis held as an axiom that ideas must be attached to concrete social interests if they were to have any effect in the realm of politics and power. The new class of managers ascended in the administrative state because it was attached to, expressed, and served the dominant interests of a complex, technological, and egalitarian civilization. Adverting to an aphorism of the old Right traditionalists, Francis wrote that "some ideas have more consequences than others, and those that attach themselves to declining social and political forces have the least consequences of all."[35] If there was still any hope for conservative resistance to the progressive liberal managerial regime, it was in the social strata of the semipopulist lower middle class—the "heartland" conservatives of "middle America." A sizable section of the society, they felt restricted and exploited by the alliance between the secular egalitarian new class and the lower-class beneficiaries of the policies that the new class managed and administered.[36] They might rise to oppose the liberal managerial regime if they were more fully awakened to issues such as "crime, educational collapse, the erosion of their economic status, and the calculated subversion of their social, cultural, and national identity by forces that serve the interests of the elite above them and the underclass below them."[37] Francis darkly elaborated this analysis in a book eventually published posthumously as *Leviathan and Its Enemies* (2016). It marked his turn to white nationalist identitarianism and, not incidentally, his rejection of both traditionalist conservatism and America's allegedly failed experiment in liberal constitutionalism. Now, supposedly, only a revolutionary who rose against the liberal managerial elites and the anachronized rule-of-law constitutional order could save the lower-middle-class white *Völk*. To chart this disturbing turn further would take us too far from our focus on mainstream conservative responses to the administrative state.[38]

As we shall see in the next section, neoconservatives reprised the concept of a managerial "new class" prior to its radical metastasization in Francis's later thought. Before turning to this development we must consider Paul Edward Gottfried's elaboration of Burnham. Gottfried sought to explicate the relationship between the relativistic and egalitarian pluralism of modern democratic culture on one hand and, on the other, the "managerial state" that so clearly placed the contemporary era "after liberalism" as it had been classically understood.[39]

Gottfried argued that the hoary notion of pluralism—according to which liberal democratic regimes balance and deliberate among competing interests to produce the public good—had helped obscure the ideological direction of modern progressive liberalism. Rather, built into the liberals' managerial state were commitments to ethical relativism, radical egalitarianism, and economic redistribution. To these ends society was to be planned, managed, and administered—ruled—by the new, elite class of expert government officials. Their power was exercised to reconstruct social relations on the new model, overcoming loyalties to family, property, local culture, religion, or ethnic identity. The state was not the "earnest or bumbling balancer of interests" of the pluralist model but the managerial means to the ideological ends of progressive liberalism.[40]

Gottfried further observed that the administrative state had moved into its therapeutic and coercive phase. In the age of relativism and multiculturalism, "public administration will decide which group receives which benefit or is forced to suffer which liability, for the sake of general self-esteem and maximal healing." Citizens become "patients" as "managerial rule" presents "itself as collectively administered assistance . . . concealing its operation in the language of caring."[41] In addition, dissent from the new order was being pathologized. Opposition to progressive liberal politics was construed as a form of deviance in need of government administered reeducation, behavior modification, and possibly the indemnification of designated victim groups.[42] Of course this expert-led reeducation and control was profoundly illiberal by the old accounting, but very much in keeping with the new managerial ideology.

Thus Gottfried too concluded that the managerial regime was a postliberal social form. Like Francis, he saw some hope of resistance in "decentralizing, populist protest movements," but any success would require many more people to reject a regime that was good at caring and providing for them.[43] Also like Francis, Gottfried criticized his traditionalist allies' insufficient attention to large-scale "structures of power." Too many traditionalists had mistakenly "confin[ed] [their] political discourse to the 'state of the soul'" and produced a "vast literature on the spiritual and aesthetic crisis that has accompanied mass democracy, but treat[ed] the managerial state as incidental to a declining 'moral imagination.'"[44] But a "managed therapeutic politics" was the more immediate threat, and for too long conservatives had elided the basic political question: Who rules and to what end?[45] Although the managerial regime of the administrative state obscured its rule and cloaked itself in virtue, Gottfried warned that this only made it the more insidious.

George Carey and Bruce Frohnen applied a different variant of the traditionalist perspective to more directly constitutional issues. Their book *Constitutional Morality and the Rise of Quasi-law* showed the ongoing development of the traditionalist perspective amid conservatives' broad reevaluation of the administrative state. To situate it, we must first briefly revisit the core claim of Carey (with Willmoore Kendall) in *The Basic Symbols of the American Political Tradition* (1970), a highly influential traditionalist interpretation of American politics and culture.[46] It set forth the central features of what traditionalists typically defined as their primary good: the communitarian, localist, and religiously rooted political culture that had long characterized America. Americans' English Protestant inheritance evolved into a political tradition aimed at deliberative and consensual government oriented to the common good. All participants understood themselves to be ultimately under divine judgment. As articulated in *The Federalist* papers, the purpose of the Constitution was primarily to establish the "mechanisms and procedures" of deliberation, accommodation, and self-limitation through which this people could realize the aims of the Preamble.[47] As noted in the introduction, Kendall and Carey borrowed the terminology of Michael Oakeshott to describe the Constitution as "nomocratic," that is, concerned mostly "with providing rules and limits for the government through which the people express their will."[48] But starting with the Civil War, the "nomocratic" Constitution of rules, procedures, and limits gradually began to transform. Over time it became "teleocratic," aimed at the ever fuller substantive realization of an abstract goal or ideal. This "derailment" of the original order came, they controversially argued, because Abraham Lincoln had misinterpreted and overemphasized the ideas of equality and natural rights announced in the Declaration of Independence.[49] Lincoln's conception of equality, in its "open-endedness and universality," bore some responsibility for the "egalitarianism that characterizes the modern, centralized, welfare state."[50] The ongoing transformation of the United States into a teleocratic regime of rights and equality became the prime goal of the administrative state, and it was this argument that was deepened in the book Carey wrote with Frohnen.[51]

Frohnen and Carey emphasized just how fundamentally the administrative state had scrambled and deranged constitutional institutions. Congress delegated its power to unaccountable bureaucracies, while the president revived the ancient prerogative power as the *vox populi*. The judiciary abetted them both and often legislated as well, having become unmoored from both the Constitution and the traditionally limited conception of the judicial function. In a helpful neologism, the authors described how the administrative state impelled each branch of government to produce "quasi-law."[52] Though garbed in the outward form of law, quasi-law lacked the generality, publicity, clarity, and predictability of true law. It was a form of arbitrary and discretionary power typically embodied in the mixed powers of an administrative agency (though several modern presidential activities also qualified). Frohnen and Carey concluded that the administrative state's reliance on quasi-law was simply incompatible with constitutionalism and the rule of law as Americans traditionally understood them.

The rise of the administrative state had also eroded the federalism and localism so important to traditionalists.[53] Only the "retrenchment of the federal government into a much smaller but more detailed and legalistic form" would allow "more actions to be taken by other institutions, be they states, localities, or associations within civil society."[54] Reform of the administrative state would involve not only abandoning quasi-law for the real thing but also abandoning "grand schemes of national greatness, uniformity, and efficiency in favor of administrative decentralization."[55]

This sensitivity to federalism, localism, and community informed the judgment that the administrative state was a new form of social order. On one level, it reflected the shift from a nomocratic order to a teleocratic one. A related difference lay between a "mediating" constitution and a "commanding" constitution.[56] The old American order, rooted in community and locality, had produced the original, mediating constitution. It was oriented toward deliberation, compromise, and restraint because law and politics were understood as limited and practical ways of ordering public life. However, pursuit of the ends of modern progressive liberalism—primarily equality and liberty as "autonomy"—had substituted a "command" constitution. It was ends oriented and so functioned through discretionary rule (quasi-law) that necessarily remade or abandoned the basic institutional relationships of the old order.

Likewise, the new social form of the administrative state and its "command" constitution were associated with a new and different "constitutional morality." As Frohnen and Carey used this term, it described the animating spirit or ethic that informed a particular regime and the political actors within it. The morality of the original, mediating constitution was one of proceduralism, duty, and limits, as befitted the old order's relatively spare conception of government's purpose. The structures and mechanisms of the old constitution enabled the pluralistic elements of American society to deliberate and accommodate one another, and thereby to secure peace, order, and civil association under the rule of law. The virtue of the good officeholder had always been to fulfill the duties of his or her position and to defend its powers within the confines of the overall constitutional structure.[57] The morality of the new, commanding constitution— the constitution of the administrative state—was one of action and achievement. Its goal was to reform existing social and constitutional arrangements so as to realize the substantive goals of equality, security, and individual autonomy as outlined by Progressivism and the New Deal. This constitutional morality entailed overcoming the separation of powers and federalism, the elevation of the presidency over a compliant Congress, and the mixing of all forms of governance in a vastly empowered bureaucracy. The formality and rule of law necessary for limited government gave way to realization of the proper ends, and politics became administration. Over time the polity came to accept this morality of action and discretionary power as the mode associated with the commanding constitution and the regulatory-welfare ends of the administrative state.[58]

While Frohnen and Cary echoed other analysts by suggesting several institutional and legal reforms, they hoped too that the older American society of robust civil association and self-government under the rule of law might somehow gradually reassert itself now that the administrative state's problems were becoming more widely understood. Needed was a renewed cultural appreciation of the "associational vision at the heart of the Framers' mediating Constitution."[59] Society was not made up of autonomous and isolated individuals under the protection and direction of the central state. Rather, it was based on families, churches, and myriad nonstate civil associations. A "return to a pluralistic form of thinking" would better respect the rule of law because it would be more aware of law's limited purposes and capacities.[60] Reform would mean that more of social life would happen at the local level and less of it would be commanded by the government. This change would occur only if, over time, dissatisfaction with the administrative state led people to resist centralized government solutions to all social problems—and to ask more of themselves and their neighbors. Such slow social change would necessitate greater circumspection about the nature and purpose of government and law, which in turn rested on a central tenet of traditionalist conservatism: "the priority of social over political life."[61]

Neoconservatives: A Partial Revolt

Neoconservatives accepted the New Deal and the necessity of the administrative state in some form but thought progressive liberals were too confident in government and sometimes utopian. Neoconservatives often warned that politicians overestimated the ability of social science to predict the future, or else ignored its findings about the past. Like traditionalists, neoconservatives attempted to diagnose and criticize the administrative state's social and constitutional theory on a grand scale, rather than to dissect its black-letter law or jurisprudence.

Also crucial to the neoconservative perspective was the belief that government had become overloaded in the wake of 1960s egalitarianism and the judicial "rights revolution." More was being asked of government and promised by it than could be delivered. Too frequently it was oblivious to the limits of social policy as a replacement for family, tradition, voluntary association, and religion, and to the unintended consequences of government action.[62] This perspective also echoed the older traditionalist view as articulated by Kirk and Nisbet, especially in neoconservatives' elaboration of Tocqueville's insight about the democratic state's threat to civil society and intermediary institutions.[63]

Yet it was neoconservatives' evaluation of progressive liberalism based on their training as empirical social scientists that initially led them to emphasize as defining ideas "the limits of social policy" and the "law of unintended consequences."[64] A famous early example was Daniel Patrick Moynihan's "The Negro Family" (1965), which he authored while serving as assistant secretary of labor. Moynihan discovered that as the unemployment rate for Black men decreased, there was an increase in the rate of women applying for government financial assistance from Aid to Families with Dependent Children (AFDC). The program was available only to single mothers, and in fact it could make them financially better off than if the father were in the home but unemployed or underpaid. Although the point has been disputed ever since, it seemed to Moynihan (and many others) that AFDC had helped subsidize the breakup of Black families, thereby encouraging the many social problems that emanated from fatherless homes. Moynihan always advocated federal jobs programs and income support in aid of African Americans, but he never doubted that the well-intentioned policy of the AFDC had failed.[65]

This approach resounded in *The Public Interest*, which began publication in 1965 as a site for liberals to offer putatively apolitical, social scientific advice "on the appropriate design for an effective modern administrative state."[66] Later scholars (and neoconservatives themselves) noted how quickly its purpose changed. Its central theme became "a comprehensive critique of social intervention."[67] Articles pointed out how social policies—in areas such as housing, education, welfare provision, desegregation, and crime and recidivism—often foundered because of false assumptions, ignorance of incentive structures or ingrained cultural practices, inadequate knowledge, or bureaucratic incompetence. Detailed social scientific analyses condemned various liberal social engineering projects for exacerbating the problems they were meant to solve, or creating new ones. Not all of the publication's authors were neoconservatives, and some disavowed the label, but as Irving Kristol wrote in retrospect: "there is no doubt that if you go around constantly chastening utopian enthusiasm, or offering reasons for curbing reformist enthusiasm, you are bound to find yourself regarded as a conservative element."[68] James Q. Wilson, who did not much like the neoconservative label, similarly reflected that "it would have been better if we had been called policy skeptics; that is, people who thought it was hard, though not impossible, to make useful and important changes in public policy."[69]

Wilson intensively studied bureaucracy and the administrative state. He was well aware of the classic constitutionalist concern that political power had been "transferred undesirably to an unaccountable administrative realm."[70] Moreover, although he thought that the American founders would likely have approved of many of the purposes of modern regulation, they "surely would be dismayed at the political cost resulting from having vested vast discretionary authority in the hands of officials whose very existence—to say nothing of whose function—was not anticipated by the Constitutional Convention, and whose effective control is beyond the capacity of the governing institutions which that Convention had designed."[71]

Wilson stated bluntly that in a democracy the seemingly inevitable tendency was for the administrative component of government to grow as resources were transferred from the private realm to the public. The United States had done so via the transformations embodied in Progressivism, the New Deal, and the Great Society. The normally slow and difficult process of change in the nation's pluralistic, separation-of-powers constitutional system meant that these liberal achievements were not likely to be undone.[72] Nevertheless, the current reality of worryingly discretionary, unaccountable, and "client-serving" bureaucratic power was not inevitable. It had developed because elected representatives wanted it, and it was shaped by the diffuse nature of the American polity.[73] Political deliberation and legislative action were never foreclosed in a free society, but Wilson doubted that any large-scale political change would come along to alter the basics of the administrative state.

Wilson was even more sternly realistic about what could be expected of government agencies amid the crosscutting demands in the United States' "fragmented and open political system." One inescapable corollary was that "you can have less bureaucracy only if you have less government."[74] Although he did not expect or advocate its abolition, Wilson did urge pragmatism about what the administrative state could achieve and caution about its risks for American political principles. Sounding core neoconservative themes, he urged that "there are inherent limits to what can be accomplished by large hierarchical organizations."[75] Some problems were irresolvable, and some absolutely necessary functions of government were difficult to do well or efficiently. The "rule of reason should be to try to do as few undoable things as possible."[76] Summarizing the neoconservative view, Wilson observed that although, often, "present circumstances are bad and something ought to be done, it is necessary to do that something cautiously, experimentally, and with a minimum of bureaucratic authority."[77]

Based on this critique and on his judgment that the administrative state was here to stay, Wilson undertook a large and influential study of government agencies.[78] He argued that US government bureaucracies were far more varied in their modes of behavior, self-understanding, and response to stimuli of all kinds than could be comprehended by any general theory. In particular, the complexity and range of bureaucratic phenomena could be explained neither by the classical Weberian notion of an institution that rationally and predictably applied general rules and was mostly impermeable to outside influence, nor by the neoclassical economists' reduction of bureaucratic behavior to utility maximization. To understand the action or inaction of a particular government agency required a full sociological, historical, and political portrait of the institution in its multiple contexts.

The factors affecting an agency included its mission, structure, funding, personnel, leadership, culture, and relationship to other government institutions. As a general matter, however, Wilson argued that an agency struggled to perform its assigned tasks when its mission was vague or self-contradictory, when there was too large a gap between the actions of frontline operatives and managers' conception of the mission, or when an agency was hamstrung by rules and procedures imposed by other government institutions. Agencies could make moderate improvements in these areas to the limited extent they acted of their own accord, though Wilson rightly observed that they were beholden to Congress (whose guidance was often unclear) and were further subject to direction and limitation by both the executive and the judiciary.[79]

Wilson hoped his insights might lead to better agency performance, and his work is rightly celebrated as an insightful and nuanced study of American bureaucracy. With the passage of time, however, some conservatives have faulted it for not directly confronting the administrative state's fundamental challenge to American principles of limited and accountable government.[80] As one scholar observed, "*Bureaucracy* is a book about agency behavior, not the recovery of the lost Constitution."[81] Wilson appears to have found utterly unrealistic any attempt to destroy the administrative state after nearly a century of its growth and insinuation into the constitutional system. Extirpation was not an option. Rather, realist that he was, he offered his argument "not as a panacea—there is no way to avoid the problem of administration—but as a guide to choice in those cases where choice is open to us, and as a criterion by which to evaluate proposals for coping with the bureaucracy problem."[82]

Wilson was characteristically neoconservative both in accepting the goals of the regulatory-welfare state and in insisting on the problems and limitations of bureaucracy and administration. Moreover, as noted above, he exempted neither Americans in general nor Congress in particular from responsibility for the administrative state and its shortcomings. Americans made it, and with the appropriate political will, they could better direct or even remake it. Yet, absent any basic reorientation of the nation's governing institutions away from the New Deal order, bureaucratic functioning could be improved by accepting the limits imposed by the context of political pluralism and the separation of powers. Indeed, Wilson was very much a constitutional conservative in defending the latter as a bedrock principle, despite his clear recognition that the resulting diffusion of governing authority complicated all efforts at efficient administration. America's open and pluralistic politics, combined with a strong legislature and the separation of powers, ensured "clumsy and adversarial regulation." Although the "fragmented American regime may produce chaotic government," rather than a larger and more efficient one on the unified European model, Wilson rejected pursuit of a "wholly different regime" as a cure for "the mischiefs of bureaucracy."[83] While liberals objected to the separation of powers because it impeded political change toward a larger, more interventionist government for egalitarian ends, Wilson accepted the high costs of "delays, confusion, and inconsistencies." He encouraged reformers to pursue methods less drastic than wholesale constitutional alteration.[84] Far better to pursue change by means other than "abolition of the principle [of separation of powers, which] is a price that two hundred years of successful constitutional government should have taught us is too high to pay."[85]

The Return of the "New Class"

The expansion of the administrative state in the 1960s prompted neoconservatives to revive the idea of a "new class."[86] The basic concept had been circulating since Burnham's *Managerial Revolution*, influencing neoconservatives and numerous other scholars (who varied in their acknowledgment of him).[87] Neoconservatives were aware that figures on the political Left were urging the emerging class of educated experts in government bureaucracies, knowledge-based professions, and the media to advance progressive liberal reform. In coalition with the underclass, this new class might achieve a centrally planned economy, redistribute the nation's surplus, and ensure a guaranteed income for all.[88] The radicalization of university education also could help turn the new class against corporate capitalism so that "these professionals and technicians will indeed bite the hand that feeds them." As a cadre in "the public sector of society" the new class could become the "conscience constituency" of the left.[89]

Neoconservatives attacked the progressive liberal version of the new class. They deplored its antibourgeois "adversary culture" (Lionel Trilling's phrase), its antibusiness egalitarianism, and its grasp for power through government regulation. It had come to include not only the managerial planning and administrative bureaucracy of the post–New Deal state but also the New Left's relativist and egalitarian indictment of American civilization. Neoconservatives saw it as a hectoring, countercultural presence whose infatuation with rationalist planning arrayed it against both middle-class values and limited constitutional government.[90] Irving Kristol wrote that the new class pursued "power in the name of equality" because its members were "persuaded they can do a better job of running our society and feel entitled to have the opportunity. That is what *they* mean by 'equality.' "[91] Neoconservatives routinely condemned the growth of the administrative state as a source of both power and employment for the new class.[92] Its reformist political ambition would mean less liberty and more government control.

Given that most neoconservatives were educated writers, political commentators and advisers, social scientists, and even sometime officeholders, they occasionally admitted their own membership in the new class—assuming that it did truly exist as a sociological phenomenon. The idea of the new class always remained somewhat "muddled" as "half analytic concept, half polemical device." It was never entirely clear whether neoconservatives defined the new class by its expertise and organizational position within contemporary institutions or by the supposedly shared liberal goals it pursued through such positions (or by both of these factors).[93] In this sense neoconservatives understood themselves as engaged in a battle for the loyalty and direction of the new class.[94] As Kristol put it in retrospect: "We are dissidents from the New Class liberal ideology. . . . [It] was nothing but a vehicle for gaining power for themselves. That is the stratagem we have unmasked, while admittedly being part of the New Class ourselves."[95] Whether or not the new class could be said to exist according to a social scientific definition of the concept, for neoconservatives the term expressed the dubious legitimacy and constant growth of the administrative state, combined with its service to the political goals of progressive liberalism.[96] Moreover, Kristol was explicit in his strategy of soliciting and facilitating business support for neoconservatives who defended capitalism and limited government—a "counterintellectual" strategy against neoconservatives' new class opponents.[97]

However, the neoconservatives did not go far enough for traditionalists such as Samuel Francis and Paul Gottfried. Both men saw some form of traditionalism as the authentic conservatism, while neoconservatives were too liberal arrivistes, interlopers in the true conservative movement. Moreover, according to traditionalists, neoconservatives had already accepted in advance the managerial and liberal statist revolution and sought only to caution and correct it but not to dismantle it. Neoconservatives were the "right wing of the New Class they criticize so much, engaged in an effort to moderate its collectivist and utopian dynamic with a strong dose of bourgeois liberalism."[98] This accommodation was rooted in a failure to acknowledge that corporate managers were part of the new class and, thus, that corporate interests often diverged from those of common, bourgeois citizens. Against this neoconservative obscurantism or self-delusion, Francis insisted that Burnham had been correct all along: the "same social force [was] in control of the state as well as the corporation." Neoconservatives ignored this point by focusing on ideological disagreements within the new class rather than on the more fundamental fact that it was a ruling class.[99] Thus they conserved only the victory that the managerial revolution had already won in the New Deal.[100] Accordingly, Gottfried observed, neoconservatism was unable to resist the administrative state when it took the lead in directing social change according to the dictates of the new relativist and egalitarian managerial elite. Likewise, since corporations who profited from the managerial revolution funded much of the neoconservative opposition to the progressive liberal new class, neoconservatives had practical reasons for limiting their engagement with the concept.[101]

The tensions among the varieties of conservatism were apparent in these competing approaches to the administrative state. Traditionalists were convinced that it was a new social form that had mostly displaced the old constitutional order. If neoconservative attempts to moderate it were complicit in its perpetuation, the traditionalist call for its abolition, though purer, was surely impractical in any immediate sense. As noted above, the latter body of thought was radicalized and racialized by Francis when he abandoned traditionalism (and constitutionalism) for a more extreme and even revolutionary form of right-wing politics. Declining to pursue that inquiry, I turn now to the libertarian perspective.

Libertarian Foundations: Hayek and Mises

Libertarian criticism was most influenced by the work of Friedrich A. Hayek (1899–1992) (who preferred to be called a classical liberal). His influential *The Road to Serfdom* (1944) rejected centralized social and economic planning in favor of individual liberty, open markets, and limited government under the rule of law. These quintessentially libertarian goals were under assault from bureaucratic administration that attempted the impossible task of a centrally directed economy. Hayek argued that only actors in the spontaneous order of the market could respond to the vast, dispersed, and ever-changing information contained in the price mechanism. Self-interest and local knowledge, not centralized planning and administration, would efficiently coordinate production and distribution. Any government attempt to displace the market necessarily would undermine the true concept of law as a set of general rules, transforming it into coercive commands aimed at particular individuals in unique circumstances. Consequently, Hayek often reiterated that authentic law had to be known in advance and equally applied—only then were individuals left free to create varied, uncoerced forms of social order.[102]

Hayek saw that the inevitability of discretion in any legal system was dangerously magnified in the dawning age of the administrative state. More specifically, because nobody could possess all the information requisite for a comprehensive socioeconomic plan, its terms and requirements could never be fully stated in general laws prior to their application. Highly discretionary, legislative authority would have to be delegated to administrators ad hoc under color of law.[103] The consequent tendency of the centrally planned administrative state was to "legalize what to all intents and purposes remains arbitrary action." The law could permit "a board or authority [to] do what it pleases" and call its actions "legal," though they "are certainly not subject to the Rule of Law."[104]

The question of doomed socialist economic planning aside, modern democracies likewise used the same kind of bureaucratic administration in pursuit of welfare, equality, or "social justice" (a term Hayek found especially vacuous). To be sure, Hayek accepted public spending on public goods and even allowed that an "assured minimum income" could be provided within a system of market exchange and the rule of law. However, "if 'social justice' is to be brought about, the individuals must be required to obey not merely general rules but specific demands directed to them only."[105] Real liberty and the rule of law would never produce any foreordained outcome. A conception of social justice, like central economic planning, must prohibit individuals from acting freely for their own ends. Instead, they would become objects of management and administration—forced to act "in the manner which according to the knowledge of the directing authority is required for the realization of the ends chosen by that authority." This approach violated not only the generality requirement of the rule of law, but also its principle of equality, because legal power was manifested as a superior's command to a subordinate.[106] The instantiation of this tendency in socialism would be the apotheosis of the administrative state as "the destruction of law in the sense of general rules of just conduct and its replacement by administrative orders."[107]

Hayek's criticism derived from the European liberal tradition of the rule of law. It had confronted the governing practices of the age of absolutism and anticipated the same general problem—liberty and limited government versus discretionary bureaucratic administration—that the United States now faced. Accordingly, the German *Rechtsstaat* merited reconsideration because "it is the power of the professional administrator that is now the main threat to individual liberty."[108] Germany had achieved more in theory than in practice the *Rechtsstaat*'s goal of assuring that independent courts could review administrative power over persons and property. The process of legal evolution had been truncated because state socialism, and then the welfare state, had obviated the classical liberal orientation toward limited government. Nevertheless, Hayek insisted that the core principles of the latter were both sound and possible: administrative courts could be constructed both to execute complex law and to defend individual liberty, as had always been the *Rechtsstaat*'s aim.

In making this argument, Hayek, like the theorists of the *Rechtsstaat*, was wary of the grave threat that administrative courts could present to the individual. Administrative courts "will always be concerned with the aims of the government of the moment and cannot be fully independent: they must be part of the administrative apparatus and be subject to direction at least by its executive head." They were constituted to realize government policy, not to protect the individual.[109] The only way to avert this danger, which had been the unrealized hope of the eclipsed *Rechtsstaat*, was to promulgate "detailed legal rules for guiding and limiting the actions of the administration."[110] This accurate and still-relevant description of the administrative state's challenge to liberty and limited government testifies to the depth of Hayek's insight about its inner logic and troubling tendency.

Hayek observed that Progressivism had introduced into American constitutionalism "Continental European conceptions of administrative powers." The resulting quest for a " 'science' of administration" threatened individual liberty, constitutional restraints, and the rule of law.[111] Indeed, Progressives had become the "main advocates of the extension of the discretionary powers of the administrative agency" and had thus prepared the way for the "paternalistic policies of the New Deal."[112] Likewise, given his understanding of the *Rechtsstaat*, Hayek was unimpressed with the Administrative Procedure Act (APA; 1946). He quoted at length Roscoe Pound's stinging indictment of it as a return to "administrative absolutism." The APA had sanctioned the destruction of the separation of powers and allowed individual rights to be subordinated to government policies in biased administrative tribunals that only mimicked an independent court.[113]

Hayek also believed that the power of the democratic principle actually intensified the dangers of the administrative state. The liberty of the citizen was no match for a social policy that carried the democratic imprimatur of the legislature into "an administrative apparatus which is given exclusive power to carry out these instructions." That was "the most dangerous arrangement possible."[114] The contemporary trend was for administrative agencies to "become a self-willed and uncontrollable apparatus before which the individual is helpless, and which becomes increasingly invested with all the mystique of sovereign authority."[115]

Eventually Hayek came to think that the potential for administrative tyranny derived from an error in the constitutional structure of modern democracy. The "miscarriage of the democratic ideal" was the erroneous belief that "democratic control of government made unnecessary any other safeguards against the arbitrary use of power."[116] Consequently, the legislature had expanded from the realm of law into that of administration and particularistic governance.[117] Legislation had become less about the general principles of just conduct, the framing of abstract legal rules, or the appropriate limitations on official power. Instead it focused on how particular governmental measures could reward constituents with special favors so that reelection was assured.[118] This derangement of the authentic legislative function was the reason that bureaucracy in the administrative state was becoming so powerful. Legislatures had become "preoccupied by what in effect is discretionary administration[, so] that the true work of legislation is increasingly left in the hands of the bureaucracy."[119]

The United States had not eluded this problem: its version of the separation of powers had failed to keep the legislature out of the details of administration. The American founders "could hardly have foreseen that, because the legislature was also entrusted with the direction of government, the task of stating rules of just conduct and the task of directing particular activities of government to specific ends would come to be hopelessly confounded."[120] Hayek was convinced that a reform of constitutional structure was necessary. He proposed a new bicameralism rooted in the *Rechtsstaat*'s attempt to separate general law from particularistic administration. The legislature, ultimately supervised by a constitutional court, should have one house that made abstract rules of acceptable conduct for general application, while the other worked out the specifics of their application in particular circumstances. This change could solve the problems of delegation and discretion that plagued bureaucracy in the administrative state. There were no "intrinsic reasons" why the regulatory matters that legislatures commonly delegated to bureaucracies, with the attendant risk of "discretionary and essentially arbitrary powers," could "not take the form of general rules." Separation of legislation proper from the control of administration would overcome the basic problem of legislative delegation that so plagued the administrative state.[121] Hayek had thus insightfully diagnosed several of the central problems of the administrative state that would continue to trouble American constitutionalism and provoke numerous later libertarian critics. His proposed cure of basic constitutional reform was a nonstarter in the United States, but the very idea testified to how fundamental he thought the problems were.

Another significant touchstone for the libertarian understanding was Ludwig von Mises (1881–1973), Hayek's one-time teacher and a more combative and deeply antistatist Austrian economist. His *Bureaucracy* (1944) was published in the same year as Hayek's *Road to Serfdom* and shared much if its perspective. Like Hayek, Mises argued that the absence of price signals and the profit motive in government institutions made economic calculation impossible and, therefore, an economy centrally planned by government bureaucrats was unworkable. Socialism, though ascendant, was thus destined to fail. Yet some measure of government bureaucracy was inevitable: every regime needed a system of hierarchy and rules to deliver public goods that could not be priced in the market, such as defense against external enemies, public order (policing), and justice according to law.[122] Mises accepted that any such government action entailed bureaucracy. The deeper problem was expansion of the state into ever more of the private realm, bringing first bureaucratization and eventually socialism and totalitarianism. Individual freedom was rapidly contracting because "the inherent trend of present-day economic and social policies [was] toward the substitution of government control for private initiative. People blame bureaucracy, but what they really have in mind are the endeavors to make the state socialist and totalitarian."[123]

Mises contrasted "profit management," the method of a firm responding to price signals in the marketplace, with "bureaucratic management," the method of government agencies that regulate through command-and-control methods. The government-bureaucratic method was always economically inefficient. This was tolerable within its proper realm, but became oppressive when official coercion displaced freely chosen forms of social order so that the state could direct social development. Firms in the market responded to the sovereignty of consumer demand—or else they perished. But bureaucracy was the tool of people who insisted they knew how best to order society.[124]

Mises observed that Americans had democratically chosen statist bureaucratization in the form of the New Deal, despite its problems.[125] This observation underscored the deeper point that the choice for statist growth led naturally to politically unaccountable bureaucracy. The problem was "not the fault of bureaucracy" but rather the "outcome of the new system of government which restricts the individual's freedom to manage his own affairs and assigns more and more tasks to the government."[126] In a democracy this choice could be reversed.[127] But liberty would be lost without a politically engaged citizenry that made the effort, with the help of its leaders, to understand the logic and tendency of statist intervention and bureaucratic expansion. Scholars and intellectuals were obligated to provide insights about bureaucracy to citizens or else "society breaks up into two castes: the ruling professionals, the Brahmins, and the gullible citizenry. Then despotism emerges, whatever the wording of constitutions and laws may be."[128] Everyday citizens could not be expected to penetrate every legal technicality, said Mises, but the preservation of liberty required them to take up the burden of self-government. The influence of Mises, like that of Hayek, would reverberate in libertarian constitutional thought for the rest of the century.

Libertarian Elaborations: The Public Choice Critique of Bureaucracy and Administration

A later but related strand of the libertarian response to the administrative state was "public choice" analysis.[129] It developed quickly in the post–New Deal era, with the ideas of Hayek and Mises as important parts of its intellectual inheritance.[130] Although the term "public choice" was often associated with libertarian or conservative politics, a leading scholar has recently argued that the core concerns and methodologies of those employing similar labels were not fundamentally distinct from public choice, nor were those associated with the various labels uniformly libertarian or conservative.[131] The parsing of labels aside, public choice is often defined as the application of economics to politics. It usually aims to produce formal models that describe and predict the strategies and choices of rational, preference-maximizing individuals who must make collective decisions amid various incentives, rules, and constraints. Libertarians have been instrumental in its development.

The field first analyzed voting and legislative behavior, with influential early studies holding that self-interested action in a majoritarian democracy undermined the realization of anything like a stable or truly "common" good. Rather, officeholders, and the organized groups who helped elect them, advanced their own goals via political bargains and government-mandated resource redistributions that were never truly efficient.[132] This general perspective was applied to the reigning theory of government bureaucracy, which since the Progressive era had treated it as the apolitical and efficient execution of clear public mandates. Public choice scholars rejected this "normative mishmash of Max Weber's sociology and Woodrow Wilson's vision of public administration."[133] On the contrary, officials in bureaucracies remained self-interested utility maximizers, just like everyone else. And, as Hayek and Mises had emphasized, bureaucracies were not subject to the discipline of the price mechanism or the profit motive. Accordingly, the thrust of the public choice version of the libertarian critique was that bureaucracies would always be hard to control or make politically responsible and that they would be aggressively growth oriented, expensive, and inefficient.

Gordon Tullock, informed by his time as a foreign service officer, was the first to apply public choice to the internal workings of a government bureau.[134] He built on a primary distinction between "political" relationships in a hierarchical order, in which superiors must be obeyed and pleased, and "economic" relationships, characterized by mutually beneficial, uncoerced exchanges between equals. His goal was to understand how a mid-level bureaucrat (the "reference politician"), who sought career advancement, would respond to incentives and constraints in relation to those above and below him and, accordingly, how a hierarchically organized bureaucracy would actually function.

Tullock argued that bureaucracies would be inherently inefficient and costly because of deficiencies and distortions in the transmission of information, the incompatibility of officials' incentives, and the resulting difficulties in compelling individual subordinates to comply with the bureau's objectives and attempts at coordination. A clarifying illustration was the game of "whispering down the lane," which exemplifies how information from a superior is distorted when its complexity and the number of people who transmit it increase. Information traveling up the chain from subordinates was also subject to their self-interested interpretation and filtering. Nor could a decision maker at the apex of the organizational pyramid possibly process all relevant information if it were simply relayed to him as raw data from the ground level.[135] As efficiencies and resources unavoidably seeped out, additional time and resources would be spent on monitoring and compliance. The thoroughly libertarian, antistatist conclusion was that "most modern governmental hierarchies are much beyond their efficient organizational limits."[136]

Another important early public choice study was Anthony Downs's *Inside Bureaucracy* (1967). Downs was not a libertarian, nor did he think that bureaucracy in America had yet become politically illegitimate or dangerously overgrown: most people still wanted its benefits and were willing to pay for them.[137] Still, like Tullock, he sought to understand bureaucratic motivation in terms of self-interest and to explain how differences in organizational structure and environment affected outcomes. A lasting contribution was his typology of bureaucratic personalities: climbers, conservers, zealots, advocates, and statesmen. The first two were almost purely self-interested, while the latter three mixed self-interest with "altruistic loyalty to larger values" that might include particular policies, the mission of the organization, or the general welfare.[138] While Downs thus allowed for some other-regarding motivations, the fundamental postulate of utility maximization meant that they would operate only if institutions were designed so that bureaucrats could simultaneously pursue their own self-interest.[139] His book put forth a series of behavioral "laws" derived from the various personality types' interaction with differing organizational structures and external environments. In charting the resulting "dialectic of supervision and evasion endemic to hierarchical organizations," Downs significantly advanced the public choice view of bureaucracy as shot through with self-serving behavior and inefficiency.[140]

A leader in the field concluded that public choice in the work of Tullock and Downs "made a stunning entrée into the world of bureaucratic theory, upsetting the good government vison of public administration and charting a bold new path for analysis."[141] Although these books successfully reoriented scholarly inquiry about bureaucracy, they did not generate the formal, testable economic models that came to characterize public choice. Nor did they address the interaction of bureaucracies with other institutions in the constitutional system as much as they did the internal workings of a single organization. The more lasting direction of public choice analysis of bureaucracy, one that built explicitly on Mises, Tullock, and Downs, was established by the "budget maximization" model of William A. Niskanen Jr. A larger budget provided more of what bureaucrats wanted: money, power, prestige, amenities, and security in office. Niskanen modeled the relationship between the legislature and the bureaucracy as a bilateral monopoly in which the agency possessed an information advantage about the true costs of its activities, derived from its subject expertise, experience, and locality. Moreover, the agency knew the preferences (demand) of the legislature and that the agency's services could not be otherwise supplied. Niskanen again reached the thoroughly libertarian and antistatist conclusion that, as these advantages were pressed, all government bureaucracies were larger and more expensive than necessary.[142]

The public choice analysis of bureaucracy developed quickly in the wake of Niskanen's pathbreaking work, in line with the rapid ascent of rational actor models in political science more generally. Scholars questioned how monopolistic bureaucracies actually could be in light of the variety of tools legislators had for monitoring and controlling them in service to their own reelection prospects. Likewise, interest groups, courts, and presidents could influence, compel, or rebuff agency actions. Accordingly, the field moved away from Niskanen's stripped-down principal-agent model toward the idea of multiple principals who nevertheless assumed "as given bureaucratic self-interest."[143] In just a few decades public choice had demolished, at least to its own satisfaction, the Progressive-era conception of a "technocratic, apolitical, professional civil service" of "robotic bureaucrats fulfilling administrative mandates handed down by public-interest-driven legislators." Rather, supposed " 'civil servants' " in public choice models "are not in any meaningful senses different from the stylized rational actors of neoclassical economic theory. They, like all human beings, are motivated primarily by their own objectives for present and future income, promotion in place, status, and other personal rewards."[144]

Public choice went a long way in explaining why government agencies were often inefficient, politically unaccountable, and entrenched. Likewise, its significant presence within political science reasserted an important aspect of traditional American constitutionalism: a deep skepticism toward officials who claimed to exercise power for the benefit of others. At the same time, public choice's abstract microanalysis and general pessimism disallowed the notion that government could ever pursue the public good. However thinly that idea might be conceived, historically it had been a prerequisite of a functional constitutional order.[145] In taking this view despite the century-long reality of modern bureaucratic government, public choice mirrored the impracticality of libertarian constitutionalists' call for wholesale rejection of the administrative state, to which we now turn.

Libertarian Conclusions: The Administrative State as Obviously Unconstitutional

Friedrich Hayek cast an especially long shadow as libertarianism began arriving in American law schools in the 1970s.[146] Some leading libertarian legalists began to criticize the administrative state from a generally Hayekian and originalist perspective. They argued forcefully and fundamentally that it imperiled liberty and property by subverting the rule of law, abandoning the separation of powers, and undermining representative government. Major figures such as Richard A. Epstein and Gary Lawson were blunt: the New Deal administrative state was unconstitutional and its victory a "bloodless constitutional revolution."[147] Independent administrative agencies were not contemplated by the tripartite separation of powers and thus were "flatly unconstitutional—there is no Article IIIA."[148] Destruction of the separation of powers was "perhaps the crowning jewel of the modern administrative revolution."[149]

Libertarian analyses of key characteristics of the administrative state advanced this basic theme. A major culprit was the death of the nondelegation doctrine, resulting in frequent congressional cession of highly discretionary, essentially legislative authority to administrative agencies both in and beyond the executive branch. Libertarians conceded that no legal regime could function without some discretion and that the boundaries between legislative and executive power were not self-evidently clear. But because the Supreme Court had not upheld the nondelegation doctrine since 1935, the organic statutes of major administrative institutions were permitted to violate the separation of powers by conferring authority in terms so vague and discretionary as to lack a discernible rule of law.[150] Not only were administrative agencies thus possessed of the power to legislate, but also their hearing and adjudicative functions usurped the power of the other two branches. This combination of rule making (legislation), investigation and prosecution (execution), and adjudication was a "conscious and complete inversion of the principle of separation of powers."[151] Finally, libertarians argued that the Court's administrative law jurisprudence had become too deferential to bureaucracies in matters of law and jurisdiction, and less predictably so in matters of fact. Under the doctrine of *Chevron*, the Court almost always deferred to an agency's own interpretation of its typically vague and discretionary organic statute, while sometimes accepting and other times ignoring its subject matter expertise regarding the APA's "substantial evidence" factual standard. Such vagaries gave the Court nearly a free hand if it so desired. Libertarians usually thought that individual liberty would be better protected if courts were less deferential to bureaucrats and more often undertook de novo review of agency actions.[152]

Both Epstein and Lawson were aware that the developing theory of the unitary executive (addressed in the following chapter) sought to increase presidential control over the administrative state. But neither thought it a very fruitful line of resistance in light of the Court's long-standing removal jurisprudence, which prevented the president from removing officers at will (without "cause") from the executive branch (let alone from independent agencies).[153] Lawson thought that the basis of a strong removal power was too ambiguous and, in any event, it had proven inadequate in practice for controlling the federal bureaucracy.[154] Epstein, by contrast, accepted that a proper reading of the Constitution permitted the president to remove officeholders even from independent agencies, yet he denied that the president could direct the actions of subordinates that were delineated by statute. Even though the famous case of *Humphrey's Executor* (1935) had wrongly truncated the removal power, Epstein argued, agencies independent of presidential control had become a "fait accompli."[155] The reality was that "Article I judges have been in office for seventy-five years, [so] we should not try to turn back the clock on a modest reform that makes good institutional sense" at least for independent agencies that did no more than "set rates, administer the bankruptcy code, decide tax cases, or resolve accident claims."[156]

Perhaps libertarians thought it was quixotic to hope for a revival of the removal power—or perhaps it seemed more like responding to a too powerful bureaucracy with a too powerful presidency. Whatever the reason, this assessment did not alter their fundamental view that the administrative state was politically dangerous and constitutionally illegitimate. When combined with public choice analyses of bureaucracy, it was clear that libertarians challenged the New Deal administrative state at the deepest levels—though their calls for overturning it remained at the level of abstract principle rather than concrete political action.

Conclusion

Traditionalists, neoconservatives, and libertarians each thought that the administrative state threatened both their distinctive principles and the health of the constitutional system. Traditionalists saw it as an elitist and managerial social form whose centralized governing bureaucracies had, with seeming permanence, displaced America's traditionally limited and locally based government, along with its historical preference for private social ordering. Neoconservatives focused on the limited capacity of bureaucracy and social science expertise to effectuate major policy change in light of the realities of human behavior, custom, and historical circumstance. Both traditionalists and neoconservatives argued that a "new class" had a vested interest in the growth of the administrative state, often favoring it at the expense of realistic policy and constitutional propriety. For their part, libertarians saw the administrative state as a quintessential expression of modern statist overreach into the market and civil society, one that was inevitably wasteful, inefficient, and plainly incompatible with the original constitutional order. Thus conservatives' diagnoses and emphases varied in accord with their own ideas, but all saw in the administrative state challenges to the elements of American constitutionalism they most valorized.

CHAPTER TWO

Straussians, the Administrative State, and the Rise of the Unitary Executive

First-generation Straussians' initial response to the administrative state was two-fold. They critiqued social science as the basis of putatively apolitical expertise, and they called for the education of bureaucratic functionaries in the principles of American constitutionalism and the practice of political prudence. The goal was adaptation to the post–New Deal reality that still preserved the distinctive virtues of the United States as a regime. Later generations of Strauss-influenced scholars abandoned this attempted reconciliation because they became convinced that the administrative state was an alien and dangerous distortion of the regime's deepest principles. This shift took shape primarily in the 1980s, just as the theory of the "unitary executive" was emerging in the Reagan administration as a way to restrain, direct, and make more politically accountable the institutions of the administrative state. Defense of the unitary executive soon migrated from the Reagan administration to the law schools and was reflected in some notable Supreme Court opinions. The administrative state continued to expand into the twenty-first century, though conservative constitutional analysis had successfully altered the political-intellectual landscape by making its legitimacy a matter of serious contention.

Attempts at Legitimation

Straussians built on their teacher's well-known attack on positivist social science and its core fact-value distinction. The premises of social science obscured the truth that politics was inevitably about the prudent pursuit of just ends, said Strauss. Politics always began in the commonsense perceptions of members of a particular community and, as such, involved some conception of the human good that could not be reduced to something else.[1] Max Weber, the father of modern social science positivism and the fact-value distinction, had not evaded this truth. In practice he recurred to exactly the value judgments he supposedly had abjured after convincing himself they were groundless.[2] Strauss and his students developed this claim in a noted attack on the premises of midcentury American political science. The discipline's attempt to derive objective laws of politics on the basis of the fact-value distinction smuggled in commonsense value judgments just as Weber had. It also assumed the norms and institutions of liberal democracy as both the standard of judgment and the protective cover for its enterprise—all while confidently denying the possibility of any ground on which to defend or criticize one set of political arrangements over another. Accordingly, behavioralist political science simultaneously deepened and obscured the modern crisis that Strauss sought to explicate and overcome.[3]

Herbert J. Storing applied this critique to the work of Herbert A. Simon, a leading analyst of public administration and defender of rational choice decision making in government bureaucracies.[4] Storing had little difficulty showing that Simon's insistence on the fact-value distinction, like Weber's, was honored only in the breach.[5] Simon also repeatedly instanced "some pre-scientific divination of the nature of man and the world." Likewise, what counted as a "problem" to be solved via some particular decision-making method resulted from a normative judgment, conscious or not, about what was worthy and real.[6] The point was not that commonsense perceptions were necessarily true or just— Strauss taught that philosophy began in an ascent from them—but rather that the political, and thus any meaningful analysis of it, occurred with reference to the principles that citizens of a particular regime regarded as true and just.[7] On this account, social science could not recognize its dependence on what surrounded and preceded it or the inevitability of prudential judgments about how to reach political ends.

Storing advanced from this critique to a careful study of the American founding. Its basic aim, he held, was a strong and effective central government capable of protecting rights by moderating democratic passion and short-sightedness.

Now the principles of American constitutionalism must be applied and adapted to the post–New Deal era of regulatory-administrative government. "To strengthen . . . those qualities of the bureaucracy that contribute knowledge and moderation to government and set an example of devotion to the public good is to defend an old position with a new institution."[8] The time had passed for unhelpful "random carping or wholesale condemnation of the bureaucracy." More politically sound was the effort to "nurture and strengthen its capacity for administrative statesmanship."[9] Storing undertook this task in several influential essays.

Encouragement for his effort came from the near universal abandonment at midcentury of the Progressive idea that politics could be separated from administration, as Woodrow Wilson had famously proclaimed.[10] Even scholars who eschewed the Straussian critique of social science recognized that political discretion inhered in administration. Accordingly, "the age-old political and constitutional problems now present themselves as problems of (or in) public administration."[11] Yet the field had not yet produced a standard, other than technical expertise, that might justify bureaucracies in moderating or limiting the democratic will.[12] Storing therefore reframed the basic problem. Having been taught to consult only "technical competence and popular will," how should the administrator judge when they conflict or are exhausted?[13]

The administrator was a political actor in a particular regime; hence his or her duty was the statesmanlike exercise of discretion in accord with its principles. The administrator's discretion must be properly schooled, and the institutional position of bureaucracy be utilized, so that the administrator's capacity for prudence, moderation, and stability would preserve American constitutionalism.[14] The nation needed administrators among its leaders, and it must educate them in this way.[15]

Storing did not have a full plan for achieving this goal, though he supported creating a cadre of senior executive civil servants. (This idea was first proposed by the Hoover Commission in 1955, and a version of it became law in 1978). In addition, he suggested that the orientation toward moderation and stability he saw in administrators could fulfill the role originally intended for the Senate before the direct election mandated in the Seventeenth Amendment. From this perspective the bureaucracy's relative distance from public opinion was an advantage because it could slow the democratic zeitgeist.[16] Although the founders had "failed to anticipate the full significance of the administrative state," there was "a close harmony between the original intention of the system of checks and balances and the political role of the modern civil service." Both aimed to "to institutionalize moderation."[17] "Cautious prudence and orderliness" helped bring about "that part of practical wisdom in which the party politician is likely to be deficient."[18] This adaptation of the founders' principles no more guaranteed success than did their original "inventions of prudence." But, Storing held—in the same mode of political realism underlying his dismissal of the politics-administration dichotomy—"if the civil service is a political institution with a political function, it does not appear unreasonable that it should have some political power."[19] He urged that this power be shaped for appropriately constitutional ends.

Storing also held that the distinctive institutional characteristics and position of the bureaucracy fostered the American understanding of justice and the rule of law. Bureaucratic preoccupation with "rules and regulations" was not merely about "orderly administration." Rather, requiring that "that there should *be* rules and regulations" manifested the American principle of "treating equals equally." Likewise was the typical bureaucratic insistence on following precedent, a practice that was generally "orderly, reasonable, and fair." Bureaucracy conduced to rule by set and standing laws.[20]

Storing's view was developed most notably by John A. Rohr and less directly by others associated with the "constitutional school" of public administration.[21] Rohr, too, saw that the Progressives had rejected leading components of American constitutionalism, especially the separation of powers, because it impeded rational administration of the popular will via the politics-administration dichotomy.[22] However, Progressives had gone too far: the founding and its central principles were normative in American politics and could never simply be dismissed as they had attempted. Rather, Rohr followed Storing in seeking to legitimate the administrative state in terms of constitutional principle.[23] He hoped that this effort would allow the administrative state to "perform more effectively" so that its "worst excesses" could be avoided or tamed.[24]

Aided by Storing's scholarship on the Antifederalists, Rohr focused on the spirit and political logic of founding-era debates rather than on the text and forms of the Constitution. American constitutionalism was said to contain a more "relaxed" and "flexible" conception of the separation of powers than had been commonly understood. Attacks on administrative agencies were "usually based on an excessively rigid interpretation of this venerable doctrine."[25] The work of the Philadelphia convention itself illustrated the true, looser, and more "pragmatic" approach. The Senate was a prime example in that it had all three kinds of governing power: legislative (in concert with the House); executive (the advise-and-consent function); and judicial (in impeachment proceedings). Rohr similarly treated *The Federalist* papers, emphasizing Madison's gloss on Montesquieu in number 47: "Where the *whole* power of one department is exercised by the same hands which possess the *whole* power of another department, the fundamental principles of a free constitution are subverted."[26] Hamilton added that the "true meaning" of separation of powers was "entirely compatible with a partial intermixture of those departments for special purposes, preserving them in the main distinct and unconnected."[27] Consequently, the mixing of governing powers in administrative agencies could be accepted: it need be met not with "formalistic" incantations of "doctrine" but rather with "prudence and accommodation." Agencies never exercised the whole power of another branch of government and were always subordinate to at least one of them.[28] The separation of powers was not wholly overcome, as the Progressives had wanted, nor need it be an absolute prohibition on the administrative state.

Rohr further developed Storing's idea that the upper reaches of the civil service could fulfill the role originally intended for the Senate. Government bureaucracies could foster moderation, stability, and balance by exercising their discretion on behalf of the foundational principles of the regime.[29] In addition, mass participation of citizens in government, as rank-and-file civil servants, could heal what the Antifederalists regarded as the grave defect of inadequate and too elitist representation in the original House of Representatives. Such a "representative bureaucracy" involved citizens in the classic political activities of ruling and being ruled. The public spiritedness and active citizenship that resulted would conduce to the legitimacy and maintenance of the regime.[30]

Rohr's attempt at legitimation was characteristically Straussian: it returned to the American founding with ancient ideas about the nature of politics and the teaching that an enduring regime must cultivate its own distinctive principles among citizens and officeholders. Indeed, Rohr's work has been noted in the field of public administration for featuring the idea, from Aristotle via Strauss, that bureaucrats should be concerned with "regime values."[31] Very much in the Straussian tradition, Rohr defined "regime" as the "best English equivalent of what Aristotle meant by a 'polity.'"[32] In the United States it was "the fundamental political order established by the Constitution of 1789" and further included social norms or values beyond the text.[33]

Given, as discussed earlier, that "*the* ethical problem for bureaucrats is how they should use their discretionary authority," Rohr proposed that they be educated in regime values—meaning constitutional principles.[34] He delineated these variously as equality, freedom, and property and, more generally, as the protection of individual rights. These principles could be taught to government officials in such things as Supreme Court decisions or contested assertions of presidential power.[35] Such a political education would enable bureaucrats to develop a *"sense* of what is constitutionally appropriate,"[36] that is, prudent judgment that served constitutionalism and individual liberty.

Rohr also appealed to the oath that public administrators took to support and defend the Constitution. It signified that while bureaucrats were subordinate to the three branches of government, they were loyal to the Constitution. The oath further represented the constitutional knowledge that Rohr wanted bureaucrats to have, and thus could authorize those empowered to exercise discretion to make an educated choice in accord with the regime's values. "Professional competence in the constitutional heritage" was the foundation of Rohr's "case for the administrator as constitutionalist."[37] Education in the principles of the regime, as well as statesmanship, was as necessary in the modern administrative state as in ancient Athens.

Rohr, like Storing, accepted the permanence of the administrative state and the necessity of integrating the New Deal into the nation's constitutional heritage. Unlike the Progressives, the "New Dealers tried to legitimate the administrative state that they were founding with arguments that were, for the most part, plausible restatements of the founding argument."[38] The Administrative Procedure Act (1946) was "akin" to a Bill of Rights for the administrative state. It had been influenced by the final report of the US attorney general's Committee on Administrative Procedure (1941), which Rohr praised for its "emphasis on rights, procedures, and participation." This report had "helped to integrate the public argument over the administrative state into the perennial American public argument."[39] Having emerged intact from the presidency of Ronald Reagan, Rohr concluded that the administrative state solidified in the New Deal was unlikely to disappear. To continually treat it as foreign or illegitimate only debased citizens and undermined self-government. Rather, wisdom lay in continuing the effort begun in the New Deal "to legitimate the administrative state."[40]

Rejecting the Administrative State

Another group of Straussians, often from the "West Coast," disagreed explicitly with Storing and Rohr.[41] Though fully attuned to the critique of the fact-value distinction and the bankruptcy of the politics-administration dichotomy, they thought the administrative state rested on principles too alien to be reconciled to US constitutionalism. This interpretation gradually developed as they examined more deeply the philosophical roots of the Progressive view of the Constitution, especially as articulated by Woodrow Wilson. In Progressivism Straussians saw historicism and organic state theory, proximately German in origin, though indebted indirectly to Rousseau's concept of the general will. They argued that from these sources the Progressives had imported an anticonstitutional administrative system whose conception of social justice informed a new version of presidential leadership and whose regulatory and redistributive functions were abetted by empiricist and positivist social science. The overall result was a disordered and distorted constitutional system that had been severed from its basis in natural rights, social contract, and the separation of powers.

Once Martin Diamond's seminal work on *The Federalist* debunked Progressives' cruder materialist attacks on the founding—that the Constitution was supposedly a tool of self-interested elites who reviled democracy—Straussians began to see the historicism that Strauss had identified as the source of so many modern political problems.[42] Leavened with Darwinian evolutionary theory but subordinate to it, historicism came with the related German conception that the state effectuated its purposes through bureaucratic administration.[43]

Some of Storing's students advanced quickly down this path, most notably Paul Eidelberg. He connected the democratizing yet statist-regulatory impulse of Progressive administration to both the historicist conception of progress and Wilson's redefinition of the presidency. When Wilson opined, " 'If [the president] rightly interpret the national thought and boldly insist upon it, he is irresistible,' " or when he asked " 'Why may not the present age write, through me, its political *autobiography*?' " Eidelberg beheld "the taint of historicism." The president becomes the "incarnation of the spirit of his people," with his powers emanating from his embodiment of the popular will.[44] Public administration effectuated the president's vision, whatever its morality or effect on the original Constitution.[45] Another of Storing's students, Kent Aiken Kirwan, argued that Wilson saw politics as having "gradually diminished in importance to the point of leaving little but merely administrative tasks for government"—a perspective grounded in a "Hegelian view of history." The science of administration would realize "an evolutionary historical process that is rational and progressive."[46] Wilson had thereby dismissed prudence from politics and reduced "statesmanship to riding the wave of the future"; it had become "management conceived as the handmaiden of history."[47]

This interpretation matured in the writing of several Straussians, perhaps most extensively in the important work of Ronald J. Pestritto and John Marini.[48] This literature indicted the administrative state as antithetical to American constitutionalism, explaining just how fundamentally and self-consciously

Progressive thinkers sought to transcend it based on a profoundly different understanding of history, human nature, and politics. Progressives thought that the time had come to create a centralized bureaucratic administration in place of the founders' regime. Realization of this vision was historically inevitable, they believed, and the Constitution was an anachronism. The rationally administered state would apply social science to advance progress through bureaucracy, displacing natural rights and limited government, along with the distinctively political activities of prudence, deliberation, and compromise.

An allied development (explored in more detail in chapter 7) was the "rhetorical" presidency. It began with Theodore Roosevelt and Woodrow Wilson and eventually dominated the twentieth century.[49] Roosevelt and Wilson thought the president's original capacity to express and shape public opinion was too confined. Wilson's leadership as "interpretation" held that the president was a "leader of men" who could reflect and articulate public opinion. With and through him, popular opinion could come to realize what the next stage of history required of government. This theory placed a premium on rhetoric that articulated a "vision" for the nation as formulated by the president as Roosevelt's "steward" of the general welfare. The new-style political party would form around this leader and his vision in a quasi-plebiscitary fashion. The leader's command of popular opinion would compel Congress to legislate accordingly. With constitutional and customary constraints on leadership thus overcome in the name of progress, the rest was detail—administrative detail—about how best to enforce the vision voiced by the president and backed by mass popular opinion.[50] This conception of the presidency ascended as American political science initially oriented its professionalization around Hegelianism and German state theory, a development scholars have long recognized.[51] In the words of John Marini, the arrival of this final stage of history transformed politics into the "organic expression of the will (or spirit) of the people; administration is the technical, rational means by which it is made adaptable and put into practice." Within this compass, political science became "the applied science of the rational state."[52]

It was, once again, Strauss's critique of the fact-value distinction and its basis in historicism that enabled his followers to argue that modern political science was founded on the same theoretical principles as the administrative state.[53] Dispensing with empirically irresolvable disputes over "values," the field established itself on the "technical and rational authority of the scientific method—the means by which to achieve social justice." Political science thus found its moral justification in helping the state achieve empirically measurable "progress." Putatively philosophical or normative questions had been transcended by the rational historical process that was being willed by the people and realized through the state. Social science merely "provide[d] the expertise to enable government, and the enlightened bureaucracy, to administer progress or change in the emerging administrative state."[54] Progressivism thus spelled the transcendence not only of natural rights, the separation of powers, and limited government but also of the distinctive political virtue of prudence. Its profoundly prepossessing character meant that there was nothing left to be truly political about.

Straussians concluded that the post–New Deal administrative state had undermined and deranged the founders' constitutionalism, though without wholly supplanting it.[55] They joined many others in analyzing its increased growth and complexity under the Great Society programs of the 1960s. However, unlike most other commentators, they always returned to the original constitutional order as a standard and source of legitimacy. For example, the legislative process and the separation of powers were fundamentally distorted by Congress's delegation of vast but vague legislative power to administrative agencies. Other major themes were the administrative state's transformation of rights into entitlements to be administered by technocratic experts; its obscuring of the responsibility for the actions of government; its relentless distancing of legislation from some conception of the common good and the consent of the governed; and its general weakening of the rule of law. As the administrative state advanced, average citizens increasingly related to their government through massive bureaucracies that progressive liberalism had created compassionately to provide their security and well-being but that in practice were sclerotic, unaccountable, and biased.

These developments only intensified as Congress reorganized itself in the late 1960s and early 1970s to pursue regulatory policy through administrative agencies that it wanted to be more accessible and democratic. More power was devolved upon subcommittee chairs, and special interest groups gained easier access to administrative agencies. The result, from the Straussian perspective, was further derangement and disorder. Congressional committees, special interest groups with their lawyers and lobbyists, and federal courts all became more deeply and competitively enmeshed. Legislators eschewed representation of dispersed but unorganized interests and authentic deliberation about the common good. Instead, Congress produced highly generalized and usually progressive statements of principle to be effectuated by bureaucrats, while its members became advocates and ombudsman for constituents and favored interest groups or corporations. National policy was less frequently public and representative and was more often focused on just servicing contending special interests. Meanwhile, the interested parties usually could litigate in federal court if they were dissatisfied with the results; indeed the regulatory statutes themselves often encouraged them to do so. Judges were quite willing to hear special interest groups through relaxed standing requirements, to second-guess both Congress and administrative agencies, and to manipulate the vague, confusing, and discretion-ridden elements of administrative law. Judges increasingly functioned, in the words of Jeremy Rabkin, as "amateur, unaccountable, episodic managers of regulatory performance."[56] The president, long ago barred from removing many administrators as a result of *Humphrey's Executor v. United States* (1935), could not coordinate the enforcement of the law in any coherent way. The executive power had been dispersed among myriad agencies, many of them having crosscutting mandates and acting with legal independence from presidential control. A rather charitable interpretation of this overall situation was that it represented a combination of American pluralism and the regime's established constitutional principles at once worked into the administrative state.[57] Nevertheless, nearly all Straussians after Storing and Rohr agreed that the administrative state was endangering American constitutionalism. In their eyes it altered political interactions in ways that strained the nation's deepest principles and created a deficit of legitimacy that sternly resisted any reform.

Laced through Straussian analysis was frequent recurrence to Alexis de Tocqueville (as with traditionalists). Indeed, a major study of Tocqueville's place in American thought called Strauss "the most pervasive conservative influence on late-twentieth-century Tocqueville scholars."[58] Tocqueville's approach was akin to the regime analysis Strauss had retrieved from the ancients. Likewise, both Tocqueville and Strauss were "friends but not enthusiasts" of democracy.[59] And both knew that politics was always imperfect and inevitably involved mores and religion, as well as reason and pride. Straussians appreciated that Tocqueville's understanding of administrative centralization derived from equality as the definitive feature of American democracy. They often recapitulated his analysis of democratic equality's tendencies toward general ideas, uniformity, material well-being, and security, which were realized when a centralized state empowered elite administrators to oversee the details of daily life. Straussians regarded Tocqueville's resulting description of "soft" or "mild" despotism as strikingly applicable to the modern United States. Pushed aside were local-level participation in political affairs and the civil associations necessary for the sustenance of self-government under the Constitution. Although in his own time Tocqueville feared the centrifugal forces of the American polity, Straussians typically agreed that, since the Progressive era, it had instead come to resemble the "despotism of administrators" he had warned against.[60]

Tocqueville's influence fit well with Straussians' response to the Progressive attack on the separation of powers, and together the two formed a powerful and ongoing opposition to the administrative state. Today no serious discussion about reforming it can avoid the depth of the Straussian critique. The earlier attempts by Storing and Rohr to reconcile the administrative state with American constitutionalism, while valiant and theoretically sophisticated, seem to have fallen permanently by the wayside.

The "Unitary Executive" in the Reagan Administration and the Law Schools

Conservative criticism did not immediately produce any momentous changes, nor did theorists and academics necessarily expect that it would. But this discourse did help move the parameters of discussion about the purpose and legitimacy of the administrative state. The election of Ronald Reagan as president in 1980 augured a more direct legal-political confrontation. Given that the Democratic Party had normally controlled Congress in the post–New Deal era while Republicans had usually held the presidency, executive power increasingly came to be seen as the best—perhaps the only—way to control the administrative state that Congress had created and that had become thoroughly entrenched in both interest group politics and Supreme Court jurisprudence. This context encouraged the emergence of the theory of the "unitary executive."

Proponents of this idea held that the text, structure, and original meaning of the Constitution gave only the president ultimate authority over officials who undertook executive functions and, along with that authority, the power independently to interpret the meaning of the document with respect to the executive branch. Although long existing in nascent form, the theory was concertedly advanced to limit and direct the administrative state by lawyers in the Reagan Justice Department, by the administrative law jurisprudence of Associate Justice Antonin Scalia, and by conservative theorists in law schools (some of whom had earlier served in the Reagan administration). The academic theory continued to develop in the 1990s and in a new form contributed to the exercise of presidential power in the War on Terror after September 11, 2001 (this latter development is treated in chapter 6).

The growth of executive branch agencies and independent regulatory commissions had earlier generated numerous proposals to cohere and control the burgeoning federal bureaucracy. They typically aimed to help the president direct, coordinate, and make the bureaucracy more efficient—though with Congress always ensuring that it retained substantial control.[61] The 1960s and 1970s brought new regulations and agencies in areas such as the environment, workplace safety, and consumer protection. Soon afterward came the economic "stagflation" that lasted for about a decade. In this situation there was substantial political support for "deregulation," which in turn prompted the administrations of Presidents Nixon, Ford, and Carter to consider more carefully both the processes and effects of federal action. In 1970, under Nixon, the Office of Management and Budget (OMB) was created within the Executive Office of the President. It oversaw the creation of the executive budget to be proposed to Congress. Over time, and largely through executive orders, OMB and the Office of Information and Regulatory Affairs (OIRA), created within OMB in 1980, became the locus of attempts to centralize the review of regulations issued by agencies in the executive branch. With varying degrees of intensity and sophistication, administrations of both parties have, since Nixon, reviewed regulations to ensure that they accord with presidential priorities and to gauge their economic impact, moving under Carter and then Reagan especially toward cost-benefit analysis.[62] After Reagan, the president's influence in the regulatory process, if not the theory of the unitary executive, became more regularized and accepted.[63] But these actions in the executive branch never contemplated the dismantling of the administrative state. Nor was there a revolution in the jurisprudence surrounding it, in part because courts were unwilling to defer to executive authority if it too substantially diminished their own role in the field.[64]

This trend toward more centralized regulatory oversight in the executive branch formed another part of the context for the unitary executive theory's emergence in the Reagan administration. Moreover, many conservatives inside and outside the administration had long thought that the constitutional authority of the presidency had been severely eroded and should be reasserted in the aftermath of Watergate and Nixon's resignation (1973–74), the War Powers Act (1973), and the creation of the office of special prosecutor in the Ethics in Government Act (1978). To justify its oversight of deregulation in the White House, the Reagan administration began to articulate the theory of the unitary executive in several venues. These included opinions by the Office of Legal Counsel (OLC), which is located in the Office of the Attorney General and provides the AG and the president with legal advice; in legal briefs; in presidential signing statements; and in at least one high-profile speech by Attorney General Edwin Meese.[65]

One of the earliest announcements of the idea was Reagan's Executive Order 12,291 (1981). It required executive branch agencies to submit to the director of OMB a regulatory impact analysis of proposed rules. It also prohibited agencies from implementing rules whose costs outweighed their benefits. The OMB, not individual agencies, was given authority over the definitions and standards of review, and rules could not be promulgated until they had been cleared by the OMB. This executive order thus sought to establish "presidential oversight of the regulatory process."[66] The OLC used a rudimentary version of the unitary executive theory in reviewing this order for form and legality. It cited the Take Care Clause (Art. II, sec. 3) as the basis of the order and explicated its meaning with a quotation from Chief Justice William Howard Taft's opinion in *Myers v. United States* (1926): the clause "authorizes the President, as head of the Executive branch, to 'supervise and guide' executive officers in 'their construction of the statutes under which they act in order to secure that unitary and uniform execution of the laws which Article II of the Constitution evidently contemplated in vesting general executive power in the President alone.'"[67] As decided in *Myers*, the Take Care Clause gave the president the "distinctive constitutional role" of "supervisory authority" and the "function of coordinating the execution of many statutes simultaneously."[68] Noting *Myers*'s doubt that the president's supervisory authority could displace a discretionary judgment conveyed by statute to a subordinate executive official, the OLC opinion also underscored *Myers*'s insistence that the president nonetheless could subsequently remove an executive official because of dissatisfaction with the exercise of such discretion.[69] Moreover, a contemporaneous, unreleased draft OLC memorandum urged that EO 12,291 be applicable to independent agencies (or commissions)—not just those commonly recognized as within the executive branch and whose heads were subject to presidential removal. That view was contrary to the statement in *Humphrey's Executor* that the president's authority over such institutions ended with his power of appointment.[70] This claim was not included in the final OLC opinion, but it shows that with the theory of the unitary executive the Reagan administration was contemplating fundamental challenges to the administrative state.

A careful study found an "identifiable version" of the unitary executive theory in seven Reagan-era OLC opinions. One near the end of Reagan's second term, signed by Assistant Attorney General Charles J. Cooper, supported the theory by appealing to the principles and structure of the constitutional text and presented historical "evidence of original intent" from the Philadelphia convention and *The Federalist* papers.[71] Cooper wrote that the president's authority "as head of a unitary executive" meant that he "controls all subordinate officers within the executive branch." Article II's vesting of "the executive power," he emphasized, meant "the *whole* executive power." Congress violated the Constitution whenever it interfered with presidential supervision or direction of subordinates who carried out "executive functions."[72]

The trend intensified once Edwin Meese became US attorney general in February 1985. Meese worked to bring more intellectual discipline and coherence to the activities of the Department of Justice.[73] A clear goal was nurturance of conservative legal ideas over the long term, particularly originalism.[74] His efforts included long-range planning, publicity campaigns, careful hiring practices, discussion groups, seminars, and invitations to external speakers. Under Meese's direction the DOJ held seminars on the unitary executive and on *Humphrey's Executor*.[75] Indeed, in a noted speech Meese mockingly attacked the language of that decision, which had insulated officials in independent agencies from presidential authority. "Federal agencies performing executive functions are themselves properly agents of the executive. They are not 'quasi' this, or 'independent' that. In the tripartite scheme of government a body with enforcement powers is part of the executive branch of government."[76] Meese made it clear throughout this speech that in undermining the separation of powers, the core challenge of the administrative state was to obscure responsibility and thus accountability for government actions.[77] The theory of the unitary executive, in contrast, meant that the president enforced the law and was electorally accountable for his actions.

The decision in *INS v. Chada* (1983), which overturned Congress's use of a legislative veto, contained a strong defense of the separation of powers that emboldened the Reagan administration's efforts. After *Chada*, said Meese, the question became, What more "can be done to increase responsibility and accountability?"[78] One answer was continued defense of the unitary executive, and the removal power specifically, in the litigation of major cases such as *Bowsher v. Synar* (1986) and *Morrison v. Olson* (1988).

Bowsher found a violation of the separation of powers in a provision of the Balanced Budget and Emergency Deficit Control (Gramm-Rudman-Hollings) Act. It had given the comptroller general the power to require the president to make specific budget cuts, even though the comptroller was subject to removal by Congress rather than by the president. For this reason the administration's brief in the case used the unitary executive theory to attack the statute. "The Framers deliberately settled upon a unitary Executive," whereas the Act, argued the brief, undermined the executive's responsibility and accountability for enforcement of the law.[79] The comptroller could not exercise executive power unless he was subject to removal by the president. The brief even suggested in a footnote that developments subsequent to *Humphrey's Executor* seemed "to have cast a shadow upon [its] premises" regarding the limits on presidential removal power.[80] Indeed, participants in the case and later commentators were well aware that the question of control of independent agencies via presidential removal lurked on the periphery of *Bowsher*. Solicitor General Charles Fried nevertheless sought to limit the reach of the unitary logic by insisting that any suggestion that the government's position endangered "those agencies or would embark this Court on some constitutional adventure is simply a scare which we don't intend to throw into the Court." Justice Sandra Day O'Conner replied: "Well, Mr. Fried, I'll confess you scared me with it."[81] Chief Justice Warren Burger's majority opinion explicitly and rather offhandedly exempted independent agencies from the decision's reach.[82] Nevertheless, the brief in *Bowsher* showed that the unitary executive was being asserted with increased vigor and frequency and that its potential for disrupting the administrative state was becoming more pointed.

All of these issues arose once again in *Morrison v. Olson* (1988), which upheld the constitutionality of the independent counsel statute. The decision reversed the District of Columbia Circuit Court of Appeals, which had repeatedly invoked the unitary executive theory to attack the statute as an invasion of the president's authority under Article II of the Constitution.[83] The DOJ made the same argument for the responsible and accountable unitary executive in its *Morrison* brief.[84] It contended that the independent counsel should be treated as an executive office subject to at-will presidential removal. *Humphrey's Executor*'s limitations on the removal power were again inapposite because "the duties of an independent counsel are purely executive in nature, and they therefore can be performed only by an officer who is accountable to the President."[85]

Chief Justice William Rehnquist's majority opinion was based on a more relaxed conception of the separation of powers than the one in *Chada* and *Bowsher* that had so encouraged advocates of the unitary executive theory. The Court held that removal of the independent counsel only for "good cause" (rather than at the will of the president via the attorney general) did not fundamentally invade executive authority, because Congress was not involved in the removal and the independent counsel was an "inferior" officer whose jurisdiction and duties were limited. Justice Scalia wrote a vehement dissent that twice mentioned the "unitary executive" by name and that subsequently became a touchstone for defenders of the idea in the conservative legal movement. Sounding the core of the theory, he wrote that Article II's vesting of executive power in the president "does not mean *some* of the executive power, but *all* of the executive power."[86] The investigatory and prosecutorial duties of the independent counsel were "quintessentially" executive, and therefore the officer should be removable at the will of the president.[87] Scalia's dissent proclaimed a grave violation of the separation of powers in the majority's acceptance of a politically unaccountable executive officer, but, as in *Bowsher*, the Court was unwilling to pursue a line of reasoning that all could see would imperil the independent agencies of the administrative state.[88]

The Department of Justice under Meese also led an initiative to use presidential signing statements as expressions of the unitary executive theory. Earlier presidents had used them to criticize aspects of a law, but the Reagan administration amplified and cohered the process. Aided by young staffers such as Steven Calabresi and Samuel Alito, the DOJ began to advance this agenda in 1985.[89] The department began citing signing statements in legal briefs and other official documents in the hope that the principles of the unitary executive would gain exposure and come to be regarded as akin to the legislative history of a statute. In 1986 Meese convinced West Publishing Company to print the statements in the "Legislative History" section of the *United States Code Congressional and Administrative News*. The phrase "unitary executive" was used in only one Reagan-era statement, but its logic was "the driving force and the constitutional rationale" for the initiative.[90]

One notable signing statement was issued in relation to the unitary executive litigation discussed above. When signing the Deficit Control Act, Reagan protested that the duties of the comptroller general were an invasion of the executive branch.[91] The majority opinion in *Bowsher v. Synar* cited this statement.[92] Likewise, in signing the reauthorization of the independent counsel statute challenged in *Morrison*, Reagan stated that the officer should be subject to "appointment, review, and removal" within the executive branch.[93]

While the issues of executive authority and removal raised in these signing statements (and then in *Bowsher* and *Morrison*) did not directly involve administrative agencies, a goal of the signing statement project all along was greater presidential direction of them.[94] Internal DOJ communications expressed this view. For example, one official wrote that signing statements "can be used to tell agencies how to interpret a statute. The President can direct agencies to ignore unconstitutional provisions or to read provisions in a way that eliminates constitutional or policy problems. This direction permits the President to seize the initiative in creating what will eventually be the agency's interpretation—an interpretation that the courts have traditionally given great deference."[95] Steven G. Calabresi, a participant in the initiative who became a prominent law professor, subsequently defended signing statements in the same terms: the theory of the unitary executive enabled the president to direct subordinates who exercised delegated executive authority. Moreover, he argued, since the president was the head of each executive branch regulatory agency, the Supreme Court's *Chevron* doctrine of deference to agency interpretations of ambiguous statutory language should be extended to signing statements that announced the president's interpretation of a particular provision.[96] Thus did the concept of political accountability at the core of the unitary executive build on a key pillar of administrative law jurisprudence in attempting to assert presidential control of executive agencies.

As a student at Yale Law School, Calabresi had been a founder of the Federalist Society for Law and Public Policy. This organization and scholars associated with it helped to develop the theory as an important component of the conservative legal movement in the 1990s and thereafter. The Federalist Society's yearly conferences frequently addressed the unitary executive and often included DOJ alumni.[97] The quickly growing law review literature elaborated themes initially sounded in the Reagan Justice Department.[98] Scholars delineated the basis of the theory in Article II's Vesting Clause, the presidential oath, and the duty to "take care that the laws be faithfully executed." "Unitarians" likewise argued that the founders quite consciously created a unitary executive in response to their experience of feeble and disordered administration under the Articles of Confederation. They often recurred to the defense of the presidency in *The Federalist* (especially number 70) and to immediate pre- and post-ratification constitutional history. Eventually, research traced the understanding of the unitarian idea in presidential administrations across US history, focusing especially on presidents' near unanimous insistence on the power to supervise, direct, and remove officers who exercised executive authority.[99] Theorists differed about whether the president could exercise all discretionary executive power directly (supplanting the actions of any subordinate), or could only nullify actions of subordinates he disapproved, or was limited to removing officers whose actions he disapproved (principal officers and perhaps even some or all inferior officers). Beyond these important disagreements, it was clear that "the practical consequence of this theory is dramatic: it renders unconstitutional independent agencies and counsels to the extent that they exercise discretionary executive power."[100]

Further details of the now vast literature need not be comprehensively reviewed here, but it is possible to make some summative judgments about the theory's place in the general conservative response to the administrative state. Most important is the recognition that prior to September 11, 2001, the unitary executive was "a relatively limited tool to critique the administration and execution of the laws in the Executive Branch." Its initial aim was "to reclaim some power from Congress vis à vis the interpretation and execution of the laws."[101] Before the "second half of the George W. Bush administration only a very small fraction" of the law review literature mentioned the theory in the context of the president's war powers or foreign policy.[102] Moreover, presidents both before and after Reagan sought to increase presidential control and coordination of regulatory bureaucracies and, likewise, undertook numerous other unilateral actions.[103] Whatever one might think of the foreign and military policies of the George W. Bush administration or the conception of executive war power underlying them, the unitary executive "had been developing long before [he] took office" and is "much bigger than any one person."[104] Nor did all unitarians agree with the new direction the theory took. Calabresi (with a coauthor) explicitly distinguished his defense of the unitary executive in the realm of domestic policy from the claims made by the George W. Bush administration in the realm of war and foreign affairs.[105] A careful critic of the unitary executive has rightly observed that the technical arguments for presidential power in these two realms proceed from "different sets of legal considerations."[106] Arguments for presidential control of executive branch agencies and officials do not automatically justify unilateral presidential war making. It is clear that the initial development of the unitary executive in relation to the administrative state proceeded for the most part separately from considerations of emergency and war. These latter topics also involve deep questions about what executive power is and how it might be reconciled to constitutionalism, questions taken up in chapter 7.

Justice Scalia and the Administrative State

The jurisprudence of Associate Justice Antonin Scalia kept on the conservative agenda the theory of the unitary executive and the problems of the administrative state. As mentioned previously, he fully endorsed the theory of the unitary executive, the consequent presidential authority to supervise and direct executive officers, and the claim that the president could constitutionally remove any officer who exercised executive authority. His administrative law jurisprudence hinged directly on the unitary executive as the primary locus of political responsibility.[107] He had developed this view prior to joining the Supreme Court in 1986, while he had been a professor specializing in administrative law, head of the American Bar Association section devoted to the field, editor of the journal *Regulation*, and a judge on DC Circuit Court of Appeals. All along he had supported more vigorous use of executive power for deregulation and endorsed the OMB clearance provision of Reagan's Executive Order 12,291, even hoping that it might be extended to independent agencies.[108] He also had questioned the validity and reach of *Humphrey's Executor*, and also wrote the DC Circuit Court opinion preceding *Bowsher*, which held that the comptroller general could not exercise executive power while being subject to removal by Congress.[109] Accordingly, Scalia's dissent in *Morrison* was a natural outgrowth from his earlier thought.

While avidly defending the unitary executive, Scalia did not think that the administrative state could be successfully checked by any thorough reinvigoration of the nondelegation doctrine. For decades modern government had come to depend on the use of statutes with general language that gave significant discretion to the administrative agencies that applied them. Scalia observed that the Court had essentially abjured consideration of the question. "What legislated standard, one must wonder, can possibly be too vague to survive judicial scrutiny, when we have repeatedly upheld, in various contexts, a 'public interest' standard?"[110] The reality was that constitutional law had developed such that "the scope of delegation is largely uncontrollable by the courts."[111]

Given that the nondelegation doctrine was dead, how could the Court help restrain the administrative state? Scalia paired support for the unitary executive with a strong defense of the *Chevron* doctrine of judicial deference to administrative agency interpretations of ambiguous statutory language. This position was rooted in both political realism and the separation of powers: since the Court would continue to accept that Congress would continue to delegate, the only hope of accountability lay in the Court's avoiding micromanagement of the agencies and instead allowing their inevitably political choices to be associated with the president, who, under the unitary executive theory, had the ultimate power to remove officers from them. The crucial first step in Scalia's approach was to recognize "rule making as politics." Broad delegation from Congress often required agencies to make political choices. If "the conferral of nontechnocratic, political judgments upon the agencies" was done to address "the modern complaint of the 'unresponsive' bureaucracy," then "the scheme of judicial review and the requirements of administrative process must permit political judgments to be made politically." Agencies should not be second-guessed by courts but rather should respond to the "popular will through the political process—the administration placed in office in the last election, the oversight and appropriations committees of Congress, the groups with political power" who appeared before them.[112] Soon after Scalia made this statement, *Chevron* was decided and its ruling included language that quite clearly harmonized with it: "While agencies are not directly accountable to the people, the Chief Executive is, and it is entirely appropriate for this political branch of the Government to make such policy choices."[113] Scalia quickly became the leading defender of *Chevron* deference as the best available way to make legislative delegations at least somewhat politically accountable.[114] He rarely explicitly coupled judicial deference with a strong defense of the unitary executive's removal power. Nevertheless, both positions are readily apparent in his jurisprudence, and later scholars have rightly recognized that together they would produce administrative agencies with substantial discretion that could be directed by and made accountable to the president.[115]

The main point of the unitary executive theory for conservative constitutional lawyers was to challenge the growth of the administrative state and its dominance by the liberal-tending "iron triangle" of Congress, interest groups, and bureaucrats. Elevation of the presidency as a standard-bearer for the conservative causes of smaller government and separation of powers orthodoxy marked a departure from older, traditionalist and libertarian criticisms of the New Deal order that remained suspicious of the presidency. This shift made sense in the context of what the Reagan administration confronted: modern, rights-based judicial review that usually yielded liberal policy outcomes and that typically deferred to regulatory bureaucrats; a Congress long controlled by the Democratic Party and dedicated to expanding the administrative state; and the success of conservatives in electing a very popular president. Moreover, reality had shown that the Progressive dream of enlightened, apolitical administration was no longer tenable. The field was open for the conservative-populist-presidential claim that the administrative state was in fact a fount of meddling overregulation that destroyed liberty. Defenders of the unitary executive successfully joined "the release of presidential power within the executive branch" with a demand for "restoration of responsibility and accountability in government."[116] The informal powers that had accrued to the presidency since the Progressive era, basing the office ever more on the rhetorical harnessing of popular opinion in the context of continued party decay, now were linked to the formalist and originalist claims of the unitary executive. This development further bolstered the constitutional legitimacy of the president against other institutions. However, the unitary executive as the latest version of presidential power raised political and constitutional concerns for conservatives. By centralizing so much power in the presidency, the unitary executive made policy victories somewhat hostage to the next presidential election. This dynamic tended to undercut the traditional conservative preference for political stability.[117] More fundamentally, as Stephen Skowronek has warned, the long-term concentration of power in the presidency, a development intensified by the unitary executive's integration of earlier such moves, illustrated the fact that "new ideas about how to assert presidential power are now fast outpacing new ideas about how to hold that power to account."[118] The conservative effort to restrain the administrative state through a rejuvenated presidency will have miscarried if it sidelines the orthodox constitutionalist concern with limits on all official power. Amid this risk, and though the unitary executive theory was often principled and cogent, in retrospect it is clear that, like the efforts of various conservative critics, it was unable fundamentally to dislodge the administrative state.

Conclusion: Continuing Conservative Criticism of the Administrative State

Conservative assessment of the administrative state should not be obscured by or conflated with the post-9/11 unitary executive justification for presidential war making. The administrative state's origins, development, and constitutional legitimacy are now matters of increasing scholarly concern.[119] Sympathetic histories treat it as a necessary modern development that nonetheless struggled to insert itself in to the constitutional system.[120] Others have been more critical, seeing it as an often anticonstitutional enterprise that undermined and distorted the nation's first principles.[121] Still others, recognizing the serious concerns about its legitimacy, reach, and efficacy, have suggested ways to improve and defend it.[122] Perhaps most provocative is the claim that modern society has well and truly arrived at the age of enlightened administration in the executive branch. Anachronized and now rightly displaced are the traditional understandings of legislative deliberation, the separation of powers, and the rule of law.[123]

This lively reevaluation addresses the basic constitutional questions that have long preoccupied conservatives and still provoke them. For example, the accomplished legal historian Philip Hamburger has argued that the administrative state corrupts the separation of powers and the understanding of law in the Anglo-American tradition because it acts outside the forms and structures that evolved for centuries to constrain arbitrary power. The combination of legislative, executive, and judicial powers in numerous agencies enables the largely unchecked pursuit of their policies. In this way much of modern government has retrogressed to the undifferentiated yet dispersed centers of power that constitutional systems evolved since the Middle Ages to oppose. The administrative state, says Hamburger, has reconstituted extralegal power akin to the royal prerogative.[124]

Another bracing indictment comes from Charles Murray, a leading libertarian who blames the post–New Deal administrative state for much of the nation's political dysfunction and irresponsibility. A Congress corrupted by its involvement with regulators and special interests is unlikely to change course; the Supreme Court will not abandon more than a half-century of administrative law jurisprudence; and the presidency under both parties does more to foster the growth of regulatory bureaucracy than to curtail it. Murray's proposed solution is selective civil disobedience of the more arbitrary and capricious diktats of the regulatory state, backstopped by a privately endowed legal defense fund and the establishment among professional organizations of insurance pools to pay fines issued by regulators. His strategy is to overburden the regulatory apparatus and the courts in the hope that eventually the administrative state will become less intrusive and friendlier to liberty. That a figure of Murray's stature could describe the founders' Constitution as irredeemably "broken" and call for civil disobedience against the administrative state is a mark of just how intense the topic had become by 2015.[125]

Some recent Supreme Court opinions also have questioned central components of the administrative state more pointedly than seen in the past several decades. In *Free Enterprise Fund v. Public Company Accounting Oversight Board* (2010) the Court refused to extend *Humphrey's Executor's* limitations on the president's removal power. The statute's limitation of removal of board members only for good cause as adjudged by members of the Securities and Exchange Commission (themselves only removable for cause and not at the will of the president) severed them from any accountability to the president. Chief Justice John Roberts's plurality opinion was no frontal attack on the administrative state, but it did keep in play the question of removal associated with it.[126]

Justice Clarence Thomas has gone much further, suggesting in several opinions that the administrative state was fundamentally inconsistent with the separation of powers. A notable concurrence indicted the Court's lax treatment of the nondelegation doctrine, which he argued has led to the exercise of legislative powers by both administrative agencies and the entities they regulate. In another case he asserted that administrative agencies could not legitimately exercise the judicial power of federal courts.[127] Thomas has also attacked judicial deference to agency interpretations as an unconstitutional transfer of the Court's own authority, one that Congress could not require of courts.[128] Another concurrence called for reconsidering the constitutionality of *Chevron* deference as a possible violation of the vesting clauses of both Article I and Article III.[129]

An earlier dissent by Chief Justice Roberts (joined by Associate Justices Anthony Kennedy and Samuel Alito) also expressed serious concern about the scope of judicial deference under *Chevron*, warning that "the danger posed by the growing power of the administrative state cannot be dismissed."[130] In *King v. Burwell* Roberts's majority opinion declined to invoke *Chevron* deference in upholding federal subsidies to federally run insurance exchanges under the Affordable Care Act.[131] Scalia also clearly indicated that he too, the great erstwhile defender of *Chevron*, was rethinking deference just prior to his death.[132] These calls for reevaluation were measured, but abandoning *Chevron* for de novo review of challenged agency actions, instead of automatic judicial deference to them, is now a readily identifiable position among conservative commentators.[133]

Halting *Chevron* would upend decades of jurisprudence, as would substantive reinvigoration of either the nondelegation doctrine or the president's removal power. Conservatives were well aware that such major reforms are not on the immediate horizon, but they did not cease raising the constitutional issues. Three more modest proposals have been offered by Christopher DeMuth. The first has circulated for several years and been approved by the House of Representatives three times: the REINS Act (Regulations from the Executive in Need of Scrutiny). It would require both houses of Congress to approve major rules issued by administrative agencies before they take effect. REINS would check the administrative state by increasing legislative involvement and accountability for often costly and controversial rules, a dynamic that would upset the current arrangement whereby Congress can avoid much of the blame for unpopular bureaucratic regulations. A second proposal is to codify in statute the requirement of cost-benefit analysis that has evolved in the executive branch since the 1980s. This move would allow courts to eschew excessive deference, because they could more readily hold agency rule making to empirical and professional standards that are harder to game or avoid. A third idea is to subject rules issued by the executive branch to a fifteen-year sunset provision. This reform would compel reexamination of rules to insure their propriety and relevance prior to their continuation or modification.[134]

These several developments make clear that conservative concern with the administrative state shows no signs of abating. As this chapter shows, when conservatives began to regroup and rethink their own principles in the post–New Deal era, they marked the administrative state as a serious threat. They criticized it based on their own varying philosophical and political loyalties, consistently highlighting the tension between the imperatives of centralized, regulatory, highly discretionary bureaucracy and the principles of American constitutionalism. The unitary executive theory that emerged from the Reagan administration was a further concrete attempt to control and direct the administrative state. Although conservative criticism helped ensure that the administrative state never wholly overwhelmed constitutionalism, neither have the two ever been wholly reconciled. Its constitutional problems remain, and conservative ideas will continue to feature in attempts at their resolution. The centralized regulatory governance of the administrative state necessarily affected federalism, to which we turn in part II.

PART TWO

THE EROSION OF FEDERALISM
An Overview

Federalism is a form of political organization that divides lawmaking authority between individual, territorially defined member states and a central government. A signal victory of the New Deal was to overcome the established conception of "dual" federalism, in which the states and the national government acted as equal sovereigns with mutually exclusive jurisdiction over different realms of law. The presidency of Franklin D. Roosevelt and the jurisprudence of the Supreme Court successfully replaced the old federalism with nationally administered regulatory policies and social welfare programs. Vast sectors of policy formerly belonging to the states or civil society came under federal control. The era's most famous and far-reaching Supreme Court decisions, which we need not recount here, ratified this shift through a broad reading of congressional power under the Commerce, Taxing and Spending, and General Welfare clauses. Their cumulative effect was decisively to centralize US government and concomitantly to restrict the states.[1] This trend continued with only minor interruptions for the rest of the twentieth century.

The New Deal also rapidly increased the use and funding of federal "grants-in-aid" to the states. Under this practice the national government transferred funds to the states for certain purposes and on certain conditions, typically requiring them to contribute their own funds and to administer programs according to national standards. While the name "cooperative federalism" was eventually given to this practice, the states became, at least for some purposes, administrative agents of a centralized, unitary government. And these purposes ranged widely, including poor relief and income support components of the Social Security Act, public works projects (especially highways), agricultural programs, environmental conservation, public housing, and specialized educational projects. Although the practice of federal grants preceded the New Deal, and although the Roosevelt administration left many traditional state responsibilities unaffected, the die was cast. Henceforth the states administered national baseline policies in areas previously left to them.[2] This pattern was also elaborated over the rest of the twentieth century.

The next surge of centralization was the Great Society programs begun in the 1960s and consolidated in the 1970s, along with the related "rights revolution" in the Supreme Court. Federal grant expenditures increased sharply between 1964 and 1968, with disbursements and conditions that frequently bypassed the states to deal directly with urban municipalities. The locally administered "national interest" expanded to include urban renewal, health care, and job training, among other programs. One new and more intrusive method of imposing national standards was "crosscutting" conditions and sanctions, in which failure to comply with rules in one program could lead to the elimination of aid from others. Another was what came to be known as partial preemption, in which Congress asserted authority over a policy domain by setting national standards and then encouraging the states to adopt and enforce them. If the states declined or failed to enforce the standards, the national government could wholly displace them from any activity in the area. Partial preemption began in the areas of environmental protection and food inspection and then spread to others like occupational health and safety and energy regulation. The Court upheld these practices.[3]

Meanwhile, after the *Brown v. Board of Education* desegregation decision (1954), the Court, sometimes following Congress and sometimes alone, remade state law and society in basic ways. It relied on the Commerce Clause, the Equal Protection Clause of the Fourteenth Amendment, and "incorporation" of much of the federal Bill of Rights to make its provisions binding on the states. The battle against racial discrimination was extended to housing policy, supervising state electoral practices under the Voting Rights Act (1965), and monitoring employment practices and guaranteeing access to public accommodations under the Civil Rights Act of 1964. Eventually the Court said that racial nondiscrimination required bussing to achieve racial balance in schools, and the use of race-based affirmative action in employment and education. The quick expansion of federal rights and the professional coordination of litigation campaigns soon drew federal courts into the monitoring and managerial oversight of not only school districts but also state and local prisons, mental hospitals, and police forces.[4]

The Court also outlawed prayer in public schools, reformed apportionment in state electoral districts on the principle of "one person, one vote," and altered the states' laws of criminal procedure by incorporating provisions of the Bill of Rights and adding its own self-created requirements (e.g., the "Miranda" warnings issued upon the arrest of a criminal suspect). It also swept aside state restrictions on obscenity and created a "right to privacy," which soon morphed into a right to abortion that overrode the various state approaches to the issue. The details of these well-known doctrinal and jurisprudential innovations are readily available elsewhere, but as one leading study has concluded, this sweeping imposition of national standards "not only promised to revive the old conflict between centralization and localism, but it also raised the question of the nature of the United States as a national community."[5]

Starting with Dwight Eisenhower, Republican presidential administrations sought to moderate the centralization of power. Their strategies, political investment, and level of success varied. None ever sought wholly to undo the centralized, bureaucratic regulation and welfare provision established by the New Deal and elaborated by the Great Society. A brief review of some of the major initiatives shows that, despite the continuation of nationalization, concern about federalism was a consistent undercurrent in post–New Deal politics, a subtheme that established the context for conservative thought on the issue.

In 1955 President Eisenhower supported Congress's creation of the Commission on Intergovernmental Relations (the Kestnbaum Commission). Initially intended to provide a blueprint for devolution of federal power and programs to the states, instead it endorsed the template of "cooperative federalism" and its primary tool of federal grants-in-aid. The Kestnbaum Commission's goal became to streamline federal-state-local programs rather than any restoration of pre–New Deal federalism. Eisenhower did support a sorting out of national and state functions, but his Joint Federal-State Action Committee (created in 1957) could agree on only two programs to devolve to the states (sewage treatment plants and vocational education). Tellingly, champions of the local beneficiaries of federal measures in each area opposed the changes in Congress, and neither became law. Moreover, Eisenhower advocated and signed into law massive new federal grant programs, including the National Defense Education Act

(1958) and National Interstate and Defense Highways Act (1956). These two, at least, he justified based on the clear national responsibility for defense.[6] The New Deal model endured amid Eisenhower's rather limited efforts at change.

The administration of Richard Nixon made another attempt at invigorating federalism. His program inevitably included a new spate of management reforms to improve the functional efficiency of interactions between the national government and states and localities. More distinctive were "block grants" that consolidated related grant programs into a single one, with fewer conditions on their use than more restrictive "targeted" grants. Another major feature of the Nixon era was the use of "general-revenue sharing," the disbursement of money to the states with virtually no strings attached. Finally, President Nixon proposed that the national government fully finance important categories of welfare provision (as authorized by 1972 amendments to the Social Security Act); the federal government also created major new regulations in areas formerly left to the states, especially regarding the environment and via the Occupational Health and Safety Act (1970). As these nationalizing actions showed, Nixon was ultimately more committed to what he understood as strong and effective government than to a decentralized federal system. He also confronted an assertive but fragmented Democratic majority in Congress that was committed to national regulation and disinclined to accept his leadership on federalism, or much else. Consequently, there was no rebalancing of federalism. Restrictive conditional grants continued to proliferate, as did intrusive regulations in several new areas. States and localities remained as financially beholden to the national government as they were subject to its regulatory and administrative direction.[7]

President Ronald Reagan's commitment both to private social ordering through markets and to moral traditionalism usually undergirded his administration's attempts to reduce the national government's domestic role and to devolve power to the states. Reagan quickly established an advisory group on federalism in 1981 to support these efforts. His administration's budget process reprioritized spending on federal grants, eliminating many, and reduced the funding for those that remained. General-revenue sharing was terminated in 1986. The administration also consolidated several restrictive categorical grants into block grants, giving states more spending discretion and requiring less federal involvement. All this occurred amid a concerted program of deregulation that perforce lifted numerous national restrictions on the states. Likewise, the looming national debt and the constraints of the Gramm-Rudman-Hollings deficit reduction process exerted an overall structural limitation on federal spending that aided that administration's small-government, pro-federalism agenda. In 1987 Reagan cohered and restated the administration's stance in an executive order "to restore the division of governmental responsibilities between the national government and the States that was intended by the Framers of the Constitution." The order directed executive departments and agencies to consider a detailed list of fundamental principles of federalism when they formulated and implemented policies or proposed legislation that might affect states and localities.[8]

The Reagan administration succeeded in cutting federal spending on grants for the first time since the 1940s and in eliminating some regulations and compulsions for national uniformity. Nevertheless, Reagan approved new national regulations that coerced the states (for example, in the trucking industry and in the national drinking age attached to highway funding), as well as new conditional federal grants. Never realized was the president's proposal in the 1982 State of the Union address for a grand "swap" of federal-state responsibilities: the federal government would assume the full costs of Medicaid if the states would take over Aid to Families with Dependent Children, food stamps, and several smaller aid programs. This proposal failed, and upon Reagan's departure both new spending and new grant programs quickly resumed their growth. His administration effectuated more decentralizing changes in federalism than any since the New Deal, but as the most detailed scholarship on the subject agrees, "Reagan pulled off no revolution."[9]

When the Republican Party gained a majority in Congress for the first time in forty years, it enacted the Unfunded Mandates Reform Act (1995). The law aimed to prevent congressional regulations from being forced on the states without the money to pay for their administration. It had some marginal effect, but exempted many extant programs and was written in a way that allowed for easy evasion. The increased national control of state education policy in the No Child Left Behind Act (2001) and in the prescription drug amendments to Medicare (among several other policies) under President George W. Bush suggested that the Republican Party had finally given up on federalism.[10]

Another important context for conservative thought about federalism was the renewed defense of it that emerged on the Supreme Court under Chief Justice William Rehnquist. This development was rather startling because, although the Court had limited the imposition of national standards in 1976, its decision was quickly overruled in 1985.[11] In *National League of Cities v. Usery* the Court held that the extension of the wages and hours provisions of the Fair Labor Standards Act (FLSA) to state and municipal employees violated the sovereignty of the states by interfering with their traditional functions of governance. It was the first time since the New Deal that the Court had relied on the principles of federalism and the logic of the Tenth Amendment to overturn an act of Congress passed under the commerce power. States quickly sued to extend *Usery*'s logic. Then *Garcia v. San Antonio Metropolitan Transit Authority* reversed *Usery*, validating the application of the FLSA amendments to state and municipal employees and seemingly withdrawing the Court from any further attempts to revive federalism. The states, said Associate Justice Harry Blackmun, writing for the majority, were adequately protected by representation in Congress (especially the Senate), by the supposedly "federal" aspects of the legislative process in Washington, and by particular constitutional provisions that acknowledged state authority. This view, earlier a part of Justice William Brennan's dissent in *Usery*, came to be called the "process" (or "political safeguards") theory of federalism. It signified judicial deference to national control of the states on the New Deal model.

Justices Rehnquist and Sandra Day O'Connor vigorously dissented in *Garcia*, predicting that eventually *Usery*'s core logic would return. To some extent it did in the Rehnquist Court's "federalism revival," which occurred in four jurisprudential categories.[12] First, the Court held that state sovereignty, the structure of federalism, and the principles of the Tenth Amendment prevented states from being required, or "commandeered," into enforcing otherwise valid federal laws.[13] Second, Congress must accept that the principle of state sovereign immunity under the Eleventh Amendment prohibited federal authorization of a lawsuit in federal court against a state government without its consent.[14] The Court extended the principle of sovereign immunity beyond the amendment's terms but, consistent with this principle (the Court argued), it did so by overturning the federal government's authorization of private suits brought by state employees in the state's own courts for overtime pay under the FLSA.[15]

A third development was a return to some judicial limitations on congressional regulatory authority over local affairs under the Commerce Clause. In overturning the Gun-Free School Zones Act's (1990) criminalization of the possession of a firearm with 1,000 feet of a school, the Court held that the activity had no "substantial effect" on interstate commerce and improperly displaced the state police power over local matters (here, the regulation of public schools).[16] The Court extended this logic to overturn a provision of the Violence Against Women Act (1994), which had authorized victims to sue their attackers in federal court.[17] The Rehnquist Court's majority clearly thought there must exist some outer limits to the reach of the Commerce Clause if a federalism with any meaningful role for the states was to endure.

Finally, the Court narrowed the power that Congress had over the states through its use of section 5 of the Fourteenth Amendment. In the leading case, the Court overturned the Religious Freedom Restoration Act (1993), whereby Congress had sought to prevent the states from burdening religious expression by compelling them to adhere to Congress's preferred jurisprudential approach to the Free Exercise Clause of the First Amendment (as incorporated through the Fourteenth). But congressional authority under section 5 was only remedial, said the Court, and only the Court itself was constitutionally empowered to define the legal meaning of the rights protected by the Fourteenth Amendment. By overstepping its authority under section 5 and displacing the Court's power to establish the amendment's reach, Congress had intruded into state prerogatives and upset the balance of federalism.[18] In a series of subsequent cases the Court ruled that Congress could not use its authority under section 5 to abrogate state sovereign immunity, thus shielding the states from private lawsuits that had been authorized by Congress in order to prevent state infringement of patents and trademarks, or to enforce against state governments such measures as the Age Discrimination in Employment Act and the Americans with Disabilities Act.

An avalanche of scholarly protest predictably greeted the Rehnquist Court for having the temerity to take federalism seriously again. And certainly its federalism jurisprudence was subject to legitimate criticism and disagreement. Nevertheless, it never came close to upending the New Deal constitutional settlement. Neither the New Deal's regulation of major sectors of the economy nor its signature social welfare programs were challenged. For example, the Commerce Clause decisions adhered to the New Deal's "substantial effects" test. The Court thus left intact congressional power to regulate virtually any economic activity, declaring merely that that activities in question were not in any sense economic.[19] On the long historical view, the Court was drawing lines only at the margins—contestable to be sure—in an era of centralized, positive government.

No real federalism revolution occurred, in part because the conservative political revival surrounding the Court, though critical of modern centralized government, was not strong enough to dislodge the New Deal (or even much of the Great Society). Nor was the Court as an institution capable of creating the political demand for decentralization that would have enabled it to go further than it did. The fact that the Court was leading on federalism testified to just how dissipated the doctrine had become. Furthermore, the Rehnquist Court decisions, unlike those that opposed the New Deal, did not challenge the basic political agenda of the nation's governing coalition. Instead they pruned what the Court's majority regarded as some of the more egregious excesses of modern centralized government, benefiting from a political environment that was newly tolerant of such action. It has been rightly concluded that the Rehnquist Court was "feeling its way toward a distinctly post–New Deal decentralization of the federal system."[20] In sum, neither the Rehnquist Court nor the attempts of several Republican administrations to rein in the use of federal grants and mandates came close to resetting the centralizing template of post–New Deal constitutionalism.

Of course the states could never be wiped off the map in favor of regional groupings or an absolutely unitary national structure. They still had their own constitutions, the authority to tax, and responsibilities that ranged from highways and prisons to schools and health care.[21] Moreover, the governing capacity and professionalism of the states had gradually improved in the second half of the century, heightening the justification for the limited forms of devolution or deference that did occur.[22]

The Rehnquist Court was yet another example of the way federalism always produced legal conflicts that found their way to the nation's highest tribunal. An additional illustration of this theme was the ongoing debate about national "preemption" of state law through the Supremacy Clause of the Constitution. It involved significant questions about the appropriate rules governing the national market, corporate accountability, and states' responsibilities, and thereby reprised issues that had consistently recurred in the federal system both before and after the New Deal.[23] This theme of perpetual conflict is also apparent in the constant stream of scholarship that sees federalism as embodying a tension or struggle (or dialogue) that is coeval with American constitutionalism.[24] This view has always been opposed at the poles: for example, in the argument that the deepest sources of American federal thought actually conduce to a nationalist mode of political deliberation; and in the opposite view that the federal union was originally based on state sovereignty until it was refounded as a centralizing nationalist leviathan because of the Civil War.[25] We can be assured that conflict and fluidity will continue to define American federalism in practice and on the Court, and that the states will continue to exist and to govern in meaningful if significantly constrained ways. Federalism endures, but it has been circumscribed within the ambit of the centralized order created by the New Deal.

This was the reality that post–New Deal conservatives faced. Federalism had precipitously and irreversibly declined, even though constitutionalists since the founders and Tocqueville had taught that the US regime needed it to survive. Moreover, analysts of various kinds still acknowledge that federalism serves important political ends that no one yet wants to consign to oblivion. Among these is the protection of liberty through the ability of states with independent powers to check the central government. In addition, government that is closer to citizens in the states and localities can be more responsive and accountable to them. Likewise, people in the states can participate meaningfully in political decisions that directly affect them, cultivating the public spirit and citizenly virtue required for republican self-government. And states often act as laboratories of experimentation for addressing new social problems long before the national government does. States also frequently compete with one another for citizens and businesses by efficiently providing what they demand. Finally, the federal division of authority between national and state levels allows for a rational sorting out, over time, of which functions are better addressed at which level.[26] Such explication and validation of the virtues of federalism have often characterized post–New Deal conservative thought. While lamenting that the polity as a whole has accepted a more highly centralized form of constitutionalism, conservatives have argued nonetheless for federalism's continued if imperiled relevance in the post–New Deal era.

CHAPTER THREE

Traditionalists, Neoconservatives, and the Erosion of Federalism

Traditionalist conservatives attributed the post–New Deal erosion of federalism primarily to modern egalitarianism, the associated "rights revolution" on the Supreme Court, and the reach of the administrative state. They argued that the resulting centralization was destroying community, local associations, and civil society. For traditionalists these were the very things that fostered the virtues of a worthwhile life—virtues that also were needed to sustain the original constitutional system. The good society was federally organized, said traditionalists, though their treatment of the principle usually remained rather general. Often their reflections conveyed a sense of loss. Major thinkers not only lamented the decay of once vibrant cultures and communities but also warned that the formerly decentralized constitutional order was transforming into something more alien, threatening, and quite possibly beyond reclamation. In marking federalism's decline, traditionalists also criticized what they saw as overemphasis on natural rights and equality. Radical reification of these concepts had empowered the federal Leviathan to remake—or destroy—self-government at the state and local level. An ugly aspect of this critique was that early opponents of desegregation invoked "states' rights" federalism to defend their own racism. After tracing the evolution of the traditionalist position beyond this association, this chapter concludes with a brief consideration of neoconservatives' relatively scant and sometimes dismissive approach to federalism.

Traditionalist Federalism as Segregation, States' Rights, and Southern Agrarianism

Federalism had long protected a local culture in the South that had never been friendly to African Americans. Racial segregation denied their claims for individual liberty, legal equality, and government by consent. *Brown v. Board of Education* (1954) and the ensuing Civil Rights Movement brought change, but southern segregationists vociferously invoked "states' rights" and federalism to defend their position. The phrase and to some extent federalism *tout court* became equated with racism. While federalism as an aspect of constitutional theory was not inherently racist, thenceforth conservatives of all kinds never quite lived down this association as they appealed to constitutional principle against centralized federal power.

The most famous appeal to federalism on behalf of segregation was the Declaration of Constitutional Principles, otherwise known as the Southern Manifesto (1956). Eventually signed by eighty-two US representatives and nineteen US senators, it sought to obstruct and delay desegregation and to protect the seats of signatories by insuring that intransigent, rabidly racist segregationists could not accuse them of acquiescing to the Supreme Court's mandate.[1] It succeeded on both counts, inaugurating the South's "massive resistance" to desegregation. The Manifesto eschewed any overtly racist arguments in the hopes of accruing political support beyond the South and because an appeal to constitutional principle as the basis of consensus was likely to gain more signatories.[2]

The text of the Manifesto did not claim that the states were sovereign or that they could nullify federal laws—that would have been too radical. Rather, it declared, the Supreme Court had encroached on "the reserved rights of the States and the people," a phrase that appeared twice more in the document, along with an appeal to the United States' "dual system of government." The text also defended the *Plessy v. Ferguson* (1896) rule of "separate but equal" on the basis of local culture and long-standing practice.[3]

More momentously at the level of constitutional theory, though only quixotically in practice, the Manifesto adverted to the antebellum idea of "interposition" (but did not name it for fear of losing moderate signatories). First articulated by Thomas Jefferson and James Madison in the Virginia and Kentucky

Resolutions (1798), the doctrine of interposition held that states could resist or ignore actions of the federal government that they judged to be violations of the constitutional rights of individuals or usurpations of the rightful authority of the states. Several state legislatures had already passed interposition resolutions, announcing that as "sovereign states" they would ignore *Brown* because it was "unconstitutional," "null and void" and of "no lawful effect."[4] As in earlier periods of American history, the South vehemently defended the most state-centered version of federalism when its racial order was threatened.

A leading advocate of both interposition and state sovereignty was James J. Kilpatrick, editor of the *Richmond News Leader*, who defended them in the newspaper and in a book entitled *The Sovereign States* (1957).[5] Kilpatrick knew that interposition could not survive a frontal confrontation with the federal government, as eventually happened in the Little Rock crisis. Nevertheless, he tirelessly promoted it as a way for the South to resist desegregation without having directly to invoke racism. He too hoped that the interposition campaign would cause enough delay for the South to organize massive resistance at the local level and produce enough visible, committed opposition to accrue allies outside the South and somehow to persuade the federal government to relent on desegregation.[6]

Kilpatrick was actively involved in the Virginia Commission on Constitutional Government, created by the state to monitor desegregation and relations with the federal government. The commission produced and widely circulated influential materials that delineated the southern position. It studiously avoided any hint of racism, offering itself as an informational resource and educational project about the first principles of American constitutionalism. Kilpatrick was similarly involved in the organized resistance to the passage of the 1964 Civil Rights Act and in supporting the states' rights position of Barry Goldwater's subsequent presidential campaign.[7] He also wrote for *National Review*, helping to persuade its editors to oppose desegregation as a matter of policy.

One study concludes that Kilpatrick's signal contribution to American conservatism was to drop his segregationism upon its political defeat and to rework states' rights into a more general and nonracial condemnation of an interventionist, centralizing federal government.[8] Kilpatrick was both racist and deeply convinced that the South must preserve federalism by preventing the nation's decline into centralized and intrusive government. The "conservative instinct" still survived in the South, he said, and it could be "a brake upon a society plunging rapidly into a statism only dimly foreseen." Halting this trend required teaching "fundamental truths about the Constitution," primary among them its basis in a state-centered union. It further required the South's intrepid opposition to the "dead hand of the impassive state."[9]

Kilpatrick understood that, well before *Brown*, twentieth-century southern traditionalists had endeavored to protect their regional identity from modern change and outside control.[10] In *I'll Take My Stand: The South and the Agrarian Tradition* (1930), southern intellectuals had warned that northern industrial capitalism and urban modernism were threatening both the high culture and folk heritage of the South.[11] Moreover, the "Agrarians" had agreed that the economics and culture of industrialism, along with the attendant centralization of power in the federal government, was an invasion from the North—just as in 1861.[12] Though oriented primarily to literature and culture, Southern Agrarianism always contained this political undertone of antistatism and localism. More frequent expression of these ideas in explicitly constitutional terms came in response to *Brown* and the Great Society. Kilpatrick helped lead the way, appreciating that the localist aspect of Agrarianism was crucial to the South's traditionalist conservatism and, if shorn of overt racism, could be linked to growing conservative criticism of liberalism's centralized national state. He helped move conservative opinion in this direction, drawing from Agrarianism while obscuring his earlier and now politically unacceptable white supremacist and segregationist positions.[13] He largely succeeded on both counts, refashioning himself into a southern-inflected conservative media pundit in the 1970s and 1980s.[14] Deeper-dyed Agrarian traditionalists of the previous generation could not so deftly detach their localism from segregationist politics.

A crucial figure here was Richard M. Weaver, who sought to fashion Agrarianism into a philosophically deeper and more explicitly Christian humanist doctrine. His efforts had a lasting effect on the philosophical dimension of traditionalist conservatism. Nevertheless, he continued to see constitutional protections for the equal rights of African Americans as inseparable from the dehumanizing, authoritarian, and centralizing aspects of modern materialism and statism. Thus it was precisely Weaver's understanding of Agrarianism, while profound and insightful, that put him on the side of segregation, rather than with the natural rights–inspired claims for legal equality being made by African Americans at midcentury. His elaboration of Agrarianism remained an antimodern protest rooted in white southern cultural identity.[15] For example, in 1957 he confidently recapitulated the traditional southern view of the meaning of the Civil War and Reconstruction, emphasizing that, in the wake of *Brown*, the South was determined "not to be assimilated to the national pattern, but to preserve her character" by resisting "nationalization and centralization of authority."[16] The South "maintained the standards of white civilization" and had no desire to be "turned into something like those 'mixed sections' found in large Northern cities. . . . For such reasons, the Supreme Court's decretal has to it the look of a second installment of Reconstruction."[17] Of course that was precisely the point when it came to the topic of legal equality, though Weaver meant it as the most profound dismissal. For this philosophically informed southern critic of modernity, federalism was a defense of the West against "the centralizing and regimenting impulse," one that still tolerated segregation.[18]

An even more extreme conflation of constitutional federalism with the southern defense of segregation was exemplified by Donald Davidson, another original Agrarian. In the 1950s he had a substantial role in "massive resistance" efforts through the Tennessee Federation for Constitutional Government. Both Davidson and Weaver also defended segregation in the pages of *National Review* and praised Kilpatrick's devotion to the cause.[19]

The Agrarian perspective culminated in the work of M. E. Bradford. Bradford also drew from both Russell Kirk and George W. Carey (treated in the following section), but did not stoop to either racism or segregation. A student of Donald Davidson trained at Vanderbilt University primarily as a scholar of southern literature, Bradford advanced Agrarianism's core themes by decrying the tawdry, soul-destroying materialism and banality of modern life and lamenting the centralization of power supposedly wrought by Union victory in the Civil War. Most fundamentally, like the Agrarians, he was a defender of southern culture.[20]

Bradford recognized that the South's self-understanding as a traditional, localist culture long subject to outside threats had produced a thorough suspicion of government, especially the federal government. He saw this suspicion and the Agrarian conception of southern civilization as two sides of the same coin. There was "no contradiction between an organic conception of society, profoundly antiegalitarian yet still dependent upon popular validation, and a restricted view of state and federal power."[21] Bradford brought together these two ideas, defending the South through a sustained inquiry into the principles of the American founding absent from the primarily literary core of Agrarianism.[22] Indeed, the most extensive study of his constitutional theory rightly understands Bradford as attempting to return the United States to the decentralized federalism it had once enjoyed. Only then would the South be left unmolested by the governing schemes of progressive national elites.[23]

Like the larger Agrarian tradition, however, Bradford's defense of the South as a regionally distinct civilization imperiled by modern statist centralization never fully came to grips with slavery, racism, or the idea of natural rights in the Declaration of Independence. Similarly to Kirk, Bradford argued that the rebellious American colonists fought to continue their practice of local self-government and to defend the traditional, common law rights of Englishmen from a distant but meddling empire. The founding of the United States was thus a conservative act, and not a revolutionary upheaval. For Bradford the famous second paragraph of the Declaration of Independence was not an announcement of the doctrine of natural rights and social contract but rather a statement about thirteen sets of corporate peoples separating, as such, from the British Empire. According to him, " 'We,' in that second sentence, signifies the colonials as the citizenry of the distinct colonies, not as individuals, but rather in their corporate capacity. Therefore, the following 'all men' [were] created equal in their right to expect from any government to which they might submit freedom from corporate bondage. . . . [They were] equal as one free state is as free as another."[24]

Following this reasoning, Bradford also rejected the claim that natural rights and human equality were the definitive American ends that the Constitution was meant to secure. The Constitution for him was not "drawn up to foster the favorite capital-letter abstractions of the millenarians" or to provide a "positive description of acceptable conduct, which is left to local and idiosyncratic definition—to society, local customs, and tested ways. Most important, it is not about enforcing the abstract 'rights of man' or some theory of perfect justice and aboriginal equality."[25]

Bradford's Constitution was essentially structural and procedural, establishing only the methods by which a religious, republican, and diverse people deliberated and governed itself under God in their various local communities. Like other traditionalists, Bradford adopted Michael Oakeshott's distinction between "nomocratic" and "teleocratic" political orders.[26] The United States had shifted from a nomocratic to a teleocratic regime, and Bradford regarded this change as the source of the nation's constitutional and political ills. Abraham Lincoln was the primary culprit. In acid and derisive language, Bradford attacked Lincoln for having wed the Union war effort to the teleology of rights and equality via centralized government. Union victory was thus the true beginning of American decline. Lincoln made the idea of natural rights into a messianic, ideological doctrine of radical individualism and egalitarianism, which together had all but effaced the true nature of American constitutionalism.[27] Now government was sovereign over what was once a Christian humanist, locally based set of regional cultures. In the late twentieth century this corruption of the original Constitution had advanced through the federal destruction of states' rights and local self-government, an end typically effectuated by the Supreme Court.

While advancing the southern perspective on American constitutionalism to forestall the decline of the republic, Bradford's attack on natural rights and Lincoln was a crucial choice that distanced him from both mainstream political culture and other forms of conservatism. It bespoke his failure, and that of the larger Agrarian tradition, to accept that slavery was the foundation of the economic and social system whose culture they so lauded. The tone of the old South was not set, as Bradford and the Agrarians would have it, primarily by middling farmers and "plain folk." Rather, the arbiters of southern culture were the aristocratic planters whose success in the international capitalist economy depended on slavery.[28] Turning a blind eye to slavery enabled Bradford to minimize freedom and equality as the core principles of the founding,[29] thus exempting modern southern thought from fully confronting them as it declaimed the rise of the modern centralized state. A major legacy of the Agrarian-cum-traditionalist inability to resolve this problem was the poisoning of appeals to states' rights, federalism, and local self-government by their association in American politics with slavery, secession, and segregation.

Although critics of conservatism continue to underscore this association,[30] opposition to centralized government in favor of a more state-centered federalism is not ipso facto racist. Although the southern perspective can never be shorn of its association with the worst offenses to American principles, neither can it be reduced to those offenses. Its tragic connection with slavery and racism need not efface the South's culturally based resistance to consumerist materialism and uniformity, or its defense of local tradition and local self-government.

Traditionalist Federalism as Communitarian Localism: Nisbet, Kirk, and Carey

Other traditionalist defenders of federalism were not so tainted by the legacy of segregation and states' rights. Localist and communitarian themes were prominent in the thought of Robert Nisbet, who went so far as to define conservatism itself as "protection of the social order—family, neighborhood, local community and region foremost—from the ravishments of the centralized political state." To preserve the social order, Nisbet argued, "conservative theories of the state have invariably stressed decentralization, pluralism, and a maximum of individual and social autonomy." But individual freedom should not be overemphasized. It was always within community and association that it thrived, and to protect it was "to protect the social ties intermediate to the individual and the state as buffers against the spreading power of governmental bureaucracy."[31] This understanding of conservatism's purpose informed Nisbet's response to the administrative state (as shown in chapter 1) but did not induce any sustained analysis of federalism or of the question whether resistance to centralization might require strong individual states in a federative structure.[32] Nisbet was a social theorist concerned with the nature of human communal association, with what threatened and sustained it, rather than with constitutional institutions and relationships as such. Nevertheless, as Robert F. Nagel has observed, Nisbet's oeuvre did convey that American constitutionalism had failed irrevocably—if not immediately, then at some indeterminate point in the twentieth century. The social changes he so bemoaned had overwhelmed the Constitution's political logic, including its approach to federalism, to create a mass society and a centralized administrative state that were destroying community and freedom.[33]

Russell Kirk's seminal *The Conservative Mind* (1953) defended federalism largely by implication. Localism and particularism were the antidote to the dawning administrative state. To oppose centralization, bureaucratic planning, and uniformity, "every attempt at local and voluntary effort must be encouraged; every suggestion of further consolidation and nationalization must be resisted with intrepidity."[34]

Federalism remained a secondary aspect of his work, but Kirk attended to it more as time went on and thought carefully about how it fit into his vision of conservatism. Always treating culture, religion, and community as philosophically and analytically prior to politics and institutions, he understood federalism as a practical arrangement that safeguarded the human goods that emerged and flourished only at the local level. Sentiment—things loved or feared in common—and a sense of place were what first bound people together. Then came politics, which was fundamentally about limitation and restraint so that a peaceful life could be enjoyed. It was certainly not about remaking settled societies based on some ideological template. Federalism should be conserved because it established the limits and protections that allowed states and local communities to govern themselves in harmony with their varying norms and circumstances. Accordingly, Kirk included in one prominent list of distinctly American conservative qualities "a suspicion of concentrated power, and a consequent attachment to our federal principle and to division and balancing of authority at every level of government."[35] Because "the American conservative is truly a federalist," he or she had to resist the modern trend toward centralized government.[36]

Kirk elaborated this position by frequently deploying Alexis de Tocqueville's well-known defense of local, participatory self-government (which need not be rehearsed here). He similarly used the organicist ideas of "territorial democracy" and the "unwritten constitution" originally offered in Orestes Brownson's *The American Republic* (1866). Brownson's terms bolstered Kirk's view that political forms emerged from the customs, mores, and culture (the unwritten constitution) of people in a particular place. Territorial democracy underscored the geographical rootedness of authority, signifying self-government by specific local communities in their respective places according to their cultural norms. Political authority, in this view, was not a transportable abstraction, nor was it derived from a higher sovereign authority and moved down to the local level. Understood in Brownson's terms, territorial democracy within the federal system reconciled local self-government with the larger structures of the states and the union. By contrast, the Rousseauean "general will" type of democracy tended toward a centralized state administered by bureaucratic elites in the name of "the people," with little room for local self-government.[37] In the United States, then, local community and authentic territorial democracy depended on a robust federalism.[38]

Kirk offered an additional reason that the preservation of federalism was crucial for the United States. The Constitution had successfully addressed "the most persistent and perplexing of all political problems": balancing order with freedom.[39] The founders knew that to do so in the 1780s had required a stronger central government beyond the Articles of Confederation.[40] Accordingly, they redefined the inherited meaning of "federalism." The Constitution "established a true general government—which, nevertheless, was not a centralized, unitary absolute government" or "a simple league of sovereign states."[41] In the founders' hands federalism had become "a voluntary and limited union for certain defined purposes, rather than a concentrated central system." This division of power had aimed to protect "local liberties and choices while securing national interests."[42] In keeping with his understanding of the relationship between society and the realm of ideas and politics, Kirk emphasized that the Constitution's federalism emerged from the "social realities and necessities" Americans had inherited.[43] It was only confirmed by theorists such as Montesquieu. "Circumstances, not books, led to the federal plan."[44] In sum, Kirk believed, again following Brownson, that America's "mission" in world history was to exemplify properly reconciled order and freedom. Owing in large measure to territorial democracy and federalism, the United States had done "as well as any society ever can, probably," in achieving such a reconciliation—though Kirk counseled against forcing American ways on other nations.[45]

In the twentieth century, however, the ongoing march of bureaucratic centralization imperiled the American achievement. Even though Kirk conceded that some consolidation of power was necessary in a complex modern society embroiled in the Cold War, he warned that the centralization of the New Deal and Great Society departed dangerously from American political principles. He located the centralizing impulse (again drawing from Brownson) in a "humanitarian" ethic that would realize a supposed "national conscience" throughout the land. Modernity's idealistic and egalitarian leveling would "cast into the outer darkness all those citizens—perhaps a majority—who do not happen to fall in with the moral judgments of the moment made by a Washington Elect."[46] Such a "vast centralized system of national planning and benefaction" was wholly incompatible with America's traditional federal arrangements and would destroy "genuine democracy—that is, the making of decisions locally and freely, by the citizens, on a humane scale."[47]

Given that the United States was not generally disposed to centralization, Kirk maintained, attempts to realize it were difficult and dangerous. For example, federal encroachment into education via financial subsidies yielded several predictable problems. It brought waste, policy incoherence and politicization, special-interest lobbying, and loss of local control—yet few demonstrable improvements in student learning.[48] More generally, centralized administration threatened US citizens in that it was "more vast, less flexible, and more difficult to restrain or amend" than state and local government in an authentic federal system.[49] Likewise, the difficulty of ruling such a large and complex country from the center created significant inefficiency, and "detailed administration" on this scale "would require from civil servants a wisdom and a goodness never experienced in human history."[50] The United States had no class of leaders competent to undertake this task and, even if it could be created and empowered, few citizens were likely to defer to it. Finally, Kirk observed, centralized, elite bureaucratic governance would fail because ultimately it needed the very "local volition and private self-reliance" it was destroying.[51] Erosion of the "sense of participation and local decision" would diminish the "really effectual and popular authority of the general government." If the true, local roots of authority were severed, "Americans are liable to become an unmanageable people."[52] Kirk advised Americans to either strengthen and defend federalism or, if it was truly obsolete, to train the new leaders who would be necessary for the "new order."[53]

Kirk also criticized the US Supreme Court for hollowing out federalism based on an unsound understanding of rights. As noted in this book's introduction, he held that the American founders conceived of rights as the inherited British liberties they had maintained in their own local, colonial communities. The source of rights was long-established custom and tradition far more than the philosophy of John Locke or the later, more abstract, utopian, and statist conceptions derived from Rousseau and the French Revolution. Now the Court had set itself up as the font of new-style rights that undermined federalism. Kirk did not explain this transformation in any detail, though he suggested, correctly, that its beginnings lay primarily in the early twentieth century with the arrival of legal realism, legal positivism, and the closely related jurisprudence of Oliver Wendell Holmes Jr.[54] With increasing frequency since the New Deal, and on some of the nation's most momentous issues, the Court had invaded the traditional self-governing authority of states and localities by creating new rights that advanced its own quasi–natural law conceptions of justice, or progress, or the national will.

Kirk believed deeply that natural law should guide individual conduct and civil lawmaking authority, but it did "not follow that judges should be permitted to push aside the Constitution or statutory laws and substitute their private interpretations of natural law."[55] American judges had no such authority, and it was likewise an error to think that the natural law tradition was specific enough to admit of such detailed use. This kind of governance—by the Court as "an infallible and omniscient body of moral authorities"—could not be reconciled to American principles.[56] In fact it was upsetting the constitutional order in basic ways. For concrete examples Kirk pointed to the Court's free speech decisions: they had "deprived state and local authorities of nearly any ground on which actions or materials may be judged obscene or blameless."[57] Adverting to the doctrine of incorporation, he argued that the Bill of Rights had been converted into "an unlimited license for the Supreme Court to meddle with states' jurisdictions in such concerns."[58] A sad result of such federalism-destroying rights creation was "the inalienable right of [the pornographer] Mr. Larry Flynt to build a lucrative Empire of Onan at the expense of public morality."[59] Neither the federal system nor the traditional morals nurtured in local communities could survive this development over the long term.

Federalism was the focus of another variant of traditionalist conservatism, one that centered on the work of George W. Carey (with occasional coauthors). Carey was a professor of political science at Georgetown University and an expert on *The Federalist*, and was involved with major conservative institutions and publications over his long career.[60] Although not as explicitly Burkean as Kirk, Carey similarly held that the Constitution had emerged from an organic, locally based, and evolving tradition whose virtues and mores were necessary to sustain it. This form of political order had been gradually displaced by the centralizing and egalitarian developments of the twentieth century. In *The Basic Symbols of the American Political Tradition* (1970), Carey (with Willmoore Kendall) set forth the central features of this communitarian, localist, and religiously rooted political culture as it had once existed.[61] Americans' English Protestant inheritance had evolved into a political tradition whose "supreme commitment and symbol has been self-government by a virtuous people."[62] Not mere majority rule, it aimed at deliberative and consensual government oriented to the common good. All participants understood themselves to be ultimately under divine judgment. As articulated in *The Federalist* papers, the purpose of the Constitution was primarily to establish the "mechanisms and procedures" of deliberation, accommodation, and self-limitation through which the people could realize the aims of the Preamble.[63] Carey too described the Constitution as "nomocratic," concerned mostly "with providing rules and limits for the government through which the people express their will."[64]

This kind of regime, like any other, needed citizens with virtues conducive to its functioning and perpetuation, but the Constitution was not designed to create or enforce them. Carey said that the founders expected virtue to be cultivated in civil society at the local level. Close human relationships were the natural setting for such character formation. "The intellectual and moral development of individuals falls primarily to society, with government assuming only that role which society assigns it."[65] So the role of a constitution in fostering communities was passive and secondary; it allowed " 'space' or 'room' for their functioning and development."[66] In practice, the existence of such space depended on the extent to which government was unitary, centralized, and unlimited or, on the other hand, was authentically federal, decentralized, and limited.[67]

Accordingly, federalism was not a mere ad hoc compromise ginned up at Philadelphia in 1787. The new Constitution naturally accounted for the traditional, community-based social structure that had long existed in the states and that inculcated the virtues necessary to perpetuate the regime.[68] As had occurred during the founding era, the balance of power and responsibility between the central government and states and localities shifted according to the citizenry's choices as a self-governing people.

The capacity for such alteration in the balance of federalism was central to

Carey's understanding of its treatment at the founding.[69] His view of organic and evolving community as the basis of political institutions, along with careful scrutiny of *The Federalist*, precluded any states' rights absolutism on the question of federalism. The founders, he was convinced, had intended Congress ultimately to set the federalism line at any given time. This was what he called "political federalism"—the resolution of federal-state conflicts by the people's representatives through a deliberative process.[70] Although *Federalist* 39 hinted that a "tribunal" might resolve federalism disputes, Carey was more convinced by *Federalist* 46, in which Publius insisted that both the state and federal governments had a common superior in the people as a whole, who would make the final determination of the governments' respective jurisdictions. "The ultimate authority, wherever the derivative may be found, resides in the people alone," who will decide which government "will be able to enlarge its sphere of jurisdiction at the expense of the other." Any such shifts would "depend on the sentiments and sanction of their common constituents." These "common constituents" would find their voice especially in Congress. Moreover, if swayed by "manifest and irresistible proofs of a better administration" in the federal government, the people might enlarge its power at the expense of the states, and this choice was legitimate. On the other hand, if the people were dissatisfied, a remedy was always available in the "election of more faithful representatives, [who could] annul the acts of the usurpers."[71]

Carey concluded that the founders' goal of increasing the power and reach of the central government in relation to the states resulted in a system with few absolute guarantees of state independence or inviolable authority. The people's deliberation within the forms and processes of the Constitution, especially in Congress, set the federalism line at any given time. Because Publius was confident that the overall structure of the constitutional system could ensure its ends, he "would not be disturbed" if "the line between the state and national spheres eventually turned out to be heavily biased in favor of the national government."[72] *The Federalist* treated federalism only broadly and somewhat ambiguously, providing no detailed script for sorting out the inevitable conflicts that would come. Carey's conception of federalism was thus in keeping with his larger view that the Constitution itself was primarily a process or mechanism for conducting deliberative self-government. Federalism's boundaries were worked out through politics.

Carey contrasted this "political" federalism with "constitutional" federalism. In the latter the Supreme Court policed vigorously and finally (short of a constitutional amendment) the federal-state line, based on a strict division of sovereignty between the two levels of government. (Scholars have more typically referred to this view as "dual federalism.") This paradigm too had support in *The Federalist*. Still, even accepting that sovereignty could in fact be divided, such division did not settle conflicts between the states and the federal government. Although Madison's *Federalist* 39 had suggested a role for the judiciary, Carey emphasized that it did not provide any clear principles to guide decision making. By suggesting that a court resolve disputes " 'according to the rules of the Constitution,' " Madison "seems to beg the question."[73] Nevertheless, the Court had pursued the "constitutional" approach for much of US history before abandoning it under the pressure of the New Deal. Then it had adopted the modern version of "political" federalism and deferred to Congress's assertion of its powers vis-à-vis the states, typically through the Commerce Clause.[74]

The result was that the decentralized order long sustained by the theoretically dubious doctrine of "constitutional" federalism did not survive the twentieth century. Although "political" federalism was more theoretically sound, Carey condemned the vast centralization of the post–New Deal era and the Court's aggressive role in advancing it.[75] In *Basic Symbols* Carey (with Kendall) argued that the deepest roots of this development reached to the Civil War, when the "nomocratic" Constitution of rules, procedures, and limits began gradually to transform. Over time it became "teleocratic," aimed at the ever fuller substantive realization of an abstract goal or ideal. This "derailment" of the original order came in part because Abraham Lincoln misinterpreted and overemphasized the ideas of equality and natural rights announced in the Declaration of Independence.[76] Lincoln's conception of equality, in its "open-endedness and universality," bore some responsibility for the "egalitarianism that characterizes the modern, centralized, welfare state."[77] The Declaration's words, abstracted and divorced by Lincoln from their limited meaning during the founding era, encouraged the anticonstitutional central-government expansions of Progressivism, the New Deal, and the Great Society.

This interpretation of the Declaration and Lincoln caused a major disagreement between traditionalists and Straussians, and likewise between traditionalists and some variants of libertarianism and neoconservatism. For present purposes, however, the point to be emphasized is that Carey understood the derailment of the old order and its transformation into a teleocratic regime as a major reason for the massive centralization of power in the twentieth century. Putting Lincoln somewhat aside, he gave more sustained attention to the Progressives' attack on the allegedly antidemocratic Constitution, and on the theories they developed to overcome the separation of powers and federalism.[78]

Progressivism was the "basic cause," the "ideological sea change" that undermined the Constitution. "Centralization of political authority at the national level" was integral to its egalitarian aims.[79] Abetted by Lincoln, the Progressive template guided the federal government, eventually including the Supreme Court, as it enforced ever broader conceptions of equality and rights on states and localities. The vastly expanded Commerce Clause, conditional federal grant-in-aid programs, and the Court's jurisprudence of rights and equality sealed the teleocratic shift. It happened in the name of the supposedly foundational principles of a regime that in fact had abandoned its Constitution as originally understood.[80]

As community and local self-government eroded, so did the regime-preserving virtues they nurtured. The Court especially had "deprived localities of their authority to handle matters at the very core of their being."[81] It "dictat[ed] to communities and local governments [a creed] of its own making, originating in sources independent of society and the tradition." Unsurprisingly, what the Court demanded closely resembled the "progressive vision of a national 'community.'"[82] Modern centralized government meant that "primary institutions and associations" at the local level had "atrophied," and the "very sources of the virtue necessary for a moral regime are no longer functioning."[83]

Carey did not shy away from concluding that the old federal order had passed and that American life was the worse for it. Nor did he deny that on some level the polity had chosen or at least accepted this change. As noted above, in his view of "political federalism" the founders had intended Congress to be the primary mechanism for setting the balance of power between states and the central government. Accordingly, he found somewhat "exasperating" those conservatives who thought this balance had been set once and for all by the supposed specificity of divided sovereignty or "states rights." Not only was this untrue to the political science of the Constitution, he argued, but it rhetorically and morally hobbled conservatives when it came to topics such as civil rights.[84] In fact, political federalism had no straightforward content or formula whereby federal-state conflicts could be automatically resolved—its point was to facilitate the deliberative choice of a self-governing people. Since the New Deal the trend had been relentless centralization, but it need not be permanent.[85] Rather than attempting an impossible return to a discredited pre–New Deal "constitutional" federalism whose basis had never been so sure or specific as the old Supreme Court had claimed, Carey urged conservatives to use the political and conceptual space available under the rubric of political federalism to convince their fellow citizens that decentralization was valuable and appropriate.[86]

To advance this view, he drew on the concept of "subsidiarity" in Catholic social thought.[87] It holds that in any hierarchical organization things should be done at the lowest or most local level that can accomplish them efficiently and well. Neither individuals nor families nor communities should be relieved by a higher authority of their responsibility and duty to do what they are able to do. The ultimate normative reason for this principle of organization was that it encouraged and reflected human dignity—the capacity of individuals to be obligated and responsible in the context of their social bonds to one another. Although the founders did not employ the concept of subsidiarity, Carey found their approach to federalism to be perfectly compatible with it. Federalism informed by subsidiarity could recognize the distinction of functions at different levels of government, respect local differences, and guard the social space needed to cultivate the virtues crucial to the regime's preservation. Carey recommended that the concept of subsidiarity be taken up as a political project to fill in the open texture of "political" federalism. "Political federalism," he observed, "was only regarded as instrumental to centralization, not as a doctrine that should determine the substance and character of policies." Its "bright side" was that "the decision-making process it sanctions is receptive to the introduction of a morality such as that embodied in the subsidiarity principle." It was possible, therefore, that subsidiarity could be " 'sold' to the people and Congress as the basis for judging policies and programs that touch upon the concerns shared by conservatives."[88]

Carey also adverted briefly and pessimistically to even more difficult structural reforms that might resuscitate federalism. These included revising revenue-sharing arrangements that subjected state policy to federal control (i.e., conditional federal grants-in-aid); inventing some " 'neutral arbiter' " other than the Supreme Court to decide federal-state jurisdictional disputes; and in general finding a better way to limit the Court's invasion of state and local prerogatives. He doubted that any such measures could be achieved, but thought that the country was at a tipping point. "Unless some structural changes are made, communities, in any genuine sense, face the prospect of extinction."[89]

Recent Traditionalist Analysis of Federalism's Demise

Carey's approach to federalism undergirded a work coauthored, just prior to his death, with Bruce Frohnen. As treated in greater detail in chapter 1, *Constitutional Morality and the Rise of Quasi-law* (2016) argued that the administrative state inaugurated in the Progressive era and aided by the modern presidency and modern judicial review had fundamentally undermined central features of the original constitutional order. Their analysis again built on the nomocratic-teleocratic distinction at the core of Kendall and Carey's *Basic Symbols of the American Political Tradition*. The centralized, bureaucratic model of modern liberalism remade nonconforming communities, associations, and states in the name of equality and rights—now redefined as autonomous self-realization. This template was elaborated primarily in modern administrative bureaucracies that necessarily dispensed with the rule of law, the separation of powers, and federalism. The old order, rooted in community and locality, had produced the original "mediating" constitution, which was oriented toward deliberation, compromise, and restraint by law and personal virtue. Pursuit of the ends of modern progressive liberalism, however, had substituted a "command" constitution whose ends-oriented discretionary rule ("quasi-law") had remade the basic institutional relationships of the old order.

A primary result of this shift was the demise of federalism and community as they had long been practiced and understood. Frohnen and Carey doubted whether this change could be reversed, in part because it was reinforced by a shift in culture, manners, and mores (what they termed "constitutional morality"). Much of the polity had come to expect a federal government solution to nearly any conceivable social problem. "Reestablish[ment] of more natural [social] relations" at the local level was possible, but "would require, at the federal level, less of everything."[90] Overcoming the Progressives' centralized, discretionary administrative state called for "retrenchment of the federal government into a much smaller but more detailed and legalistic form that allows more actions to be taken by other institutions, be they states, localities, or associations within civil society."[91] Such decentralization might invigorate the local, communal order and the older constitutional morality that had sustained it. Both barely clung to life in the modern United States. Moreover, there was a growing recognition that the utopian aims of progressive liberalism, though they had dominated the twentieth century, were both impossible and anticonstitutional. The authors concluded that "a richer life is available to most of us at the local level if we are willing to disempower the center from usurping the roles of our fundamental associations."[92] To revive federalism required reinvigoration of the traditionalist view that social and communal life was prior to politics.[93]

At the end of the twentieth century and into the twenty-first, traditionalists' localist, religiously oriented, and communitarian conservatism had not altered the basic balance of post–New Deal federalism. Moreover, American culture had become more secular as government grew more centralized. Nevertheless, the decentralist orientation of traditionalist conservatism was woven too deeply into America ever to be wholly eradicated.[94] It endured on the margins of political life as a self-conscious, critical withdrawal from the mainstream. In this form it was neither marred by the old association with racism and segregation nor engaged directly with constitutional federalism. For example, Wendell Berry's anticonsumerist, antimaterialist commitment to community, decentralization, and local knowledge was congruent with much of traditionalist conservatism (including many traditionalist criticisms of the market). Berry drew explicitly on the principles of the original Nashville Agrarians and can reasonably be placed within the general "alternative tradition" of American political thought associated with communitarianism and republicanism.[95] Likewise, Rod Dreher's portrait of "Crunchy Conservatives" used this neologism to highlight a trend among often younger traditionalists toward older, communal, and faith-based ways of living that rejected much of modern mass consumer society. Dreher knew the history of American conservatism well enough to recognize that Russell Kirk could be claimed as the "patron saint" of this newly named type of traditionalism.[96] One of its tenets, which Kirk surely would have approved, was that "Small and Local and Old and Particular are to be preferred over Big and Global and New and Abstract."[97] Both Berry and Dreher were primarily cultural critics, so their analyses did not on their own terms consider federalism as such. At a basic level, though, it would not have made sense for such thoughtful defenders of the things once sustained by a decentralized federal order to continue in the great contest of constitutional debate. Their position had been routed in that arena, and for the time being it could proceed only as a kind of underground, countercultural movement.

Neoconservatives

One basic reason that the traditionalist conception of federalism lost so much ground, as in the case of the administrative state, was that the emerging cadre of neoconservatives accepted the New Deal expansion of national power as quite properly settled and irreversible. The centralized regulatory-welfare state was to be conservatized to the extent possible, and the excesses of the Great Society moderated, but "the neoconservatives were trying to repeal the 1960s, not the New Deal."[98] As a viewpoint born primarily of eastern urban intellectuals, neoconservatism simply did not register federalism as a pressing issue. Consequently, none of the major studies of neoconservatism accord it much attention.

Although the decline of public-spirited republican virtue was an enduring theme in the thought of Irving Kristol, he expressed it under the rubric of the "urban crisis," rather than in the classic constitutional language of federalism. More urbanization meant that the agrarian provincialism supposedly relied upon by the American founders as the basis of virtue was irretrievably lost. Despite the founders' suspicion of cities, and irrespective of their complex federalism—which Kristol did not analyze—"the challenge to our urban democracy is to evolve a set of values and a conception of democracy that can function as the equivalent of the republican morality of yesteryear."[99] Defense of federalism in the constitutional métier undertaken by other kinds of conservatives did not find its way into Kristol's view of the problem.

Even though neoconservatives themselves rarely argued in terms of federalism, later scholarship shows that important aspects of their thought at least implied support for the United States' traditionally decentralized federal system. For example, the characteristic neoconservative critique of ambitious, Great Society–style programs was that centrally administered social engineering foundered on the realities of human nature, culture, and local circumstance. A more modest and moderate approach would do less based on the hubris-inducing social science of federal officials, and more to account for the complexities and incentives of individuals, families, and local communities.[100] In addition, interventionist federal policies with grand reformist aims inevitably required bureaucracies to administer them. The usual result was the erosion of authority. Often it happened because government overestimated its capacity to effectuate change and because it relied on bureaucratic discretion that could not be made accountable to local citizens and officeholders.[101] Small-bore, incremental reform that was sensitive to local context had a better chance at success. This perspective was consistent with typical conservative defenses of federalism, even though neoconservatives did not normally articulate it in those terms.

To the limited extent that neoconservatives engaged federalism, then, they had varied and sometimes opposed postures. The tension between their acceptance of the modern centralized state and their criticism of its overreach into local and private affairs is evident in a brief comparison of Daniel Patrick Moynihan and Edward Banfield. Both have been categorized as neoconservatives, though the thought of each was complex enough that the label can be questioned. In them we see that the neoconservative persuasion was too loose and multivalenced to have a typical position on federalism—even on the rare occasions when the topic did come specifically into view.

Moynihan was an early critic of the results of the Great Society programs he had helped design as a policy adviser in the Johnson administration. His criticism sounded the characteristic neoconservative themes. Government was overloaded and had overestimated its capacity to direct social change; it relied too much on social science expertise and self-aggrandizing bureaucracy; and it underappreciated the complexity of the social order. The community action programs administered by the Office of Economic Opportunity were a notable subject of his criticism. In an influential 1967 speech, he combined these themes with his sensitivity to localism and federalism, stating bluntly that "liberals must divest themselves of the notion that the nation—and especially the cities of the nation—can be run from agencies in Washington." This approach was even more especially "false" in regard to "the kind of social change liberals generally seek to bring about." No amount of legislation and its attendant administrative bureaucracy could simply remake reality at the grass roots.[102] Moynihan's understanding of the diversity and complexity of American society kept him attuned to the importance of federalism throughout his career, even as he eventually drifted away from the neoconservative dispensation. As he stated in a 1985 speech, "Federalism is not a managerial arrangement that the framers hit upon because the country was big and there were no telephones. . . . Federalism was a fundamental expression of the American idea of covenant."[103]

Moynihan understood federalism as a structure that protected the basic human good of community, allowing it to endure and to enrich the lives of people in numerous ways. He condemned the interventionist bent of modern liberalism because, in overcoming federalism, it destroyed community and undermined the authority and efficacy of government at all levels. He found support for this view in several sources. These included (among others) the Catholic doctrine of subsidiarity, the work of Robert Nisbet on community, and the insights of Tocqueville on local self-government.[104] Moynihan never let his hard-won realism about the limits of social policy push him into antigovernment quietism, but his thought was the most self-conscious connection between federalism and the neoconservative criticism of government overreach.

Banfield too was noted for his political realism, even pessimism, but his view of federalism significantly differed from Moynihan's.[105] His study of urban politics and intergovernmental relations had convinced him that there was nothing inherently good about a government close to the people. The quality of local governance, rather, depended on the quality of citizens and their culture. The fact that citizens at the grass roots were attached to local government as their own did not necessarily mean they governed themselves well or justly.

Banfield also observed that the centralization of authority in the national government had been ongoing and "inevitable" in the United States since the founding. Centralizing sentiment combined with political circumstance had rather quickly created a variety of new national powers beyond the textual limits of the Constitution. This process had accelerated during the Progressive era and the New Deal, and especially via the rapid growth of conditional federal grants-in-aid. Banfield did not "deplore the growth of federal power. It would be pointless to deplore what one maintains is inevitable."[106] The reality was that "state governments are well on the way to becoming mere administrative districts (what many of the Founders wanted them to become!)."[107] The ultimate, Hobbesian reason for this trend was that people could not be relied on to keep their own agreements, even about the basics of their own political order. Banfield therefore held that there was "an antagonism, amounting to an incompatibility, between popular government—meaning government in accordance with the will of the people—and the maintenance of limits on the sphere of government."[108] Government by popular will would deliver what the people demanded or acquiesced to, and the concept of constitutionally limited government ultimately would give way. Banfield concluded arrestingly that "nothing of importance can be done to stop the spread of federal power."[109]

This view also led him to argue that ongoing centralization should not be seen simply as an alien imposition from Washington. For example, a realistic view of federal revenue sharing, whether direct or through conditional grants, must accept that states and localities wanted it—despite conservatives who bemoaned the effects on federalism. This argument was not meant to justify federal aid in practice: Banfield was critical of the central government's excessive faith in expertise and its own efficacy, its frequent waste and inefficiency, and its capacity to warp local government priorities. But he insisted nevertheless that such national financial involvement–cum–direction of local affairs likely would continue. Federalist scruples could not endure against either the large public demands on government in the mass democratic age or the various political interests of those who benefited from the status quo. Banfield accordingly concluded (accurately) that the current approach would persist. Its many problems and its very real centralizing effects were not enough to stop it.[110]

Conclusion

Traditionalists defended federalism first as overt states' rights segregationists, then as more erudite heirs of Southern Agrarianism, and from outside the South as communitarian localists. None of these perspectives held out much hope of stopping the continued centralization of American governance, and contemporary traditionalists appear convinced that the older, more decentralized order is gone and never to be retrieved.

While federalism attracted some attention from neoconservatives, its modern erosion was never more than a minor concern for them. As chapter 7 shows, in the 1990s they turned more directly to foreign affairs. With traditionalists having mostly arrived at a posture of resignation and withdrawal, libertarians assessed federalism in light of their own basic principles. Their analysis is the focus of chapter 4.

CHAPTER FOUR

Libertarians and the Erosion of Federalism

Libertarian attention to federalism built on midcentury theorists and advanced quickly in the last few decades of the twentieth century.[1] Libertarians' characteristic affirmation of individual liberty, competition, and voluntary choice guided their approach. Often their arguments called on the rapidly developing field of public choice in economics and political science. The libertarian vison of federalism was cogent, but sometimes labored in its attempt to connect to the established tenets of American constitutionalism. The goal was always to maximize individual freedom, minimize coercion, and make government as limited and accountable as possible—amid the underlying libertarian conviction that government always overreached.

Early Approaches

Prior to the ascendance of public choice, Frank Meyer well illustrated the early libertarian perspective on federalism. He was an editor at *National Review* who aimed to "fuse" elements of libertarianism and traditionalism into a lasting basis for modern conservatism. The details of that project aside, Meyer understood federalism in the way Americans suspicious of government traditionally had: it was part of the constitutionalist attempt to limit and disperse power so that liberty could be preserved from an overly centralized and distant government. Meyer's attention to federalism was episodic and not especially deep, but he did help keep the issue on the agenda of libertarian thought.[2]

Federalism was also a secondary concern for Friedrich A. Hayek, though he sketched the general direction that libertarians eventually took. Hayek argued that a federal system could limit the economic coercion of individuals if member states competed with one another for mobile citizens and capital. Concomitantly, a supranational system with shared rules for ordering free economic interactions (but without the power of central direction) could limit the effects of member states' bias toward planning and protectionism.[3]

Further foundations of the libertarian approach were laid in two now classic works by Charles Tiebout and Albert O. Hirschman. Tiebout applied market analysis to the service, revenue, and expenditure situation confronted by municipal governments who faced varying demands for public goods from mobile citizens. Simply put, Tiebout posited that communities must take some account of citizens who, as consumers with a choice, could move to places that best met their desired level of service and cost (taxation).[4] People could "vote with their feet." Hirschman added that, when confronting an unsatisfactory situation in a state or organization, the essential options for action were "exit," "voice," or "loyalty." An individual or group could leave or choose a competitor (exit) or attempt to persuade the powers-that-be to change (voice). The third option, more ambiguous and multivalenced than the other two, was to use voice and limit exit in the hope that the entity improves or reforms (loyalty).[5]

Federalism as Competition and as a Principal-Agent Problem

Calling often on Tiebout and Hirschman, the libertarian case for federalism came to center on the idea of competition among jurisdictions and on the closely related capacity of citizens and capital to move from one place to another. These factors would generate choice and efficiency. In turn, different levels of demand for diverse public goods and services could be satisfied, while the size and cost of government were kept within limits acceptable to citizens.[6] The basic "exit" hypothesis was explored and extrapolated in numerous ways.[7] Analysts also wrestled with the tension in federal systems between the democratic imperative of recognizing and representing within the central government member states as self-governing political units, on the one hand, and the economic imperative of efficiently allocating responsibilities between the central government and the member states, on the other.[8]

No less a figure than James M. Buchanan (sometimes with coauthors) advanced these ideas as part of the general reconsideration of post–New Deal centralization in the 1980s.[9] Buchanan's core, eminently libertarian premise was that every state acted as a Leviathan, always hungry to extract more private resources from the citizenry. Explicit constitutional limits were always necessary, but Leviathan could also be limited by a federal system that permitted migration and competition.[10] In this view "the principle of federalism emerges directly from the market analogy" because "only a federalized political structure can effectively exploit the forces of competition."[11] "Competitive federalism" was the aptly chosen name for the libertarian position. A central government with enough authority to guarantee that all members of the federation respected not only liberty and property but also freedom of trade, investment, and movement would thereby foster competition for citizens through the members' differing offers of public goods and services. The result would be more choice, efficiency, and liberty—and less government coercion.[12]

From this perspective libertarians also responded to the Rehnquist Court's revival of federalism. For example, law professors John McGinnis and Ilya Somin applied public choice's principal-agent analysis to competitive federalism to suggest that the courts could often resolve the problems this analysis identified. The basic idea was that the interests of elected officials (agents) frequently diverged from those of their constituents (principals) in ways that undermined federalism's distribution of governing power and the competition it encouraged. The liberty of citizens and the accountability of government would be diminished unless elected officials were restrained by judicial enforcement of the federal structure, as the Rehnquist Court was doing.

A prime example and inspiration for this argument was *New York v. United States* (1992). It held that the federal government could not compel (commandeer) the state into enforcing a federal statue by requiring it, in certain instances, to take title to nuclear waste. The Court observed that such a scheme was attractive to both state and federal officers because it allowed them to avoid responsibility: given the choice, federal officials would prefer that the state be required to choose where to site a nuclear waste dump; state officials would be happy to say they were directed to do so by Congress. The Court highlighted "the precise theme" of principal-agent analysis when it concluded that " 'powerful incentives might lead federal and state officials to view departures from the federal structure to be in their personal interests.' "[13]

Federalism frequently presented the classic principal-agent problem exemplified in this case. McGinnis and Somin extended this analysis to a variety of federalism contexts, including congressional action under the Commerce Clause and section 5 of the Fourteenth Amendment, arguing that often it was state officials who preferred enforcement of federal uniformity so that they did not have to compete with one another, or so that they could take credit for advocating a popular cause.[14] Only the Court could enforce the federal structure in instances when it was not in the interest of the states to demand it. Likewise could the Court enforce an open national market (via the dormant Commerce Clause, for example) when Congress was unwilling to act against the states' tendencies toward pursuing protectionism or shifting the costs of government to others.[15] The aim was not to protect "states' rights" but rather to secure individual liberty and government accountability by prompting the Court to defend competitive federalism.[16]

The Rehnquist Court's questioning of the dominant "process" theory of federalism also gave hope to Michael Greve, then director of the Center for Individual Rights, a public interest law firm that litigated before federal courts. Greve noted that the Court had once again raised the long-lost doctrine of enumerated powers, especially in *Lopez* and *Boerne* (discussed in the introduction to part II). This doctrine was potentially the basis for a lasting judicial resuscitation of real, competitive federalism. Although not a frontal challenge to the New Deal paradigm, the Court's move might encourage a "Leave Us Alone" political coalition to defend liberty by resisting further intrusion into states and localities. The Leave Us Alone coalition consisted of "populist, grassroots constituencies" that, for varying reasons on several issues, were reliably opposed to federal intervention. While not wholly libertarian on all issues nor always in favor of federalism, members of this coalition were "fiercely antinationalist and anti-elitist and, in that elementary sense, federalist."[17] The hope was that this coalition would provide political support, and file appropriate lawsuits, that over time would sustain the Court's defense of competitive federalism based on enumerated powers. In Greve's view, the idea of state sovereignty that so far had been the primary basis of the Court's federalism revival could not sustain a return to competitive federalism. It limited only the means (commandeering, most particularly) by which Congress could pursue essentially unlimited ends. Without any effective judicial limits on congressional power under the Spending Clause, for example, the Court's occasional intervention on behalf of the traditional powers of state and local governments was not enough to resurrect the more authentic, decentralized and competitive federalism that had been abandoned in the New Deal.[18]

Greve expanded these arguments in *The Upside-Down Constitution* (2012), a major expression of the libertarian, competitive federalism view. It ultimately placed more hope in the sort of judicial defense of constitutional structures that fostered jurisdictional competition than in judicial resurrection of the greatly eroded doctrine of enumerated powers.[19] Building on Buchanan's libertarian modeling of the state as a Leviathan and the basic Tiebout exit hypothesis, Greve argued that, prior to the New Deal, government had been constrained by an authentically competitive federalism (though it had not yet been self-consciously articulated as such). This older, competitive system was rooted in the preservation of a national market and the jurisdictional competition induced by the Constitution's text and structure. From these sources the Court had also generated crucial pro-competitive doctrines, including the dormant Commerce Clause (derived from *Gibbons v. Ogden* [1824]) and the federal common law (derived from *Swift v. Tyson* [1842]). Government was limited and liberty protected because the legal regime let market forces discipline and restrain both the states and the federal government. But after the New Deal, federalism became essentially a cartel system. The states gratefully accepted and often administered federal regulatory policies, federal entitlements, and transfer payments that the central government formulated and frequently subsidized. Moreover, Greve argued, once *Swift v. Tyson* was overturned in *Erie Railroad v. Tompkins* (1938), states could apply their own common law in self-serving ways. They discriminated against out-of-state companies and disrupted interstate commerce for the sake of in-state constituencies.

Over time these developments enabled the routine circumvention of constitutional limits. States were relieved from having to compete with the central government or one another, yet were allowed frequently to interfere with the free flow of commerce, or to transfer their economic burdens elsewhere. This shift—the inversion of the book's title—was from competitive federalism, as the system that maximized individual liberty, to centrally enforced cartel federalism as the system that maximized the states' extraction of economic surplus from citizens and corporations.

Greve's analysis included several bracing challenges to long-established conservative ideas. For example, he rejected the typical view that the New Deal merely "centralized" power in the federal government. Power was indeed centralized, but it was used not only against the states but also to enforce, as noted, anticompetitive cartel arrangements on behalf of states as Leviathan-extractors that exploited individual citizens. The federal government also still tolerated substantial legal authority in the states that resulted in predatory regulations and lawsuits. What the New Deal had wanted more than anything else, said Greve, was not centralization as such but rather to replace limited government and competition with more government regulation, direction, and economic redistribution "at *all* levels." Conservatives would remain incapable of reforming the pathologies of post–New Deal federalism so long as they continued simply to equate decentralization of power to the states with less government intrusion.[20]

Likewise, Greve's competition-cartel distinction, rooted in the insights of public choice, rejected the age-old description of federalism as a "balance" of powers and responsibilities between the states and the central government. That view had always aimed to avoid both disintegration and wholly unitary consolidation. But in the post–New Deal era, including on the Rehnquist Court, it was unable to contend with the many anticompetitive results of cartel federalism. The problems at hand emerged from the states, the central government, and their interactions, and they could not be solved by the Supreme Court's episodic defenses of the "states as states" in the name of balance. Moreover, the relatively few explicit protections for the states in the Constitution meant that the concrete expression of federalism in any era ultimately would be determined not by some preset balance but rather by the interaction of constitutional structures and institutions with historical circumstance and political choice.[21] Abandoning the fixation on balance for a clearer appreciation of constitutional structure, and the judicial doctrines appropriately derived from it, would encourage better governance because "the commitment to competition is hardwired in our Constitution's structure."[22]

As discussed in chapter 10, Greve also sought to advance competitive federalism by reworking originalism into a more assertive form of judicial review that could advance his theory. This task was becoming more urgent because the old-style conservative originalist loyalty to American federalism had not forestalled the contemporary crisis of fiscal sustainability and institutional inefficacy. The affluence of the twentieth century had obscured the pathologies of New Deal cartel federalism, but that era was over. Greve hoped that if an acute crisis did arrive, his theory of competitive federalism would stand as an option for judicially led reform.[23]

Greve emphasized that a major reason for the crisis besetting the New Deal's so-called cooperative federalism was that federal grants and subsidies to states fundamentally distorted the fiscal and governing logic of American federalism. Libertarian public choice analysis had been making this point for some time.[24] By the end of the twentieth century, federal money had become a sizable source of income for many states. The result was federal oversight of numerous basic policy areas. Both before and after the New Deal, conservatives of various stripes were concerned about this practice, but their criticism was episodic and not always consistent.[25] Greve described conditional federal payments to states as the "Achilles' heel" of competitive federalism. In the language of public choice, these payments created "fiscal illusion": they hid the true cost of government by severing the link between what states were willing to tax their own citizens and the actual cost of what citizens consumed.[26] Government became larger and more expensive than what people were willing to pay for it, while substantive policies applied at the local level were beyond local control. Nevertheless, a state would be foolish to forgo the federal money (to which it had contributed) if others were accepting it. The resulting policy uniformity stifled both jurisdictional competition and any accounting for numerous differences among states and localities. Summarizing the public choice position, Greve concluded that "the central fact is that *any* intergovernmental arrangement that authorizes one level of government to spend money raised by another level is intrinsically corrosive of fiscal discipline and political responsibility. Thus, the constitutional, competitive solution is to disentangle federal and state programs and to realign taxing and spending authority."[27]

Accordingly, most libertarians supported some form of competitive federalism because it derived so directly from the broader philosophy's emphasis on market competition and individual choice.[28] Other aspects of federalism that conservatives traditionally appreciated were not wholly absent from libertarian analysis. These included the ability of different subnational governments to account for differing noneconomic citizen preferences; the greater ability of citizens at the local level to affect government policy; citizens' increased capacity to monitor government officials; and the ability of decentralization to limit the power and cost of government.[29]

But of course the defense of individual liberty was always the most fundamental basis of libertarianism, and it was endangered if federalism permitted states and localities themselves to violate individual rights. Indeed, libertarians were well aware of the statement in 1964 by William H. Riker, one of the first scholars to apply public choice analysis to federalism, that the "main beneficiary [of federalism] throughout American history has been the Southern Whites, who have been given the freedom to oppress Negroes. . . . [I]f in the United States one approves of Southern white racists, then one should approve of American federalism."[30] Such "persecution of local minorities" by "grassroots tyranny" was an inherent risk of federalism that could not always be solved by competition and exit.[31] The case of state-imposed segregation for African Americans was the most infamous, but libertarians also highlighted the threat that local majorities could pose to immobile assets. For example, property rights in land could be quashed by confiscatory taxation, restrictive zoning, or eminent domain.[32] Consequently, several leading libertarians pointedly paired support for exit and competition in a federal system with insistence that a central authority, typically the federal judiciary, was sometimes necessary to protect rights from oppressive local majorities.[33]

Vincent Ostrom's Federalism as Polycentricity

Libertarianism's competitive federalism and public choice strictures were somewhat relaxed in the influential work of Vincent Ostrom. Trained as a political scientist and scholar of public administration, Ostrom drew his ideas from the intellectual milieu of public choice and its characteristic suspicion of centralized, bureaucratic government. He had been a founder and president of the Public Choice Society but eventually became dissatisfied with the subfield. He found it too fixated on economic efficiency, too reductive in its view of self-interest, and too distant from reality in its formal modeling of rational choice. Instead, he turned to *The Federalist* papers and Alexis de Tocqueville to deepen his understanding of federalism as a form of political order. Rendered properly as a "compound republic" rather than as the decentralized administration of a national sovereign will, federalism could promote liberty and coordinate authentic self-government. Still, the libertarian focus on liberty, competition, and voluntarism always informed Ostrom's critique of the overconfident, overcentralized, and overintrusive post–New Deal state. Eventually he elaborated an entire social theory about the nature and potential of human association as rule-based self-governance. That large enterprise cannot be fully analyzed here, but we shall see that his understanding of federalism always retained a clear connection to libertarian concerns.[34]

Ostrom (with Charles M. Tiebout and Robert Warren) initially challenged mainstream political science with the concept of "polycentricty" in a noted article on the provision of public goods in metropolitan regions. The conventional wisdom had been that such regions would be better served by more centralized, bureaucratic planning, along with more coordinated allocation of public goods from a unitary authority that exercised hierarchical control. This view assumed that "the multiplicity of political units in a metropolitan area is essentially a pathological phenomenon."[35] Ostrom and his coauthors turned this proposition on its head, arguing that having multiple and overlapping providers of public goods and services might better satisfy varying constellations of citizen desires. The opposite of unitary, hierarchical governance, the "polycentric" approach "connot[ed] many centers of decision making that are formally independent of each other." Multiple jurisdictions in a metropolitan area could "take each other into account in competitive relationships, enter into various contractual and cooperative undertakings, or have recourse to mediating mechanisms to resolve conflicts," thus "function[ing] in a coherent manner with consistent and predictable patterns of interacting behavior."[36] This idea drew from Tiebout's earlier work on competition and the possibility of "exit" from municipalities, thus connecting Ostrom to the later libertarian elaboration of the theory of competitive federalism. As one review of Ostrom's legacy put it, "A polycentric order generalizes Tiebout's voting-with-the-feet model by enabling individuals or communities to choose among alternative producers of public services without having to move from one jurisdiction to another."[37]

Abandoning the assumption of unitary control and hierarchical ordering enabled a clearer distinction between production and provision of public goods, making it possible to see that they need not be undertaken by the same entity. Individuals or jurisdictions could demand or provide goods at different levels, in different combinations, from various producers; producers in turn might be corporations, other jurisdictions, or nongovernmental organizations. The metropolitan region could be understood as functioning like an industry or "public economy," retaining "much of the flexibility and responsiveness of market organization."[38] A concrete example that informed this analysis was the experience of the community of Lakewood in Los Angeles County, California. It incorporated as a city to avoid being politically subsumed by the county, and then successfully negotiated with the county to purchase from it the combination and level of public services its residents wanted. Other communities in that county and elsewhere soon did the same, providing a working instance of what contemporary polycentric governance might look like.[39]

Upon developing the idea of polycentrism, Ostrom sought to establish that it was true to the American constitutional tradition. He revisited *The Federalist* to specify the design principles and political logic of the Constitution, especially with regard to federalism, as they were expressed by Publius. He offered not so much a work of history as an attempt to infer and restate more sharply the concepts of federal association contained in Publius's essays. This accomplishment could be deployed in turn against the overly centralized and intrusive bureaucratic state of the post–New Deal era. Ostrom said that the federalism of Publius, properly understood, was indeed polycentrism. It was the basis of the founders' response to the unitary, hierarchical, and ultimately absolutist understanding of sovereignty in the philosophy of Thomas Hobbes, as well as to the problem of majority faction that was unavoidable even in a republic. The American founders turned to federalism "to conceptualize how a system of government with multiple centers of authority reflecting opposite and rival interests could be held accountable to enforceable rules of constitutional law." They rejected the single Hobbesian sovereign, above the law and not bound by it.[40]

Ostrom saw in *The Federalist* a defense of governments whose jurisdictions were concurrent, overlapping, and limited. He also analyzed the shared state-and-federal authority over taxation, administration, and even defense. Neither in these modes of institutional interaction nor in any of these issue areas was there a single or unchecked source of authority. This system, grounded in the founders' historical experience, was the solution to their practical and theoretical quandary. Only federalism could adequately diffuse and check power to protect liberty while still coordinating the realization of common goals on a consensual basis. In Ostrom's reading of *The Federalist* "no single monopoly of public authority exists in a compound republic." Instead, multiple authorities represented diverse communities and interests and were able to compete, bargain, and cooperate on the scale and for the ends that they as self-governing entities found acceptable.[41]

Ostrom similarly engaged Tocqueville's thought.[42] Tocqueville helped him to see how democratic society exacerbated the dangers of centralized, bureaucratic government and how a decentralized, "polycentric" form of democratic administration could combat these dangers via association at the local level. Citizens organized themselves to achieve common goals they saw as serving their own self-interest "rightly understood." They also learned both the practicalities and virtues of true self-government as lived among themselves and their neighbors. Ostrom's excursion into Tocqueville thus complemented his earlier one into *The Federalist*. Together these sources supported the idea of polycentric governance to the extent that they showed that "democratic administration, through a system of overlapping jurisdictions and fragmentation of authority, acquired a stable form that provides an alternative structure for the organization of public administration."[43]

Ostrom accepted that liberty was insecure and collective action likely impossible without constitutional rules that structured cooperation and conflict and, at the same time, set limits on rulers. Although his libertarianism was more moderate than some, his rejection of the Hobbesian unitary sovereign in favor of federalism as a method of social ordering—one without a final or absolute seat of authority—ultimately led him to reject the idea of the state. This position was nascent in the early argument that metropolitan regions should be understood as containing "collective consumption units" within a "public economy" whose activities were not coordinated by any central authority. The resulting interactions might look chaotic compared to one-size-fits-all commands issued from a central sovereign authority, but the resulting competitive rivalry and freedom of choice better served the differing needs of the people in the region. Ostrom thus expanded the very notion of what could be considered "governance" beyond the actions of a sovereign state. In fact, one observer concluded that for Ostrom "government was an abstract noun that is used to denote polycentric processes of human interaction."[44] Federalist association and interaction enabled people to "break out of the conceptual trap inherent in a theory of sovereignty that presumes there must exist some single center of supreme authority that rules over society."[45] Federalism as polycentric governance was the alternative, Ostrom concluded, because the "conceptualization of sovereignty informing the ideal of the State reflects ideological commitments that are out of step with the normative and practical requirements of self-government."[46] Against the statist model of command and control, federalism could be a mechanism for human social interaction that fostered deliberation, problem solving, and conflict resolution.[47] It is therefore appropriate that the use of polycentricity to defend genuine self-government against "state-centered paradigms" has been credited as a "critical contribution to libertarian ideas in the social sciences."[48]

Ostrom's Critique of Martin Diamond

Ostrom's commitment to federalism as an antistatist form of social order generated a critique of Martin Diamond's influential interpretation of federalism in *The Federalist* papers. As more fully explicated in chapter 5, Diamond had argued approvingly that, to ensure ratification, Publius had artfully obscured the founders' preference for increased national power and the Constitution's orientation toward it. He said that *The Federalist* regarded the Constitution as a somewhat unsatisfying admixture of national and federal principles that over time would become more national, with the states likely serving as decentralized administrative departments that applied national policy. Publius's masterful political rhetoric also had successfully redefined federalism to include features of the Constitution that were significantly more nationalist and centralizing than would have been acceptable under any previous definition but that eventually would become the accepted modern definition.

Taking *The Federalist* more at face value than Diamond, Ostrom argued that Diamond had overestimated its commitment to centralizing nationalism and the Constitution's capacity to realize it. On Ostrom's reading, the founders had positively endorsed the new, compound kind of federalism as an improvement over the older choice between a simply unitary national government and a league or association of independent states. Their new federalism did not rely on mere decentralized application of the national will but rather on concurrent jurisdiction over territory and policy that permitted states and, by implication, municipalities to be authentically self-governing. Ostrom's painstaking reconstruction of the theoretical principles in *The Federalist*, he said, revealed that its "position on federalism is much more defensible than Diamond suggests."[49]

A central element of Ostrom's theory was in tension with the premises of *The Federalist* and Diamond's interpretation. As noted above, Ostrom said that analysis should "abandon reference to a theory of sovereignty" understood as the assignment of "unlimited and undivided authority to some sovereign entity that has the last say and rules over a society."[50] He wanted to replace it with the idea of covenantal authority that need not be legalized in government institutions, yet stood outside them and empowered them.[51] However, despite the confusion and imprecision in sovereignty as a concept, it was central to *The Federalist*'s defense of a system in which the people, as its source, could divide it between the state and federal governments.[52]

Ostrom knew that his theory of federalism as polycentrism pushed beyond *The Federalist* as it presented itself in its own historical and political context.[53] "Perhaps it is enough to recognize that *The Federalist* makes a major contribution toward a theory of constitutional rule and federalism. . . . We are the ones who bear the burden of advancing beyond what was done in the late 1780s."[54] He elaborated on this point in a response to critics who had defended Diamond. "The point at issue," he wrote, was "the relative weight to be given to historical circumstance or to coherence of a theoretical argument in assigning meaning to terms."[55] Ostrom more heavily weighted his own theoretical reconstruction of the logic of Publius's argument for federalism than he did the concrete circumstances and purposes that gave rise to it. Those circumstances did not wholly settle what it could mean, nor did the work's authors supply the "computational understanding that would enable us to specify the necessary and sufficient conditions for creating and maintaining a federal system of government."[56] That was Ostrom's proffered contribution as a theorist who built on the theoretical insights of the founding.

Ostrom's commitment to federalism as a way of protecting liberty and self-government was admirable, as was the intellectual ambition of the theory he built to defend them. And while he consciously distanced himself from the more extreme and reductive features of libertarianism and public choice, like those, his enterprise was too self-referential and internally concatenated fully to accept

American constitutionalism on its own terms. Consequently, Diamond had the better of the historical argument about the extent of the founders' commitment to centralized national power.

Yet, like Diamond, Ostrom too was entirely convinced that Progressivism had severely undermined the traditional federal order. The administrative theory of Woodrow Wilson was a major target. It was the epitome of the unitary sovereign approach in that it rejected the separation of powers and insisted on the politics-administration dichotomy. Nothing should obstruct the rigorous execution of the national sovereign will.[57] Accordingly, the effort of Wilson and his followers might better "be viewed as a degenerative rather than a progressive development. The erosion of basic constitutional understandings, the nationalization of American government, and the inability of the national government to keep its own house in order can be viewed as the correlatives of efforts to eliminate fragmentation of authority and overlapping jurisdictions."[58]

There was a vast difference between the approaches to public administration represented by the Wilsonian unitary sovereign–bureaucratic state and Ostrom's federalism-polycentricty.[59] The latter approach made it possible for "systems of public administration [to] be put together in different ways other than relying primarily on the principles of bureaucratic organization."[60] However, the logic of the modern administrative state, which called for minutely bureaucratized execution of the national sovereign will down to the local level, overwhelmed local self-government as traditionally practiced in American federalism.[61] Ostrom left no doubt that the administrative state destroyed federalism, as well as the separation of powers and the rule of law at the national level.

The Supreme Court too had done much to erode federalism, and Ostrom took aim at its jurisprudence of so-called "process federalism" as articulated in *Garcia v. San Antonio Metropolitan Transit Authority* (1985). On one level, said Ostrom, the decision merely marked the ongoing "centralization and nationalization of the American system of government" that had been under way for decades. Yet its explicit rejection of limits on Congress also seemed to augur the final abandonment of constitutional self-government in favor of omnicompetent central power.[62] "Process" federalism jurisprudence was the polar opposite of the thoroughgoing federalism Ostrom advocated.

He also thought that the erosion of federalism brought on by the nationalization and centralization of the administrative state fostered a dangerous increase in executive power. Basic precepts of bureaucratic management that the Wilsonian paradigm derived from the principle of unitary sovereignty pushed in this direction. "Strengthening of the government is viewed as the equivalent of increasing the authority and powers of the chief executive."[63] Plans for reorganization of the executive branch that recurred over the twentieth century fit this pattern—their overall goal was to accrue more managerial and discretionary power to the president.[64] The Watergate crisis itself was simply the most momentous symptom of the trend toward unified command-and-control authority in the modern administrative presidency. Whatever was identified as a problem in need of a government solution became the province of the executive, and the presidency increasingly took on monarchical overtones of eminence, command, and secrecy. Ostrom argued pointedly that the approach to administration embodied in the modern presidency was anticonstitutional. It tended toward autocracy because it lacked any limiting principle.[65] Such was the trend of American constitutionalism when true federalism was effaced.

Ostrom's melding of characteristically libertarian concerns with classic elements of American political thought strove to decenter the modern state's monopoly on governance by challenging its unitary conception of sovereignty with his own theory of federalism as polycentricty and voluntary association. Although this endeavor built on the resources of American constitutionalism, it could not always be reconciled to it at the deepest level. Nevertheless, the insight and theoretical ambition of Ostrom and his collaborators influenced and inspired a broadly libertarian and public choice defense of federalism in the last several decades of the twentieth century and beyond.[66]

Conclusion

Many core principles of libertarian thought were readily deployed to explain and affirm American federalism. The liberty of citizens who were free to move around could be better secured if states could be induced to compete with one another and if the federal government could be stopped from extorting compliance to one-size-fits-all norms via conditional grants-in-aid. Likewise, federalism practiced as a polycentric order of voluntary exchanges might displace the classic understanding of sovereignty, and with it the power of the state to command and control. These were powerful ideas, but libertarian thinkers sometimes struggled to root them in the historical experience and political theory of American constitutionalism, as Ostrom's engagement with Diamond illustrated. This problem limited the practical reach of libertarianism, but did not extinguish its intellectual influence.

CHAPTER FIVE

Straussians and the Erosion of Federalism

In the 1960s the first generation of Straussians did not join with traditionalists in defending a state-centered conception of federalism or with later libertarians in their emphases on competition and polycentricity. Rather, they typically argued that the American founders had intended federalism, and the states themselves, as subordinate aspects of a constitutional system that was fundamentally nationalist in its basis and orientation. The Constitution had accepted federalism out of necessity, integrating it somewhat awkwardly into a system designed from the beginning, carefully but irrevocably, to increase national power at the expense of the states. This claim was advanced by characteristically Straussian attention to political rhetoric, the virtue of prudence, and the centrality of natural rights. As it continued to develop, however, Straussian thought evinced greater appreciation of federalism's capacity to protect liberty from the reach of national power, to foster the civic virtue necessary for republican government, and to resist the centralizing thrust of the administrative state.

Defending a Strong National Government

Martin Diamond initially rose to prominence by refuting the reigning Beardian-Progressive claim that the Constitution was simply antidemocratic. Next, he turned to the established scholarly consensus about the meaning of federalism.[1] Mainstream scholars' views lauded what they took to be the founders' federalism, which they understood as a division of sovereignty, powers, and functions between one central and several local governments. Although this became the accepted definition, Diamond argued that it was not what the founders truly thought federalism was. They claimed not to have invented anything but merely to have combined opposed national and federal elements. In light of the older definition of federalism that Diamond traced from the Greeks to Montesquieu, the US system "constitutionally graft[ed] some pre-modern federal institutions onto a national government." The premodern definition that the founders inherited was that local member governments retained their primacy and included themselves in what was in essence a league or association of sovereign states—but not a government with legal authority over members' citizens or internal affairs. Member states participated equally in making the decisions of the central authority, while such agreements were executed locally by the members themselves.[2]

By 1787 this inherited understanding was a threat to individual liberty and the future of the nation amid the need for more national, centralized power. The states themselves were acting against liberty and property, proving the inapplicability of Montesquieu's claim, relied upon by old-style federalists, that republican liberty was safest within a small state. James Madison successfully convinced the delegates at Philadelphia that what was wanted from union— primarily and especially republican liberty but also peace, prosperity, and better administration—could be achieved only by increasing national power at the expense of the established conception of federalism.[3] Diamond acknowledged that the Convention had worked elements of the old view into the Constitution, but said that this "view survived only after having first been shaken to its very root, and hence that it survived only in a permanently weakened condition."[4]

Diamond's close reading of *The Federalist* confirmed this view, even though the rhetorical context of the ratification debate demanded that it sometimes be veiled or obscured. He analyzed how Alexander Hamilton, especially in *Federalist* 9, altered the criteria and historical examples associated with the traditional definition of federalism, while also misappropriating passages from Montesquieu, "so that the new Constitution could be deemed to belong to the federal class."[5] By the time he was done, Hamilton had lowered the bar so far that federalism could be said to exist so long as the states were not abolished and continued to exist for local purposes.[6] Designedly obscured was the extent to which the Constitution departed from the traditional understanding of federalism. Accordingly, "the great teaching of *The Federalist* is not how to be federal in a better way, but how to be better by being less federal."[7]

Diamond's patient sifting of *The Federalist* revealed for the "careful reader" the essayists' "superb rhetorical skill" in indicating their true nationalist position. Despite all the superficial and "mollifying assurances" about the persistence of traditional federalism amid the nationalizing drive, *The Federalist* "does not expect the federal elements to predominate."[8] The primary reason Diamond teased out, as indicated especially from *Federalist* 17, 27, and 45, was that the political approbation and support of the people would accrue to whichever level of government, state or federal, better attended to and administered their deepest concerns. As the parochialism of the states gradually diminished and the central government slowly became more active and visible in governing national affairs that extended into localities, the states' power and influence would decrease. "In short, the national government will be competing with the state government in circumstances that will increasingly tilt affairs to the national plane."[9] Nor did Madison's famous approach to remedying faction in *Federalist* 10 in any way depend on the federal aspects of the extended republic. Rather, said Diamond, Madison's logic of representing diverse interests across a large territory worked quite as well for a unitary system as for a federal one. The states existed, and *The Federalist* observed that they might properly resist national overreach, but they were not necessary to resolve the problem of faction as Madison presented it.[10]

In these early essays Diamond carefully deferred judgment about how the founders' nationalizing project had worked out over time. He insisted only that an accurate understanding of it should inform any contemporary discussion. Assessing Diamond's "nationalist" view of federalism along with his "democratic" rejoinder to the Beardian-Progressive claim that the Constitution was oligarchic, one scholar concluded that Diamond saw the founders as "far more like us, like post–New Deal America, than earlier scholars had made them out to be."[11]

Diamond's interpretation appeared amid the traditionalist conservative resistance to the Great Society and the Civil Rights movement analyzed in chapter 3. As discussed there, that approach often had invoked "states' rights" and the compact theory of the union, or else "territorial democracy," to criticize the growing power and reach of the national government. Diamond did not directly address these concepts, but one of his first essays on federalism appeared in *A Nation of States* (1963) alongside three others by Strauss's students.[12] Each supported national power and criticized the traditionalist conservative approach to federalism.[13]

Herbert Storing's contribution to this volume held that the framers of the Constitution "deliberately chose a strong national government" based on their understanding of the underlying moral and political union of Americans as one people.[14] As he put it in a subsequently published speech from 1967, "We Americans have not merely grown into Big Government; we were born as Big Government."[15] The Antifederalists and their heirs throughout US history who insisted on a state-centered union and a weak national government had failed to bridge the contradiction between their desire to have common interests adequately protected and their fear of increasing the power of the national government. Storing repeatedly stressed this point by adverting to *Federalist* 23: "For the absurdity must continually stare us in the face of confiding to a government, the direction of the most essential national interests, without daring to trust it with the authorities which are indispensable to their proper and efficient management."[16] He found this argument "massively persuasive" and justifiably extrapolated beyond its original context of national defense.[17] No constitution could wholly foresee what powers might be needed in the future.[18] In the post–New Deal, Cold War context, this principle dictated not only thorough national direction of defense but also regulation of the economy and labor, welfare state provision, funding of education, and enforcement of civil rights. Storing regarded these as proper national commitments in the modern era— ones that should not be revoked even if they could be.[19] "The basic reason for the centralization has not been carelessness or federal grasping, but the nationalization of our lives" that necessitated more government.[20]

While affirming the nationalist-unionist interpretation of the Constitution, Storing acknowledged that the founders had imperiled "some genuine values associated with the small community," values that should be strengthened.[21] He also agreed that "decentralization of administration" was necessary, as was the continuation of state and local government.[22] But traditionalist conservatives' path to these ends was imprudent and impossible. Storing dismissed as mostly irrelevant Russell Kirk's recurrence to Orestes Brownson's notion of "territorial democracy" (discussed in chapter 3). Kirk's treatment, he said, was a mere "incantation" of the idea. Brownson was sometimes consonant and other times utterly incompatible with the founders, but Kirk did not delve deeply enough to say what was worth keeping from Brownson, or why. This was not entirely true of Kirk, who was sounding a general idea rather than exploring the whole of Brownson. But Storing rightly observed that if Brownson's understanding of territorial democracy as a rigid division between the general and particular were fully restored, much of contemporary government would be deemed unconstitutional. And that would be unrealistic folly.[23] A proper solicitude for federalism did "not require, or even permit, a doctrinaire commitment to a species of localism or states' rights that is even less relevant to the conditions of Union now than when it was first rejected as its governing principle."[24]

Neither politics in general nor federalism in particular could be reduced to any once-and-for-all formula. Prudence was needed.[25] Storing thought that Brownson himself had indicated that view without properly applying it. In reality, definition of a national problem that demanded national action, or the extent to which such action should involve states and localities, was not settled in advance by the Constitution, the principles of federalism, or the history of American government.[26] Moreover, though Storing pointedly acknowledged that the twentieth-century rise of centralized, regulatory, bureaucratic government brought substantial risks for constitutionalism, it was "pointless merely to object to these things." The prudent course was "to be conscious of difficulties and dangers and always alert to what can be done to avoid the bad and promote the good that our circumstances make possible."[27] One way Storing attempted to do this, as noted in chapter 2, was to bring constitutional principles more explicitly into the conduct of the administrative state and the education of its leaders.

Just as prudence should guide conservatives' approach to specific modern policy questions, it should also inform their basic posture on federalism now that the national government had become so centralized, democratic, and bureaucratic. If these developments were more or less inevitable and politically irrevocable, as Storing believed, then they should be guided as constitutionally and prudently as possible. The alternative was complete political irrelevance based on adherence to a lost cause. Conservatives were mistaken, he wrote, to retreat to redoubts in the states or attempt to resist modern presidential leadership adventitiously from their longtime base in Congress. In the "only yesterday" of the New Deal, when conservatives sought to "shackle" the national government from addressing "social security, agricultural policy, and labor relations" because supposedly they were mere local issues, they succeeded only in depriving themselves of "any influence in deciding how the nation would meet what were manifestly national problems."[28] A similar "rigid insistence" on localism in the face of national problems in the post–New Deal era would have the same consequences. Again adverting to prudence in the face of reality and necessity, Storing advised conservatives devoted to localism to contemplate Hamilton's warning in *Federalist* 25: "Nations pay little regard to rules and maxims calculated in their very nature to run counter to the necessities of society. Wise politicians will be cautious about fettering the government with restrictions, that cannot be observed." Too many conservative analysts of federalism inadequately appreciated that constitutional government must be not only limited but also effective; avoiding this fact undermined their own capacity to affect political developments and steer the course of the nation.[29]

A Nation of States also contained strongly nationalist essays by Harry V. Jaffa and Walter Berns. They aimed directly at strict construction, state sovereignty, the compact theory of the union, and the Tenth Amendment as the bases of a putatively authentic, state-centered federalism. These ideas, earlier relied on to justify nullification and secession, were being invoked in the 1960s by conservatives such as Barry Goldwater and James Kilpatrick to resist national authority in several areas, especially civil rights.

Jaffa first argued that this narrow reading of national authority was utterly inadequate to national defense in the Cold War, as it had been to national economic recovery during the Great Depression. On the contrary, the proper reading of the Commerce Clause and the Necessary and Proper Clause provided ample national authority to act on behalf of the general welfare and the common defense as a constitutional majority of the nation determined was necessary in any given circumstance. Moreover, the imperative of national defense could properly extend national power into realms ranging from education to urban planning. Jaffa observed that the strict states' rights view was undermined by *any* concession to implied powers, as, for example, the use of an air force for national defense or the well-known desire of several leading founders to establish a national university. This was confirmed by historical experience, beginning with Thomas Jefferson's contradiction of his state-centered views by approving the Louisiana Purchase. "*No American statesman has ever attempted to govern in accordance with the doctrine of State-rights.*"[30] Accordingly, Jaffa judged that such appeals had been "intrinsically no more than a rhetorical principle upon which to oppose action by the national government deemed undesirable," and instead his essay concluded with a ringing endorsement of national power.[31]

Berns advanced the nationalist position by arguing that advocates of state sovereignty who invoked the Tenth Amendment logically implied the abandonment of their defining doctrine. If the states were truly intended to be sovereign and therefore capable of judging finally the extent of national power, "they would not require a tenth amendment to remind them that they intended, when they established the Constitution, to set limits to their agent's (that is, the federal government's) power."[32] The amendment made no sense as an admonition to the states if they were in fact sovereign, so it could be only an "accessory to interpretation" by the Supreme Court and thus an acceptance of "the right of the national government" to "arbitrate federal-state relations." Yet such arbitration could not be based on the terms of the amendment, because it contained no rule of law as such. Berns thus explicitly endorsed the statement in the famously nationalizing New Deal case of *United States v. Darby* (1941) that the amendment " 'states but a truism that all is retained which has not been surrendered' " by the states to the national government.[33] He then went on to delineate how the word "expressly" had been very carefully kept out of the amendment. Consequently, Congress legitimately had implied powers, despite several later attempts by advocates of state sovereignty to interpolate the word back into the text.[34] Next came a supportive analysis of John Marshall's expansive reading of the Necessary and Proper Clause in *McCulloch v. Maryland* (1819) and a condemnation of James Kilpatrick for still supporting the losing side. Kilpatrick was also wrong to claim that *Martin v. Hunter's Lessee* (1816) had been incorrectly decided: it rightly had upheld section 25 of the Judiciary Act of 1789, which permitted the removal of state court decisions for review in federal court. Berns urged Kilpatrick and his traditionalist compatriots to quit fighting lost battles and accept once and for all that the Constitution and the laws made pursuant to it were supreme over the states.[35]

Not long after the publication of these essays, Jaffa responded to Frank Meyer's attack on Abraham Lincoln in *National Review*. Meyer said that by defeating state sovereignty and secession, Lincoln and Union victory in the Civil War had brought on the modern centralized Leviathan of the New Deal and the forced egalitarianism of progressive liberalism.[36] Jaffa countered this position by briefly recapitulating, as he would relentlessly for more than a half century, the root of consent-based constitutional government in the natural rights possessed equally by all human individuals. Lincoln made it plainer than the founders had, said Jaffa, that sovereignty rested in the people, not the states, as "an inference from the primordial tenet of human equality."[37] Constitutionalism as limited government did not, as Meyer had argued, ultimately rest on some supposedly inviolable but now destroyed tension or balance between the sovereign states and the national government. Rather, it rested on "the recognition that *all* men have rights which *no* government should infringe."[38]

Slavery clearly had been the gravest conceivable affront to natural rights and constitutionally limited government, yet Meyer was appealing to the arguments that had defended it. Lincoln had never pursued the destruction of the states in order to end slavery, Jaffa observed, but he had argued that national power could and should be used to prevent its westward movement. And likewise only national power could maintain the indissolubility of the Union, as had been advocated by James Madison, Daniel Webster, and Andrew Jackson.[39] Jaffa thus explained why the natural rights basis of American constitutionalism could not be sacrificed to the spurious logic of state sovereignty and the compact theory of the union; rather, these ideas were precisely what had to be defeated by national power so that the natural rights of all were secure. As he emphasized much later, John C. Calhoun and the secessionists had clung to the pre-*Federalist* understanding of federalism, rejecting the national-federal redefinition wrought by the founders.[40]

The exchange between Meyer and Jaffa was an important landmark in the development of postwar conservatism. It dramatically illustrated the conflict between traditionalists' old-style states' rights federalism and the Straussians' support of national power exerted on behalf of natural rights.[41] Jaffa's rejoinder likely was the first thorough defense of Lincoln in *National Review*, heretofore mostly libertarian and traditionalist, and sometimes neo-Confederate and openly hostile to federal action on behalf of civil rights. But Jaffa's position, derived from his *Crisis of the House Divided* (1959), gradually reoriented both scholarship on Lincoln and many conservatives' assessment of his statesmanship and legacy.[42] Indeed, Jaffa's understanding of Lincoln helped sway William F. Buckley Jr. away from the view represented by Meyer. In this context it is telling that just prior to his death, Buckley said that "I once believed we could evolve our way up from Jim Crow. I was wrong: federal intervention was necessary."[43] As was clear to Meyer at the time, the Straussian natural rights–equality view supported a more robust exercise of national power over states and localities than was acceptable to libertarians or traditionalists.[44] Concomitantly, Jaffa's arguments helped reorient much conservative opinion away from the traditionalist emphasis on hierarchy and prescriptive liberty.[45] Federalism as such garnered little attention in either Jaffa's subsequent scholarship or his frequent quarrels with other conservatives. As with several other Straussians, he directed his attention primarily to philosophical analysis of regime principles.

In sum, first-generation Straussian assessments of federalism were favorably disposed to national power. They resisted any definition of federalism that involved immoveable limitations on that power or that portrayed the union as fundamentally state centered. They openly derided federalism understood as "states' rights" approval of secession or segregation. Accordingly, later Straussian scholars judged that Storing was "no great fan of federalism." He "occasionally offered an obligatory defense" of the principle even though "his heart was not in it." Diamond too was described as a "Big Government nationalist" who thought the Constitution created a "national government lightly laced with an occasional federal principle."[46]

Straussians' nationalist orientation reached something of a high-water mark in the work of Morton J. Frisch, who wrote several works in defense of Franklin Roosevelt and the New Deal. His general argument was that the New Deal regulatory-welfare state was a prudent and conservative reworking of the American political tradition—it did not amount to a revolutionary break with the regime's basic tenets. Economic regulations and social welfare programs were necessary elements of the national government's new role: serving the New Deal's now properly enlarged conception of liberty as security. In response to the conditions of modern life, government was to furnish "not only the conditions of happiness, but, to a considerable extent, the enjoyment or possession of material happiness which may properly be called *well-being.*"[47] The democratic nature of the regime was retained, said Frisch, even as he conceded that the ascent from "merely the securing of political freedom on the lowest level" to the "guaranteeing of equality of opportunity through governmental provision for welfare or economic well-being" was a move that "transcends some of the limitations of liberal democracy and even enlarges its horizons."[48]

Based on this capacious view of national authority and responsibility, the New Deal had rightly displaced the older understanding of federalism. Frisch's judgment of the Hughes Court of the 1930s applied a measure articulated by Diamond and Storing: the Court had failed to see that "whether to do a thing nationally or locally (in this case the proper extent of government control over the economy) must always be a prudential decision made at the particular moment in view of the particular circumstances."[49] The older conception of liberty and federalism had simply become outmoded. Frisch thus endorsed the conception of the general welfare and national power in the New Deal's broad reading of the Commerce Clause, by whose expansion the Court displaced the old federalism and validated the modern regulatory state.[50] While this view of the 1930s retained some purchase in the 1970s, it received little if any further elaboration among later generations of Straussians and marked Frisch as an outlier.

Defending the Virtues of Federalism

Straussians' generally nationalist posture did not make them mere apologists for post–New Deal centralization. The elaboration of modern progressive liberalism in the Great Society of the 1960s prompted some rethinking. Central to this development, also evident in the work of Storing and Diamond, was the characteristically Straussian point that the United States was a fundamentally modern regime rooted in self-interest and commerce and, therefore that the extended commercial republic might fail at the local level to instill the citizenly virtues necessary for its own preservation. Moreover, Straussians saw that, although the founders increased national power to protect liberty from abuse at the state and local level, liberty also had come to be threatened by the centralization of power in the federal government over the course of the twentieth century. Mitigation of these problems required retention of at least some meaningful political authority in states and localities, where the virtues necessary for self-government were cultivated.

Storing turned to the Antifederalists to reconsider some of the defects of the victorious Federalist-nationalist approach, even though the Antifederalists too were liberals in the most fundamental sense. They defended the states as self-governing republics that were necessary to prevent the consolidation of power at the national level and thereby the destruction of liberty. Moreover, they taught that civic virtue and affective attachment to the regime, though not addressed by the Constitution's reliance on interests and institutions, could be fostered only by the states, local communities, and associations of civil society that federalism made possible. Only in the small republics of the states could people know and judge one another; only there could they participate meaningfully in public life. The state's smaller scale afforded the degree of homogeneity and shared moral understanding required for people to remain self-governing citizens, whose attachment to institutions and obedience to laws was voluntary. Likewise, government was close enough to the people that it could remain responsible to them, and in turn the people could mold and educate themselves into the kind of citizens who understood their government and were dedicated to its preservation.[51] "The Anti-Federalists saw, although sometimes only dimly, the insufficiency of a community of mere interest. They saw that the American polity had to be a moral community if it was to be anything, and they saw that the seat of that community must be the hearts of the people."[52] They agreed with the Federalists that the protection of liberty was the purpose of government, but they also believed that "there was an inherent connection between the states and the preservation of individual liberty."[53] Union of course was absolutely necessary for some purposes, but liberty "depended on republican virtue, which in turn depended on maintaining the primacy of the states."[54]

The Antifederalists thus remained relevant to Storing's understanding of federalism, despite his acceptance of "big government."

That earlier emphasis did not entail any denial that politics was about public and moral commitments or that it would always require prudence to balance and moderate government at both the national and local levels.[55] The Antifederalist indictment of the Constitution for its overreliance on private interests fostered in the large commercial republic, which they said tended to undermine citizens' public-spirited support for the Constitution, "was never wholly laid to rest" and thus remained central to US history. "Do we not require, to put it in its most elementary terms, patriotism, devotion to a common good, a moral community, in order that our political system shall survive and be worth surviving?"[56] These aspects of small-republic federalism underscored the continued importance of Antifederalist thought in the post–New Deal age of national power: "There is a need to look for approximations to the small republic in the midst of Big Government—for subordinate communities that can serve some of the functions that men like the AntiFederalists saw were possible only in relatively small, 'human-sized' communities. These can only mitigate the hugeness of Big Society and Big Government, but they can help."[57]

Similar themes were apparent in Martin Diamond's thought as he moved toward a more positive view of federalism.[58] Like Storing, he remained convinced that the founders fully intended to tilt the constitutional system toward increased national power, yet he too extolled the older and more locally rooted conception of federalism in light of post–New Deal centralization. It had become clearer that the continued "vitality" of American government and politics required "keeping interest, affection, power, and energy alive and well at the state level of politics in an otherwise homogenizing and centralizing age."[59] An important part of the problem was that the doctrine of delegated and enumerated powers had "eroded" and the scope of national government had "vastly expanded." Any defense of federalism would have "to restore the moral and intellectual *bona fides* of the constitutional doctrine of enumerated powers" in order "to limit the growth of national government relative to the states."[60] Diamond warned that reformers' appeals to efficiency or compassion to overcome limitations on national power encouraged further departures from constitutional federalism. For it to endure, states' policies would have to be allowed to differ.[61]

Federalism was needed to limit and moderate the democratic trend toward plebiscitary national politics. This logic was an important component of Diamond's defense of the electoral college, which was under attack in the late 1960s and early 1970s. As a federal element incorporated into the structure of the central government, the electoral college compelled political parties and presidential campaigns to account for differences of opinion among the states. The planks of the resulting political platform, thus federalized, were more moderate and representative than if there were a national popular election. Likewise, the electoral college's federal aspect required large-scale political participation across the geographic span of the country, whereas in a national election conducted in the age of mass media, candidates would focus mostly on large advertising markets.[62]

Federalism helped in other ways to address the problem of participation in political life and to encourage the virtues of citizenship that participation relied on and reinforced (as Storing too had argued). Diamond used Tocqueville to express this understanding. Political participation and civil association at the local level taught democratic man, based largely on his self-interest, how to be a republican citizen and—somewhat despite himself—to act for the public good. Tocqueville's "self-interest properly understood" explained how federalism mandated the "administrative decentralization [that drew] democratic man out of private, individualist isolation into political life." Individualistic self-involvement would always be a primary feature of the democratic age, but with federalism's administrative decentralization it could be the basis for public-regarding action. "And thus the idea of virtue, on a lower but surer foundation, is to be re-established in the political world."[63] Tocqueville helped Diamond to see this effect. The United States, though definitively individualistic and modern, was worthy of preservation because its federal arrangements produced citizens and politics that had a kind of modern virtue, if not nobility in the ancient sense.[64]

These themes in the work of Storing and Diamond were the basis of the renewed Straussian appreciation of federalism that gained momentum in the Reagan era. Gary L. McDowell, a onetime student of Storing, brought this view into Reagan's Department of Justice (DOJ) as associate director of the Office of Public Affairs.[65] The conception of federalism that began with the Antifederalists and that emphasized civic virtue, responsible self-government, and the limitation of national power was "not an outdated relic of a distant past."[66] It echoed throughout US history and was again apparent in Reagan's commitment to federalism as the remedy for overcentralization—the cure for what the Antifederalists had called "consolidated" government.[67]

In the DOJ, McDowell helped advance Reagan's agenda by writing speeches for Attorney General Edwin Meese and by organizing conferences and seminars to educate career attorneys on the principles of federalism, among other foundational constitutional ideas.[68] He also served on the Domestic Policy Counsel's Working Group on Federalism, which produced a detailed report titled *The Status of Federalism in America* (1986). This report contained a historical overview of the principles of federalism, a discussion of its decline due to the centralization of modern American government, and recommendations for how it might be restored. Suggestions in this latter category ranged widely, even holding out the dim prospect of a constitutional amendment. For example, within the legislative branch the proposals included a requirement for a federalism impact statement for all congressional legislation; restrictions on the use and conditions attached to federal grants to states and localities; and an explicit statement of intent from Congress before any preemption of state laws took effect. For the executive branch the recommendations included revision of executive orders for greater control of regulatory agencies' impact on the states, and the advancement by the DOJ of a pro-federalism litigation strategy.[69]

Such reforms would help, but, the report argued, the primary reason for the decline in federalism was the Supreme Court's post–New Deal jurisprudence (as McDowell's earlier work had also argued).[70] Consequently, judicial reform was an important part of the Reagan administration's federalism agenda. Although Reagan administration policies sometimes worked at cross purposes to its own federalism goals, the elevation of William Rehnquist to be chief justice and the Court's ensuing focus on federalism were very much a part of Reagan's legacy.[71] In addition, alumni of the Reagan DOJ were significantly involved in the Federalist Society's support of federalism litigation before the Supreme Court as it took off in the 1990s.[72] (A more detailed treatment of jurisprudential developments is included in part IV's analysis of how conservatives responded to the rise of modern judicial review.)

Certainly Straussians contributed to the intellectual rejuvenation of federalism and had some influence on the Reagan administration's approach to the issue. But Ralph Rossum, another prominent Straussian scholar, rightly observed that there were severe limits to the Rehnquist Court's supposed "federalism revolution." Building on Diamond's argument that the founders expected federalism's boundaries to shift through an ongoing political negotiation, Rossum further underscored that the states had originally been protected in this process by their legislatures' power to choose US senators. The founders' vast increase of the powers of Congress was acceptable in large measure because the states could guard their own interests in the Senate. But the Seventeenth Amendment's requirement for popular election of senators negated this original structural protection. Henceforth the states were hamstrung in their ability to resist centralization, and as Congress began relentlessly to expand national power, the Supreme Court became the sole arbiter of changes in the balance of federalism. Its attempts to "legalize" a process that the founders knew was always political could never be principled or consistent: there were no judicial standards for measuring the questions involved. Indeed, Rossum wrote, the Court had "candidly confessed on numerous occasions" that it could not "determine exactly where the wall of federalism should go, i.e., it cannot identify a principled line demarcating federal from state powers."[73] The Court was thus fated to incoherence as it alternately and severally undermined individual rights, self-government in the states, the will of national governing majorities, and its own authority as an institution.

Rossum urged his readers to recognize that the original federal design was dead. The Court's efforts to revive it "by drawing lines between federal and state power that the framers denied could be drawn and that they never intended for the Court to try to draw—are merely futile attempts to breathe life into a corpse."[74] He applied this critique to the Rehnquist Court's federalism jurisprudence. Although he sometimes sympathized with the decentralizing results of particular decisions, there was no denying that the states were much reduced from the position they had enjoyed under the original Constitution.[75] Perhaps this melancholy conclusion was the reason that federalism subsequently attracted little direct attention from Straussians.

More recent Straussian analysis of the administrative state has gradually come to appreciate that it too has threatened federalism.[76] After the second wave of administrative expansion in the late 1960s and early 1970s, its pronounced centralizing trend dramatized the corollary threat to federalism. Straussians did not typically treat this theme in great detail, but they repeatedly recognized both the reduction in the traditional powers of the states and the concomitant undermining of the virtues associated with local self-government. This view was expressed in an early, though brief, form in Paul Eidelberg's influential study of the Progressive genesis of the administrative state. The Progressives' egalitarian and statist drive centralized power in the national government, as exemplified by Woodrow Wilson's view that the Commerce Clause justified a national police power over the states. This move necessarily would "subvert the principle of federalism." Wilson's proffered endorsement of federalism notwithstanding, "the logic of his political thought," as in his view of the Commerce Clause, "cannot but eventuate in a unitary system."[77] The most detailed Straussian study of Wilson extensively documented his hostility toward federalism. Wilson held that federalism had no principled basis but rather was the result of the founding's particular historical circumstances. It was destined to be overcome as part of history's progress toward greater national unity and the clear expression of the national will. Simply put, "Wilson saw federalism as a system that was too outmoded to handle the problems that emerged from the development of history."[78]

As chapter 2 shows, Straussians' knowledge of the history of political thought attracted them to Tocqueville's influential diagnosis of "administrative centralization" and the resulting malady of "soft," democratic despotism as the central problem of the administrative state. Concomitantly, then, Tocquevillian themes featured in Straussian analyses of federalism. When a distant power undertook administration at the local level, said Tocqueville, not only was it usually inept and unresponsive to local needs, but it also atrophied citizens' capacity for self-government. Over time the central power intruded into an ever greater number of aspects of life, while people lost the habits and virtues needed to govern themselves—and eventually the ability even to recognize what it would mean for them to do so amid the enveloping power of the state. This use of Tocqueville was included in the work of John Adams Wettergreen, one of the first Straussians to consider the administrative state's threat to federalism; in a book by John Marini that significantly influenced all later Straussian thought on the subject; and in a penetrating indictment of modern American governance by Paul A. Rahe.[79] If there was ever to be a reversal of centralization in favor of the states, Rahe argued, it would be rooted in Tocqueville's recognition that "human dignity is bound up with taking responsibility" and, more especially, with the "ordinary and honorable human desire to take responsibility for one's own well-being and that of one's family and local community." Only in this way could people have a "bulwark against the soft despotism that is modern democracy's drift."[80]

Conclusion

The initial Straussian engagement with federalism in the 1960s emphasized the nationalist orientation of the Union against "states' rights" conceptions of it that historically had helped trample natural rights and justify secession and segregation. But Straussians' awareness of the complexity of federalism and its place in the founders' political science, along with sensitivity to their own post–New Deal political context, gradually led them to a more robust appreciation of federalism in the 1980s and 1990s. The growth of the administrative state and its accompanying centralization of power showed that federalism must be defended if liberty and local self-government were to endure. Nevertheless, by the end of the century most Straussian analyses of federalism feared that Tocqueville's warning about administrative centralization and soft despotism had gone unheeded.

THE MODERN PRESIDENCY
An Overview

The power and influence of the presidency grew substantially as a result of the New Deal, World War II, and the Cold War—a transformation that has been among the most salient and studied developments in all of US constitutional history. Part III focuses on conservatives' varied postures toward the growth of presidential power in the realm of foreign affairs and their enduring concerns about the president's subordination of Congress through shaping and leading public opinion. Modern presidents increasingly communicated directly with the people to further a vison of the national interest, but conservatives were leery that this development tended toward a plebiscitary and anti-republican mode of politics—one that frequently called for more government intervention, regulation, and war making. These trends sat uncomfortably with the long-established conservative suspicion of executive power.

Scholars typically speak of the "modern" presidency as having been formed under Franklin D. Roosevelt, albeit with important antecedents, especially in the Progressive era. After Roosevelt, the president, rather than Congress or the political parties, came to be seen as the embodiment of popular rule. He was encouraged and expected to be (in the words of Theodore Roosevelt) the "steward of the public welfare."[1] This view developed in part because the New Deal institutionalized in the executive bureaucracy the powers Franklin Roosevelt had used to address the national emergencies of the Great Depression and World War II. Unilateral presidential action became more frequent in both domestic and foreign affairs. The "security and well-being of the nation" were now said to be basic presidential responsibilities. The chief executive was expected to present a legislative agenda to Congress, to manage the national economy, and generally to articulate in public speech the direction of national life.[2]

Roosevelt's unilateral actions during the approach of World War II—the last war formally declared by Congress—set the template of the modern presidency in foreign affairs.[3] The Cold War soon multiplied the instances of presidential war making. There were also numerous covert operations that ran the gamut from disinformation to assassinations and coups d'etat. A Rubicon of sorts was crossed in June 1950 when President Harry Truman committed US forces in Korea without congressional consultation or authorization. In 1951 Truman also sent US forces to Europe to support the North Atlantic Treaty Organization (NATO). This action, in light of the growing conflict in Korea, lead to a major debate in Congress about the extent of unilateral presidential power (analyzed in chapter 6). As strikes in the steel industry threatened to hamper the Korean War effort, Truman issued an executive order to have the government take possession and operate much of the nation's steel industry. That action was subsequently overturned in *Youngstown Sheet and Tube Co. v. Sawyer* (1952).[4] In that case the Supreme Court attempted to delineate a continuum for legitimate unilateral presidential actions vis-à-vis Congress, an action's place on the continuum depending on preexisting congressional authorizations or prohibitions. *Youngstown* significantly influenced the way that legal-political actors argued about presidential war making in the twentieth century, but did not halt it.

President Dwight Eisenhower instigated numerous covert operations but was more circumspect than Truman when it came to direct military engagements. He consulted Congress and received from it a joint resolution authorizing the use of force in the Formosa Straits crisis of 1955. Another such resolution, preceded by more delay and negotiation, was passed in 1957 to authorize intervention in the Middle East. Nevertheless, a new pattern of presidential initiative had been set and was apparent in actions across the remainder of the twentieth century. Congress was mostly supine in the Cuban Missile Crisis (1962), nor did President John F. Kennedy understand himself to need its approval for the actions he took. The infamous and loosely worded Tonkin Gulf Resolution (1964) allowed President Lyndon B. Johnson to conduct the Vietnam War as he saw fit. Johnson willingly took responsibility for the conflict, Congress continued to fund it, and his presidency collapsed as Vietnam polarized the nation.

Scholars have long observed that, prior to the denouement in Vietnam, the modern presidency found resounding support in liberal political and academic opinion. Prominent liberals who endorsed the "heroic" modern presidency often regarded Franklin Roosevelt as the model. He was lionized for overcoming the fragmentation and parochialism of American politics as represented in Congress. He also successfully abandoned or transcended the constitutional limits that originally had constrained the presidency in both domestic and foreign affairs. One analyst described the "textbook presidency" advanced by leading liberals of the 1950s and 1960s as a "cult" that placed a "halo" over the office. It elevated the chief executive to the status of "omnipotent" fixer of all national problems and the "moralistic-benevolent" totem of the nation.[5] Accordingly, noted liberal scholars such as Henry Steele Commager and Arthur Schlesinger Jr. rushed to defend President Truman's intervention in Korea. They were opposed at the time by figures such as the political scientist Edward S. Corwin of Princeton, Senator Robert A. Taft of Ohio, and later by Louis Fisher, a leading recent critic of presidential war making.[6]

Mainstream liberal opinion was well represented by Clinton Rossiter, who endorsed presidential power in sometimes fawning prose that was little concerned with constitutional limitations.[7] Even more influential was Richard Neustadt's instruction on how a shrewd president, if skilled in manipulation and persuasion, could accrue more power and influence at every possible turn.[8] Neustadt essentially equated good governance with this approach. In an afterword to a later edition, he clarified the import of his views for Cold War foreign policy. Nuclear weapons had altered the original constitutional requirement of congressional involvement in war making, he said. "Technology has modified the Constitution: the President perforce becomes the only such man in the system capable of exercising judgment under the extraordinary limits now imposed by secrecy, complexity, and time." The president had in many respects become the nation's "Great Initiator. When what we once called 'war' impends, he now becomes our system's Final Arbiter."[9] Summing up, Corwin's seminal study concluded, in a line endlessly repeated by scholars (though not always in full), that, "taken by and large, the history of the Presidency is a history of aggrandizement, but the story is a highly discontinuous one." As a liberal who supported the New Deal, Corwin was an outlier in being somewhat critical of this trend. A more recent study has rightfully observed that, at midcentury, "aggrandizement was generally well received and even applauded."[10]

Liberal opinion turned sharply due to Vietnam and the administration of President Richard M. Nixon. Now the presidency was said to be out of control.

It must be restrained in the wake of Nixon's conduct of the war (particularly the bombing of Cambodia), his confrontation with Congress over spending and regulatory policy, and of course the Watergate affair. At this time Schlesinger famously reversed course to warn of the "imperial presidency," as he titled his 1973 book. Congress passed the War Powers Resolution over Nixon's veto in 1973. It provided that, absent a formal declaration of war, a president should consult with Congress about US troop deployments whenever possible. Further, he could initiate hostilities only under certain specified conditions. The president was required to report to Congress the necessity for any such action and the authority that justified it. Deployments must be for a limited time and could be extended only with congressional approval. Congress could also pass a concurrent resolution to remove armed forces engaged in hostilities.

As Congress thus sought to restrain the president, the Watergate investigation revealed a host of illegal and unconstitutional actions that had been intended to destroy Nixon's radical and liberal opponents. The House of Representatives prepared to impeach the president for obstructing justice, abusing his power in derogation of the rights of citizens, and failing to comply with congressional subpoenas (a proposed charge related to the bombing of Cambodia was not advanced). Watergate and Nixon's resignation, combined with the War Powers Resolution, thus marked Congress's concerted response to modern presidential power. Other measures in a variety of areas soon followed. Many concerned domestic policy and included restrictions on executive branch secrecy, surveillance, budgetary discretion, and campaign finance. The Ethics in Government Act (1978) created an office outside the direct control of the Department of Justice, the special prosecutor (later known as the independent counsel), to investigate possible malfeasance in the executive branch.[11] Numerous investigations of executive branch officials were undertaken through the 1980s and 1990s, including most notably that of President Bill Clinton, which resulted in his impeachment, trial, and acquittal (1998–99).

Nevertheless, a close study of this post-Watergate congressional "resurgence regime" concluded that it receded as executive power again ascended in the 1980s and 1990s.[12] Indeed, it would be difficult even to list exhaustively for these decades all of the airstrikes, ground invasions, covert operations, nation-building efforts, and peace-keeping missions that presidents ordered. They ranged geographically from Central America and the Caribbean to Africa, the Middle East, and Eastern Europe. In undertaking them, presidents continually denied the constitutionality of the War Powers Resolution, and while usually citing it in regard to their actions, they insisted that the commander in chief power was not limited by its provisions. When presidents did seek and gain formal congressional support for large-scale military engagements, as in the Gulf War of 1991, they denied it was constitutionally necessary. Indeed, President Clinton dispatched thousands of ground troops to Bosnia for several years in the late 1990s. He also bombed the Serbs in Kosovo in 1999 without explicit authorization or endorsement by Congress.[13]

The various strands of conservatism responded to and interacted with these developments. As conservatism became more variegated and internally contentious, its approach to executive power became more complex. This process accelerated in the context of the antipresidential congressional resurgence. Moreover, the election of Ronald Reagan in 1980 and 1984, a president as charismatic and rhetorically gifted as any in the twentieth century, further complicated the conservative position. As discussed in chapter 2, the "unitary executive" theory emerged to reassert presidential power in domestic affairs as a way to control the administrative state. Chapter 6 shows that the other side of this theory, an emboldening of presidential power in foreign affairs, developed among conservatives in the aftermath of Watergate and the War Powers Resolution. It percolated in the Department of Justice during the 1980s, cohered in response to the Iran-Contra affair (1986–87), and developed further in the 1990s. Its basic elements were in place well before the terrorist attacks of September 11, 2001.

As presidential power expanded, waned, and then expanded again, traditionalist conservatives remained largely consistent. They opposed the modern presidency in both foreign and domestic affairs, regarding it as inconsistent with the deepest principles of American constitutionalism. But the salience of traditionalists diminished after Watergate and amid the rise of Reagan and the unitary executive. Meanwhile, libertarian attention to the presidency was rather sparse between the New Deal and 9/11. The few extensive libertarian analyses attacked the office for having long been overly "imperial" and statist, though some libertarians grew more realistic and nuanced after the Cold War. Straussians studied the presidency more comprehensively starting in the 1960s. They came to see it as a form of modern (post-Machiavelli) executive power inherently in tension with constitutional government. Its orientation toward emergency and necessity, as well as its potential for populist demagoguery, were unavoidable yet also potentially salutary. On this basis, Straussians usually supported an assertive presidency in foreign policy. This orientation sometimes associated them, more sensationally than accurately, with neoconservatism as it advanced this general position in the last decades of the twentieth century.

CHAPTER SIX

Traditionalists, the Modern Presidency, and the Rise of the Unitary Executive

Traditionalists consistently criticized the growth of presidential power. Their characteristic affirmation of culture, morality, and locality opposed the modern presidency's soaring rhetoric, grand policy leadership, and international adventurism. Traditionalists did not think that the president's status as the highest nationally elected official justified subordination of Congress or that the United States' military forces should go abroad without congressional assent. In taking these positions, traditionalists understood themselves as hewing to the long-established and orthodox constitutional principles inherited from the founding: Congress was the nation's representative and deliberative institution; executive power tended to be expansionist and thus suspect. Their view typified American conservatism until well into the 1960s. But soon thereafter a new development emerged: the theory of the unitary executive. It arose among establishment conservatives in the Republican Party and the Reagan administration to reinvigorate the presidency after the debacles of Watergate and Vietnam. The theory was then nurtured in the nascent conservative legal movement in law schools in the 1980s and 1990s. Amid this development, traditionalists maintained their long-standing views, but with waning influence. Here it should also be noted that, both before and after the rise of the unitary executive, traditionalists confronted the modern presidency with thorough defenses of Congress that are only limned in this chapter. They are revisited in the conclusion along with the various other conservative perspectives.

Traditionalists from the Birth of the Cold War to the Rise of the Unitary Executive

In 1946 the Republican Party won majorities in both houses of Congress for the first time since 1928. Conservatives offered a variety of measures to pare back the New Deal in general and the presidency in particular, including the Twenty-Second Amendment (proposed in January 1947). It provided that a president could be elected only twice (including a president who had succeeded to the office in the first two years of the predecessor's term). On one level, it was a partisan Republican rebuke of Franklin Roosevelt that passed quickly in both houses with relatively little discussion. Anti–New Deal southern Democrats also supported it, in many cases because they feared presidentially led federal intervention related to civil rights. On another level, however, the amendment was relatively uncontroversial because it formalized the two-term tradition that Roosevelt had violated. Supporters understood it as restoring constitutional "balance" and reinforcing "restraint" among the institutions of government.[1] This limit on the president's term of office proved to be conservatives' one formal constitutional victory in their battle to constrain the post–New Deal executive.

Amid the amendment discussion, C. Perry Patterson presented one of the first post–New Deal traditionalist scholarly reassessments of the presidency.[2] At heart a southern Jeffersonian advocate of states' rights, Patterson argued that the long evolution of political parties had, during the New Deal, finally succeeded in creating a presidency unconstrained by constitutional limitations and in control of the majority in Congress due primarily to the president's leadership of public opinion. The legislature's unlimited reach, now under the executive's direction, had in turn been confirmed by the Roosevelt Court's revolution in jurisprudence and personnel. These changes ratified the new era of presidential supremacy. "As head of the nation, head of his party, mouthpiece of the American people, and political executive of the Government of the Day, he is in position to govern the nation."[3]

Moreover, the administrative state had displaced the Jeffersonian tradition with its own "positive theory of the state" and the "planned economy." Both further empowered the presidency, though the president was never fully in control of the bureaucracy.[4] The New Deal had massively empowered government in the executive branch but, at the same time, had made it less responsible, instantiating a "highly regulated and socialistic type of society [that] forces centralization and requires an executive type of government for its administration."[5]

The long-term trend in foreign affairs was similar, said Patterson. The treaty-making power, the increased use of executive agreements (which did not require Senate ratification), the conduct of diplomacy, and the unilateral power to make war all aggrandized the presidency and diminished Congress. He concluded that the ancient warnings about the tendency of most governments to end in executive despotism or monarchy had seemingly come to fruition.[6] Later traditionalists and some libertarians would reiterate this charge.

Contemporaneous with the Twenty-Second Amendment's final phase of ratification in 1950–51, Senator Robert A. Taft of Ohio became the most prominent traditionalist conservative to oppose both President Harry Truman's foreign policy and his use of executive power. Taft had earlier criticized Roosevelt's interventionism in the years before World War II. Although he was never truly an "isolationist," as some of his political critics alleged, he was relatively inexperienced in foreign affairs. And he was dedicated to preserving the constitutional powers of Congress. He continued to favor noninterventionism as much as possible, and although he supported several military deployments in Europe and Asia, he consistently upheld the traditional conservative resistance to presidential power.

Taft supported Truman's confrontation with communism in Korea in June 1950, but he protested the president's failure to seek congressional authorization for sending troops under the aegis of the United Nations, let alone a formal declaration of war. The president simply lacked the authority to go it alone. Taft urged Truman to seek a joint resolution to authorize action and averred that he would support it. But, up to that point, the Korean War had been "a complete usurpation by the President of authority to use the Armed Forces of this country." This mistake must be protested or else "we would have finally terminated for all time the right of Congress to declare war."[7]

A more direct and extended clash resulted from Truman's plan to deploy several divisions to Europe in early 1951 (as part of a NATO agreement). Former president Herbert Hoover and former ambassador Joseph P. Kennedy publicly questioned any anticommunist policy that might lead to land wars in either Europe or Asia. Their position helped initiate the so-called Great Debate, which lasted for several months in both the House and Senate and included pro-presidency attacks on Taft by Henry Steele Commager and Arthur Schlesinger Jr. (and a more measured statement by Clinton Rossiter).[8] Both chambers considered various resolutions and amendments that would have constrained presidential action by delimiting the use of congressional appropriations, or mandated presidential consultation with congressional committees, or required congressional authorization for military deployments. Ultimately, the Senate managed to pass only a legally nonbinding "sense of the Senate" resolution which held that any additional divisions deployed to Europe be sent only with the prior approval of Congress.

Taft's contribution to the debate stands as a major statement of the traditionalist position. He gave a long speech in the Senate on January 5, 1951, and another in March. He disputed the necessity of more ground troops in Europe and insisted that internal debate on foreign policy, rather than cession of all control to the president, was healthy for the nation's politics. The time had come for Congress "to assert clearly its own constitutional powers unless it desires to lose them."[9]

Taft criticized a report from the executive branch to the Senate that appears to have been one of the first articulations of the pro-presidential arguments that recurred for the rest of the century. It did not use the phrase "unitary executive" but advanced the core claims of what later became that theory. The president's authority to send troops into battle in Korea or station them in Europe was said to reside in the Commander in Chief Clause and the requirement to "take care that the laws be faithfully executed." In addition, vesting of "the executive power" in the president brought further unspecified powers in foreign affairs "which are not conferred expressly by the Constitution but are derived from the fact that the United States is a sovereign nation." The report concluded that the "need for speed and the growth in the size and complexity of the armed forces have enlarged the area in which the powers of the Commander in Chief are to be wielded." Congress might be asked for its support, but the pace of events had turned prolonged debate and a formal declaration of war into dangerous anachronisms.[10]

Portions of Taft's speeches in these debates were included in his book *A Foreign Policy for Americans* (1951), which used the report to summarize Truman's position. Taft said that it contained "the most unbridled claims for the authority of the President that I have ever seen written in cold print."[11] Based on its logic, "whenever in [the president's] opinion American foreign policy requires he may send troops to any point whatsoever in the world."[12] Congress was relieved of any power to act on its own and was reduced to being "simply given the right to support the President after the President has acted."[13] On the contrary, Taft held that Congress's Article I, section 8, power to declare war and appropriate money for the armed forces reflected a "certain and definite suspicion of a possible desire on the part of some President to set up a great permanent military force."[14] Taft sincerely thought that the country had reached a precipice that endangered its constitutional principles.[15] His resistance to presidential unilateralism in foreign affairs anticipated the principles of the War Powers Resolution, which came two decades later.[16]

Taft also rejected Truman's use of the Korean conflict to justify his infamous attempted takeover of the nation's steel mills in April 1952: "The President once again is usurping power which is not conferred on him." In fact, Congress had explicitly rejected giving the president this power when passing several recent laws dealing with strikes. Nor could the president's assertion of a national emergency enlarge his constitutional authority. The illegitimate and dangerous idea of "inherent powers" did not permit the president to "go around the country seizing people's property." This episode, like the other recent events in foreign policy, advanced "the general philosophy of the New Deal and the Fair Deal, that if there is any way to avoid coming to Congress for authority to act, it will be immediately adopted."[17]

The Supreme Court's negative response to the attempted presidential steel seizure suggested that further limitations might succeed.[18] In late 1951 Senator John Bricker of Ohio, a conservative ally of Taft who had been the Republican nominee for vice president in 1944, proposed a constitutional amendment to provide that no treaty could conflict with the Constitution and that Congress must legislate in order for a treaty to have domestic effect. It also provided that Congress could regulate executive agreements with foreign governments or international organizations. The Bricker amendment responded to long-standing discontent with a treaty's capacity to override domestic law, with executive foreign policy unilateralism, and with the possible reach of the new United Nations. The proposal was debated and revised throughout 1952 and 1953 in the context of Truman's foreign policy actions. President Dwight Eisenhower and Secretary of State John Foster Dulles eventually opposed the amendment as too much of an intrusion into executive control of foreign affairs. In February 1954 an attenuated version failed in the Senate by a vote of 60 to 31—one vote short of the two-thirds needed for approval.[19]

Both the Bricker amendment and the steel seizure case helped dissuade Eisenhower from as much unilateral action as had occurred under Truman or Roosevelt. Nevertheless, the amendment's failure was the high-water mark of Taftite conservatives' reproach to the modern presidency. Taft had endorsed the concept of the amendment (though he thought its text might need changes). But he was physically ailing and died in July 1953. The Democrats regained control of Congress in November 1954 and several pro-amendment Senators were defeated. Bricker himself was defeated in 1958. The Taftite Republican old guard was defunct.[20] Consequently, serious congressional attempts to restrain the modern presidency abated for a generation. When they did reemerge, it was from the progressive liberal side of the political spectrum in the aftermath of Vietnam and Watergate.

In the 1950s and 1960s, however, opposition to the modern presidency remained central to traditionalist conservatism, even though Congress itself had seemingly capitulated. *National Review*, founded in 1955, held this general view into the 1970s. The magazine warned of executive overreach, defended Congress, and supported the Bricker amendment. Its writers lamented actions of the executive branch that "usurp[ed] functions constitutionally assigned in whole or in part to the Legislature" and utterly rejected modern liberalism's tendency to "destroy the balance of powers and center authority in a plebiscitarian Leader-President."[21] Clinton Rossiter's study *Conservatism in America* (1955) rightly concluded that "as to the Presidency, even the sight of one of his own kind in the highest office does not allay [the conservative's] suspicions of executive power."[22]

James Burnham, a founding editor and central figure at *National Review*, advanced this view in his seminal work *Congress and the American Tradition* (1959). His position was situated within two other, more comprehensive analytic frames (both treated in chapter 1 of this book). The first was the "managerial revolution," in which a new elite administered the post–New Deal state in the name of the democratic masses ("democratism"). The second was the twentieth-century ascendance of the liberal strand of American political culture over the conservative one. Currently the dominant "liberal-democratist ideology" fostered a centralized, bureaucratic state that justified itself by advancing egalitarianism in the name of the democratic mass. The president was the crucial leader of this program and, since Franklin Roosevelt, had stood at the head of an often unaccountable bureaucracy. Burnham held that the current alignment of pro-presidency liberals and pro-Congress conservatives was not necessarily permanent or inherent, but he doubted it would change any time soon.[23]

He also diagnosed what later scholars called the "plebiscitary presidency," which had become "the primary democratist institution."[24] The president was a "plebiscitary leader, who embodies the true general will."[25] This change clearly spelled the "breakdown of constitutional government."[26] "Intermediary institutions," Congress chief among them, were for the president mere "interferences."

"If they contradict the President, then they are necessarily contradicting the general will, and their actions are anti-democratic. . . . The President is the voice of the general will; therefore the law is what he proclaims."[27] The legislature increasingly served "merely to approve," and perhaps to tinker with, the program now "initiated, formulated and presented by the executive."[28] Having been thus reduced, Congress "best serves the national interest by waiting to be told by the President what to do, and then obediently doing it."[29]

Nevertheless, Burnham was a deep-dyed Cold War anticommunist and accepted that modern conditions required a more active presidency in foreign affairs. He similarly acknowledged that the size and complexity of the military, along with technological advances (especially nuclear weapons), had in some respects obviated congressional limits on military appropriations and the delay involved in formal declarations of war.[30] However, the recent actions by Truman in Korea and Eisenhower in the Middle East amounted to "an assumption of the power to declare war." As such they were "obviously not an extension but a contradiction of the traditional content of the Constitution."[31] Burnham described Truman's seizure of the steel mills as clearly unconstitutional. These actions were the "substance of democratic despotism." Truman's operative principle appeared to have been that the "sovereign executive claims to embody the will and interest of the people" and "decides whether an emergency exists. If he so decides, he acts as he sees fit to solve the emergency. Such an action so taken becomes lawful, without regard to any previously existing law."[32]

Willmoore Kendall, another founding editor at *National Review*, similarly rejected the rise of the presidency (and defended Congress). Kendall wanted to develop a thoroughly American, traditionalist, and constitutional conservatism that was not beholden to either Edmund Burke or Russell Kirk.[33] An important part of this effort was the cabining of executive power, as expressed in "The Two Majorities" (1960), a now canonical article in political science.[34] One majority associated with the presidency as a national office chosen by the mass electorate; and the other, with Congress as the representative of numerous and diverse local constituencies. The mass democratic constituency for modern presidential elections had made the office essentially "plebiscitary." The "people" were invited to give the president a "mandate" for programmatic action. The trend was to "glorify and enhance the office of President, and [to] try to make of presidential elections the central ritual of American politics."[35] This dynamic positioned the president as the embodiment of both "lofty and enlightened principle" and "professional expertise" that overcame the crude and backward rubes in Congress.[36] The president spoke of grand plans and high ideals to the nation's elites and those they influenced, while Congress was cast in opposition to "the moral imperatives that the nation's proper teachers urge upon us."[37] Yet the reality of a national campaign in the age of mass media meant that the terms of the plebiscitary mandate were vague, abstract, and hortatory. As candidates moved from "whistle-stop to whistle-stop and television studio to television studio," voters were offered only "the policy platitudes that constitute the table talk in our faculty clubs."[38] The winner claimed a mandate from the supposed national majority but inevitably would "overestimate [the electorate's] dedication to the pleasant-sounding maxims that have been poured into its ears."[39] Of course Congress typically resisted the result in the name of its differently constituted, more local, and more conservative majority. Kendall concluded that "plebiscitary presidential elections cannot become the central ritual of our system without destroying the system."[40]

In addition, Kendall observed that if the president was to lead the statist-egalitarian program of modern progressive liberalism, the United States' traditionally locally based, fragmented party system must be remade. Following the path charted by Woodrow Wilson, which in turn had become the conventional wisdom of the political science profession, liberals had long yearned to transform the parties on the model of a centralized and majoritarian parliamentary democracy. Both recalcitrant representatives and the separation of powers should yield to a "disciplined" and "responsible" majority in Congress that carried out the program of the president and his party. This transformation would " 'bridge the gap' between President and Congress—and so would insure unified, responsible and concerted action." Such a basic alteration of the constitutional system would advance liberal goals. Accordingly, "the advocates of a 'strong' President, or of greater coordination between Congress and President, all plead for measures that would in fact serve to advance the ends of the disciplined party theory." Such advocates included the American Political Science Association in a well-known report published in 1950. Another was the noted scholar James MacGregor Burns, whom Kendall publicly debated. He described as revolutionary Burns's call for reforms that would ensure the dominance of a liberal presidential electoral majority that had been culled from both major parties. This idea was a desperate and doomed attempt to change the rules of the constitutional game because they had for so long frustrated the progressive liberal program.[41]

Kendall also was wary of Harry V. Jaffa's monumental study of Abraham Lincoln in *Crisis of the House Divided* (1959). Kendall praised the book as learned and philosophically profound but warned of the Caesarist potential in Jaffa's rendering of Lincoln. If Lincoln had improved or transcended the founding by justifying the United States according to natural rights and equality, Jaffa had not recognized how expansive this enterprise might become. Lincoln himself had eschewed the dictatorial destruction of self-government in the crisis of the Civil War, using his power to center constitutionalism on the foundation of equality as the core of American national identity. But what of those who followed Lincoln? Kendall said that Jaffa's Lincoln may well have laid the groundwork for "a political future the very thought of which is hair-raising: an endless series of Abraham Lincolns, each persuaded that he is superior in wisdom and virtue to the Fathers, each prepared to insist that those who oppose this or that new application of the equality standard are denying the possibility of self-government."[42]

Kendall (with coauthor George Carey) later expanded this critique in *The Basic Symbols of the American Political Tradition* (1970). Jaffa responded with a decades-long series of attacks that wrote off Kendall as a neo-Confederate who rejected the basis of American government in natural rights and equality. This debate is by now well known to students of American intellectual conservatism and repays careful attention from anyone interested in the subject. But it tended to obscure Kendall's deeper concern that a powerful presidency armed with egalitarian sentiments could direct both popular opinion and Congress against the more conservative grain of most Americans.[43]

Conservative criticism of the presidency in the 1960s went beyond *National Review* and the well-known figures of Burnham and Kendall. For example, both men were aware of a French observer, Amaury de Riencourt, who suggested that the United States had begun to succumb to a democratic Caesarism that appeared to be advancing throughout Western civilization.[44] Another noted critic, Alfred de Grazia, similarly contended that the rise of the "executive force" was threatening the very existence of republican government in America.[45] In 1967 at the American Enterprise Institute in Washington, DC, de Grazia publicly debated Arthur Schlesinger Jr., who then represented the liberal establishment's endorsement of the modern presidency. De Grazia cogently advanced many of the themes analyzed above. He also recommended that the presidency be limited to one six-year term, that the president's unilateral war power be reduced, and that Congress assert more control over the federal bureaucracy by reducing its size and discretionary power.[46] He characterized Schlesinger as offering only opportunistic endorsement or condemnation of the presidency, depending on whether a particular action or policy achieved liberal results. After having defended the liberals' powerful presidency for so long,

Schlesinger now appeared to have been in the midst of an adjustment due to his disapproval of Lyndon Johnson's policy in Vietnam.[47] But in de Grazia's judgment, Schlesinger's pragmatism was too shallow to grasp the deeper principles of constitutional governance involved and, thus, the reality that "the office of the President will not cure itself of its tendencies towards a cult of personality and rampant activism."[48]

The lines of conservative-versus-liberal debate about presidential power thus seemed quite solid in the 1960s. Accordingly, Willmoore Kendall and George Carey concluded in 1966 that the two sides "appear to have made permanent and well-nigh irreversible commitments" on the issue. For them to "switch sides" would assuredly "take some doing."[49] This judgment was accurate from the New Deal into the 1970s. However, conservative and liberal approaches to the office began to realign once the "unitary executive" emerged to contest the diminished status of the presidency after Vietnam and Watergate. The following section considers this theory and how its emboldening of executive power became the orthodoxy of Republicans in Washington, DC, though not of traditionalist conservatives.

The Unitary Executive Emerges, 1970s–1990s

As noted in chapter 2, the theory of the unitary executive first developed in the 1980s as a rejoinder to the administrative state. The Reagan administration was simultaneously pursuing a more assertive foreign policy in the Cold War. Administration officials and allies in Congress, along with supportive law professors, began asserting that the president had the constitutional authority to use military force, conduct covert operations, and take other foreign policy actions independent of congressional approval. The concept and the nomenclature of the "unitary" executive gradually emerged in the realm of foreign affairs, but the label was not routinely used in this way until the mid-1990s.

Many Reagan administration officials came to Washington, DC, convinced that the War Powers Resolution and other post-Watergate reforms had dangerously and likely unconstitutionally diminished the presidency. Some were veterans of the Gerald Ford administration, where the sense of siege from Congress had been palpable.[50] To be sure, neither Ford nor Jimmy Carter wholly ceased actions abroad based on the independent constitutional authority of the executive branch, including the use of force.[51] Perhaps most famous was the *Mayaguez* incident in spring 1975, when Ford ordered military action without congressional approval in response to an attack on a US cargo ship by the Khmer

Rouge off the coast of Cambodia. Ford later insisted that the "imperial Presidency" was rightly gone, "but neither can we afford an imperiled Presidency."[52]

But Ford's room for maneuver was always severely limited, while conservatives thought Carter's presidency had failed utterly to address the problem of the hobbled executive. His foreign policy they opposed especially as weak and feckless. Moreover, they judged that Carter had too readily acceded to congressional invasions of executive authority over foreign affairs and national security, as in the Foreign Intelligence Surveillance Act (1978).[53] One telling anecdote from this time was Dick Cheney's response to Howard Baker's query for advice when, in 1980, Baker became Ronald Reagan's chief of staff (a position Cheney had held under Ford). Amid more routine issues, Baker's notes reveal, Cheney had told him: "President seriously weakened in recent years. Restore power and authority to Executive Branch—Need strong leadership. Get rid of War Powers Act—restore independent rights." Baker added that this was a "central theme we ought to push."[54]

Like his two immediate predecessors, Reagan deployed armed forces without seeking congressional approval (for example, in Lebanon and Grenada). However, it was in the battle for control over policy in Central America that the burgeoning conservative desire to reassert executive power, along with Reagan's staunch Cold War anticommunism, combined to produce a major conflict between the executive and Congress. The result was the Iran-Contra affair of 1986–87. This well-known episode involved officials in Reagan's national security apparatus who secretly sold weapons to Iran in the hope of garnering its aid in negotiating the release of American hostages in Lebanon. They then diverted some of the money to fund the Contras' resistance to the Marxist regime in Nicaragua—which Congress purported to forbid in the second Boland amendment.[55] Here we need not fully measure this particularly acute instance of the institutional conflict and political struggle that the separation of powers imposes on the conduct of US foreign relations. Instead I examine how Iran-Contra catalyzed conservative constitutional defenses of executive authority in foreign relations that eventually came to be known as the unitary executive.

One important example was a memorandum to the attorney general from Charles J. Cooper, then in the Office of Legal Counsel (OLC). It cited the Article II Vesting Clause, the commander in chief power, and the Take Care Clause to claim executive independence and discretion for delayed notification to Congress of covert diplomacy and arms sales to Iran. It also relied heavily on Justice George Sutherland's influential claim that the president was the nation's "sole organ" in the arena of foreign affairs (which itself was a quotation of John Marshall from 1800).[56] Accordingly, the memorandum concluded, "the president possesses inherent and plenary constitutional authority in the field of international relations," which accorded him "virtually unfettered discretion" about precisely when to report covert actions to Congress under statutory standards for "timely notification." While Congress possessed some oversight authority, it could not attach "conditions to Executive Branch appropriations that require the President to relinquish any of his constitutional discretion in foreign affairs."[57] The phrase "unitary executive" did not appear in this memorandum, but the rudiments of the theory clearly did.

The Minority Report of the Iran-Contra investigation repeated several of these points, analyzing much the same historical evidence and legal precedent (plus more), though with added detail and a more confrontational tone.[58] Most importantly, it cast the Iran-Contra affair as a controversy over constitutional first principles and supported the president as the authorized leader in foreign policy. The Minority Report repeatedly rejected as unconstitutional the use of the congressional spending power to invade the Article II powers of the president, as was done in the Boland amendments that prohibited aid to the Contras.

Two chapters in the report adduced historical evidence from the records of the Philadelphia convention, *The Federalist* papers, and examples and defenses of the exercise of presidential power in foreign affairs from across US history. A consistent theme was that the president was no mere "clerk" who simply carried out the will of Congress.[59] Rather, he was the head of an independently constituted branch of government tasked with sensitive and dangerous responsibilities that Congress was neither capable of conducting nor authorized to encroach upon. The executive branch, and ultimately the single person of the president, was both capable and politically responsible for foreign affairs that required diplomacy, secrecy, prompt decision, and military force.[60]

The Minority Report, like the Cooper memorandum, thus laid out the basic logic of the unitary executive without actually using the phrase. Both documents often spoke in terms of "inherent" or "plenary" powers in foreign affairs, or an inviolable area of executive "discretion." They aimed to secure "core presidential foreign policy functions" and "the President's constitutional independence and authority in the field of foreign relations."[61]

The Department of Justice (DOJ) similarly attempted to shield Oliver North from the criminal prosecution generated by the independent counsel investigation into Iran-Contra. It argued that North's actions were taken pursuant to legitimate executive authority, which wrongly had been invaded by the congressional spending power (in the form of the Boland amendments). The Vesting Clause of Article II made "plenary" the president's power over foreign affairs, including covert diplomacy, which "could not constitutionally be limited by any congressional enactment."[62]

The nascent unitary executive theory also was discernible in a paper Dick Cheney prepared for a conference in March 1989. Its primary purpose was to condemn Congress's overreach into Reagan administration foreign policy decisions. Cheney praised the Minority Report for illuminating the issues involved and referred to the limits placed on Congress by the "inviolable powers inherent in the presidential office."[63] The presidency was designed by the Constitution's creators "as a one-person office to ensure that it would be ready for action."[64] That the substance of the unitary executive theory continued to precede the label was apparent insofar as the published conference proceedings contained only two matter-of-fact usages of the phrase or a cognate—by the constitutional historian Jack N. Rakove. His contribution ruminated on some of the "consequences that flowed simply from the creation of a unitary presidency charged with the oversight of the subordinate departments of the executive branch." Rakove doubted that the historical record could justify extravagant claims of presidential power, but he un-self-consciously referred to the "principle of a unitary executive" and noted that nearly since the birth of the republic there had been tension over foreign affairs between the presidency and Congress.[65]

The "unitary executive" label was haltingly applied to presidential foreign affairs power in law review articles of the late 1980s and early 1990s, often by Reagan administration officials and members of the Federalist Society (who were sometimes one and the same). The usage was rare and not yet paired with the historical and theoretical arguments analyzed above. For example, Bruce Fein, who had been a lead researcher on the Minority Report, wrote an article that advanced several of its arguments. In this context he referred to the Constitution's creation of a "unitary executive responsible for international negotiations."[66] Geoffrey P. Miller, a law professor who had been an attorney in the OLC from 1981 to 1983, made conclusory mention of the president as "the official who oversees and supervises warmaking" based on the "Commander-in-Chief clause, and the clause giving the executive power to a unitary President."[67] Still, as the most detailed study of the topic concludes, the academic development of the unitary executive theory was at this time in its infancy and relatively immature.[68]

More direct and substantial expressions appeared in two books that marked the endorsement of a strong presidency among Washington, DC, establishment Republicans. *The Fettered Presidency: Legal Constraints on the Executive Branch* (1989) included contributions from many such figures with connections to the various camps of conservatism. One was Theodore B. Olson, previously an assistant attorney general in the OLC, who made an originalist historical case for the unitary executive akin to the Minority Report. He then detailed several examples in which Congress had, since the 1970s, invaded presidential foreign affairs powers.[69] Two other, Strauss-influenced authors with experience in the Reagan administration similarly argued that the Constitutional Convention of 1787 had intended the separation of powers to institutionalize the core functions best suited to each branch. In establishing "a largely independent and unitary office, the framers were signaling their intent to move decisively away from the incompetence of congressionally dominated government, particularly in the areas of war and foreign affairs."[70]

A second landmark book, *Energy in the Executive*, was by Terry Eastland, who had also worked in Reagan's DOJ. He later became the publisher of the *Weekly Standard* and is properly categorized as a neoconservative. Like the writers analyzed above, Eastland recurred to Alexander Hamilton's description of "energy" in *Federalist* 70 as the definitive quality of the executive branch. The framers "saw energy *and* responsibility as the two sides of the same coin of 'unity.'" Having a "single person" as president ensured both qualities.[71] Eastland hoped to persuade conservatives who favored limited government that they should endorse a strong presidency on the ground of constitutional principle rather than mere short-term political expediency.[72] Although the "unitary executive" nomenclature was not a central feature of his book, Eastland left no doubt about his views. The president had ample authority under the Constitution "to use force without congressional approval."[73] Moreover, "no attack is needed to create the kind of 'national emergency' that the President may legitimately respond to."[74] Eastland thus anticipated the strong form of the unitary executive in foreign affairs: the president "may wage preemptive war in the nation's defense, and he cannot be limited to waging a strictly defensive war in that effort."[75]

Development of the unitary executive idea thus continued apace, despite the end of the Cold War and the subsequent debate about the overall purpose of US foreign policy. For example, the administration of President George H. W. Bush, with Dick Cheney as secretary of state, used presidential signing statements aggressively, if often briefly, to defend the commander in chief power from any incursions by Congress. It resisted information disclosure and reporting requirements about military affairs, as well as involvement in the more fundamental issue of deployment of military equipment and personnel.[76]

A strong view of presidential power also guided the administration's conduct in the Persian Gulf War of 1991. Bush used his executive authority to hasten the conflict through both diplomatic and military actions.[77] At the same time, he successfully secured a United Nations resolution that authorized the use of force, and then a joint resolution of Congress, while also readying for military invasion.[78] But neither Cheney nor Bush accepted the notion that congressional authorization or a declaration of war was constitutionally necessary. Cheney explicitly said so in hearings before the Senate on December 3, 1990.[79] In signing the joint resolution into law in January 1991, Bush said, "My request for congressional support did not, and my signing this resolution does not, constitute any change in the long-standing positions of the executive branch on either the President's constitutional authority to use the Armed Forces to defend vital U.S. interests or the constitutionality of the War Powers Resolution."[80]

By the early 1990s, then, the unitary executive had emerged in practice, *avant la lettre*, to justify presidential war making without congressional authorization. The administration of President Bill Clinton did not elaborate the theory as such, though it certainly continued the unilateral presidential use of force abroad.[81] One of the first law review articles to advance the theory in foreign affairs was by Steven Calabresi (an alumnus of the Reagan DOJ and a founder of the Federalist Society). He accepted that in foreign affairs it was never entirely clear where to draw the line between the general concepts of congressional "policy making" and presidential "implementation."[82] But he urged a deeper appreciation of these basic functions and the reasons for which the founders had separated them as the best way to decide "when to insist on congressional authorization and when to insist that the President have a free hand."[83] Calabresi's brief treatment defended the key unitary claim that the president had core functions in foreign affairs that could not be invaded by Congress, but it did not offer the theory as the basis for unilateral presidential war making.

That move came decisively in an influential and lengthy article by John C. Yoo in 1996. It made an originalist argument for the unitary executive, claiming that the president was constitutionally authorized to initiate war without congressional approval. Yoo held that historical evidence had been misinterpreted and overlooked by mostly liberal scholars who opposed presidential unilateralism, while mostly conservative pro-presidency scholars had not yet adequately investigated it. Accordingly, analysis of founding-era sources made up most of the article. Yoo said that the presidency had been originally intended to retain more of the monarchical prerogative in war making than had been commonly understood in the pro-Congress view. The founders "proceeded to marry an independent, unitary President to the substantive war powers exercised by King, colonial governor, and state executive."[84] And that substance was "a system which was designed to encourage presidential initiative in war."[85]

While Reaganites had emphasized that Congress could not use the appropriations power to invade definitively executive functions, Yoo added that declining to spend at all was the primary tool available to Congress for halting presidential war making. Another was impeachment. Based on these momentous options, he described the war power as one shared in a process of dialogue and negotiation. Forced brinksmanship would be a less sanguine description. To this kind of objection Yoo responded that "although one might feel some disappointment at Congress' failure to take advantage of its funding powers, a failure of political will should not be confused with a constitutional defect."[86]

A congressional declaration of war was not the only way to bring it about, nor was presidential war making limited to defensive efforts in an emergency. Yoo readily accepted that the unitary executive validated President Clinton's use of force in Kosovo in 1999. Nor did he think that international law properly could induce or limit presidential war power, as Clinton's action in Kosovo appeared to have demonstrated. Yoo's criticism of the Kosovo conflict was that Clinton had placed US troops under the command of a foreign power via the UN. That action violated the unitary executive powers of the president, as well as the Appointments Clause (Article II, section 2) and the principle of nondelegation. Despite this problem, Yoo observed that congressional funding of Kosovo and other military engagements under a Democratic president while most liberal pro-Congress commentators remained silent seemed to have ratified a bipartisan consensus in favor of presidential initiative in war making according to the theory of the unitary executive.[87]

Prior to 9/11 Yoo's vision of the unitary executive and his interpretation of the historical evidence received some criticism, to which he responded.[88] At this point, then, the theory appeared as a pointed salvo in the well-rehearsed debate over war powers between "presidentialists" and their pro-Congress opponents. After 9/11, however, Yoo was in the OLC, where he helped extrapolate the unitary executive theory, as developed in his own and others' publications, into a justification for highly controversial and constitutionally suspect presidential war powers.[89] The ensuing legal-constitutional firestorm included renewed arguments that the historical evidence for the unitary executive could not justify the contemporary use being made of the theory and that the scholarly standards of the student-edited law reviews that had published it were perhaps inadequate.[90] These serious questions aside, Barack Obama's succession of George W. Bush, like Clinton's succession of George H. W. Bush, marked no end to presidential unilateralism. A careful study of the endurance of the unitary executive concluded that it has seemingly been normalized, and with it the presidential war powers that traditionalists had resisted for decades. Both developments moved "from being almost unthinkable, to being controversial, to being more common but still not quite normal, to being the way things are done."[91] The unitary executive theory as the basis for a strong presidency in foreign affairs (and in domestic policy) clearly was well in place before 9/11.[92] Whether any defensible version of the theory justified the actions of the George W. Bush administration in the War on Terror is a problem of an entirely different magnitude and beyond the scope of this book. Addressing it at the deepest level would entail asking whether the unitary executive, or any theory, can successfully constitutionalize the realm of necessity, emergency, war, and self-preservation.[93]

The Pro-presidential Critique of Congress

Many of the new conservative supporters of a strong presidency advanced two related themes that were incompatible with the older traditionalist view: frequent disparagement of Congress as an institution, combined with calls for presidents to outflank it politically with rhetorical appeals to the public. Both moves were apparent in several of the sources analyzed above. For example, documents from the Reagan and first Bush administrations described Congress as fragmented, inconstant, and meddling, with a crabbed political perspective that made it beholden to special interests and petty constituent services. An important 1986 policy memorandum to Attorney General Edwin Meese about how to handle separation-of-powers conflicts described many members of Congress as having "tunnel vision." Structural and procedural reforms since the 1970s had diffused and confused Congress's lines of authority, while individual members were often merely "ombudsmen for parochial spending interests."[94] The image was of an unruly and self-serving crowd that could and should be put in line by a strong president.

The Iran-Contra Minority Report bluntly advanced similar views. Serious problems in foreign policy (and elsewhere) often resulted from Congress's "ever-changing policies" and its propensity for both blame avoidance and crude last-minute intervention. Often the result was "intentionally ambiguous laws or amendments that postpone the day of decision." The executive branch was then left to make sense of vague and mutually conflicting imperatives. Another all too common form of irresponsibility was eleventh-hour spending resolutions to ensure the funding of basic government operations, a form of "legislative hostage taking."[95]

A negative view of Congress was long held by Dick Cheney, a veteran of the Ford administration, a former representative from Wyoming, and a major force behind the Minority Report. In his eyes Congress had become an overly aggressive, often dysfunctional institution that frequently endangered US national interests by interfering with executive powers.[96] It was rightly geared toward deliberation and compromise, he observed, but when it "steps beyond its capacities, it takes traits that can be helpful to collective deliberation and turns them into a harmful blend of vacillation, credit claiming, blame avoidance, and indecision."[97] As such it was "ill equipped" to address many issues of foreign policy.[98] Similar characterizations abounded in conservative writing of the late 1980s and 1990s.[99] Perhaps the most pointed and confrontational work was a collection of essays entitled *The Imperial Congress* (1988). The general view of the contributors was that "a Constitution-restoring presidency will require taking on the Congress."[100] In a different but related vein, a major academic defense of the unitary executive deployed a public choice idea to describe Congress as facing an insuperable "collective action" problem when confronting the growth and expense of modern interventionist government. Individual members seeking reelection could not decline to bring federal largesse home to their constituents, and the institution as a whole had no way of halting this dynamic. The result was "an unmitigated redistributive disaster . . . that as a practical matter can only be ameliorated by strengthening presidential power."[101]

Now that prominent conservatives were portraying Congress as a problem, a possible solution was presidential rhetorical leadership of public opinion. An important forecast of this shift was written by Jeffrey Hart for *National Review* in late 1974. Explicitly distancing himself from Willmoore Kendall and James Burnham, Hart argued that there was no longer a national majority in favor of a liberal presidency. Moreover, the pervasive mass media pulled public attention in whatever direction it chose. Only the president had "the capacity to contest the mass media where the focusing of opinion is concerned." For future centrist or conservative presidents the "key struggle" would be with the media. Such pressure also could be brought to bear on the entrenched bureaucracies of the administrative state "through the action of a powerful President who is willing virtually to go to war within his own executive branch in order to carry out his mandate." Hart concluded with an assessment of the broad historical context that proved prophetic in light of the developments traced above: "Conservative distrust of the strong Executive is a legacy of the 'oppositional' phase of American conservatism, a legacy of the New Deal hegemony."[102] It is notable that a few months later William F. Buckley Jr. sounded a note of caution about "conservative theorists who reason that only a strong Executive can summon the public power to contest an irresponsible Congress backed by the huge bureaucracy it feeds." At this point he continued to prefer that Congress take responsibility for curbing its own excesses rather than relying on the "re-establishment of a dominant Executive."[103]

Nevertheless, the eloquence and popularity of Ronald Reagan encouraged support among many conservatives for the soon to be named "rhetorical presidency."[104] To give only one example from the above-cited 1986 administration strategy memorandum to Attorney General Meese, the president was encouraged to use the "bully pulpit" in response to separation-of-powers conflicts with Congress. If direct communication with members did not work, "public statements" should be considered on the theory that " 'if you can't make them see the light, make them feel the heat.' "[105] The Minority Report of the Joint Iran-Contra Committee agreed. It faulted Reagan for failing to take up the task of "democratic persuasion" in defense of his position on the issues, despite his reputation as a " 'communicator.' "[106] "Persuasion is at the heart of a vigorous, successful presidency," and only "persistent leadership" could produce a "lasting change in the public's understanding and opinions."[107]

Advocacy of the rhetorical strategy was a major theme of the essays collected in *The Imperial Congress* (1988). Following the template of Franklin Roosevelt, a president committed to the conservative program should use his unique position as "party leader, national figure, and occupant of the 'bully pulpit' " to oppose the modern progressive liberalism advanced in Congress. No one else was so positioned.[108]

Terry Eastland's *Energy in the Executive* made a more detailed and careful case for presidential rhetoric (though he regarded the phrase "rhetorical presidency" as a pejorative). He acknowledged that the founders feared demagogic presidents, but argued that in modern times the founders' overriding goal of deliberative government required the president to shape and lead public debate. Presidential rhetoric should be "used to promote reason and deliberation about public policy" and aim at "arguing, not merely asserting, or sound biting," the president's positions.[109] Eastland pointedly distinguished this view from the progressive liberal heroic model of the president as the avatar and leader of inevitable historical "progress" toward continually more government intervention and regulation. Such visionary but vapid rhetoric undermined rather than promoted the informed debate crucial to deliberative self-government.[110] Nevertheless, the nineteenth-century days of the president as the usually silent chief magistrate were gone. Eastland urged conservatives that the modern rhetorical presidency could and must be reconciled to the central tenets of American constitutionalism.

Traditionalists in the Era of the Unitary Executive: Marginalized but Enduring

The new embrace of presidential power sidelined the established traditionalist view. The change happened as the Republican Party resumed the control of the presidency it had enjoyed since 1968 (with only the interlude of the Carter administration). Meanwhile, the Democratic Party had usually retained majorities in Congress despite the erosion of its coalition. Liberals also became more suspicious, if only episodically, of the "imperial" presidency they had previously encouraged. Scholars have pondered this shift. Often it was said to confirm the inevitably partisan nature of constitutional law and institutional loyalty. Alternatively, it might be ventured that if conservatives too had joined liberals as "presidentialists," the urgent task was restoration of a more balanced constitutionalism and therewith a reassertion of congressional authority.[111] These questions endured, though clearly the new conservative endorsement of the unitary executive ascended because it was both "plausible" and "timely."[112] That is to say, the unitary executive had historical and theoretical roots in American constitutionalism that could not be dismissed out of hand, and they were asserted and cohered just as the constellation of political forces conspired to provide a fertile context. Traditionalist opponents of this development, not to mention liberal constitutionalists with second thoughts, were compelled to respond with constitutional arguments of their own.

While traditionalist assessments of the presidency after the rise of the unitary executive and before 9/11 were fewer than previously, they voiced the same basic perspective.[113] At the level of social theory, the expanded presidency appeared as a symptom of the nation's continued devolution from a constitutional regime into a centralized, bureaucratized, and increasingly militarist "empire." Robert A. Nisbet expounded this view in his 1988 Jefferson Lecture (sponsored by the National Endowment for the Humanities). He observed acidly that the presidency was increasingly taking on the aspects of "royalism" in both policy and image.[114] Often this trend traveled under the banner of "national security, that ancient refuge of despotic monarchs." Like the ancient notion of *"raison d'état,*" which had "conceal[ed] crime, heresy, or treason, or all three in a given kingly court," national security had become a "wonderful umbrella for extensions of the presidential-royal power." Nisbet skewered the Iran-Contra affair as "perhaps the ultimate thus far in *raison d'état* in the name of the higher patriotism and morality that is above the law."[115]

Claes G. Ryn, a well-known traditionalist at Catholic University, offered a correlative assessment amid the initial surge of post–Cold War triumphalism. He warned that a "new Jacobinism" was discernible in the contemporary push to make democracy "a world-wide moral crusade." It was all the more odd that this view was advocated by "people called 'conservatives.'"[116] Their efforts echoed the "missionary zeal" of the original Jacobins of the French Revolution in the desire "to replace historically evolved societies with an egalitarian order."[117] Like the humanitarian, Rousseauean democracy it echoed, the new Jacobinism was a morally universalistic creed that exuded confidence in its own conception of virtue and justice. As a "democratist ideology," it advanced the rule of "plebiscitary or majoritarian democracy" over the restraining forms and institutions of the United States' established constitutionalism.[118] This posture led Ryn to predict that "one likely avenue for the attempted expansion of virtuous power is a vigorous presidency."[119] The future portended more "international adventurism" based on the notion that America was "the instrument of universal right."[120]

The new direction was unwelcome among the few traditionalist academics who specialized in the presidency. One observed that in the Reagan era "many conservatives began to spout arguments about executive prerogatives and power that were reminiscent of F.D.R.'s New Dealers."[121] This turnabout was unprincipled "constitutional instrumentalism." Its focus on short-term policy victories threated the authentic constitutionalism of balance among the branches of government.[122]

It was only after these trends culminated in the post-9/11 War on Terror that George Carey, a leading traditionalist, directly attacked the conservative endorsement of presidential power, though his core position remained utterly consistent both before and after that event. The reason was that the founders had intended Congress to be the most powerful branch. The modern aggrandizing presidency was obviously a mistaken deviation, traceable ultimately to the Wilsonian notion that the president should lead a party that spoke for "the people" to advance "progress."[123] Accordingly, Carey's earlier, seminal book on *The Federalist* had contained no sustained treatment of executive power (other than the presidential veto). In a later brief but pointed observation, Carey adduced Willmoore Kendall as having gleaned from the founding the proper position for conservatives: they should "defend the Congress against the intrusions of the executive and his unilateral assumptions of power." This principle should not bend with the political winds when Republicans controlled the presidency.[124] "Disillusioned and disgruntled traditionalists" like Carey rejected the "aggressive foreign policy" of the George W. Bush administration (he termed it "Wilsonianism on steroids") and the conception of executive power used to pursue it. The Republican Party had too quickly bent to this view.[125]

Traditionalists understandably focused on the growth of executive power in foreign affairs, but concern about the plebiscitary, "rhetorical" presidency was not entirely absent. Gary L. Gregg traced appeals to mass public opinion in the Progressive era, through the New Deal, then in the midcentury liberal "heroic" view of the presidency, and finally to the increasing attraction they had for conservatives.[126] The modern approach had consistently undermined the representative and deliberative politics that traditionalists saw as properly embodied in Congress. The houses of the legislature were "reduced at best to the handmaids of the president and at worst to outright obstacles in the way of progress and the march of the people's will through their government. The complex representation of the deliberative republic is replaced by the unitary representation of presidential leadership."[127] The political message was that "Congress can add nothing with extra time to think, discuss, and weigh alternatives" but must give way to the "presidential plebiscite."[128] The original intent had been that, within the dynamic of deliberation and consent, the "chief executive's voice is to be one among many" because "ours is not a system geared toward the efficient representation of a single national will."[129]

Such long-standing traditionalist views, though diminishing among scholars, also informed the statements of established figures who wrote in high-profile publications. *Policy Review*, then published by the Heritage Foundation, featured an article by Mickey Edwards, a Republican member of Congress from Oklahoma, a founding trustee at Heritage, and a former national chairman of the American Conservative Union. He attacked the "new monarchism" as an "abdication" of authentic conservative principles. Conservatism properly understood was not "the philosophy of kings and great concentrations of power." On the contrary, it was "diffusionist" in affirming the separation of powers against any form of centralization.[130] Edwards accepted that the founders intended a "strong, vigorous, energetic president," and he opposed the War Powers Resolution. He likewise conceded that the president had substantial latitude in the conduct of foreign affairs and that the borders of this power with Congress were ambiguous.[131] But he could not accept "today's conservatives [who] have begun to assign preeminence to the executive in matters of foreign policy."[132] No such dominance or "singular authority" was originally intended.[133] Rather, the president "does not have the final word on spending decisions nor does he have the authority to decide on his own to go to war."[134] Edwards urged conservatives to cleave to their old principles and abandon the newfound "royalist impulse," as well as to avoid undermining constitutionalism based on the delusion that they would hold the presidency forever.[135]

William F. Buckley Jr. likewise warned that presidential power should be reassessed in the 1990s. Recent Republican dominance of the presidency had produced in many conservatives "a dangerous attachment to executive supremacy." His advocacy of a more circumspect and "realistic" foreign policy for the post–Cold War world generated a somewhat droll suggestion to conservatives of the "hypothetical possibility that there might someday be a military adventure which we do not endorse." Conservative thought had become "spastically pro-executive" and should instead revisit James Burnham "to remind ourselves that Providential absenteeism might at some point in the future result in the election of a Democratic President who will enter office citing paeans by conservatives to executive supremacy."[136]

Samuel Francis also went to the fundamentals of conservatism and constitutionalism. He lauded Edwards's effort and also recurred to Burnham. Francis argued that the presidency was advancing the managerial-bureaucratic revolution on a global level, increasingly through supranational institutions (such as the UN) that undermined American sovereignty. Consequently, "congressional conservatives today [should] resist the monopolization of foreign policy by the executive." Congress had long been the traditional break on such grandiose executive schemes.[137] He concluded that conservatives in office were now moving in precisely the wrong constitutional direction—one that ultimately enhanced the managerial revolution he was so fixated on. The antistatism promised by Reaganism was being forsaken amid the "the beginnings of a theoretical justification on ostensibly conservative grounds of the mega-state and of the centralized power of the Presidency at its core. In recapitulating the liberal defense of the 'Imperial Presidency,' conservatives may soon find themselves metamorphosing into something they never wanted to be."[138] Francis's position was all the more urgent because, at the beginning of the Reagan era, he had argued that a presidency seized by the rising conservative movement might finally displace the managerial elite in favor of the old Right's constituency of "middle American radicals."[139] But by the late 1980s that hope was clearly disappointed. Instead,

Republicans had used weak constitutional arguments to embrace presidential power and thereby abandon the traditionalist position. This "conversion" was evidence that, far from upsetting the managerial regime, mainstream conservatism had been assimilated to it.[140] Consequently, Francis became increasingly disgusted with the conservative half measures and accommodations of the Reagan era, as exemplified by the presidency: "The Old Right, whether libertarian or traditionalist, was the real enemy of the imperial presidency from its origins, and it is a tribute to the shallowness of the post-Reagan conservatives that no sooner was their own candidate the ostensible captain of the presidential flagship, and they and their buddies were let in on a share of the swag, than they promptly forgot every word" that the older conservatives (many analyzed above) "had ever written or said in resistance to the new monarchy."[141]

Although the presidency had failed for the moment to advance Francis's hoped-for traditionalist-cum–middle American revolution, he and others associated with the traditionalist-paleoconservative magazine *Chronicles* saw the end of the Cold War as an opportunity for a more modest foreign policy—and a concomitantly reduced presidency. They sought to revive the concept of "America First" that had undergirded the traditionalist old Right's noninterventionism prior to World War II. Patrick Buchanan became the standard bearer for this view during his presidential campaigns of the 1990s.[142] The nation's plunge into the Gulf War both invigorated and sidelined this effort. Francis characteristically urged the America First approach as a rebuke to the managerial revolution's supposed global ambitions. Along with immigration and trade restrictions and several other "nationalist" polices, he advocated dismantling the Cold War national security state and embracing "a clear recognition of congressional supremacy in foreign affairs," along the lines of the Bricker Amendment, to prohibit US troops from entering combat without congressional approval.[143] Thomas Fleming, editor of *Chronicles*, supported this view while also sounding the traditionalist emphasis on locally rooted culture. "We cannot be free or prosperous at home, so long as our Presidents continue to gratify their vanity with international power games."[144] Bill Kauffman, a traditionalist with a libertarian bent (or perhaps vice versa), also analyzed the America First theme across the history of the nation's culture and politics. He concluded that this recrudescence in the 1990s rejected the assertion of Washington, DC, Republicans or conservatives that the "executive possess[ed] virtually unlimited powers in the conduct of foreign affairs" and could use them "blithely [to] invade sovereign nations without a declaration of war from the Congress." Reviving "some form [of] the Bricker Amendment" to reassert congressional control over troop deployments abroad was a necessity that nonetheless suggested "just how dead a letter our Constitution is."[145]

Conclusion

The traditionalist view of the presidency stood as conservative orthodoxy for the first few decades after the New Deal. It was marginalized by the long-term growth of presidential power associated with the Cold War and by Republican officials and conservative law professors who supported it with the theory of the unitary executive. The old traditionalist arguments never wholly disappeared, but neither could they disrupt the larger trend of expanding presidential power in foreign policy and war making. Whether the United States was best served by presidentially led military interventions abroad, or by a single officeholder claiming to embody the nation's true interests, is a question that traditionalists raised continuously and that still persists. The following chapter considers how the other major schools of American conservatism related to the modern presidency.

CHAPTER SEVEN

Straussians, Neoconservatives, Libertarians, and the Modern Presidency

Leo Strauss did not write directly about the American presidency, but his students took up themes in his oeuvre to do so. They argued that a strong presidency was needed to defend the nation and, domestically, for effective government administration. Yet they also cautioned that executive power was inevitably in some tension with constitutionalism. It was required in the face of necessity and emergency but might dispense with the rule of law. Furthermore, modern presidential rhetoric potentially could sway mass public opinion to disregard constitutional authority or limits. Straussians' generally pro-executive posture eventually contributed to a vituperative controversy about their influence on the post-9/11 conduct of the War on Terror, which is considered later in this chapter but need not cloud our initial examination. We shall see that the Straussian position was very much in place well before 2001. Likewise, while some Straussians in the 1990s supported the burgeoning neoconservative call for a more interventionist post–Cold War foreign policy, this discourse simply assumed the decades-old unilateral war power of the modern presidency. That power was amply demonstrated in the 1990s under President Bill Clinton while neoconservative thinking was developing. Hence neither Straussians nor neoconservatives had any specific burden of justification for the established practice of presidential war making, however one may ultimately judge its constitutionality. Nor, despite some overlap, were Straussians and neoconservatives convertible categories, as sometimes portrayed in the media, and indeed they sometimes disagreed with each other. This chapter concludes with a brief explication of the libertarian assessment of the foreign policy presidency, which consistently did see it as both imperial and frequently unconstitutional.

Themes from Strauss

Strauss's writing contained several themes relevant to executive power that others later elaborated.[1] (Here no attempt is made fully to place these themes in Strauss's complicated effort to resurrect the disagreement about natural right that divided ancient and modern political thought.) A core problem was that the modern redefinition of politics as the rational pursuit of self-interest, security, and acquisitiveness could not wholly channel or control *thumos*, as the Greeks named the spiritedness that was natural to human beings. This insistent self-assertion could be manifested as courage and nobility, or vainglory and destruction. *Thumos* often appeared politically as ambition for power and the desire for fame based on heroism and great deeds. Strauss taught that no regime could completely subdue or blithely ignore it.[2] A related concern was how statesmen could through public speech direct and restrain politics in light of a regime's principles and the demands of circumstance.

Strauss also addressed the inevitable gap between a regime's established principles and procedures and what might be necessary for its survival. This issue came to the fore especially in the realm of foreign relations and war. In circumstances of extreme danger, self-preservation could override the rules of justice that abided in normal times. Moreover, what was necessary for the preservation of a regime could never be wholly foreseen—in fact, necessity might require the exercise of discretion or force against the established rules of justice.[3] This logic applied equally to the practice of espionage and to the control of subversives within the homeland. Accordingly, "in extreme situations the normally valid rules of natural right are justly changed, or changed in accordance with natural right; the exceptions are as just as the rules."[4] Nor was it possible to define with precision the difference between the extreme and the normal situation in a way that could account for all actions of people who were bent on evil. Here Strauss drew a pointed contrast. In contradistinction to Machiavelli's fixation on the liberating necessity of the extreme situation, the properly Aristotelian statesman "takes his bearings by the normal situation and by what is normally right, and he reluctantly deviates from what is normally right only in order to save the cause of justice and humanity itself."[5] Actions in extreme conditions could be judged after the fact, but they could not be proscribed beforehand, precisely because they emerged in particular circumstances.

Executive Power: Necessary but Dangerous

Strauss's students initially addressed executive power in relation to self-preservation, necessity, and war by studying John Locke, the philosopher who so influenced the American founders.[6] The basic idea was that, however much Locke veiled it, the state of nature was a state of war that could not be escaped once and for all. Recourse to some form of executive power was constantly necessary to maintain or reestablish security. Citizens warred against one another in violating the laws meant to protect life, liberty, and property; a prince or a legislature warred against citizens if the social contract was violated and their rights thereby endangered; war was the more or less constant state of affairs in the anarchic realm of foreign relations. While Locke held that the legislative power was primary in domestic affairs because it made laws carried out by the executive, and although there was a distinct "federative" power that dealt with war and foreign relations, in practice the security of individual rights and of nations required a single executive to use force and discretion.[7]

Each nation had to execute the law of nature—self-preservation—for itself. Consequently, the federative power exercised by the executive proceeded according to no set rules, as compared to the usually straightforward execution of everyday domestic laws. Often the executive's dealings with foreigners depended on what they themselves were doing and so had to be "left to the prudence and wisdom of those whose hands it is in, to be managed for the public good."[8] As Richard H. Cox insightfully concluded, Locke here reduced the ancient political virtue of prudence to the service of peace as "security" amid a world of "anarchy and disorder."[9] In foreign affairs especially, prudence became no more than "proper calculation of the means which will satisfy the natural desire for security, independence, and the comforts of life."[10]

Executive power had a similarly momentous role in domestic affairs. Even when the legislature was not in session, standing laws must be enforced, and the executive was the "power always in being" that did so.[11] Likewise, sometimes it would be necessary to act for the public good when the legislature was not in session or had left no law to guide action.[12] Locke named this type of power the "prerogative," defining it as the "power to act according to discretion, for the public good, without the prescription of law, and sometimes even against it."[13] In some ways it was akin to the juridical concept of equity, insofar as prerogative could mitigate the inflexibility of the law or pardon worthy offenders.

At a more basic level, prerogative accounted for the reality that "it is impossible to foresee, and so by laws to provide for, all accidents and necessities, that may concern the public."[14] As Locke goes on discussing it, the prerogative becomes quite broad—enough to justify "God-like princes" whose actions the people accept (or not) as undertaken for the public good.[15]

As in so many other areas, Herbert J. Storing was the first of Strauss's students to analyze the presidency based on this understanding of executive power.[16] His direction was set by the time of his sudden death in September 1977, having just assumed a professorial chair at the University of Virginia and the directorship of a center devoted to the presidency. One example was Storing's brief but rich introduction to Charles Thach's *The Creation of the American Presidency* (originally published in 1923). There Storing highlighted the founders' awareness of the tension between the monarchical derivation and tendency of a single executive, on one hand, and the principles of limited constitutional government on the other, as well as Alexander Hamilton's attention to this problem in *The Federalist*. The president enforced through energetic administration the will of Congress, the republican legislature. Yet the president also had the power to check, resist, and lead Congress and the people, as well as the duty as commander in chief to defend the nation. In an influential dictum, Storing said that the first idea implied "executive subordination to the legislature" while the second implied "an equality (if not, indeed, a superiority) of the executive in the constitutional scheme. The beginning of wisdom about the American Presidency is to see that it contains both principles and to reflect on their complex and subtle relation."[17] Furthermore, "energy" in the Hamiltonian sense of *Federalist* 70 put the presidency and its tensions at the center of the constitutional system. By directing and protecting it, he had a chance at greatness and fame. The independence of the office meant that the president "was to be no subservient administrator, no timeserver, no mere doer of the will of Congress or the people." The office had far greater responsibilities and possibilities. Understood in this way, it was "the crucial feature of the Constitution" because it had the most difficult duty in a popular government: "to reconcile the wants of the people and the needs of the Republic."[18]

As in Locke, the president's duty was particularly acute in the area of foreign relations and war. Disputing Arthur Schlesinger Jr.'s understanding of the "imperial presidency" as exercising a prerogative power *outside* the Constitution, Storing reevaluated the Lockean idea in its American context. He found "massively persuasive" Hamilton's logic in *Federalist* 23 and 25, which echoed Locke: there must be an unlimited power of self-defense and authority in the government to command whatever resources were required, because no nation could foresee what might be necessary to defeat an enemy.[19] But to meet inevitable and potentially boundless necessity by treating prerogative as outside the Constitution was too dangerously to set it against the Constitution. Over time this approach would make the Constitution irrelevant, undermining the respect and reverence needed for it to endure. The nation would be forced to ask itself: "Do we want to save our Constitution by admitting that we must at times resort to nonconstitutional, plebiscitary dictatorship?"[20] Storing said the founders had consciously rejected this path.

Instead, he argued, they held that "the Constitution must be broad enough to provide a place for the impulse of self-preservation."[21] It "must lie with the grain of nature; it must 'constitutionalize' prerogative, so far as any law can do that," and therefore provide "room for whatever powers would be necessary."[22] Accordingly, the vesting clause of Article II, the Take Care Clause, the commander in chief power, and the presidential oath together provided a "noble spaciousness" suitable to most any exigency. The Constitution was meant to be "commodious and elastic enough to meet the demands of necessity and yet retain its character as law."[23]

The case of Abraham Lincoln in the Civil War was paradigmatic: in an emergency the president exercised powers of dubious constitutionality but subsequently justified them in constitutional terms to Congress and the people, who accepted. The existential threat of war similarly but temporarily sidelined the rule of law posture of the judiciary, but, as in *Ex parte Milligan* (1866), the Court could "restore or tighten up the rule of law when the pressure of necessity is off."[24] In such dangerous situations there were no guarantees, and the judgment of statesmen and engaged citizens was needed. Moreover, tyranny was conceivable in an extreme situation where the laws were somewhat in abeyance and the fate of the regime was determined by one person.[25] But over time, if not at any one particular moment, the system of checks and balances could and did reestablish itself. A "dynamic balance" functioned "to make the rule of law work: 'work' here means do the things that have to be done, while yet keeping government within the limits of law."[26] As in the Lockean analysis, citizens would have to judge over time whether the system was out of balance in a way that was fundamentally unconstitutional.

The Straussian understanding of a strong presidency was developed most influentially in Harvey C. Mansfield Jr.'s *The Taming of the Prince* (1989). This book considered the basis and purpose of the presidency by tracing the idea of executive power in Western political thought. Beginning with Aristotle's intimations of the natural kingship of virtue, it worked up to the central figure of Machiavelli, and then through the development of liberalism in Hobbes, Locke, and Montesquieu. This rich and difficult work has become a landmark in the field, and though a full explication is not appropriate here, we must appreciate how some of its major points advanced the general Straussian view. Mansfield also undertook the characteristically Straussian work of instructing and improving liberal constitutionalism by, in this instance, pointing out how its theoretical base had weaknesses that required the executive as their remedy.

Mansfield elaborated with philosophical insight and detail many of the themes treated in the foregoing discussion of Locke. For example, executive power was what enabled the United States to overcome republicanism's history of weakness and failure by calling on and integrating aspects of monarchy.[27] The energetic executive could take initiative, focus political attention, and consistently direct the efforts of society to "extensive and arduous enterprises," such as the New Deal or the Reagan Revolution.[28] Another key element of executive strength, as discussed earlier, was the ability to use force for preservation of the nation in cases of emergency that were not contemplated by the law or even violated it. Following Machiavelli, Mansfield argued that these aspects of the modern executive answered the primary human need for security.[29]

Further drawing on Machiavelli, Mansfield showed that since no body of law was perfectly reasonable or self-sufficient, force and discretion were entailed in all governance, not merely in cases of national self-preservation. Law could not make all the distinctions and allowances needed for exact justice in every case. Nor could inevitably general (and therefore unjust) legal rules induce obedience from recalcitrant, self-interested individuals.[30] Discretion and force were required. But the harsh Machiavellian prince who induced compliance through such vile means as sensational executions had gradually been "domesticated" or "tamed" as early modern liberal constitutionalism evolved toward the American founding. Executive power was thus "regularized and legitimated" in large measure by obscuring the violence and even terror that could never be wholly eliminated from government in general and self-preservation in particular.[31] In underscoring the relation of executive power to unavoidable necessity, Mansfield was defending American constitutionalism by reminding liberalism that its own principles of individual rights, consent, and the rule of law were insufficient for its own survival.[32]

It was through the executive that the Constitution recognized necessity: those aspects of political life that could not be chosen but that would inevitably appear. Unchosen necessities would always emerge because of unruly human nature and the possibility of war. "Those necessities limiting our choice, which we would like to wish away, are brought into the Constitution so that the people, through their government, can choose how to deal with them after having anticipated the necessity of doing so." This was a primary purpose of the executive power in the office of president. "In its 'energy' or quickness, the executive deals more than any other branch with the accidents and force that may thwart or disturb republican choice. By dealing with such necessities, the executive actually represents them in the Constitution." The creation of a strong executive and the election of a president to exercise this power "reflect[ed] a realistic recognition by the people" that "emergencies will arise that may confound their choices."[33]

By another measure, the presidency was also the founders' attempt to contain for the benefit of the Constitution the thumotic political ambition that naturally arose in any regime. The power and fame made available in the office would attract the " 'noblest minds' " who wanted the glory and responsibility of undertaking " 'extensive and arduous enterprises for the public benefit.' " Unlimited reelection to the presidency allowed the satisfaction of such ambition and the esteem of success to foster the steady administration of government over the long term. Equally important, argued Mansfield, was that the kind of person who aspired to greatness was the kind who was needed when crisis or necessity presented challenges that only the executive could meet. In this sense, not just stability and survival but also greatness could come to depend on "these extraordinary men who will make or break the republic." The presidency was the Constitution's provision for the possibility that it may need such men to survive by calling on "their preeminent virtue and abilities to become great. Here the constitutionalizing of necessity is elevated to the appreciation of greatness."[34]

But what if the urgent need for an extraordinary man fell on one whose aspiration for greatness was sated by tyranny rather than by defense of the republic? As the previous quotation suggests, this possibility became a question of virtue. Therefore, Mansfield offered another Straussian lesson to improve liberalism: it could not dispense with virtue, no matter how hard it tried. Moreover, there was no guarantee that virtue would be exercised when it was most needed. Virtue was thus "indispensable and undependable," its indeterminacy confirming that neither politics nor liberalism could be fully comprehended or adequately defended by modern social science methods that took liberalism for granted.[35] The problem of virtue could not be eluded, because "no law or system can actually ensure the behavior it summons without depending on an executive who is at least in part outside the law and not explained by the system."[36]

The possibility that virtue might not emerge from the constitutional structure designed to elicit it from a president was a standing reminder to Americans that self-government was both delicate and demanding. The institutions created by the Constitution were no mere mechanisms: to work, they needed virtuous statesmen and citizens. Thus the Constitution attempted to realize a people's capacity for self-government by asking human beings to take responsibility for themselves, that is, to act virtuously in ruling both themselves and others.[37]

The executive's ambiguous relation to constitutional self-government was further illustrated by Mansfield's treatment of the famous Pacificus-Helvidius debate that followed President George Washington's Neutrality Proclamation in 1793. Writing under these respective pseudonyms, Hamilton and Madison disputed whether the president had the constitutional authority unilaterally to abrogate a treaty with France and declare, without congressional approval, that the United States was neutral in France's war with Britain. Hamilton defended a broad interpretation of "the executive power" as conveying inherent authority beyond the text of the Constitution to act on behalf of the nation. The executive, he said, was the mode of interaction between the United States and other sovereign nations. The president was responsible for protecting and preserving the nation in its relation with others in ways that could not always be spelled out ahead of time and need not be preapproved by Congress. For his part, Madison condemned this view as a dangerous and anti-republican extrusion of executive power. Questions of war and peace were the constitutional province of the legislature, and the president was there to execute the legislative decision.

The Pacificus-Helvidius exchange expressed paradigmatically the debate that always recurred when an extreme and unforeseen situation required the constitutional republic to use the necessary but dangerous executive power. Both positions could deploy resources from the constitutional tradition and appeal to the logic of whatever circumstance the nation might confront. No outcome was foreordained because each would depend on the political situation and personal characteristics—virtue or its lack—in the actors involved. The presidency thus tamed the prince to the extent that virtue could rule: "When executive power is made constitutional and republican, it gives Machiavellian necessity its due by maintaining some of the maneuverability and flexibility of the prince. But it does so, at its best, without loss of responsibility for acting with virtue."[38]

Mansfield's book stood as the most thorough and influential grounding of the Straussian advocacy of a strong presidency. In the 1980s others advanced the same general argument with remarkable consistency, using much the same sources as Mansfield's book and the articles that preceded it. It would be redundant to redisplay such evidence and analysis, though sometimes other authors expressed the general argument with refreshing candor. For example, Morton J. Frisch wrote that the executive discretion Locke identified as outside the law "must be given leeway if the President is to fulfill his constitutionally specified duties, but this discretion must somehow operate within the framework of the law." Yet to ensure his effectiveness in foreign affairs, "he was understood to have implied nonenumerated powers over and above the expressly enumerated powers in the executive article."[39] Straussians who took care to acknowledge the legitimate role of Congress in foreign affairs nevertheless made the same general argument for a strong presidency capable of responding to emergency and making war.[40] Likewise, Richard H. Cox expressed particularly well the unavoidable danger that executive power presented to constitutional government. There was a type of human ambition that "will have fame at any cost, even that of destroying a free political order. Hamilton's seeming confidence [in *Federalist* 72] in joining interest to duty in the soul of those thirsting for fame, and coming, at last, to the exercise of 'the executive power,' particularly in conditions of alleged or real exigency, should give adherents of constitutional governments pause."[41]

We have seen that Straussians recognized this danger but still thought that a strong presidency was needed. This view is borne out by commentary on several constitutional controversies involving the presidency from last few decades of the twentieth century. The sampling that follows illustrates their usual stance, without of course claiming that all Straussians agreed with every position described.

One prime example was the War Powers Resolution. It was said to err in both political logic and constitutional authority, despite being an understandable attempt by Congress to reassert itself after Vietnam. The reality was that no legislature could ever provide for all circumstances wherein necessity might require the president to act alone or quickly, and perhaps without the explicit sanction of law.[42] Another evaluation stated more bluntly that the War Powers Resolution was "gloriously unconstitutional" insofar as it rested on the "assumption that Congress, as opposed to the Constitution itself, is the fount of presidential power."[43]

Another topic was executive privilege, whereby a long line of presidents had claimed authority to withhold some kinds of information from Congress. Gary J. Schmitt, who later served as executive director of the Foreign Intelligence Advisory Board under President Reagan, argued that it was an inherent part of the executive power. Enforcement of the law and effective administration would suffer amid public deliberation or transparent decision making. Nor could the president properly conduct his constitutional duties if the information and advice he received from subordinates was constantly open to public inspection. Executive privilege was thus an "essential component" of the founders' intent "to create an independent and energetic executive branch." Still, there was no avoiding the inherent and necessary tension between executive privilege and the principle of consent that was central to democratic government. Secrecy was sometimes required, but democratic public opinion ultimately would set an outer limit to how much officeholders were allowed.[44]

Executive secrecy in espionage and covert operations found support from Schmitt and Abram Shulsky, who worked in the Department of Defense under Reagan and later in the administration of George W. Bush. They argued that reforms after Vietnam and Watergate had produced a congressional oversight regime and, with it, public scrutiny that endangered national security by interfering with core executive functions—a trend that threatened to intensify after the Iran-Contra affair. Covert operations were hamstrung because Congress had "infused its own institutional tendencies to compromise and deliberate into a mechanism whose design should be to maximize secrecy, decision, and dispatch."[45] But neither public opinion nor Congress could at any given time avert or control a necessity or emergency that fell into the lap of the executive.[46]

A call for stronger presidential direction of the national security apparatus in the aftermath of the Iran-Contra affair came from Carnes Lord, who served on the staff of the National Security Council (NSC) in the first Reagan administration.[47] He argued that the overall process for making national security decisions was insufficiently responsive to the president because it was overly bureaucratized and thus too uncoordinated. The Iran-Contra affair was a case in point. The White House's resort to use of the NSC for a covert operation illustrated the dysfunction of a system not properly organized to respond to presidential direction. Lord recommended a series of technical organizational and policy changes that would recast the NSC and the role of national security adviser as more direct extensions of the president's constitutional authority and political will. The NSC should coordinate and lead the decision-making process among all federal security agencies, ensuring that the president's overall foreign policy was being followed. At the core of this vision was "a recovery of the Hamiltonian conception of the presidency as an institution uniquely capable of decision, activity, secrecy, and dispatch."[48]

Iran-Contra and the rise of terrorism in the Middle East also provided the context for Walter Berns's rendition of the established arguments for the president's broad executive power as having derived most proximately from Locke's prerogative. Of course there were some constitutional limitations on the president, but "in times of crisis or danger, these limitations prove to be few indeed."[49] The proper avenue for post hoc political judgment was the impeachment process. Berns concluded that while the constitutional power to respond to grave threats was fully available, the more pressing question was whether Americans any longer had a "sufficiently strong commitment" to "the cause of free government" to support the use of such power when it was needed.[50]

The Rhetorical Presidency: The Dangers of Mass Public Opinion

While Straussians defended energy in the executive for steady administration, national defense, and emergency action, they thought nevertheless that the presidency had become dangerously plebiscitary and anticonstitutional. One reason was twentieth-century alterations in the method of presidential selection. Closely related was the emergence of the "rhetorical presidency," a major new interpretation that Straussians took the lead in developing. It sought to explain how the prominence of direct presidential appeals to mass public opinion affected the office's constitutionally mandated powers and duties and the political system as a whole. Straussians were attuned to these issues because of their characteristic attention to both political rhetoric and the principles and health of the constitutional order.

One element of the context for this interpretation was the ongoing reevaluation of the presidency after Vietnam and Watergate; another was renewed proposals in 1977 to abolish the electoral college in favor of direct popular election of the president. Both Herbert Storing and Martin Diamond opposed the latter idea in testimony before Congress. They raised several points later elaborated by others who examined the questions of selection in relation to the rhetorical presidency. Storing described the proposal for direct popular election as a "simplistic" and overly majoritarian understanding of democracy. Good government was more than immediate responsiveness to whatever a majority might want at the moment, which might in fact "tend toward instability, ignorance, and indifference to minority rights."[51] American government was designed to inform, moderate, and check the majority will, not simply to reflect and satisfy it. The electoral college as it interacted with the two-party system had produced a method of choosing presidents that had long and successfully served this and other crucial ends. Its decentralized federal mechanism also moderated factional conflict and avoided the fragmentation and polarization of extreme political disagreement. An open, national direct election would make politics more volatile and ideologically fractious because it would become "less rooted in state and political organizations, less influenced by party professionals or quasi-professionals, and dominated by shifting personal alliances of nationally oriented personalities, ideologues, interest-group spokesmen, and media specialists."[52]

Diamond stressed that direct popular election would aggrandize the presidency by diminishing the moderating effects of competition between the two major parties. More direct reliance on public opinion also would further liberate the presidency from legal-constitutional restraints. The electoral process would come to be defined by the mass media, a candidate's personal organization outside the party, and the "freewheeling search for popular votes." The proposed change would substantially increase "the national and plebiscitary foundations of the presidency" just when "so much fear [has] been expressed about the 'imperial presidency.' "[53]

These concerns were incorporated into the theory of the rhetorical presidency as rendered especially by James W. Ceaser and Jeffrey K. Tulis, both of whom were influenced by Storing (Tulis had been a student and Ceaser briefly a colleague). This chapter focuses on the work of these two authors without undertaking a full exploration of the larger debate about the rhetorical presidency in the scholarly literature.

Ceaser argued that changes in the system of presidential selection had come to encourage plebiscitary appeals to mass opinion and even demagoguery, thereby overcoming the founders' careful attempt to avoid just this outcome.[54] The original system aimed to garner popular support for someone who already had a national reputation for merit, and without forcing him to directly court public opinion. The office would thus not attract figures opposed to republicanism, and once in office, the president might need the discretion to check or ignore public opinion. The emergence of political parties soon skewed this system, though in practice they acted as a filtering and moderating mechanism that achieved roughly what the founders intended. The decisive move toward the rhetorical presidency came with Woodrow Wilson and the Progressives. The president was reconceived as the visionary spokesman of historical progress who would rally mass opinion, his party, and Congress around his program, starting with candidate selection via direct primary elections. Nevertheless, Ceaser showed that parties retained substantial influence in the selection process, continuing to shape and cohere presidential politics until the late 1960s and 1970s. Then a series of changes further sidelined party professionals, organizations, and platforms in favor of open primaries and direct public appeals by individual candidates.

The outcome was "what can be termed a plebiscitary system" that elicited "a new method of generating support in presidential campaigns: 'popular leadership,' or the attempt by individual aspirants to carve out a personal mass constituency by their own programmatic and personality appeals and by the use of large personal campaign organizations of their own creation."[55] And, crucially, this dynamic continued when the president took office. The authority for governing rested on the president's ability to reflect, control, or lose the support of public opinion—rather than in the constitutional definition of the office. The Wilsonian presidency heightened expectations of what a single person could accomplish while being neither beholden to his party nor able to depend on it for gathering public support. In the twentieth century an office originally constituted against demagoguery had gotten much closer to it, in both the selection process and the kind of rhetoric presidents used.[56] Ceaser warned that, given these developments, "we should not be too surprised by the eventual recurrence of imperial tendencies in our highest office."[57]

Ceaser, Tulis, and two coauthors wrote a seminal article that further elucidated the "rise of the rhetorical presidency."[58] This work and Tulis's subsequent book, plus Ceaser's book previously discussed, oriented much of presidential studies for decades.[59] Each elaborated the points Ceaser had set out and adduced additional historical evidence for the basic transformation he had identified. Study of the rhetorical presidency advanced the Straussian goal of ministering to the health of the constitutional order as a modern regime in need of ancient political science. In this light, the primary danger was demagoguery in everyday politics, and both Ceaser and Tulis gave sustained attention to this idea.[60] The founders had "fear[ed] that mass oratory, whether crudely demagogic or highly inspirational, would undermine the rational and enlightened self-interest of the citizenry" on which the constitutional system and its stability depended.[61] To the extent that presidents and the nation had accepted the transformation of the office into the "'voice of the nation'" and its "'moral leader,'" politics centered on a "form of presidential speech that soars above the realm of calm and deliberate discussions of reasons of state or appeals to enlightened self-interest."[62]

Both Ceaser and Tulis made it clear that they were not advocating a weak presidency cut off from popular support as a source of political authority. Rather, they wanted a presidency whose modulated rhetoric was not constantly exhorting the public beyond normal restraints. Success was more likely if grand political rhetoric was reserved for moments when the nation needed to achieve large purposes or meet extreme challenges. As Tulis put it, in the founders' design "popular leadership was proscribed, but statesmanship was not."[63] Moreover, in this context rhetoric could not be "distinguished from demagoguery by a clear standard." In fact there was a kind of "rhetorical prerogative" that pushed beyond the confines of regular political processes and could be used to reorient the regime's priorities, upend the regime, or save it from ruin in trying times.[64] There had to be room for maneuver so that such rhetoric could be effectual, but the necessary discretion of the statesman was endangered if it was always beholden to public opinion as such.[65] Consequently, the rhetorical presidency, like Mansfield's conception of executive power, was dangerous but sometimes absolutely necessary. And the threat of the rhetorical prerogative in the hands of a true demagogue could never be forgotten.[66] The pressing problem was normalization of rhetoric that tended toward demagoguery. The "continual or routine use of the 'crisis tool' of popular leadership" was erasing any distinction between normal and crisis times.[67] It was becoming normal for presidential speech to manipulate the public mood with frequent appeals to grand ideals or invocations of emergency (or a policy of "war" on something or other). Thus, while tending to lift constitutional norms and restraints, the rhetorical presidency was actually making everyday government more difficult. It was burdening the office with a type of policy-making leadership it was not constituted to deliver.

Moreover, to attack the failure of presidential rhetoric to constantly realize policy change threatened to undermine the president's core responsibility for the conduct of foreign policy and the defense of the nation in emergencies.[68] The rhetorical presidency's demand for a persuasive policy leader in everyday domestic affairs had forgotten "the tougher side of the executive's role—the exercise of the executive power where the president acts within his own realm and where rhetoric may consist more of explaining actions taken rather than mobilizing support for future proposals."[69] Currently there was too much focus on the inability of presidential speech to do something it was not designed for, while as a result of Vietnam and Watergate, the president simultaneously battled Congress to maintain his constitutional authority to act in foreign affairs.[70] A major problem with the rhetorical presidency was to risk "turning the presidency into an institution that is all talk and no action."[71]

Straussians also considered how the now entrenched rhetorical presidency might be adapted and redirected to the benefit of a sounder constitutionalism. A reformed version could serve the ends of the regime by directing public attention to its principles and especially by fostering deliberation in Congress. The nation needed rhetoric that "connects this generation with the moorings of our political system," not a president who sought plebiscitary authority to transcend them. "Presidents must recapture the capacity to address the nation's enlightened self-interest no less than its sense of idealism and the related capacity to approach Congress directly rather than through the people."[72] Presidents should eschew not only "utopian visionary speech that overpromises" but also policy prescriptions that "preempt and preclude legislative deliberation."[73]

Tulis developed this theme most thoroughly, outlining how presidents could advance a "rhetoric that is popular and constitutional" through speech that "makes sense of the polity, its constitutive principles, and its political tendencies."[74] Presidents should lay out more realistic but general goals and invite Congress to deliberate about how to achieve them. Moreover, the president should be willing to let Congress take the policy-making lead, explaining to the public that the legislature is better suited for deliberation, while the energetic executive primarily served other ends. The aim was "to encourage more deliberation as a corrective to excessive energy."[75] The president could further encourage better deliberation with a "conditional veto" that promised approval of legislation if it met conditions he laid out. The State of the Union address could be repurposed to hold Congress responsible for its action or inaction. Finally, presidents could elevate public discourse by raising questions about the constitutional basis or justification for certain lines of policy being considered in Congress. All of these changes might reinvigorate an older and healthier form of politics that reasoned more clearly, prompted by "the president [who] interprets the Constitution as a window on American identity and uses that interpretation to change (and improve) the terms of public debate."[76]

Analysis of the rhetorical presidency and the understanding of the nature of executive power discussed above convinced Straussians that the "modern presidency" had arisen well before Franklin Roosevelt and the New Deal. As noted in chapter 2, almost universally they pointed to Woodrow Wilson as its deepest theoretical source (though it had been anticipated in practice by Theodore Roosevelt). One important exception was David K. Nichols's *The Myth of the Modern Presidency* (1994). It contended that the best rendering of the founders' political science, bolstered especially by the concrete examples of James Wilson and Gouverneur Morris, had seen popular opinion as a source of strength for the presidency. The office was not just a potential fount of demagoguery to be managed but also a democratized form of executive power that helped reconcile it to liberal government.[77] Nichols argued that the mode of election was essentially popular and, therefore, had adapted easily to political parties as expressions of public opinion; while Article II plus the veto power enabled the president to set the political agenda and shape debate in light of public opinion and his own views. Although time had assuredly brought changes, Nichols held that "for the most part the development of the office can be understood as logical outgrowths of the constitutional Presidency" and thus "the Constitution is largely responsible for the character of the modern Presidency."[78]

From this perspective, Wilson and the Progressive version of the modern presidency had not revolutionized the office by using rhetoric to lead public opinion, something that had always been contemplated by the Constitution. Rather, it was the opposite, mistaken belief "that a powerful modern Presidency could exist only if the President escaped the constraints of the Constitution."[79] This move was part of Progressives' overall reconceptualization of government for ends that were fundamentally anticonstitutional and unlimited: to realize the democratic will of the national community more or less immediately. Having separated the democratized presidency from the Constitution, "the Progressives eliminated the basis for restraint. The Progressive Presidency needs no limits, because for the Progressives democracy needs no limits."[80] Because the core problem was the post-Progressive orientation of the rhetorical presidency toward statist growth, not the original presidency itself, "the solution cannot be a mere lowering of expectations for the Presidency, but it must be a lowering of expectations for the government as a whole."[81] In fact, a strong rhetorical presidency could help trim government overreach, as Andrew Jackson and Ronald Reagan exemplified.[82]

While the depth of the rhetorical presidency's roots in the Constitution was an "intra-Straussian debate," participants agreed that the presidency was always intended to be strong.[83] Its relative weakness in the nineteenth century had been a matter of historical contingency rather than constitutional design. Indeed, as the concept of the rhetorical presidency developed, both Tulis and Ceaser stated more pointedly their agreement that the framers of the Constitution had always expected some level of popular leadership from the presidency. To an extent, then, the contemporary rhetorical presidency was consistent with the original Constitution, perhaps even "built into the constitution's 'genetic code.'"[84] Of course, the crucial political question always remained: To what ends was presidential rhetoric being employed as the means?

More generally with respect to executive power, Straussians agreed that the presidency had always been modern insofar as it included some version of what had developed since Machiavelli. The Constitution was built for a national government of continental scope that could defend its interests on the world stage—hence it contained the strong executive requisite to meeting national challenges at home and abroad. "Big government" too was in this sense always latent in the Constitution. Tulis urged, therefore, that "we need to disconnect the problems of plebiscitary leadership from the development of big government. To be sure, big government requires a strong executive, but it is not clear that it entails a democratized presidency."[85] A noted scholar in the field rightly observed that Straussians (and others) understood the powers of the modern presidency as having "been there all along," needing only "to be recovered in their full significance."[86]

Neoconservatives, Straussians, and the Debate over Post–Cold War Foreign Policy

There was every reason to expect that the established Straussian support of a strong foreign policy presidency would persist after the Cold War. After the defeat of communism, conservatives, including some Straussians, began to debate both their overall political identity and the nation's foreign policy. This debate included a new generation of neoconservatives who argued that American principles and interests would be served by a strongly interventionist foreign policy. The United States should aim to foster democracy abroad, by force if necessary. A leading advocate of this view was William Kristol, a Straussian who had studied with Harvey C. Mansfield Jr. Kristol founded the *Weekly Standard* in 1995 and a think tank called the Project for a New American Century (PNAC) in 1997. In the late 1990s the *Standard*, PNAC, Kristol, and various other neoconservatives advanced their foreign policy program and, as a particular application of it, the toppling of Saddam Hussein in Iraq.[87] After 9/11, neoconservatives had some measure of influence in the counsels of the George W. Bush administration and its decision to invade Iraq in 2003. Subsequently, there was an eruption of charges from journalists and some academics that Strauss, who died in 1973, was the guru of a belligerent, nihilist-elitist cult whose disciples supposedly had seized control of the Bush administration, via neoconservativism, to make war as part of their larger ambition to rule. These charges were in turn met with substantial scholarly rejoinders in defense of Strauss and against the wilder and more conspiratorial allegations aimed at those he was said to influence.

It would take us too far from the Straussian understanding of the presidency fully to reconstruct the foreign policy debates of the 1990s, let alone to sort out the by now sprawling and detailed literature on the alleged nefarious plotting of Strauss and the Straussians. However, since we have been following the influence of Strauss's ideas throughout this study, it is worth widening the focus slightly to consider the developments that put them at the very center of national discussion. A primary point to be noted here is that the neoconservative prescriptions of the 1990s were cast in terms of foreign policy and its relation to national purpose and identity, not in terms of the constitutional authority of the presidency or the nature of executive power.

Neoconservatives wanted a "broader, more enlightened understanding of America's interests" that avoided a return to the more isolationist, less engaged posture they associated with traditionalists like Patrick Buchanan.[88] They advocated a "benevolent global hegemony" in which the United States guaranteed international order and actively promoted its universal principles of natural rights and government by consent as announced in the Declaration of Independence.[89] In practice such promotion meant that "a principal aim of American foreign policy should be to bring about a change of regime in hostile nations."[90] This "remoralization of American foreign policy" would make possible true "national greatness" and "restore a sense of the heroic" to public life.[91] Lauding Theodore Roosevelt's idea of a "civilizing" national mission, and insisting that their prescriptions were "not Wilsonian idealistic whimsy," neoconservatives argued in terms of policy and national purpose.[92] They simply assumed the vast foreign affairs and war-making powers of the modern presidency. This was understandable insofar as the debate of the 1990s occurred while President Clinton repeatedly used military force abroad on his own authority. Neoconservatives thought these actions were too often truncated and their humanitarian and multilateralist impulses misconceived, but they did not raise constitutional objections as such.[93] Instead, they aimed for an expansion of the definition of "national interest" that went "beyond material security and prosperity" to include "honor and greatness in the service of liberal principles."[94]

After 9/11, complaints about the "imperial presidency" predictably re-emerged. They came in response to actions that the Bush administration justified with the "unitary executive" theory, which, as the previous chapter shows, was already well developed prior to 9/11. A forceful rejoinder to such complaints came from Harvey C. Mansfield Jr. He remained consistent in reasserting his well-established view of executive power amid both the occupation of Iraq and the controversy over the Bush administration's domestic electronic surveillance policy. His arguments appeared in both the neoconservative *Weekly Standard* and the Straussian *Claremont Review of Books*.

Mansfield repeated that the Constitution had successfully accounted for necessity in the presidency, and that critics were confused in thinking that every necessity could be provided for by law and ahead of time. Consequently, to accuse the Bush administration of acting unconstitutionally in the surveillance program was to misunderstand the proper terms of judgment, thereby undermining both constitutionalism and the president's capacity to act. "The president can be held accountable and made responsible, but if he could be stopped, the Constitution would lack any sure means of emergency action. Emergency action of this kind may be illegal but it is not unconstitutional; or, since the Constitution is law, it is not illegal under the Constitution."[95] The charge of an "imperial" presidency was wrongly leveled at actions taken by the president for purposes of national self-defense. Moreover, if the United States had overstepped in Iraq, it was from a too sanguine hope that Iraq could follow America's example and advice, not from "imperial ambition."[96] Historically, isolationism rather than imperialism had proven to be the great danger for America, and "if America is an empire, it is the first empire that always wants an exit strategy."[97]

James W. Ceaser later noted that Mansfield had responded to the "imperial" charge with what in essence was an originalist argument about the nature of executive power under the Constitution—one that comported with the theory of the unitary executive. Both Mansfield and the unitarians concluded that "much of what Schlesinger's followers reflexively call 'imperial' is not imperial at all, but constitutional."[98] Accordingly, said Ceaser, the imperial charge was not sustained by a proper understanding of the history and theory informing the Constitution's text. Rather, the charge was "used to provide (false) constitutional warrant to promote a passive or neo-isolationist view of international relations."[99] Here we see a rare but clarifying awareness of the commonalities between the Straussian support of a strong presidency, the theory of the unitary executive, and an interventionist foreign policy. This conjunction was consistent with Mansfield's long-standing views. But those views did not depend on either the emergence of the unitary executive or neoconservatism—both of which proceeded on their own tracks and neither of which he claimed to follow.

Nor, as we have seen, was the Straussian case for a strong presidency part of neoconservatives' advocacy of the policy of "benevolent global hegemony" in the 1990s. When considering the relationship between Straussians and neoconservatives, it is clear that, despite some affinities and overlap of the kind apparent in Mansfield, these were never convertible categories. Strauss was not the fount of neoconservatism as such. Nor were Straussians in control of the actions and rhetoric of the Bush administration after 9/11, even if some (but not all)

Straussians sometimes supported them. Some consideration of these issues is necessary to distinguish between the established Straussian support of a strong presidency and misattributions of Straussian responsibility for or uniform approval of post 9/11 developments.

Neoconservatism was a multifaceted political orientation that moved through several stages from the mid-1960s to the early 2000s. It is notable that Strauss is not mentioned in either the first serious study of neoconservatism in 1979 or in the book's updated foreword (2013). However we might understand neoconservatism—a careful recent study concludes that it "is such a diverse thing that the term has always been close to meaningless"—it was too variegated and its development too contingent to be attributed to the thought of Strauss. To do so is "fundamentally erroneous" and simply "does not work."[100] Moreover, the condition of American constitutionalism as such was not an initial motivation for neoconservatism. The movement's limited attention to legal-constitutional issues in its formative years was the purview of frustrated liberal social scientific policy analysts with no connection to Strauss or the way his students thought about American constitutionalism. To the extent that Straussian constitutional theory and its concern with nature as a standard of right became associated with neoconservatism, it did so by displacing the original neoconservative approach to the topic, not by inspiring it.[101]

None of this is to deny that there were some commonalities and connections between Straussians and neoconservatives, as all serious studies of the subject accept.[102] Certainly, Strauss's work helped neoconservatives (and others) to speak respectfully of the nation's basis in natural rights and government by consent, and to question the viability of liberal democratic regimes amid the radical intellectual movements and violent horrors of the twentieth century.[103] Reflective, non-Straussian criticism readily acknowledges the presence in neoconservatism of Strauss's concern with transhistorical human nature in relation to legitimate government—while still rejecting partisan distortions of Strauss's thought or the putative Straussian takeover of Bush administration foreign policy.[104] Strauss's work was too philosophical and thus "underdetermined" to generate any straightforward political program among those he influenced, either during his lifetime or since his death.[105]

Consider the case of Irving Kristol, who was heatedly attacked as the major intellectual conduit between Strauss and the supposed neoconservative direction of the Bush administration.[106] Kristol, a founder of neoconservatism, sometimes acknowledged the influence of Strauss (and one of his students, Martin Diamond). He even once described his overriding political concern in rather

Straussian terms as the "tendency of democratic republics to depart from . . . their original, animating principles, and as a consequence to precipitate grave crises in the moral and political order."[107] That thought, along with the appeal to natural right, fairly describes much of the overlap between Straussians and neoconservatism.[108] But Kristol was also a realist in foreign policy. He denied that the United States could or should export democracy through armed intervention. For example, he defended the limited objectives of the first Persian Gulf War, stating that "no civilized person in his right mind wants to govern Iraq" and that America's national interest had "never implied a commitment to bring the blessings of liberty to the Arab world."[109] One must either read Irving Kristol out of neoconservatism or acknowledge that engagement with Strauss's ideas did not necessarily produce advocacy of the United States' recent invasions and attempts at remaking foreign nations.

Another pertinent example was Nathan Tarcov, a prominent Straussian who rejected neoconservative foreign policy. Considering the international situation in 1991, he wrote that America's founding principles had always made it a "revolutionary power with positive, potentially global, aims, albeit ones that limit the means of their own actualization by dictating respect for the consent of other peoples."[110] The sole remaining superpower could not withdraw from the world stage and should not shrink from its principles, but neither should its objectives "involve doctrinaire crusading or reckless disregard for the value of American resources, the costs and risks of particular policies, and the choices of other peoples."[111] While this stance was somewhat abstract in the immediate post–Cold War period, Tarcov opposed the 2003 invasion of Iraq and found no support in Strauss for any such enterprise. In fact, he argued, closer attention to Strauss's views "might have served as warnings against some of the missteps that have plagued U.S. policy in recent years."[112] Tarcov examined two of Strauss's unpublished lectures given in the 1940s in comparison to his later published work. Without recapitulating Tarcov's full findings here, it was clear that his conclusion aimed at contemporary American policy. Strauss "stressed the impossibility," Tarcov observed, "of imposing a lasting form of government through conquest, the obstacles to the democratic education of one people by another posed by differences of political tradition and intellectual climate, and the need for re-education toward liberal democracy to be the work of the people involved rather than of foreigners or exiles."[113]

As Tarcov's conclusion suggests, the fallacy in blaming the United States' post-9/11 actions in the Middle East on Straussian ideas can be seen through a comparison of the concept of "regime" in Strauss's thought with "regime change" and "nation building" commenced through military force. Strauss famously retrieved the Aristotelian concept of regime (*politeia*) as the central object of political science, understanding it as both a system of government and way of life. A regime consisted of not only government offices but also the culture and customs that validated the predominant authority of certain human types, most especially the claim to justice they represented and legally enforced. All parts of society were shaped by and reflected the ruling principle of the regime, whatever its mix of nature and convention. Both individuals and institutions assumed its basic outlook and conformed their conduct to its principles and laws. From here, the Aristotelian political science Strauss revived began to consider such basic questions as what the best regime according to human nature was, what the best practical regime was, and how philosophy might improve and defend a decent regime. Those large questions aside, the concept of regime always carried with it a sense of pervasiveness, if not complete intractability, in that regimes formed their peoples so deeply and fundamentally that they were not easily altered.[114]

Nevertheless, William Kristol (with a coauthor) recurred to Strauss's retrieval of "regime" in the context of Bush administration policy. This effort first accurately restated the concept's insistence that "political life always partakes of both the universal (principles of justice or rule) and the particular ('our' borders, language, customs, etc.)." And then this: "President Bush's advocacy of 'regime change'—which avoids the pitfalls of a wishful global universalism on the one hand, and a fatalistic cultural determinism on the other—is a not altogether unworthy product of Strauss's rehabilitation of the notion of regime."[115] But is it? This statement might be interpreted neutrally as a use of the concept that merely highlighted the distinction between a tyrannous regime and the liberal democracy that United States has always hoped to see proliferate. But it was mistaken if it meant to claim the sanction of Straussian analysis for any specific foreign policy or military action in the Middle East.[116]

Other notable Straussians and at least one prominent neoconservative recurred to Straussian regime analysis precisely to dispute the possibility of enduring "regime change" in Iraq through either conquest or subsequent democratic "nation building." Closer attention to the limitations imposed by the perdurable features of a political regime, as Strauss understood it, might have cautioned "some of the more exuberant supporters of the war" about the unlikelihood that it could "bring democracy to Iraq."[117] Charles R. Kesler, editor of the *Claremont Review of Books*, judged that neoconservatives had overestimated the capacity of a forced change in political form to reshape a regime's culture.

Neoconservatives were too readily "carried away by the apparent ease with which democratic transitions took place around the world," especially after the collapse of the Soviet Union. But the Arab Middle East was not simply the next in line, because "there were cultural, religious, and political factors that had made it resistant to the democratic wave—and would continue to do so." While Kesler was persuaded that the toppling of Saddam was in the US national interest, he concluded that "the decision to turn that deterrent, punitive, and preventive action into the occasion for elaborate democratic reconstruction was, alas, ill-conceived."[118]

Thomas G. West agreed that Iraq deserved military defeat and punishment, but his examination of the lessons about foreign policy that Strauss had gleaned from the ancients (especially Thucydides) convinced him too that nation building there was doomed for the foreseeable future. The primary purpose of foreign policy was national security and self-preservation for the sake of peace, which in turn was the precondition for a people's pursuit of virtue in a well-ordered regime.[119] Furtherance of that end was arguably served by the removal of Saddam, but, West wrote, "from Strauss's point of view, . . . the case against nation-building in Iraq is strengthened by the fact that neither Iraq nor any of its major regions has ever in history been governed democratically. It appears that Iraq lacks the elementary preconditions of constitutional democracy."[120] This fact about the Iraqi regime could not be altered by a quick, forced process. "Words on a piece of paper (an Iraqi Constitution, for example) will have zero political effect if there is no strong support for their enforcement, and no understanding of why their enforcement is a good thing."[121] The attempt to compel the desired democratic change "may well cause more harm than good," particularly in lives unnecessarily lost on both sides.[122]

Neoconservatives' confidence that liberal democracy could be forcefully implanted in a historically inhospitable locale like Iraq reflected their willingness to claim at least some level of inspiration from Woodrow Wilson. Spreading liberal democracy advanced the national interest, they said, though they rejected Wilson's view that supranational organizations should have a say in US decisions. Numerous observers, including some conservatives, agreed that this approach was incompatible with older and more properly realist versions of conservative foreign policy.[123] Some Straussians too judged that the Wilsonian idealism of neoconservatism overwhelmed its claim of compatibility with a realist view of the national interest. It was irreconcilable to either a prudent regard for concrete American interests or any principle derivable from Leo Strauss. According to Charles Kesler, a more properly realistic view was that "the primary question for us is to make the world safe for American democracy." Therefore "it is a judgment of prudence, not of categorical moralism, which countries are worth our blood and treasure. (In principle most neocons would agree, but they do not draw the right conclusion regarding Iraq.)"[124] In a condemnatory echo of the neoconservative credo, Thomas West declared, "The foreign policy of Strauss and the classics seeks neither *hegemony* over other nations nor *benevolence* toward other nations, unless, accidentally, one or the other is a means to survival."[125] West accepted that Saddam had presented an authentic threat that merited removal, and that the United States could legitimately attack preemptively to defend itself in any similar situation. Those were judgments rooted in traditional foreign policy realism, but "Americans should not confuse matters by engaging in enthusiastic talk about national greatness and restoring a sense of the heroic by sending their own soldiers to die in battles that perhaps serve the interests of others, but not our own."[126]

In sum, Straussians can neither be simply equated with neoconservatives nor be held responsible for the neoconservative approach to foreign policy and whatever influence it had on the Bush administration. The Straussian defense of a strong presidency, like the growth of presidential war making and the theory of the unitary executive, long antedated the neoconservative advocacy of benevolent global hegemony and regime change in Iraq—policies whose advocates did not think required any new defense of executive power. Nor did Straussians who supported a strong presidency uniformly approve neoconservative or Bush administration policies once they were in motion. Consequently, it is clear that one can simultaneously accept that executive power will always be both necessary and dangerous while holding too that the rise of the modern presidency unbalanced the constitutional system. Neither position requires assigning responsibility for Bush administration foreign policy to Leo Strauss or those who learned from him.

Libertarians

Like the neoconservatives they reviled, libertarians argued more often about foreign policy than the presidency as such. Like their sometime allies in the traditionalist old Right, libertarians wanted a noninterventionist policy that restrained the presidency from initiating foreign involvements. Here libertarianism was most pronouncedly in its purist and rejectionist mode, standing on principle to condemn America's conduct in the Cold War and the powerful presidency associated with it. Consequently, it was politically sidelined and increasingly silent on these topics from the 1960s to the 1990s. Moreover, while previous chapters show that public choice theory helped advance libertarians' defense of federalism and their critique of the administrative state, the presidency and executive branch garnered very little attention from this perspective. One summation from 2004 concluded that public choice analysis of the subject remained in its "infancy," and accordingly it need not detain us here.[127] Until quite recently, the most salient libertarian statements on foreign affairs and the presidency were at once deeply principled, unrealistic, and marginalized.

The impassioned work of Garet Garrett in the early Cold War era was an important example. Garrett was a financial journalist, author, and editor whose work appeared in major publications from the 1910s until his death in 1954. He remains an inspirational figure for libertarians. Criticizing President Truman's policy in Korea and Europe, he said that the president had unconstitutionally seized from Congress the power to declare war. He pointed in particular to the historical significance of the document (analyzed in chapter 6) titled "Powers of the President to Send the Armed Forces outside the United States" (1951). He noted especially its declaration that " 'constitutional doctrine has been largely moulded by practical necessities' " and its concomitant conclusion that " 'use of the congressional power to declare war, for example, has fallen into abeyance because wars are no longer declared in advance.' " This pronouncement Garret regarded as more befitting Caesar's Rome than a constitutional republic. "If constitutional doctrine is moulded by necessity, what is a written Constitution for?"[128] In fact, Garrett argued that this new extrusion of executive power, following those of the New Deal and US entry into World War II, confirmed the nation's conversion from a republic into an empire. Although the old institutions and slogans remained, there had been a "revolution within the form."[129] The president's capacity to declare war and to move troops anywhere he wished formed the primary evidence. Likewise did the presidency now exhibit the plebiscitary aspects of Caesarism, with the president claiming that a " 'mandate from the people' " empowered him to speak for them.[130]

Garrett thus exemplified the trope of the " 'lost republic,' " overcome by imperial executive and plebiscitary debasement. This refrain circulated among the libertarian old Right in response to both World War II and the birth of the Cold War.[131] Less vituperative echoes recurred with diminished frequency and potency.[132] Nevertheless, the defeat of the Bricker amendment in 1954 proved to be the same crucial loss for the libertarian wing of the old Right as it had been for the traditionalist wing.[133]

In addition, the anticommunist conservatism that cohered around *National Review* rejected the isolationism that emanated from antistatist libertarians or anyone else. Before the magazine was even founded, William F. Buckley Jr. declared that "we have got to accept Big Government for the duration—for neither an offensive nor a defensive war can be waged . . . except through the instrument of a totalitarian bureaucracy within our shores." Victory in the Cold War amid the threat of nuclear war would require extensive taxation and centralization.[134] This position was anathema to libertarians. Indeed, two stalwart libertarian noninterventionists, Murray Rothbard and Justin Raimondo, wrote histories of the movement that used this quotation to emphasize just how fundamentally mainstream conservatism offended their principles.[135] Nevertheless, *National Review* held this view throughout the Cold War, articulated especially in the columns of James Burnham. The magazine's criticism of libertarians also endured. In 1979 it devoted a derisive article to the recent founding of the Cato Institute, a libertarian think tank. It took particular aim at Rothbard's noninterventionism and his sympathy for disarmament, even though others protested that this was not uniformly the position at Cato. The article found the foreign policy views of those writing for Cato to be unrealistic and woolly-headed apologies for America's enemies. They should not be taken seriously by anyone who actually cared about national defense.[136]

Both Rothbard and Raimondo recognized that as long as the Cold War continued, there was no place within conservatism for their radical libertarian brand of noninterventionism or for that of a figure like Garrett.[137] Protests against the Vietnam War presented an opportunity to win libertarian adherents, but even then, antistatist radicalism was not particularly attractive amid the worldwide conflict with communism. Nevertheless, Rothbard's pointed attempt to capitalize on antiwar sentiment ostentatiously rejected American constitutionalism: "The idea of binding down power with the chains of a written Constitution has proved to be a noble experiment that failed"; therefore, "some other, more radical means must be found to prevent the growth of the aggressive State."[138] Such radicalism helped ensure the irrelevance of libertarian foreign policy views.

The end of the Cold War finally afforded libertarians the chance to raise anew the prospect of a noninterventionist foreign policy and, with it, a more restrained presidency. To do so, Rothbard (who died suddenly in 1995) allied with the populist traditionalism of Patrick Buchanan and the renewed discourse of "America First" that circulated around his presidential campaigns of the 1990s. Libertarians joined traditionalists-cum-paleoconservatives, such as Samuel Francis and *Chronicles* magazine, in ineffectual opposition to the Gulf War and the military campaigns of the Clinton administration.[139] Likewise, while the 1990s did bring somewhat more receptive audiences among the Washington foreign policy establishment for the Cato Institute's noninterventionism, there was no illusion at Cato that any radical policy reorientation was afoot.[140]

Libertarians produced few focused analyses of the presidency prior to 9/11. However, there were occasional renewals of Garrett's and Rothbard's purist-rejectionist attack on America's supposed decline into a presidentialist empire. Llewellyn H. Rockwell Jr., president of the radically libertarian Ludwig von Mises Institute, virulently attacked the presidency in the pages of *Chronicles*. The office was "the worst outgrowth of a badly flawed Constitution, imposed in a sort of coup against the Articles of Confederation." Corrupt from its very inception, the presidency had always had "too much power" and had always "been an instrument of oppression." Rockwell cataloged the supposedly unlimited powers and unlimited sins of presidents over the centuries, bemoaning that the older conservative suspicion of executive power had given way to neoconservatives' use of the presidency to remake the world. The office was now "by definition in violation of the Constitution." For those who loved liberty, the time had come for "our plebiscitary dictatorship [to] be reined in or tossed out."[141]

A related book published by the Mises Institute likewise found little consonant with libertarian values in the history of the US presidency.[142] The book barely engaged either the nature of executive authority or the founders' intent in creating the office of president. Instead, chapter after chapter argued that flawed and misguided presidents had used their ambition and guile to aggrandize power in a central government that dominated both citizens and foreigners. Moreover, the whole sad spectacle appeared to be pretty much inevitable—yet another confirmation of the libertarian precept that the state always grows in power at the expense of liberty. Amid other contributing factors, the presidency was most to blame for "the transformation of America from a constitutional federal union to an empire."[143] Yet again, the Constitution was deemed a "fateful error" that had proven incapable of securing liberty by prohibiting immoral scoundrels from gaining office and exploiting power.[144] Salvation would come from piecemeal secession by towns and cities that refused to abide by federal law, gradually realizing the radical libertarian goal of a stateless "anarcho-capitalist" social order. Private insurance agencies would then emerge to provide the security and services historically monopolized by the state, obviating the need for taxation, legislation, and of course executive power.[145] Although perfectly consistent within libertarian theory as such, in the real world this line of thought was of course utterly utopian.

The Bush administration's exertion of executive power in response to 9/11 prompted some rethinking among libertarians, as it did among others, as well as some more direct and realistic attention to the presidency and the surrounding questions of foreign policy. Some prominent libertarians even supported the invasion of Iraq. Although the Cato Institute opposed it and still advocated a generally noninterventionist foreign policy, it eschewed the more radical libertarian approach to foreign affairs, such as the privatization of national defense.[146]

Cato's Gene Healy also abandoned the more extreme and rejectionist approach in an important libertarian study.[147] His book was conversant with the history of the presidency and addressed the central debates within the scholarly literature on the subject. A severe indictment of the "heroic" modern presidency, it especially criticized the plebiscitary approach to public opinion and unilateral war making. Healy was disappointed that conservatives had begun to embrace presidential power in the 1970s, after having opposed it for so long, and he predictably rejected its bold reassertion by the Bush administration. These positions certainly reflected libertarian principles, and Healy likewise favored a noninterventionist foreign policy. Significantly, however, he claimed justification in the original meaning of the Constitution. Both liberals and conservatives, he argued, had wrongly accepted a modern presidency that had corrupted and abandoned it. Its original meaning should now be recaptured and enforced, not dismissed as a mistake or failure, as prominent libertarians earlier had.

Accordingly, he adopted the critique of the plebiscitary, "rhetorical" presidency analyzed above, agreeing that it vastly exceeded what the founders had intended. He also used evidence from the founding to attack the theory of the unitary executive and the writings of John Yoo in particular. His summary statement was blunt: "The 'executive Power,' as understood by the Founding Generation, was hardly the bottomless fount of royal prerogative radical unitarians envision."[148]

Healy felt compelled to suggest some legal-constitutional "fixes" for the pathologies of the modern presidency, but he doubted there was much chance of success. He diagnosed the fundamental problem as acceptance, by both everyday citizens and political elites, of the modern presidency itself—along with the inflated expectations and inevitable disappointments accompanying it.[149] American political culture had seemingly forsaken the "skepticism toward power that is our constitutional birthright." There was little hope of change until "we free ourselves of our atavistic tendency" to see the president as "responsible for our economic well-being, our physical safety, and even our sense of belonging."[150] Perhaps without fully recognizing it, Healy here echoed an ancient idea that was well understood by the American founders: maintenance of a republic ultimately depends on the virtue of its citizens and their ability to govern themselves. This thought again marked Healy's distance from more radical forms of libertarianism that rejected the constitutional order *tout court*. Healy now saw the problem as a "century-long drift away from the Framers' vision." Together with a political culture that demanded ever more from government, this gradual abandonment had produced "a presidency that is a constitutional monstrosity: at once menacing and ineffectual."[151]

A similarly nuanced analysis of the presidency and the politics surrounding it was apparent in Richard Epstein's magnum opus, *The Classical Liberal Constitution* (2014). This comprehensive study argued that as a matter of original understanding the Constitution was informed more by the principles of classical liberalism than by any other theory—no radical libertarian rejectionism here. As one would expect, Epstein too dismissed Yoo's unitarian endorsement of unilateral presidential war making. He likewise insisted that foreigners detained in US custody should be able to challenge any jurisdictional classification that automatically denied them access to the writ of habeas corpus. Nevertheless, Epstein accepted that there were few bright lines separating congressional and executive powers when it came to war. Generally speaking, of course, Congress had the authority to determine the scope of any conflict, while it was left to the president to conduct operations. But "in the end, a political accommodation has to be reached, informed by the relative spheres of authority." In this area the Constitution "was best understood as a framework for future elaborations [rather] than as a perfect contingent state contract. Classical liberal theory cannot pull rabbits out of hats." Epstein thus conceded that libertarians would always find it easier to identify rights than fully to map, amid political disagreement and contingency, the proper interactions of the institutions designed to protect them.[152] Here was a mature libertarian acceptance of the fact that the presidency existed in a milieu where the maximization of individual liberty against state action could not always be the primary concern.

Conclusion

Straussians' understanding of Lockean prerogative and Machiavellian necessity convinced them that executive power was intrinsic to modern politics, and they held that the presidency had accounted for this reality as much as possible. The tension between executive power and constitutionalism must be wisely managed but could never be wholly resolved. Straussians were likewise concerned that the rhetorical-plebiscitary presidency had the potential to dispense permanently with other foundational components of the constitutional system. Its tendency toward demagoguery threatened the Constitution's limits and forms, concomitantly undermining deliberative self-government and the rule of law. If carefully used, however, it might buttress constitutional norms. While Straussians undeniably advocated a strong presidency, their position did not equate to the neoconservative call for "benevolent global hegemony" as the United States' proper post–Cold War foreign policy. Nor did Straussians commandeer neoconservativism—a political dispensation difficult to define in the best of times—to rule via their supposed control of Bush administration foreign policy. Such sensational claims overstate the immediate effects of constitutional discourse and discount the decades-long reality of presidential war power. The growth of that power convinced many post–New Deal libertarians that the republic was lost or, alternatively, that the Constitution had been a mistake and a failure from the start. Some more recent libertarian evaluations were more moderate in arguing that the modern presidency was more of a corruption of the original Constitution than a confirmation of its inevitable failure—though of course still eminently capable of traducing individual liberty. The awesome power and influence that had accrued to the presidency ensured that it would remain an abiding concern for all varieties of American conservatism.

PART FOUR

MODERN JUDICIAL REVIEW
An Overview

The Supreme Court's validation of the New Deal both reflected and advanced momentous changes in judicial review that had been brewing for decades. Together, pragmatism, Progressive political science, and legal realism redefined how law, interpretation, and the Constitution itself were understood. Judging was now said to be just another form of legislating, one that balanced social interests and rights against each other. Law was an especially obscurantist form of politics in that judges always retained the capacity for discretion and choice. The Progressive rubric of the "living Constitution" came to signify that the Court would accept and help define a Constitution that changed over time and adapted to new social circumstances and values—primarily through the growth of government and the protection (or invention) of new rights. The Court approved the New Deal according to this modern reconceptualization of law and the Constitution. Its endorsement entailed an obvious rejection of the older view that the Constitution had a fixed meaning that bound interpreters. The new Court would defer automatically to federal regulation of large swathes of the economy and society, but its capitulation also contained the seeds of the "rights revolution" and the egalitarianism advanced so vigorously under Chief Justices Earl Warren, Warren Burger, and even William Rehnquist. This basic story of the New Deal revolution and the concomitant rise of modern judicial review has been told with detail and insight by many scholars, and another full re-counting here is unnecessary.[1] Instead, this overview distinguishes the lodestars of modern judicial review, emphasizing the Court's revised understanding of the Constitution and its powerful, highly discretionary role within the New Deal order. This approach clarifies the basic parameters of what conservatives responded to in the second half of the twentieth century.

A crucial building block of modern judicial power was long known as the "preferred freedoms" doctrine, but is now often referred to as "bifurcated review" or the "double standard." It was offered tentatively in the now famous "footnote four" of *United States v. Carolene Products* (1938).[2] That decision upheld a regulation under the Commerce Clause and stated that the Court would generally defer to Congress's judgment about the necessity of such actions and presume them valid. It did not invalidate another federal law under the Commerce Clause until the 1990s. But the Court signaled that it might cease deference and use more "exacting judicial scrutiny" for legislation that affected the Bill of Rights, or inhibited the functioning of the political process, or targeted "discrete and insular minorities" on the basis of race, religion, or nationality. At first this logic was applied episodically to protect some political radicals, labor groups, and religious minorities as they undertook picketing, leafleting, and public protest. Eventually it became the Court's template, often effectuated through the Equal Protection Clause of the Fourteenth Amendment, for establishing what it saw as the proper "balance" between social needs as expressed in legislation and what it defined as a "fundamental" right.

Closely related was the practice of "incorporation," by which the Court used the Fourteenth Amendment to apply portions of the Bill of Rights to the states. Although it had started somewhat earlier, its lasting expression was Justice Benjamin Cardozo's opinion in *Palko v. Connecticut* (1937). In that decision, the Court said that the states would be bound by provisions of the Bill of Rights that the Court determined were "implicit in the concept of ordered liberty" or that expressed the "fundamental principles of liberty and justice which lie at the base of all civil and political institutions."[3] These rights would be "selectively" incorporated. Other justices and commentators advocated "full incorporation" of all of the Bill of Rights, or all of it plus other, unspecified rights they deemed fundamental. Gradually over the decades these various postures combined to make most of the Bill of Rights, as well as other rights not delineated there, binding on the states. This change fundamentally recalibrated the federal system. Now the Tenth Amendment was said to express a mere "truism that all is retained which has not been surrendered."[4]

The new model of review was not at first zealously elaborated. Progressives in the mold of Oliver Wendell Holmes Jr. and Louis Brandeis had been calling for judicial self-restraint and deference to legislatures for decades prior to the New Deal. If law and interpretation boiled down finally to subjective political choices, surely the nation's democratic norms required that those choices normally be made by legislatures. Judges should not overly indulge their inevitable discretion. This point loomed especially large as Nazi totalitarianism and Soviet communism focused attention on the need for democracy and consensus.[5]

In the 1940s and 1950s the older tradition of judicial self-restraint fed into the "legal process" jurisprudence pioneered at the Harvard Law School (and widely taught elsewhere). Felix Frankfurter was the leading proponent of the process-restraint view on the Court until his death in 1962. Operative primarily in statutory interpretation and administrative law, this jurisprudence deployed its master concepts of "institutional settlement" and judges' "reasoned elaboration" of "purposive statutes" to cabin the more radical implications of legal realism and to assimilate the new administrative state into the constitutional structure. On the premises of this jurisprudence, even though deeper philosophical foundations were lacking, the democratic processes of lawmaking certified the legitimacy of legal outcomes. Judges were to apply democratically generated norms and aid the functioning of the legal institutions (including administrative agencies) created to achieve society's ends. The integrity and persuasiveness of this project required tightly reasoned judicial opinions that demonstrated their bases in preexisting principles. Judges should in no way attempt to inaugurate social reform or move the law sharply beyond the present social consensus. Judicial authority was limited and must be husbanded so that it would be obeyed.

The most important expression of the process-restraint tradition in the constitutional context was Alexander M. Bickel's *The Least Dangerous Branch* (1962). Bickel cohered the components of the tradition to urge that the Court should only rarely and carefully assert its authority on behalf of a grand constitutional principle like equality. To do so too frequently, or too much ahead of public acceptance, would endanger the Court and expose the vast discretion that the process-restraint tradition had always quietly reposed in judges. The book was Bickel's attempt to integrate his moral approval of the *Brown v. Board of Education* desegregation decision (1954) into the process-restraint tradition so the crisis of the 1930s was not replayed.[6]

The Warren Court's plunge into renewed liberal reform jarringly sidelined the process-restraint tradition.[7] Several members of the Warren Court were informed by legal realism and held a frankly result-oriented and instrumentalist view of constitutional law. As a whole, and under Warren's leadership, the Court undertook to "update" the "living Constitution." Often it did so on the *Carolene Products* model of "strict scrutiny" and "equal protection" under the Fourteenth Amendment, "balancing" vigorous protection of equal rights for "discrete and insular" minorities against other social interests. *Brown* had inaugurated the end of racial segregation with an opinion whose emphasis on social and psychological factors in lieu of constitutional analysis was controversial at the time and has been ever since. When predictable and often racist grassroots resistance quickly materialized, it prompted the Court's most extreme statement of judicial supremacy in *Cooper v. Aaron* (1958). That decision seemed to equate the Court's interpretation of the Constitution with the thing itself, insisting that anyone who took an oath to the Constitution must cease disagreeing with the Court and promptly obey.[8]

There soon followed other momentous reforms based on controversial reasoning or precedent-shattering opinions, or both. Starting with *Baker v. Carr* (1962), the Court abandoned its long-standing adherence to the political questions doctrine as a bar to evaluating the apportionment of state legislatures. Eventually states were compelled to organize their legislative districts substantially on the basis of population. No longer was much of anything considered to be a "political" topic and therefore insusceptible to judicial resolution.[9] The Court similarly revolutionized state criminal procedure by incorporating various components of the Fourth, Fifth, and Sixth Amendments over the course of several decisions. Overall, the admissibility of evidence and the practices of interrogation and trial were made more favorable to the accused. This trend was encapsulated in the now famous *Miranda* warnings given to arrestees, which were announced with a statute-like particularity whose provenance in the constitutional text was not readily discernible.[10] The decisions in the areas of desegregation, reapportionment, and criminal procedure showed that modern judicial review was now exercised not only to protect rights but also positively to command detailed reforms of institutions and practices to the Court's satisfaction.

The liberal reformist project continued in various aspects of the Warren Court's First Amendment jurisprudence. It became more difficult for government officials and nongovernment public figures to sue for libel or defamation. The Court also gave greater protection to obscenity while simultaneously prohibiting prayer in public schools. It called on the First Amendment and several others to mint a new right of "privacy" that allowed married couples to use contraceptives.[11] The Court's numerous new departures were far-reaching and unsettling. As one authority put it at the end to the decade, "The list of opinions destroyed by the Warren Court reads like a table of contents from an old constitutional law casebook."[12] Several decades later a leading study concluded, with some understatement, that the Warren Court advanced values that were "deemed political and wrongheaded by a significant sector of [the nation's] politicians and electorate."[13]

Given such quick and deep changes in constitutional law, some kind of retrenchment was widely expected when Richard Nixon nominated Warren Burger to be chief justice in 1969, especially as three more new appointments soon followed. The Court did take a more conservative stance on criminal procedure. It likewise resisted expanding equal protection and due process doctrines into additional aspects of social reform and welfare provision. But there was no reversal of any landmark Warren Court decision. Nor was there any rethinking of the basic jurisprudential elements of modern judicial review. The double-standard, strict scrutiny approach and the telltale balancing of rights and interests remained very much in place. As one critic put it, "In 1969 something was supposed to happen, and didn't."[14] A later scholarly analysis aptly summarized the Burger Court as "the counter-revolution that wasn't."[15] Moreover, the Court followed through on *Brown* by upholding school bussing as a remedy for segregation.[16] It then entered its own divisive set of racial controversies by validating affirmative action in university admissions, various employment contexts, and federal contracting.[17] And, most divisively and controversially of all, it built on the dubiously generated right of privacy to proclaim a new constitutional right to abortion.[18]

In the more technical and lawyerly realm, the Burger Court acceded to an expansive conception of standing to sue that allowed anyone in the "zone of interest" of a federal regulatory statute to bring a lawsuit for its enforcement. Various "public interest" litigation firms were encouraged to sue on behalf of the numerous new regulations announced during the expansion of the administrative state in the 1960s and 1970s. The upshot was that the Court involved itself in federal policy in areas ranging from environmental protection and workplace safety to automotive design and the management of endangered species.[19] The expansion of standing, combined with the earlier demise of the political question doctrine, made it all but impossible to avoid modern judicial power on any issue of consequence.

William Rehnquist became chief justice in 1986, joined that year by Antonin Scalia and by Clarence Thomas in 1991. Despite this trio's orientation toward originalism and formalism, the core tenets of modern judicial review remained firmly in place (including in some of their own opinions). Still, this solid conservative bloc affected the direction of decisions in some areas. A primary example was property rights under the Fifth Amendment. The Court rejected state permit conditions and regulations that extracted public goods (e.g., beach access or a bike path) from property owners without just compensation. It further held that a "regulatory" taking was compensable when a state law deprived a property owner of all value in land even though there was no physical taking.[20] Aspects of affirmative action and race-conscious policy making were narrowed in employment, government contracting, legislative districting, and university admissions—but in each area the core principle remained intact.[21] The Court routinely declined to review the numerous death penalty cases that came to it on appeal. In addition, a bare majority went some distance in reviving the seemingly moribund idea of federalism that earlier had been so central to American constitutionalism. But, as discussed in the introduction to part II, the so-called federalism "revolution" of the Rehnquist era was decidedly limited. At no point were the major economic regulations or social welfare programs of the New Deal or Great Society under threat. Likewise, in limiting Congress's reach into states and municipalities via the Commerce Clause, the Court stayed well within the jurisprudential parameters of the New Deal settlement.

Moreover, it was in the context of federalism that the Court pointedly reiterated its conception of judicial supremacy. It rejected the congressional attempt in the Religious Freedom Restoration Act (1993) to prevent states from burdening religious expression by compelling them to adhere to its preferred jurisprudential approach to the Free Exercise Clause of the First Amendment. Echoing *Cooper v. Aaron* (1958) and likewise citing *Marbury v. Madison* (1803), the Court declared that it alone was the supreme constitutional interpreter and could limit Congress.[22]

A similar assertion was central to the Court's defense of abortion in *Planned Parenthood v. Casey* (1992). This decision said that constitutional government itself depended on the people's willingness to cease disagreement and obey the Court's holding. It had "the authority to decide their constitutional cases and speak before all others for their constitutional ideals." *Casey* dropped *Roe*'s outmoded trimester rubric in favor of determining whether state restrictions placed an "undue burden" on abortion. Equally amorphous and distinctly unusual was *Casey*'s claim that abortion should remain protected because "at the heart of liberty is the right to define one's own concept of existence, of meaning, and of the mystery of human life."[23] It was unclear how far these imprecisions would stretch, though it was far enough for the Court to uphold the gruesome procedure of partial-birth abortion.[24] Decisions regarding homosexuality tended in a similarly permissive direction. *Romer v. Evans* (1996) overturned a Colorado referendum that had prohibited the treatment of homosexuality as a specially protected category under state or municipal law. The Court dismissed the principles of the Colorado majority as nothing more than "animosity towards the class of persons affected." It then extended the right of privacy to overturn a state law that had criminalized homosexual conduct.[25]

Even amid these decisions, however, the Rehnquist Court marked an end to judicial review as a thoroughly reliable adjunct to New Deal–Great Society liberalism. Nevertheless, modern progressive liberalism still set the boundaries within which the Court operated. None of the farthest-reaching liberal precedents were overturned, and yet again there was no counterrevolution or fundamental alteration.[26] From the perspective of conservative-leaning commentators, changes occurred only at the margins. The Rehnquist Court could at most be described as "moderately conservative."[27] The Court retained its highly discretionary jurisprudential methods and its confidence that judicial review could resolve just about any political issue.[28]

Conservative criticism of modern judicial power paralleled and sometimes overlapped directly with the emergence of "originalist" jurisprudence.[29] At its most basic level, originalism held that the meaning of the Constitution (or later amendments) at the time of enactment should remain authoritative. To interpret the Constitution was to recover its original meaning, and since the Constitution is law, this meaning should guide and limit officeholders and citizens. This understanding was inherited from English jurisprudence and the natural rights, social contract basis of the American Revolution. Originalism was always latent in American political discourse and Supreme Court decision making in the eighteenth and nineteenth centuries, though it was usually untheorized because it was so thoroughly accepted. The intellectual and political developments that culminated in the New Deal successfully eclipsed the originalist idea. It remained a submerged aspect of the process-restraint tradition, but only truly reemerged in response to the Warren Court. Commentators, intellectuals, dissenting justices, and everyday discourse began to recur to the originalist idiom as a way of arguing that the Court's farthest-reaching and most controversial decisions were inadequately rooted in the Constitution. By the late 1970s three major figures, Robert Bork, Raoul Berger, and William Rehnquist, had shaped originalism as distinctively judicial restraintist, legal positivist, and majoritarian. This version of originalism stood for the view that a Court more properly tethered to the original meaning of the Constitution would do less and would more often defer to the decisions of democratically elected legislatures. Originalism thus claimed deep roots as a neutral method of constitutional interpretation. The timing and context of its reemergence, however, affirmed that it was expected to yield more conservative results in judicial decision making.

Originalism became a major force in the constitutional politics and jurisprudential debates of the 1980s. Academic constitutional commentary increasingly centered on originalism and its detractors, displacing the briefly dominant nomenclature of "interpretivism versus noninterpretivism." The Department of Justice under Attorney General Edwin Meese publicly and frequently defended originalism as a matter of policy. The Department's Office of Legal Policy issued reports that advocated originalism and analyzed constitutional law from this perspective. A group of conservatives led by James McClellan formed the Center for Judicial Studies and published the quarterly *Benchmark* to subject judicial decisions and academic debate to originalist criticism. In 1982 a group of conservative and libertarian law students formed the Federalist Society as a way of countering liberal ideas. From its inception, the organization supported originalism. Federalist Society chapters quickly emerged nationwide and began hosting conferences, supporting journals, and credentialing young lawyers for service in Republican administrations and the federal judiciary. The nomination of Robert Bork to the Supreme Court in 1987 heightened the ferment that originalism had induced and firmly associated it in the public mind with both conservative politics and the call for limits on modern judicial power.[30]

The defeat of the Bork nomination did not mark the demise of originalism. Instead, it both accelerated and expanded in the 1990s and thereafter. Its staying power was illustrated when some liberal theorists switched from attacking originalism to trying to appropriate it for their own ends. Originalism also endured because new personnel on the Court continued to write originalist opinions. Historical research into the original meaning of constitutional provisions increased, while originalist jurisprudential theory rapidly grew more refined and complicated.[31]

A full consideration of the many complexities in the so-called "new originalism" would take us too far from the present inquiry, but its major tenets must be briefly delineated as part of the context for conservatives' ongoing response to modern judicial review. It referred less often to the concept of intent as the object of interpretation and more to the Constitution's "original public meaning." Another change was to emphasize the duty of fidelity to this original meaning, rather than insisting on judicial restraint or deference to the legislature. When original meaning could be known, said most new originalists, courts should not shy from adhering to it. An additional crucial innovation was to distinguish between interpretation as the attempt to recapture original meaning and "construction," defined as a more political and contestable process undertaken when interpretation was impossible or indeterminate. New originalists also attended more explicitly to the methods and standards necessary to sustain the theory's jurisprudential claims and to the knotty problem of nonoriginalist precedent. These developments made originalism in the early twenty-first century a lively and respected enterprise in constitutional jurisprudence. It has attracted a new generation of defenders (and critics) and affects the Court's decisions with some frequency. Some observers have suggested that all of this energetic development has fragmented and diffused the originalist project, making it hyperacademic and intellectually incoherent. This may indeed be its fate. It is also possible that, like any other kind of jurisprudence, originalism can be insincerely manipulated in the pursuit of desired results. However originalism may continue to develop, its core claims have endured with remarkable continuity. Among recent theorists they have been described as centering on the concepts of "fixation" and "constraint." Nearly all originalists, old and new, would agree that the meaning of the Constitution was fixed at the time of its adoption and that this meaning should guide and limit later interpreters, constraining what they can say and do under its authority.[32]

The various schools of conservatism shared this basic view both before and during the development of jurisprudential originalism. Beyond their differences and disagreements, different types of conservatives understood themselves as loyal to the original meaning of the Constitution and thought that judicial review should be based on it. Conservative intellectual and political criticism of the Court intensified and intermingled with originalism as it became the dominant jurisprudential way of saying that judicial decisions had become too liberal and too distant from the actual Constitution. Accordingly, although explicitly originalist discourse began and remains centered in jurisprudence and lawyerly technique, the core idea's substantial influence and deep grounding in American principles oriented conservatives as they assessed modern judicial review from their own distinctive perspectives.

Traditionalists, Neoconservatives, and Modern Judicial Review

Apart from the technicalities of jurisprudence and interpretive method, traditionalist conservatives advanced their own self-understanding through a defense of original constitutional meaning. They insisted on a distinction between interpretation of the actual Constitution and the power to legislate or amend. Especially early on, traditionalists expressed this view quite un-self-consciously—as the received wisdom that the Court was ignoring in its rush to remake American politics and culture. Original meaning properly applied, said traditionalists, would prevent judicial decisions from undermining localism, a religiously informed culture of community and moral self-restraint, and the right to life. In the immediate aftermath of *Brown v. Board of Education* (1954), the traditionalist position was not readily separable from states' rights segregationism. Traditionalists gradually developed more detailed and deeply theorized analyses of modern judicial power in the last decades of the twentieth century. Increasingly they saw it as a force that degraded American life by legislating the values of a liberal elite. As the century drew to a close, however, there was pessimism and a sense of loss among traditionalists who feared that judicial corruption of the Constitution was irreversible.

Neoconservatives too criticized the increasing "legalization" of public policy, but only occasionally did they address modern judicial review as such. As erstwhile liberals and social science policy analysts who became frustrated by the Great Society, they were not centrally concerned with constitutional legitimacy or interpretation. Accordingly, their analysis and mode of discourse tracked their own logic far more than they did originalism in the manner of other conservatives. Still, notable neoconservatives clearly thought that modern judicial power was a novel and disturbing departure from courts' traditional and proper role.

Traditionalists from the 1950s through the 1970s

As noted in chapter 3, southern traditionalists saw in *Brown* an affront to federalism and states' rights (which of course had long shielded racial segregation). Some of the original literary and philosophical Agrarians from *I'll Take My Stand* (1930), such as Donald Davidson and Frank Owsley, defended segregation and "massive resistance," as did Richard Weaver. But they did not delve deeply into constitutional issues. Partly this avoidance was a matter of training and intellectual orientation. Partly it was because, like many conservatives in the early Cold War, they saw the supposed "regimenting" of centrally imposed desegregation as a stalking horse for communism. At another level, *Brown* seemed only to confirm that the United States was rushing headlong into statism and uniformity, due ultimately to the failure of secession.[1]

This line of thinking did occasionally induce quasi-originalist comments. In a lecture originally delivered in 1955, Owsley argued that too frequent modern abandonment of the Constitution was due to neglect of the limits imposed by America's principles of natural rights and consent, which were meant to limit government, not to legitimate a Supreme Court that "remodel[ed] the Constitution by interpretation." It plainly had not occurred to Owsley that it was precisely these foundational American principles that undergirded the gathering challenge to segregation. Still, although Americans had always debated judicial review, surely the founders had never intended to bestow "legislative powers on the judiciary."[2] In assessing the South's relationship to American conservatism, a relationship that, in the 1950s, *National Review* was eager to promote, Davidson wrote that "as to government we [southerners] are all thoroughgoing constitutionalists." He advised northerners that the Court appeared unlikely to stop at the type of "social legislation" mandated in *Brown*. Therefore, constitutionalist resistance to the judicial advances of the "Leviathan government that we have allowed to grow up in Washington" was "one of the tasks of conservatism in our time."[3]

Other early opposition to *Brown* frequently claimed that the Court had gone beyond the original meaning of the Constitution. Most such expressions were superficial, but some were detailed. In the first category was the "Southern Manifesto" (1956), which protested that *Brown* was a "clear abuse of judicial power." The Court was said to have seized legislative power from Congress and, based on its own "personal, political and social ideas," to have issued a decision "contrary to the Constitution."[4]

Soon thereafter Virginia created its Commission on Constitutional Government to resist desegregation, and then the Warren Court more generally. Originalist thinking was prominent in the commission's efforts. It reprinted a brief submitted in the *Brown* litigation by the commission's chair, David J. Mays, a Richmond lawyer who also used it in his testimony on the decision before Congress. Mixing terms that later jurisprudential originalists would parse theoretically, Mays premised that " 'the fundamental principle of constitutional construction' " was " 'to give effect to the intent of the framers of the organic law and of the people adopting it.' " He canvassed the historical record for the intent of the framers of the Fourteenth Amendment and the understanding of the states that ratified it; this review convinced him that the amendment was not meant to affect racial segregation in public schools. The only way of reversing the Court's error and "restoring the original meaning" of the amendment was for Congress to begin the amendment process.[5] Another expression of originalism as traditionalist segregationism was a widely noted speech by James F. Byrnes, a former associate justice of the US Supreme Court, secretary of state in the Truman administration, US senator, and governor of South Carolina. Byrnes held that the Court had in essence amended the Constitution against the demonstrably limited original meaning of the Fourteenth Amendment. He declared that southerners rightly respected the written Constitution, but they should not be expected to abide by wholesale change of the fundamental law through the Court. This would transform the Court into a "constitution maker instead of a constitution defender."[6]

In this early period one of the most detailed such indictments of the Court came from James J. Kilpatrick, editor of the *Richmond News-Leader*. As noted in chapter 3, Kilpatrick was a member of the Virginia Commission on Constitutional Government and the leading advocate of state "interposition" against federally enforced desegregation. His position often was straightforwardly originalist: unless the Constitution's words were "exact and enduring, the test for official conduct vanishes."[7] Kilpatrick aimed to show that "the meaning, the object, the intention, and the end" of the Fourteenth Amendment's creators had positively excluded school desegregation.[8] But the Court had transformed constitutional interpretation into amendment.[9]

Kilpatrick confidently raised the banner of the original Constitution with respect to states' rights and segregation, but outside this context he was an inconsistent exponent of the idea.[10] Moreover, his interposition campaign was quixotic and doomed, its basis in state sovereignty having been defeated in the Civil War. It could be distinguished from slavery and segregation at a theoretical level, but not within the context that Kilpatrick reasserted it. A similar problem confronted the commission despite its lawyerly and originalist criticisms of the Court and the Civil Rights Movement (including, along with Kilpatrick, the Civil Rights Act of 1964). Indeed, Kilpatrick and Mays strove to disassociate the commission from more reactionary and racist elements. But such efforts suffered amid the images of hissing white mobs and the John Birch Society's "Impeach Earl Warren" publicity campaign, with its assumption that the undeniable leftist presence in the Civil Rights Movement necessarily made desegregation a communist plot. The commission never could shake its segregationist roots and was disbanded in 1968.[11] Even the more genteel states' rights segregationism of Kilpatrick and Mays associated conservative constitutional criticism of the Court—and to some extent the originalist idea—with racism.

The incipient originalism in the traditionalist response to modern judicial power was not, however, the sole preserve of racists or segregationists. Recurrence to the limiting power of the written Constitution and the distinction between interpretation and legislation (or amendment) were fundamental to American constitutional thought. Other, more mainstream conservative voices naturally and uncomplicatedly expressed the originalist idea. For example, the editorials of David Lawrence in *U.S. News & World Report* frequently took aim at the Court, arguing that "true liberalism" stood for a "government of laws under a written Constitution." He wondered rhetorically "do we believe that nine Justices may re-write the Constitution as they please?"[12] Lawrence sometimes stumped for the bygone notion of state sovereignty and also, rather forlornly, urged that the Fourteenth Amendment had not been legitimately ratified, but the root of his protest was that "it was never intended by the Founding Fathers that the American people should be governed by five men, sitting as a majority of the Supreme Court."[13] He reiterated these themes throughout the late 1950s and early 1960s, believing it was "time for a crusade to restore the constitutional system our forefathers gave us."[14]

Similar proto-originalist responses to the Court were broadcast by Clarence E.

Manion, a former dean of the University of Notre Dame Law School who hosted a nationally syndicated radio program from 1954 to 1979.[15] Manion and his guests usually used loose and colloquial language to say the Court had flouted the limited meaning of the original Constitution and overstepped the limited judicial role as understood by the founders. Primary targets included the school prayer decisions, the seeming irrelevance of the Tenth Amendment and states' rights, and eventually the judicially created rights of privacy and abortion.[16] By 1975 the criticism of modern judicial review was summarized by Governor Meldrim Thomson Jr. of New Hampshire, who asked: "Who today can read the words of the Founding Fathers and believe that they ever intended that an omnipotent Federal government should exercise control over abortions, capital punishment, busing, schools, wages and hours of state and local employees, and levy penalties in factories and shops, all without due process?"[17]

Manion organized the publication of Arizona senator Barry Goldwater's influential *The Conscience of a Conservative* (1960), in which the need to protect the original Constitution from judicial mistreatment was a running theme. The Constitution's commitment to limited government, said Goldwater, was "at the heart of the Conservative philosophy."[18] He too noted that the Court in *Brown* had asked the litigants to discuss the history of the Fourteenth Amendment only to dismiss the results, thus "expressly acknowledg[ing] that they were not being guided by the intentions of the amendment's authors."[19] The Court had thereby turned American constitutionalism on its head: "The Constitution is what its authors intended it to be and said it was—not what the Supreme Court says it is. If we condone the practice of substituting our own intentions for those of the Constitution's framers, we reject, in effect, the principle of Constitutional Government: we endorse a rule of men, not of laws."[20] Similar views were included in *Conservatism: A Guide to Its Past, Present, and Future in American Politics*, a political primer that featured an introduction by Goldwater. Aimed at a popular audience in advance of the 1964 election, the book ranged widely and expressed concern that the Supreme Court was becoming untethered from the Constitution. What normally had been a conservative institution was now "wielding its power with an energy not surpassed in this century." Conservatives were urged to continue their reverence for the fundamental law amid the recognition that the original Constitution could be entirely different than what the Court said about it.[21]

Traditionalist scholars made similar, though more erudite, points. One early example was Charles S. Hyneman, who taught and influenced such prominent traditionalists as Willmoore Kendall and George W. Carey. He noted criticism of the "readiness with which judges have rejected both the plain meaning of constitutional language and evidence of original intent in order to announce an ideal which is declared more binding than either language or intent," as if the Constitution were "a series of hints which invite the Supreme Court to write a new constitution."[22] Hyneman thought that the Court was lifting itself to a "new peak of judicial power" that perhaps entailed a "new constitutional regime."[23] The constitutional order's normal mechanisms for orderly, consensual change were unbalanced by judges who were pursuing their own reformist program.[24]

A similar response to the school prayer decisions came from Charles E. Rice, a law professor at the University of Notre Dame (and sometime guest on the *Manion Forum*).[25] He traced religious expression in American public life from the colonial era to the Warren Court, arguing that the First Amendment had ratified the accepted practice of nonpreferential government acknowledgment of and support for biblical monotheism. Rice frequently insisted that the original meaning of the Amendment, as revealed by the intent of its creators, should control judicial interpretation.[26] He recommended a constitutional amendment "not to change the Constitution, but to restore it" and thus rescue it from the Court's mistaken insistence on government "neutrality" between religion and irreligion.[27] Rice's attempt to correct the Court was rooted in the traditionalist view that a morally decent culture and a properly limited politics were equally impossible absent the sustaining force of religion.

Modern judicial review was not Willmoore Kendall's central concern, but his views still significantly influenced traditionalist thinking. He judged that the Court was undermining the Constitution's original purpose: to realize, through institutions designed for consensus building, the considered judgment of the people on national issues. Any "judicial fiat" that validated the uncompromising and immediatist goals of the Civil Rights Movement, for example, would disrupt the Constitution's slower and more deliberative way of addressing new political demands. The Court's move into desegregation, school prayer, and reapportionment truncated the compromise needed to absorb and moderate new claims of justice. On the contrary, the matured and cohered "deliberate sense" of the people—as much "government by consensus" as possible—was "to be preferred at all times to the immediate acknowledgment of any set of hitherto-unacknowledged rights, or the immediate stepping-up to the federal level of any particular power hitherto reserved to the states." To hamstring properly constitutional politics by "governmentally-induced drastic change" would hasten a constitutional crisis.[28]

While Kendall thought that the original meaning of the Constitution should be respected at the level of political theory, he advised conservatives to cease arguing with the Court about the historical meaning of discrete constitutional phrases. While the Court "hardly keeps up even the pretense, these days, that it is not legislating," Kendall still thought it was a losing battle to appeal to original meaning when the Court had for so long used the Fourteenth Amendment, which was "never intended for the purpose," to "incorporate" most of the Bill of Rights against the states.[29] Neither attacks on specific interpretations of constitutional language nor a frontal assault on judicial review itself could successfully restrain the Court. The sounder approach was to attack the political prudence and actual enforceability of the Court's decisions and to underscore how those decisions offended the American tradition of local decision making. At the same time, Congress should either amend the Fourteenth Amendment or constrict the Court's appellate jurisdiction via the Exceptions Clause of Article III, section 2. Kendall here again returned to the original design of the Constitution, understood as the set of institutional processes that effectuated the "deliberate sense" of the people, in this case through the mechanisms available for them to correct judicial misinterpretations of the Constitution.

Kendall influenced L. Brent Bozell's *The Warren Revolution* (1966). The Court, Bozell wrote in Kendall's terms, was causing a "crisis in the consensus society." It did so by moving difficult and divisive issues from the realm of debate and compromise (the "unwritten" or "fluid" constitution of principled political negotiation) to the realm of legality and compulsion (the "fixed" textual Constitution). Until the Warren Court, the political theory of the original Constitution embodied in this distinction had worked, "our fixed constitution survived more or less intact, according to the framers' original plan and apparent expectations." But now the Court's highly disputed claims about the original Constitution were quickly upending the slow and organic evolution of political-constitutional change. The Court was dangerously ignoring the fact that "meaningful provisions of the written Constitution must have the support of a broadly based consensus." Neither the Court nor the Constitution could create "change in society's underlying ethical substructure."[30]

Despite Kendall's advice, Bozell also contested the historical accuracy of the Court's claims about the meaning of constitutional provisions. His premise was that according to the long-established cannons of jurisprudence the primary question for any interpreter was: "What did the framers of the Constitution intend?"[31] He found inadequate evidence to support the results reached in the Court's decisions on segregated schools, school prayer, and legislative reapportionment. Given the Court's demonstrably incorrect rulings, the question of legitimate authority inevitably arose.[32] To determine whether the Court must be obeyed as the sole and final arbiter of constitutional meaning, Bozell offered an extended historical inquiry into the basis for "judicial supremacy" of the type announced in *Cooper v. Aaron* (1958). He concluded that, on the contrary, the founders originally intended what later scholars have called "departmental" or "coordinate" review. Each branch of government was meant to share in the practice of constitutional interpretation, with none understood as supreme over the others. In this sense, hearkening to Kendall's conception, the Constitution was the nation's "consensus machinery" that facilitated the negotiated resolution of political disagreement. The system was a "summons to every department to exercise energetically and resolutely the rights and duties the Constitution had confided to it."[33] But now the Court was undermining the Constitution's political theory based on erroneous claims about the original meaning of its text.

Bozell opposed segregation, but, as is well known, *National Review* initially supported it in hopes of resisting the Court's egalitarian zeal for displacing legislative compromise and local authority. At first the magazine let Kilpatrick shape and articulate its endorsement of states' rights and gradual, orderly, and white-led reform. Yet the editors also wanted to avoid identification with a merely sectional perspective and so eventually quit speaking in the southern states' rights idiom. Instead, *National Review* settled on the position rooted in Kendall and elaborated by Bozell. The Constitution was originally intended to effectuate the "deliberate sense" of the people as expressed primarily through their representative institutions—in which African American votes too should count—while the Court should refrain from usurping legislative power.[34] This defense of the original Constitution in response to the Warren Court helped renew post–World War II conservatism. This trend was in place well before the dominance of originalism in later jurisprudential debates about constitutional interpretation.[35] Consequently, as George H. Nash's pathbreaking history has observed, resistance to the Warren Court gave conservatism a much stronger claim to American roots and helped link it with the growing majoritarian resistance to modern elite-dominated, interventionist government.[36]

As noted in the introduction to part IV, the self-conscious move toward jurisprudential originalism in the 1970s was generally legal positivist and majoritarian. Leading figures such as Robert Bork, William Rehnquist, and Raoul Berger (a New Deal liberal, not a conservative) all insisted that judicial interpretation true to the Constitution's original meaning would necessarily yield more space for the rule of legislative majorities. Nevertheless, many traditionalists were moral realists and religious believers who ultimately rejected the legal positivism and majoritarianism they saw in lawyerly originalism. At the same time, traditionalists were especially morally appalled at the constitutionalization of abortion in *Roe v. Wade* (1973), which even the noted liberal commentator John Hart Ely declaimed as having no discernible basis in the Constitution.[37] Yet the conservative response to *Roe*, often led by Catholic exponents of natural law, was always legal-constitutional as well as moral.[38] Accordingly, amid both the more general ascendance of originalism in the 1970s and the avalanche of attacks on *Roe*, the originalist idea was gaining credence among traditionalists who were not themselves preoccupied with originalist jurisprudence.[39]

For example, Robert Byrn, a law professor at Fordham University who had long been active in antiabortion politics and litigation, said that "the Supreme Court made its own value judgment, one that is contrary to the intent of the framers of the fourteenth amendment."[40] Joseph O'Meara, former dean of the Notre Dame Law School, agreed that the majority opinion in *Roe* "contains no syllable concerning the genesis, purpose, and adoption of the Fourteenth Amendment." Nevertheless, it was clear that "the drafters did not intend to have [it] withdraw from the States the power to legislate," and instead "the Court simply legislated the legality of abortion."[41] An extensive study by John T. Noonan Jr., another conservative legal scholar, began with the premise that readers of the Constitution would "seek to comprehend the purposes of its framers." But the abortion decision had shown that "instead of developing the purposes of the framers, the Court can subvert them."[42]

Charles E. Rice also responded extensively to *Roe*. He was one of the first commentators to argue that it paralleled *Dred Scott v. Sandford* (1857), the infamous decision that justified slavery. Both decisions had placed a class of human beings beyond the Constitution's protection for legal "persons." This point soon became a regular component of traditionalist criticism.[43] Rice straightforwardly asserted the originalist idea: "In reaching the conclusion that the child in the womb is a 'person,'" he wrote, "we are construing the intent of the framers of the fourteenth amendment."[44] Moreover, even if the framers did not have abortion specifically in mind, or if previous medical knowledge had not recognized the personhood of the unborn, technological advances now made it clear that prenatal life was fully human and therefore covered by the text and intent of the amendment.[45] Rice therefore concluded that abortion was the killing of an innocent human being for the convenience of someone else and "manifestly repugnant to the intent and purpose of the equal protection clause of the fourteenth amendment."[46]

In a longer study, Rice not only condemned the Court for ignoring limited original meaning but also criticized the Constitution itself for being overly permeable to modernity's positivist and secular trends. The Declaration of Independence had embodied a concept of higher law, but John Locke's philosophy had made the regime vulnerable to the rule of mere majority will. Rice deemed "inevitable" the "degenera[tion into] positivism" exhibited in *Roe*, because, though the Constitution "implicitly recognized a natural law," its "defect was its failure to specify a moral arbiter, external to the state, to interpret the meaning of that higher law in particular situations." The Court had now assumed this role. Its decrees in the name of the Constitution were law, no matter how demonstrably incorrect they might be in terms of either the text or natural law—or both. Rice recommended recourse to the moral teachings of the Catholic Church as the most authoritative standard by which to measure judicial decisions like *Roe*, though of course he accepted that the pope could never have a veto over the actions of the US government. Abortion was an extreme case in which the polity must appeal to the Declaration's " 'laws of nature and Nature's God' " against what the Court had made of the Constitution.[47] Rice had no illusions that the Court would reverse itself on the basis of such arguments, and like Noonan, he advocated a constitutional amendment to overturn *Roe* (though they differed on what exactly it should say).[48]

Another important example of traditionalist originalism was M. Stanton Evans, a journalist long involved with conservative organizations and publications (including *National Review*) and president of the American Conservative Union. He argued that modern liberalism had rejected the religious and ethical culture of the West in the name of secular humanist progress, a transformation that necessarily entailed overcoming the "first principles of the founders" as embodied in the Constitution. "The founders' intentions, quite simply, had to be disposed of."[49] A judicially updated living Constitution was a major component of this process. Evans traced the Court's advancement of the liberal program not only in the case of abortion but also in the incorporation doctrine, the diminished protection for property compared to the expansion of civil liberties, and the validation of centralized regulation at the expense of the states.[50] Disputes in constitutional interpretation were inevitable, "but that variation is quite different from the enunciated doctrine of the liberals—that the Constitution means exactly what they wish it to mean in any given set of circumstances."[51]

George W. Carey, always a leading traditionalist constitutionalist, published two essays on judicial review in the mid-1970s that applied the logic of his and Willmoore Kendall's *Basic Symbols of the American Political Tradition* (1970).[52]

It had noted briefly that the Supreme Court was more frequently enforcing the liberal expansion of rights and equality over the old constitutionalism, whose foundation was in legislative deliberation and consensus building amid shared religious norms.[53] Having now fully exceeded the founders' understanding of the limited scope of judicial authority, as explained in *The Federalist*, the Court was creating a regime of judicial supremacy that typically effectuated the ideals of "secular, materialistic liberalism."[54] The hypertrophy of rights especially drew it into the governance of many formerly local issues. Carey singled out the judicial installation of nationwide abortion on demand as the most egregious manifestation of the "breakdown of the traditional American political order."[55] The state, through the Court, was now bestowing new rights on citizens and issuing quasi-legislative positive commands that mangled the relations of civil society, disrupted local communities, and flouted the established forms of self-government. A restoration of constitutional and moral propriety concerning the question of abortion, for example, would require either an amendment or legislation by Congress under section 5 of the Fourteenth Amendment. Carey doubted either would succeed anytime soon.[56]

As in the sources examined above, *National Review* had for decades advocated originalism before the label existed, in varying forms and levels of specificity (though of course not solely by traditionalists).[57] The magazine's support for Raoul Berger's hugely influential *Government by Judiciary* (1977) helped bring the broader and more diffuse forms of conservative originalism together with Berger's jurisprudentially focused, judicial restraint version. Berger had argued that the original meaning of the Fourteenth Amendment was limited and that it had positively excluded federal intervention into school desegregation and state control of suffrage. Thus the Court had illegitimately amended the Constitution under the guise of interpretation. William F. Buckley Jr. hosted Berger on his television program *Firing Line* just as the book was being released. Buckley noted that Berger was a liberal and a Democrat, so his originalism could not be dismissed as conservative partisanship or segregationism. Noting that one of Berger's previous books had defended the legitimacy of judicial review amid attacks prompted by the Warren Court and that another had undergirded the case for Richard Nixon's impeachment, Buckley observed that this one was "bound to embarrass those who have simply accepted the Supreme Court as the agent of their social concerns."[58] Berger's intervention made it harder to dismiss the long-standing conservative defense of the original Constitution as mere short-term partisanship.[59]

National Review positively reviewed the book and allotted space for Berger to rebut several liberal academics who had attacked him and originalism.[60] In doing so, he emphasized that judicial adherence to the limited original meaning of the written Constitution was a fundamental prerequisite of self-government, which should occur primarily in the legislature. "Were the people aware that the rules imposed upon them represent choices of the Justices, not the Framers, they would insist upon a return to self government" as opposed to "to the ungoverned, illimitable law-making of the Justices."[61] Berger reminded his readers that a certain political result's desirability did not mean it was constitutional. The distinction between law and morals should be respected, in part because "there are wide differences over what is moral—as witness the current abortion controversy."[62]

Abortion was not Berger's focus, though the evidence offered above indicates that his generally legal positivist originalism would have found little basis for the Court's decision in *Roe*. Irrespective of the potential conflict between legal positivism and natural law, traditionalist opponents of *Roe* invoked Berger's originalism. In a book that railed against legal positivism, Charles E. Rice quoted Berger to say that in *Roe*, too, the "Court has replaced the choices of the framers by personal predilections of the Justices."[63] John T. Noonan Jr. noted Berger's book as justification for opposition to *Roe* and subsequent abortion decisions because "the Court could not add to the written Constitution."[64] *Human Life Review*, a journal founded in response to *Roe*, featured an article in which Berger's originalist method and criteria were applied to cast the Court's abortion decisions beyond the pale of constitutional justifiability. In these decisions the Court had exhibited the same judicial " 'usurpations' identified by Berger in the contexts of desegregation and voting."[65] Such developments showed that originalism was becoming more prominent among traditionalists just as the Reagan administration was about to feature it in the 1980s.

Neoconservatives

Neoconservative analysis of judicial review and the Supreme Court was episodic and occurred in its own intellectual register. Accordingly, its tendency toward originalism was far less pronounced than other forms of conservatism.[66] One prominent example was Nathan Glazer's suggestion that the nation was moving toward an "imperial judiciary" (1975). He noted that the historic reforms mandated by the Warren Court had not been followed by a period of quiescence under the successor Burger Court, as often had occurred in US history. Instead, the Court had continued its interventions into numerous controversial policy areas. Moreover, the Court's new and perhaps now permanent role was positively to command what government must do, and how—not simply to announce limits on government power as before. It now set basic policy in education, housing, prisons, and mental health facilities, as well as environmental standards. Glazer read the new form of judicial review as consistent with the core neoconservative tenet that government overreach was self-defeating.[67]

Other characteristic neoconservative themes were manifested, including minute attention to policy outcomes, skepticism of social science, and diagnosis of a self-serving "new class." Glazer considered the effects when courts intervened in the administration of social services explicitly "from the point of view of the analyst of social policy" but left to others assessment of "the legitimacy and constitutional basis of this expansion of judicial power."[68] Overall there was a negative impact. A primary reason was the judicial discourse of "rights," especially as courts had come to discern or invent new rights. The logic of rights contained a deontological insistence that, in practice, tended to hamstring and erode the discretion, authority, and responsibility of administrators at the grassroots. The stated goals of social policy often foundered as a result.

As with their view of the administrative state, neoconservatives thought that courts too had become overconfident in social science. This mode of inquiry was simply too underdeveloped to justify judicial remaking of so many policies and institutions. Instancing questions about, for example, deterrence and the death penalty, and the requisites of student learning, Daniel Patrick Moynihan concluded that it was "a melancholy fact that, recurrently, even the most rigorous efforts in social science come up with devastatingly imprecise stuff."[69] Moreover, what counted as a "problem" to be solved by social science was inextricably linked to the "pronounced 'liberal' orientation" of practitioners in the various disciplines.[70] But none of these factors had prevented social science from touting its supposed findings and judges from relying on them.[71] Glazer also was blunt about how this hubris had corrupted the judicial process. Reformist judges bent on fixing social ills sought and found justification in social science expertise, even though "in many of these areas of social policy there is no clear knowledge of what the root of the problems is."[72] Thus, all that was really needed was a judge with the will to act upon his conviction "that the services in question are inadequate, or that they violate the constitution, or the laws, or the health code, or equal treatment, or whatever, [and] he will find some expert who agrees with him."[73]

Glazer also squarely associated his criticism of modern judicial review with the "new class," whose lawyers deployed the grammar of rights and the logic of fair procedure in order to litigate against any institution or practice that offended its principles. True to its self-replicating logic, new class litigiousness always demanded more lawyers. And the thrust of its action was always for more managerial intervention to be directed by them: "government should be forced to do more—more regulating, more enforcing, more monitoring."[74]

An important element of the new class dynamic, said Glazer, was that judges often yearned for the approval of the right-thinking, educated public opinion represented by this class. The liberal faculties of elite law schools, the clerks they sent to federal judges, and the amicus briefs judges read, all transmitted new class values to the judiciary. At this elite level, law was "much closer to the 'new class' in its orientation to government and business." Consequently, Glazer concluded that "lawyers are indeed important members of the 'new class,' if we consider that its essential character is to call for, to defend, and to benefit from the expansion of government."[75] His influential study of affirmative action similarly held that judges were swayed in this fashion. They felt "the weight of educated opinion, an educated opinion which is convinced that morality and progress lie on the side of the broadest possible measures of intervention," which in this case meant statistically proportional representation by race in employment, public schools, and housing.[76]

At the end of the 1970s, neoconservatives criticized modern judicial review based on what they understood as constitutional orthodoxy. This stance perforce drew them into quasi-originalist reasoning, though not to the soon dominant lawyerly and jurisprudential version that focused on the nature and object of constitutional interpretation as such.[77] Rather, their arguments were cast in general terms about the true meaning of constitutional principle and tradition, with less and decidedly subordinate consideration of the original meaning of the constitutional text. Glazer's book on affirmative action was again a leading case in point. While mostly sociological and policy oriented, it did argue that affirmative action breached constitutional norms by shifting the governing template from individual rights to racial and ethnic group rights. This shift opposed what was "intended by the Constitution and the Civil Rights Act [of 1964]." The American tradition codified in those texts, said Glazer, was neither forcible assimilation of all groups to one pattern nor formal division of social goods according to group identity. Yet the latter approach now defined affirmative action, and the Supreme Court had encouraged the change in league with federal administrators and new class proponents. Thus was the United States abandoning liberal individualism.[78] Glazer saw a long period of argument and persuasion to reestablish the original principle that most people still accepted:

that "rights attach to the individual, not the group, and that public policy must be exercised without distinction of race, color, or national origin."[79]

A similar argument was made in *Counting by Race* (1979), one of the first studies to criticize affirmative action after the Court's validation of it in the *Regents of the University of California v. Bakke* and *United Steelworkers of America v. Weber* decisions (addressing university admissions and employment, respectively). Terry Eastland and William J. Bennett dug more deeply than Glazer had into American political philosophy, history, and Supreme Court decision making. But even these two Harvard-educated lawyers (who would soon join the Reagan administration) aimed at a general audience and specifically declined to pursue specialized legal analysis.[80] Accordingly, their book described the debate about affirmative action as a contest between the ideas of "moral" and "numerical" equality. The first was rooted in the American political tradition of natural rights. It stretched from the Declaration of Independence to Lincoln, and onward, and they described it in historical detail and at the level of principle. Numerical equality was a policy mandate that required some form of proportional group representation, a process they also traced from its beginning in the 1960s. Their overall argument was that, after having for so long failed to live up to the idea of moral equality in law and practice, the United States was now repeating the error through affirmative action—and this despite and against the achievements of the Civil Rights Movement that had rightly affirmed moral equality. This argument was well researched and powerfully made, but it anticipated originalism only in insisting that the constitutional problem of affirmative action should be resolved by the historically verifiable meaning of individual equality as found in the texts of the American political tradition, including of course the Constitution itself. It was not an originalist argument aimed at the historical basis or jurisprudential manner of the Court's decisions or at constraining the now large role of the Court in the constitutional system. It was more akin to a remonstrance or jeremiad that called on the Court and the broader culture to reconnect with the core principles of American political thought.

Daniel Patrick Moynihan also practiced this quasi-originalist but largely nonjurisprudential mode of analysis in asking, "What do you do when the Supreme Court is wrong?" (1979).[81] Of course his very title premised that the Constitution had a true and recoverable meaning that the Court could misinterpret. Moynihan said that in practice, however, the Constitution was what the Court said it was. If other elements of the polity thought it had erred, they bore the burden of persuading it to change. The methods available included scholarly debate and criticism, ongoing litigation, and sometimes congressional legislation. Moynihan applied this rubric to the Court's First Amendment Establishment Clause jurisprudence, arguing that it was utterly incorrect by originalist standards to have prohibited nondiscriminatory state financial aid to religious schools. The truth was that "the meaning of the term 'establishment' as used in the First Amendment is altogether accessible and quite unchanged.... It is not too much to ask that persons who profess to care about the Constitution take the trouble to learn the language in which it is written."[82] Recurrence to the demonstrable original meaning was but one way of entering a constitutional dialogue that would ideally prompt the Court to change course, but Moynihan was not offering originalism as the basis of jurisprudence. Nevertheless, as with the other neoconservatives examined here, he could not wholly avoid the pull of the originalist idea in a regime based on a written text—even as neoconservative analysis was more fundamentally built around other concerns.

Traditionalists in the Age of Reagan and After

In the 1980s the Reagan administration helped to orient most conservative discussions of judicial review toward the originalist idea. In this context traditionalists defended originalism against both the liberal-reformist trajectory of the Supreme Court and the theorists who rationalized it. An example was Richard E. Morgan's *Disabling America* (1984), a work welcomed by numerous conservatives. Morgan was a traditionalist political scientist who had been observing the Court for decades. Written with wit and insight, the book indicted modern judicial review's abandonment of the Constitution for the "disaffected idealists of the left."[83] Morgan expressed core elements of the traditionalist view: the liberal reform program not only was "in conflict with the attitudes of the majority of Americans" but also frequently failed to root itself in the original meaning of the Constitution.[84] That meaning would not answer all contemporary questions, to be sure, but "to qualify as constitutional interpretation an argument must give weight to what can be known of the intent of the framers and must take into account what previous generations of constitutionally literate persons conceived the words at issue to mean."[85] Morgan catalogued various methods by which liberal judges and theorists sought to emancipate the Court from the limits of the Constitution, noting that the results had offended traditionalist principles (e.g., church-state relations, criminal law enforcement, local control of schools). Judicially created public policy in such controversial areas typically advanced elite liberal opinion through interventions in the private or local realm that could not be effectuated through normal democratic politics.[86]

A similar understanding of originalism was part of Robert Bork's off-the-bench pronouncements while he was a federal judge in the 1980s. Bork was of course a central figure in the development of jurisprudential originalism. During the 1970s he had abandoned his earlier libertarianism (discussed in chapter 10) for a more traditionalist form of conservatism (he eventually converted to Catholicism). Like Morgan (who cited him), Bork took aim at liberal constitutional theorists who rejected originalism as they urged the Court toward new reforms. Liberals' competing antioriginalist theories, despite their complex tergiversations, all ended up advocating the same result: "a constitutional law which is considerably more egalitarian and socially permissive than either the written Constitution or the state of legislative opinion in the American public today."[87] Liberals rejected the public morality of the majority in favor of the "moral relativism and egalitarianism" that dominated the nation's elite, especially its law schools.[88] By the alchemy of modern judicial power "the politics of the professors becomes the command of the Constitution," which Bork described as a process of "gentrification." Hewing to the limited original meaning of the Constitution, and with it the limited role of the judge, would entail the rule of the more conservative public morality of America's legislative majorities.[89]

There was further evidence in the mid-1980s of the traditionalist embrace of originalism. A scholarly symposium, "The State of Conservatism," featured appeals to originalism in brief assessments by two major traditionalist figures (both of whom are treated in more detail later in this chapter). George W. Carey insisted that conservatives' primary goal "ought to be the restoration of the constitutional order bequeathed to us by our Founders." Judicial imposition of liberal ideology had "skirt[ed] the deliberative political processes" and "shown utter contempt for the basic principles inherent to and underlying our constitutional system."[90] M. E. Bradford agreed that traditionalists would benefit from a reversal of "the modern trend in misinterpretation of the Constitution." It was a "palpable absurdity" to claim that "the intent of the Framers cannot be known, that the Constitution is a blank check." Judges appointed by Reagan, Bradford hoped, would recognize that constitutional government under the rule of law necessitated "a Constitution which limits what, through the law, may be attempted."[91]

That thought was put to the test as conservative criticism came together spectacularly with originalism in Reagan's nomination of Robert Bork to the

Supreme Court in 1987. Bork continued to present originalism as a jurisprudence of judicial restraint and as a democratic public philosophy: it left to legislatures whatever contested policy questions had not been clearly resolved by the original Constitution. His opponents crudely but effectively maligned his character and distorted his record while casting originalism as some sort of strange atavism. But what mattered most in this event was not the nuances or limitations of originalism as either jurisprudence or political theory. Rather, Bork had to be attacked and defeated at any cost because his fifth vote in place of the retiring Justice Lewis Powell threatened liberal judicial victories—especially regarding abortion. Although the whole story of Bork's nomination need not be recounted here, originalism featured prominently in the hearings and subsequently endured despite his defeat.[92]

The massive, though skewed, attention to originalism in the Bork hearings further identified it with conservative resistance to judicial decisions that achieved liberal policy results despite legislative majorities or public opinion. For example, the conservative publisher Henry Regnery judged that Bork's nomination had raised such a dishonest frenzy among liberals because his originalism stood in opposition to continual judicial erosion of traditional morality in areas such as abortion, homosexuality, and pornography.[93] A longtime editor of *National Review* described its editorial stance in defense of Bork and originalism as defining its core position on the relationship between conservatism and judicial review. It reflected and reiterated Willmoore Kendall's basic position: the Constitution was originally understood primarily as a mechanism for debating and cohering the "deliberate" sense of the people as expressed through their representatives; it was never intended that the Court twist the text to impose the values of an elite minority on the rest of the nation.[94]

Bork's best-selling *The Tempting of America* (1990) explained that the core issues remained what they had long been: "The orthodoxy of original understanding, and the political neutrality of judging it requires, are anathema to a liberal culture that for fifty years has won a succession of political victories from the courts." The originalist orthodoxy was rejected because liberals "have moral and political agendas of their own that cannot be found in the Constitution and that no legislature, or at least none whose members wish to be reelected, will enact."[95] There was simply no grounding in originalism for the liberal position on such issues as affirmative action, abortion, homosexuality, or the death penalty, irrespective of one's moral or political views about them. Originalism thus prevented the moral or political theories of liberal elites from entering the Constitution under the guise of interpretation.[96]

By the dawn of the 1990s, then, traditionalists had clearly gravitated to originalism to resist modern judicial power's threat to their principles.[97] This trend was confirmed in some of the final work of three major traditionalists, all of whom were deceased by the mid-1990s. Although Robert Nisbet, M. E. Bradford, and Russell Kirk never focused extensively on the topic, each marked the challenge that modern judicial power presented to their respective versions of traditionalist conservatism and to the constitutional order as they understood it.

Nisbet assayed the judiciary from within his focus on the displacement of traditional, communal social bonds by centralized bureaucracy and egalitarianism. The judiciary had become a leading component of the "clerisy" that advanced statist control.[98] His Jefferson Lecture of 1988 invoked the originalist idea as a rhetorical device to measure the distance between the founders' conception of limited government and the invasive reach of the modern state.[99] Nisbet was not a constitutional scholar, but he was an acute social theorist who knew a major shift when he saw it. "The Supreme Court is the single most glittering prize to be had in America for the activism-, reform-, or revolution-seized political mentality," because it could quickly bring results without the bother of the legislative-executive lawmaking process the founders had created.[100] The founders had not intended the Constitution to install judicial supremacy, and "repeatedly the Supreme Court has shown itself to be misinterpreting when it claimed to be interpreting tradition or the real will of the people," all the while generating government control over ever more aspects of American life.[101]

Bradford's Southern Agrarian traditionalism similarly condemned the Court for abandoning the original Constitution. Trained professionally as a literary scholar, he undertook a sustained study of the American founding that culminated in *Original Intentions* (1993). In one sense, the book's title embodied his claim that the state ratifying conventions had never uniformly endorsed the vastly centralized government that some members of the Philadelphia convention had wanted. In another sense, it was intended to situate within the ambit of original meaning the southern traditionalist commitments to local self-government and Christian morality. As noted in chapter 3, Bradford thought that the original, decentralized constitutional order of process and restraint so conducive to southern traditionalism had been "derailed" by Union victory in the Civil War. It had supposedly enabled the federal government to elaborate a rigid egalitarianism from Abraham Lincoln's valorization of the Declaration of Independence. The Supreme Court had played a major role in advancing this deleterious trend against the states and their historic solicitude for religious morality, especially through its First Amendment jurisprudence and the "incorporation" of the Bill of Rights through the Fourteenth Amendment. The Court's numerous modern misinterpretations amounted to a "formula used to transform the Constitution of the United States into a purpose-oriented (that is, teleological) blank check for redesigning American society according to the advanced opinions of our savants."[102] Bradford's originalism sought to restrain the Court's egalitarian interventionism so that the rule of law could shield the moral traditionalism of the South from modern corruption.

Specifically judicial questions attracted little attention from Russell Kirk for most of his career, but that changed as they loomed more ominously over traditionalist concerns.[103] His assessment was rooted in his long-standing and deeply Burkean insistence that the nation had an unwritten constitution of inherited custom, habit, and ideals that surrounded and informed the documentary Constitution. He cautioned conservatives not to eschew the unwritten constitution for a pedantic focus on the text, as if it could replace the prudential judgment about contemporary questions that politics always required. This point made, he affirmed "the necessity for a doctrine of original intent" as a recognition that the Constitution had real and binding meaning. "If this solemn pact we call the Constitution should come to be regarded as a mere formula of words to be set aside for present convenience whenever a temporary majority or strong-willed minority may choose, the peace soon would be breached."[104] Still, Kirk wisely accepted that textual meaning would eventually run out and, similarly, that the framers' intentions could not always be known. Prudent, Burkean adaptation to changed circumstances would always have to draw from the cultural norms of the unwritten constitution.

Within this awareness of the inherent limitations of any documentary constitution, Kirk condemned modern judicial review. Only a "reasonable attachment" to the text as law could prevent "the domination of American public policy, and much of American private life, by the impulses, prejudices, and ideological dogmata of the nine justices of the Supreme Court."[105] Recent constitutional changes had not welled up organically from local communities or been properly deliberated in representative institutions. Rather, it was the Court that was altering the Constitution.[106] Kirk attacked the Court's modern jurisprudence of obscenity and pornography and the allied doctrine of incorporation of the Bill of Rights against the states through the Fourteenth Amendment, because local communities were thereby barred from enforcing traditional moral norms. We shall see presently that he also took part in a lively discussion among traditionalists about the proper relationship between natural law and the Court's role in the constitutional order.

That dialogue emerged most proximately from the presence of such issues in the Bork nomination and in Bork's subsequent best-selling book.[107] He had been criticized by Christian conservatives and Straussians for defending originalism in terms of majoritarian legal positivism.[108] Like the Straussians, whose position the following chapter treats in more detail, traditionalists questioned the philosophic basis of Bork's positivist-majoritarian conception of originalism. Did it entail a rejection of the moral realist foundations of the United States in natural rights? Could it be reconciled to Thomistic natural law, or was his stance necessarily that of a moral skeptic and conventionalist (or perhaps even a nihilist or cultural relativist)? Bork addressed these issues in an exchange with interlocutors in the journal *First Things* in 1992.

He argued that because the content of natural law and its application to changeable circumstances were always matters of prudence and discernment, it was imperative that under the US constitutional system they be left to legislatures rather than judges. This was legal positivism, to be sure, but he denied that he was therefore a moral skeptic or any kind of relativist. "The judge, when he judges, must be, it is his sworn duty to be, a legal positivist. When he acts as a citizen, he, like all other citizens, must not be a legal positivist but must seek moral truth."[109] In another formulation of his position, Bork wrote that "natural law, morality is the stuff out of which legislation and constitutions are made. Positive law is the application of those legal documents to decide specific controversies in court."[110] Judges freed from the constraints of the Constitution might reach morally proper results (or not), but the result could not justify the usurpation of constitutional authority from the legislature. If under the proper forms and limits of the Constitution "the people have enacted an immoral law, it is the judge's duty to enforce it or resign. He may resign because he agrees, as he should, that there is 'morality outside the positive law,' but that morality is not his business while on the bench."[111] Legal positivism need not insist that there was no moral law beyond the positive law. Bork averred that perhaps a "misperception arises because when I speak of the judge's obligation to rid his judging of moral principles not found in the law, some readers think I am denying that there are such principles."[112]

It gradually became clearer that traditionalist defenders of natural law were not as hostile to Borkian positivist originalism as they might first have imagined. Russell Hittinger, who had criticized Bork in the *First Things* exchange, agreed with him that "a natural law theory of law and politics can be distinguished from the issue of whether legislatures or courts should have the principal authority to render the natural law effective."[113] Robert P. George likewise noted that, according to the Thomistic view, the judge's role in relation to the natural law was determined by the positive law of a given regime. It was not a matter derived directly from the natural law. Bork's originalist-positivist limitation on judges was sound, said George, because the Constitution placed "primary authority for giving effect to natural law and protecting natural rights to the institutions of democratic self-government, not to the Courts, in circumstances in which nothing in the text, its structure, logic, or original understanding dictates an answer to a dispute as to proper public policy."[114] Accordingly, "Bork's idea of a body of law that is properly and fully (or almost fully) analyzable in technical terms is fully compatible with classical understandings of natural law theory."[115]

To highlight the fact of disagreement about moral truth or the requirements of natural law in a specific circumstance, as Bork often did, was not proof of their nonexistence, as he understood.[116] Hittinger and Russell Kirk thought that in underscoring such disagreement Bork tended too readily to dismiss centuries of discussion about the natural law or slighted its importance for informed reasoning about the common good. Still, like George, they agreed with Bork that the basic originalist imperative was best cast in terms of the limited constitutional authority of the judge. As Hittinger put it, the strongest version of Bork's point was that "whatever the degree of knowledge about the natural law, the judge must judge within the bounds of the authority conferred upon his office."[117] Kirk too believed deeply that there was a divinely wrought order discernible by the principles of natural law and that it should guide individual conduct and civil lawmaking authority. But from this precept it did "not follow that judges should be permitted to push aside the Constitution or statutory laws and substitute their private interpretations of natural law."[118] It was a misunderstanding of the Constitution to think that judges could use natural law reasoning for settling concrete cases over and against the text of the document, and a misunderstanding of the natural law tradition to think that it was specific enough to admit of such detailed use. When the Court invoked some version of natural law to rule as "an infallible and omniscient body of moral authorities," it could not be reconciled to American principles.[119]

The relationship between morality and judicial review was the topic of a *First Things* symposium published in 1996–97, which produced a massive response and constituted probably the highest-profile conservative engagement with the subject in the 1990s. The journal's editor, Fr. Richard John Neuhaus, and various contributors (not all of whom would identify themselves as traditionalists) pointedly raised the themes traced in the foregoing discussion.[120] Major controversy ensued in part because the symposium questioned whether religious believers who adhered to traditional morality could any longer assent in good conscience to the regime of modern judicial power. A few previous contributors to the journal resigned from their association with it. Neoconservatives especially were critical of the symposium for raising the issue of legitimacy. They thought it had been done in an incendiary fashion, though they somewhat obtusely conflated rejection of modern judicial review with anathematization of American government as a whole. In turn, several observers detected strains or even a crack-up of the conservative coalition. To the extent that *First Things* had included and been sympathetic to neoconservatives, the symposium suggested growing disagreement on sociocultural and moral issues that perhaps betokened a more traditionalist (or "paleoconservative") direction. Without getting bogged down in either minute distinctions of intellectual-political categorization or the full anatomy of the symposium controversy, here the analysis focuses on why conservative adherents of traditional morality thought the judiciary had become dangerously unmoored from the original Constitution.

The *First Things* editors wrote in their introduction that for decades the judiciary had been usurping the role of democratic institutions and ruling without the consent of the governed. This violation of the separation of powers was undertaken to advance secular liberal policies on the role of religion in public life, abortion, homosexuality, and the then dawning issue of euthanasia. In reaching its decisions in these areas, the Court had not only violated the Constitution but also "declared its independence from morality." Currently "morality—especially traditional morality, and most especially morality associated with religion—has been declared legally suspect and a threat to the public order."[121] This development pressed the age-old question of obligation when the positive law as announced by government officials violated the moral law as understood in the Western tradition. Such fundamentals were at stake amid the contemporary "displacement of a constitutional order by a regime that does not have, will not obtain, and cannot command the consent of the people."[122]

The editors cited several passages in recent Supreme Court decisions that illustrated the pathologies of the new regime. One was what became known as the "mystery" passage in *Planned Parenthood v. Casey* (1992). Reaffirming the constitutional right to abortion while reworking and abandoning much of the trimester logic of *Roe*, the Court said abortion should remain protected because "at the heart of liberty is the right to define one's own concept of existence, of meaning, and of the mystery of human life." Traditionalists regarded this passage as announcing a fundamentally illimitable and antinomian concept of self-legislation incompatible with established moral norms. Similarly, in *Romer v. Evans* (1996) the Court overturned a Colorado referendum that had forbade the treatment of homosexuals as a specially protected class in state or municipal law. The Court wrote off the moral views of the Colorado majority, informed by millennia of Judeo-Christian teaching, by declaring that "laws of the kind before us raise the inevitable inference that the disadvantage imposed is born of animosity towards the class of persons affected." In *Lee v. Weisman* (1992), the Court overturned a nonsectarian prayer by a rabbi at a public school graduation as an establishment of religion forbidden by the First Amendment. Any state action derived from "an ethic and morality which transcend human invention" was tantamount to an imposition of religion on others. Moreover, in *Casey* the Court had quite directly staked the legitimacy of constitutional government itself on the people's willingness to accept the Court's continued defense of abortion. Such acceptance was supposedly required by the rule of law because the American people's "belief in themselves as such a people [under the rule of law] is not readily separable from their understanding of the Court invested with the authority to decide their constitutional cases and speak before all others for their constitutional ideals." This conflation of abortion with the rule of law and what the Court said about the Constitution appalled the *First Things* symposiasts and their allies.[123]

The symposium took up *Casey's* invitation to measure the legitimacy of modern judicial review, but used the original meaning of the Constitution as its standard. Indeed, the symposium was offered in the originalist idiom as an attempt to "revive the republic bequeathed us by the Founders."[124] The modern form of judicial power was far more ominous than mere complaints about an errant or "activist" decision here or there. Rather, "judicial usurpation involves a redefinition of the constitutional order" that forced "the question of whether ours is still the form of government constructed by the Founders."[125] Reflecting on *Casey's* nexus of abortion, constitutional authority, and judicial legitimacy, Neuhaus held that in fact "the Court's legitimacy is undermined when it is perceived that the Court is not interpreting but is rewriting the Constitution."[126] Robert Bork complained, "The idea that the Constitution should be interpreted according to that original understanding has been made to seem an extreme position. That is convenient for those who want results democracy will not give them, but the truth is that violation of original understanding ought to be the extreme position."[127] Robert George concurred that the proper response to judicial usurpation was "to reassert the true principles of the Constitution and to reaffirm our allegiance to this nation, under God."[128]

As noted above, traditionalists associated with *First Things* were concerned that in moving beyond the restraints of the Constitution, the judiciary was secularizing and degrading the nation's religiously rooted morality. Within months of the symposium, another best-selling book by Robert Bork marked his full embrace of traditional-cum-cultural conservatism. He saw American cultural decline across a range of subjects, attributing it to the amoral hedonism and leveling egalitarianism of the liberal cultural elites who came of age in the 1960s. The judiciary was the "enforcement arm" that served to "advance the agenda of modern liberalism."[129] The Supreme Court's First Amendment jurisprudence in particular was well beyond the confines of original meaning. Almost any form of lewdness or obscenity could be displayed in public, while most expressions of even the mildest theism were banned.[130] As Neuhaus wrote in the symposium's immediate aftermath, nonestablishment was now "taken to mean that religion be confined to the strictly private sphere of life; that wherever government advances, religion must retreat. And today government advances almost everywhere."[131] The journal's editors thought that "perhaps the most ominous development is the growing explicitness with which the judiciary rejects any moral law superior to the law of the state, as defined by the courts." On the contrary, Neuhaus averred that any enduring society needed some understanding of god. But with the encouragement of its courts the United States seemed to be abandoning the old god for the new. "If we accept the jurisprudence of recent decades, the public square is filled with the god of the Leviathan State, whose laws are definitively framed by the courts, and by the little gods of the autonomous, imperial Self, for whom liberty is indistinguishable from license."[132]

On one hand, the symposiasts and *First Things* more generally were confident that the nation's long-established Judeo-Christian moral culture opposed the Court's onslaughts against it and the Constitution. On the other hand, it sometimes appeared to them that many Americans were content to be governed at the Court's behest by the new gods of postmodern solipsism—whether from apathy or approval (or both). Several respondents to the symposium, and the editors, observed that the lack of any sustained or successful resistance to judicial usurpation bespoke at least such acquiescence, and perhaps even tacit consent. Everyone involved understood that the law always had an educative effect: what public officials such as judges deemed constitutional shaped citizens' conception of acceptable behavior. Despite the general agreement that the Court was acting without constitutional warrant, there was a grim recognition that many people were too politically disengaged or ignorant to recognize the usurpation—or that they were not in fact morally offended by the policy results.[133]

George W. Carey offered a similarly fundamental and pessimistic assessment. He had been observing American politics for decades, and his conclusions serve as a fitting summation of the growing dismay among traditionalists at century's end. Carey agreed that the extent and duration of judicial power now presented basic "regime"-level questions about the survival of the original constitutional order. The Court had long been an active participant in the radicalization of rights and equality that he thought had been adumbrated by Lincoln and then extended by Progressive ideology through the New Deal and the 1960s.[134] In retrospect it was clear that *Brown v. Board of Education* (1954) "provided the opening for the forces of progressivism to use the Court as a vehicle to reinterpret the Constitution and our tradition in a manner congenial to their basic tenets."[135] Modern judicial power was "an ideology hostile to the basic principles of the Founders' Constitution." In fact it was tyrannous from the perspective of the founders' political science.[136] This distortion meant that the original Constitution was dying.[137] On another occasion, Carey said that the victory of modern judicial power (in addition to other factors) meant that the "Philadelphia Constitution is dead because, even though the institutions and processes it established are still there, its character—one might say its 'essence'—has changed to such an extent that today it bears only a nominal connection to its 1789 version."[138]

If the original Constitution was dead or dying, Carey said that the new progressive liberal constitution of judicially enforced rights–as-autonomy, centralization, and leveling egalitarianism had not yet produced a full theoretical account of itself. Nowhere was there something on the order of *The Federalist* papers that could persuade the public of the new regime's acceptability at the level of both philosophy and politics. Instead, its adherents were "seemingly content to operate within the shell of the older regime, pretending as if they are its true heirs."[139] The result was increased strife and recrimination as the two constitutional regimes, with their conflicting ends and claims to legitimacy, abutted and contested each other. This was a sad and dangerous "state of 'limbo' where the most basic questions about the placement of authority cannot be answered, not even by reference to the Constitution itself."[140]

Conclusion

Brown's challenge to the constitutional status quo provoked originalist rejoinders from segregationists, but the originalist idea ran deeper than their claim on it. A broad array of traditionalists across the decades found no justification in history or theory for an active, reforming court that too readily overturned majority decision making based on strained or plainly invented renditions of the Constitution. Traditionalists thus made originalism an organizing concept in their critique of modern judicial power, while neoconservatives stood at a greater distance from this discourse in their more policy-oriented criticism. In addition, the policy results of numerous unpersuasive judicial decisions were disastrous from both the traditionalist and neoconservative points of view. The judiciary had become a major force in disrupting self-government and the religiously informed culture of community and moral self-restraint that America had historically sustained at the local level. Perhaps most blatantly, the Court's invention of a constitutional right to abortion and subsequent staking of its own legitimacy on the nation's respect for the decision was especially destructive for both the Court and traditional culture. Traditionalists thus retained their understanding of a natural and moral order but denied that judges legitimately could invoke it to violate the Constitution. In the last decade of the twentieth century many of them were concluding mournfully that modern judicial power was so ingrained in American constitutionalism that their protestations were of little effect.

CHAPTER NINE

Straussians and Modern Judicial Review

Leo Strauss taught that politics was best understood by studying a regime's deepest principles as revealed especially at moments of founding and grave crisis. His students returned to thinkers of the past, tried to understand them as they understood themselves, and then sought "useable" political lessons for the present. This prescription guided the first Straussians to study the American founding and American constitutionalism.[1] They anticipated originalist thinking by inquiring into the true meaning of the Constitution (and its limits). Others eventually gravitated to originalist discourse to limit modern judicial review. An early theme was that the founders had intended the Court to moderate and ennoble the regime beyond its low but sturdy liberal foundation. The Court was keenly placed both to limit and to educate, thereby preserving the regime by defending its principles and perhaps by retrieving virtues from beyond the liberal horizon. Later Straussians rethought and sometimes abandoned this approach in response to the Warren and early Burger Courts and liberal constitutional theorists. This shift generated a more textualist and judicial restraintist form of originalism, along with some pointed interventions in the originalist jurisprudential debates of the 1980s and 1990s.

Storing and Diamond

Herbert Storing and Martin Diamond oriented later Straussians toward the originalist idea. Storing straightforwardly focused on "the great architectural principle of the American government as it was conceived by its framers" and more particularly delineated "the ends of any system for electing the president, as the framers saw them."[2] His study of federalism said that "the 'basic intent of the founders' is indeed the place to begin." As Strauss himself had taught, past thought need not be accepted uncritically, nor would it necessarily provide ready-made answers to contemporary political questions. But before making any such determination, it was necessary "to investigate not only the intention of the founders but also the reasons that lay behind that intention."[3]

Similarly, Diamond's influential response to the Progressive attack on the founding was a study of *The Federalist* subtitled "A Reconsideration of the Framers' Intent." He too allowed that the founders' thought may have been mistaken, or perhaps even finally outmoded by modernity, but agreed that, before judging, it was first "absolutely necessary to understand what they said, why they said it, and what they meant by it."[4] Observing that the politics of the 1960s often resembled a "debate on the intentions of the founding fathers," he warned conservatives that their current anti-establishment, majoritarian politics was no more compatible with the original Constitution than Progressivism had been earlier in the century.[5] Still, conservatives were attacking "the abuse of the power of judicial review," not the idea of law or the Court itself. To call for better interpretation was "to presuppose the possibility of true judiciality and hence to deny the fundamental claim of sociological jurisprudence."[6] By the mid-1970s Diamond was even more directly originalist when bemoaning most scholarly consideration of federalism for not having even attempted to engage the original meaning of the Constitution. While constitutional interpretation had always been contested, "there formerly had always remained at least some notion that the Constitution had an objective meaning and had some binding authority upon us. [Absent] some sort of fixed, objective, intelligible, and accessible meaning, we cannot say that we govern ourselves under a constitution." Again, the notion of adaptation was likewise part of American constitutionalism, "but for 'it' to be adapted to changing circumstances, 'it' must first exist; that is, it must have some persisting meaning of its own which is to be aptly applied in those changing circumstances."[7]

Walter Berns and the Court of Virtue

Walter Berns was the first Straussian to study the Court extensively. He argued that First Amendment jurisprudence had strayed from the founders' sounder understanding of speech and public morality informed by religion, though he was not yet writing explicitly in terms of original constitutional meaning. He understood the United States as a modern regime of natural rights and consent that the Court could help perpetuate by incorporating ancient political wisdom. Properly instructed, the Court could infuse America with the virtue and prudence needed to avert the self-destruction of liberal constitutionalism—even if judges must sometimes push beyond the confines of the Constitution to do justice.[8]

Berns argued that both libertarian free speech absolutists and majoritarian judicial restraintists were trapped within the liberal horizon. Neither could distinguish between speech that was intrinsically good or bad. Against the libertarians, Berns insisted that not all free speech was good speech; against the majoritarian restraintists, he insisted that a standard other than public opinion was needed to limit bad speech. The root of the problem was that liberalism's basis in rights and consent lacked the capacity for substantive judgment about which speech conduced to a good life in a good regime. Reality inevitably intruded to show that "freedom and justice are not always compatible."[9] With respect to speech, "one cannot say that a law that grants people the freedom to speak is a good law unless he examines what people do with that freedom."[10] First Amendment jurisprudence within the confines of liberalism was thus ill-equipped to contend with the claims of virtue or justice or with how to perpetuate the regime.

Calling on Aristotle, Berns thought that the Court could help reorient American law beyond its liberal, Hobbesian individualist roots. Contemporary First Amendment law had been so defined by the conflict of individual rights versus majority will that it ignored the law's responsibility to foster virtues that preserved the regime. The problem was exemplified by obscenity, which was not political speech and should be more forcefully restricted, and by communism, which might be proscribed if it advocated the destruction of the regime.

In these areas (and others) Berns dissected decisions of the 1940s and 1950s to illustrate the dilemmas and limitations of liberal free speech doctrine. All along, the Court had been slighting the preliberal principles of virtue and prudence necessary for the very survival of the United States, as well as its aspirations for justice. It is striking just how much responsibility for improving

American liberalism Berns gave the Court. Even amid the limits of a written constitution, a judge might have to "transcend the system of which the law or ruling forms a part" and invoke criteria "beyond the precedents and beyond the Constitution in deciding many cases coming before him . . . [and] look to justice, to 'the ideal relation among men.'"[11] In a move that is jarring given Bern's later advocacy of a judiciary restrained by the cognizable original meaning of the Constitution, here he favorably invoked Charles Evans Hughes's notorious dictum that "'the Constitution is [necessarily] what the Supreme Court says it is.'" In practice, this meant that the Court's purpose was not to make "justice conform to the Constitution. It is rather to make the Constitution conform to justice."[12] Judicial interpretations of the First and Fourteenth Amendments especially "permit, but do not guarantee, a further opportunity for wisdom and prudence to be introduced into the American Constitution." The regime could be improved because "judicial review provides virtue with, as it were, a final chance."[13] As is shown below, Berns subsequently revised his estimation of how much latitude the Court should have.

The Court as Republican Schoolmaster, Judges as Statesmen

First-generation Straussians did not immediately follow Berns in focusing on the Supreme Court.[14] While a few saw a subtly moderating legal-judicial statesmanship in William Blackstone, and more directly in Alexis de Tocqueville, the role of the Supreme Court was not yet frequently considered in this light.[15] Soon, however, Tocqueville's famous observations on the topic helped several early Straussians to see the Court as a teacher of republican virtue. Tocqueville had argued that lawyers' attention to forms, procedure, and the weight of precedent could restrain, rationalize, and elevate democratic public opinion. Federal judges in particular "'must not only be good citizens and men of education and integrity'" but also "'statesmen; they must know how to understand the spirit of the age, to confront those obstacles that can be overcome, and to steer out of the current when the tide threatens to carry them away.'"[16] Ralph Lerner argued that leading architects of the federal judiciary shared the Tocquevillian view. Judges were originally intended to take on the role of "educator, molder, or guardian of those manners, morals, and beliefs that sustain republican government."[17] Lerner adduced substantial evidence from the founding era, including debates at the Philadelphia convention, a close reading of *The Federalist*, and federal judges' charges to grand juries in the 1790s.

Since the United States was founded on the democratic principle, *The Federalist* was necessarily subtle in supporting a judiciary that could limit and educate the popular will. Still, Publius was said to have advocated courts as "a locus of high statesmanship—cautious, politic, yet able and willing to cope with popular excesses." Publius's treatment of the judiciary, Lerner argued, intimated that judges "would view themselves as teachers of republicanism using the text of the Constitution and the national laws, interpreted in a judicial spirit of moderation and fairness."[18] Salutary outcomes were possible but never guaranteed. In naming what became for several Straussians the project of the Court as "republican schoolmaster," Lerner acknowledged this contingency: "Teaching is inseparable from judging in a democratic regime. But whether the Justice has taught well" was "highly debatable."[19]

The republican schoolmaster idea was readily apparent in early Straussian studies and was often used interchangeably with the idea of judicial statesmanship (as expressed by Tocqueville and in Lerner's original exposition of the subject). For example, Paul Eidelberg argued that the founders' original intent was a Constitution that instantiated an Aristotelian "mixed regime." The separation of powers and the composition, selection, and responsibilities of various offices introduced principles of justice that checked and balanced the modern, natural rights–derived basis of American popular sovereignty. The Supreme Court could restrain democratic opinion and reinforce the principles of the regime as it elaborated and applied them. Manifesting the statesman's virtues of prudence and judgment in the service of justice, judicial opinions were a form of political rule that taught citizens what the Constitution required and more firmly attached them to it.[20]

A similar conception of the judicial role was notable in the first Straussian study of Chief Justice John Marshall by Robert K. Faulkner. He saw Marshall as operating in a modern liberal regime of natural rights and consent rather than in Eidelberg's Aristotelian mixed regime, but similarly described Marshall as fulfilling the founders' original intent in practicing judicial statesmanship. Marshall fulfilled the founders' design by safeguarding life, liberty, and property under the rule of law while also exhibiting "traces of an older and nobler aristocratic republicanism" in his thought.[21] Marshall did not attempt to redirect the liberal American regime toward ancient virtue, nor did he think that it was possible to do so. But he did seek to limit and shape democratic opinion via the Constitution so that the regime might be preserved and perpetuated. Adverting to Lincoln's recommendation in the Lyceum Address (1838) that America make reverence for the laws its political religion, Faulkner wrote that "if Marshall's sobriety would never let him recommend a 'political religion,' his judicial endeavors went toward much the same instruction."[22] Marshall understood the delicacy of preserving a modern regime of rights and consent by going somewhat against its grain while also linking this endeavor to the original meaning of the Constitution as the basis of national politics. "Statesmanship employing rhetoric is still required. It must be of a kind that constructs the political edifice on the foundations provided by common opinion, and thus is able to shape the public mind," thereby creating "a kind of shield defending the Constitution, so far as rhetoric can."[23]

These early versions of the republican schoolmaster project were theoretical and historical inquiries that did not directly address contemporary Supreme Court jurisprudence. Others eventually followed Berns in criticizing the Court's approach to obscenity under the First Amendment, most notably Harry M. Clor in 1969. He explicated recent decisions, the fundamental philosophical question of the law's relationship to morality, and the extent to which the United States as a liberal state could concern itself with this issue. Clor defended judicial statesmanship and called for censorship more stringent than that permitted by the Court's increasingly libertarian decisions.[24]

Following Aristotle (and citing Berns), Clor too said that law inevitably shaped the character of citizens and that it should therefore do so in ways that supported the regime instead of undermining it. America needed the public spiritedness of citizens, a virtue rooted in the sacrifice of immediate desires or prejudices, as well as the citizen morality that the law helped to form. Thus the older republican responsibility of forming citizens remained despite the nation's deeply liberal and individualistic orientation. From these premises, judicially enforced censorship of some obscenity was both politically necessary and constitutionally permitted under the original meaning of the First Amendment. It cultivated the wise use of freedom among "republican citizens [who] are subjected to a mild form of moral discipline so that they will not have to be subjected to physical coercion. If this is a paradox, it is one which republicans can and ought to accept."[25] Clor carefully weighed how best to define obscenity, and he was well aware that any centrally imposed or draconian formula was both impossible and unworkable. But he nevertheless insisted that the law and the Court must curtail obscenity in order to promote "public standards of civility." These were particularly appropriate in "a regime of liberty" because "ethical and political prerequisites" were needed for its preservation rather than "the mere extension of individual rights and privileges."[26]

Like many other observers, Clor also saw the "moralizing role of law" exemplified in the Supreme Court's desegregation decisions. They had helped change attitudes about race and encouraged the landmark civil rights legislation of the

1960s. Here the Court had shown that the law "can point the way toward moral improvement by holding up a standard somewhat higher than that upon which many persons are acting."[27]

A few Straussians continued to champion the Court as a republican schoolmaster into the 1980s, often by invoking the idea of judicial statesmanship. Gary J. Jacobsohn devoted a book to the subject (1977), adopting the generally Tocquevillian conception sketched above.[28] He opposed the dominant pragmatism and legal realism derived from Oliver Wendell Holmes Jr., because its rootless evolution lacked adequate continuity with established norms. It could not foster statesmanship in the American grain because it rejected the nation's definitive commitments to natural rights and a Constitution of fixed, settled principles.

Still, Jacobsohn accepted the idea that judicial statesmen must adapt constitutional principles to the complexities of modern society. The tired categories of activism versus restraint could not capture how statesman confronted new circumstances with the regime's deepest principles as guiding ends. More or less "activism" or "restraint" might be required at a given moment in order to reinforce the political wisdom embodied in the Constitution. Any necessary activism was still in a profound sense preservative in that, "unless judges act so as to impose restraints on whoever chooses to innovate on that wisdom, they are not performing the high tasks of statesmanship."[29] Jacobsohn thus averred that authentic judicial statesmanship was fundamentally originalist at the level of theory and could be in the actual decision of cases, as well, because it involved "intensive examination into the intent of those who gave us the Constitution."[30] Judicial statesmanship made "available to us the wisdom of the founders, which is to say, the original will of the people."[31]

Jacobsohn's work was insightful and typically Straussian in seeking to house the idea of judicial statesmanship within the original meaning of the Constitution. It was likewise so in affirming the United States as a regime of natural rights, in rejecting the Holmesian-Progressive-pragmatic onslaught, and in tendering the statesman's prudence and wisdom as the way to preserve and adapt the nation's mostly liberal Constitution. Consequently, Jacobsohn's exemplar of twentieth-century judicial statesmanship was somewhat surprising: Charles Evans Hughes's majority opinion in *Home Building and Loan Association v. Blaisdell* (1934). That decision upheld a state law that extended the time for debtors to repay creditors in order to avert home foreclosures—in essence a "stay" law of the kind that shielded debtors in the 1780s and prompted inclusion of the Contract Clause in the Constitution. But the Court held that this law was permissible as a legitimate exercise of the state's police power during the Great Depression.

Jacobsohn argued that Hughes sought both to abide by and escape the authority of the founders and the original meaning of the Contract Clause. Hughes insisted that as a response to novel conditions the law was "consistent with the spirit and purpose of the constitutional provision, and thus [could] be found to be within the range of reserved power of the State to protect the vital interests of the community."[32] For Jacobsohn this was a "model of judicial statesmanship." Hughes struck just the right balance between change and continuity, eschewing "judicial absolutes" while also respecting "fixed political-constitutional principles," adapting the Constitution "to changing socio-economic conditions" without abandoning "the vision of the founding fathers."[33]

This interpretation showed just how expansive judicial statesmanship could be. Justice George Sutherland's dissent had pointed out the founders' condemnation of stay laws while affirming the traditional understanding of constitutional interpretation as the attempt "to discover the meaning, to ascertain and give effect to the intent, of its framers and the people who adopted it."[34] Like Sutherland, many observers at the time and since took *Blaisdell* as an indication of the demise of the established constitutional order and its conception of interpretation, not the statesmanlike salvation of either.[35] Some Straussians treated later in this chapter also rejected *Blaisdell* (and in some instances Jacobsohn's defense of it). They were unconvinced that it could be reconciled to the founders' solicitude for the sanctity of contract as an expression of the natural right to property, or to the original meaning of the Contract Clause, or to the traditional understanding of what it meant to interpret the Constitution as law.[36]

Other defenses of judicial statesmanship sought to distinguish it from the judicial supremacy that had come to typify the Court since the 1960s. The latter was an illegitimate monopoly on interpretation that displaced the older and healthier constitutional dialogue among all government branches and citizens. John Agresto urged the Court to cease this usurpation but nonetheless remain the "institutionalized theoretician of the nation." At its best the Court could articulate constitutional principles "as they unfold themselves in time."[37] Harry Clor also defended judicial statesmanship, just as the nomenclature of the debate between "interpretivists" and "noninterpretivists" was morphing into the conflict between originalism and its opponents. The interpretivism-cum-originalism of Robert Bork and Raoul Berger overly confined the discretion necessary for judicial statesmanship, said Clor. But he rejected even more emphatically the eruption of post–Warren Court liberal constitutional "theory" that betrayed the idea of judicial statesmanship by constantly urging the Court to ever greater reform. The abounding varieties of liberal theory had seemingly lost all contact with the Constitution and the political tradition that sustained statesmanship under its aegis. The possibility of judicial statesmanship depended on judges to persuade citizens that decisions grew from the regime's constitutional principles, if not always from a strict reading of the constitutional text.[38]

A more extreme and therefore marginal type of judicial statesmanship was part of Sotirios A. Barber's call for an "aspirational" constitutionalism that fulfilled the aims of the Preamble. Barber attacked what he took to be the moral skepticism of judicial restraintist originalists, holding that the founders did not exclude "moral judgments from decisions in constitutional cases."[39] Judges had no monopoly on constitutional interpretation, though the judiciary supposedly had the reason needed to educate the nation about the requirements of constitutional values and the meaning of rights.[40] Judges and all public officials should strive to interpret the Constitution according to "the best feasible conception of justice" within the circumstances they confronted.[41] In practice this meant that judges would frequently take an active role in expanding rights, and perhaps even in inventing new ones.[42] In Barber's account, "not every fair-minded observer has to believe that the Warren Court offended Publius's constitutionalism."[43]

By the late 1980s Barber's conception of judicial statesmanship was an outlier among Straussians, and the idea in general was waning. A brief but important introduction to Straussian analysis of the judiciary described Barber as encouraging the polity, and judges in particular, to range "far beyond the Founders' vision." Barber's judges were to advance new rights in a "moralistic agenda without any duty of deference to popular will as expressed through the elected representatives."[44] Before turning to Straussians who criticized or rejected judicial statesmanship and the Court as republican schoolmaster, it is important to address an important version of this project that nonetheless opposed modern judicial review.

According to Paul O. Carrese, Montesquieu was the crucial early modern source of a subtle argument for judicial statesmanship wherein judges could gradually and subtly liberalize and moderate regimes that were beginning to base themselves on natural rights and consent. Carrese traced Montesquieu's deep influence on William Blackstone, who so influenced the American founders. Publius and Tocqueville leavened Montesquieu's effort with the quasi-Aristotelian virtues of aristocratic character and prudence then still available in the common law. Carrese's detailed textual support for this argument stands as the most thorough claim that the founders pursued a "republican schoolmaster" project rooted in canonical works of political thought. This concept and the complementary notion of "judicial statesmanship" informed his analysis and helped to express its conclusions.[45]

Crucially, however, Carrese further argued that Montesquieu had made possible the radical contemporary judicialization of politics. The door that he left ajar was kicked open by Holmesian legal realism and pragmatism, which derived most basically from modernity's skeptical rejection of nature for history and progress. The corrupt form of judicial review that followed brought chronic legal instability, continued erosion of the separation of powers, and the decline of republican government. Modern America had lost the "distinction between judicial statesmanship and judicial legislating" that applied particularly to moral issues.[46] The now overly judicialized constitutional system needed the older, more moderating and ennobling form of judicial statesmanship—which had better understood its own limits. With respect to moral issues, but not only there, "we judicialized matters that, while in need of moral principle and order, nonetheless properly lie either largely or completely outside the competence of courts of law, in the domains of legislative and executive power."[47] A truer constitutional statesmanship would better "promote the community's concern for such issues in a way that fosters deliberation and a comprehensive public policy."[48]

Criticism of the Schoolmaster-Statesman Project

Having diminished over time, the republican schoolmaster–judicial statesmanship project was vigorously criticized as it ebbed. This development responded to the Warren Court and its successors and, likewise, to liberal commentators who urged further expansion of modern judicial power.[49] A leading figure here was again Walter Berns, whose shift has been noted by others.[50] In 1976 Berns expressly criticized the Court as a " 'republican schoolmaster,' " saying that too often it allowed "sophistry to be brought to bear on public law, and there is inevitably more sophistry than philosophy at large in the intellectual world."[51] The Court's First Amendment decisions had only worsened: it was still undermining the decency, self-restraint, and reasoned discourse that nurtured republican government. But now Berns was more convinced that the Court was incapable of doing otherwise with the discretion it possessed. "Instead of remembering or conserving, the Court has been inclined to see its role as an innovator or pathfinder."[52] By 1987 Berns was echoing Raoul Berger in complaining of "government by judiciary." He called for the republican schoolmaster project to return to the founders and early Supreme Court justices for "instruction in constitutional government rather than in the constitutional law of our times."[53] A decade later he pronounced the schoolmaster project a failure. Instead of orienting its decisions to the ends of the regime and the social conditions that sustained those ends, the Court systematically favored radical individualism and secularism. As "schoolmaster" it "has taught us to despise the very idea of censorship," and the result was a precipitous decline in public morality. Berns wondered, "Can people be trusted to govern others if, by acting on every impulse, sexual or otherwise, they prove to be incapable of governing themselves? Some of us might live long enough to learn the answer."[54]

He was not alone in reevaluating the schoolmaster project. Ralph Rossum agreed that in several areas the Court had "not always realized this noble intention" and that at times "what it has taught the citizenry has served more to jeopardize than to sustain republican principles."[55] An egregious example (also noted by Berns) was *Cohen v. California* (1971). The Court upheld the display of a four-letter expletive emblazoned on the jacket of a protester who was on public property, based in part on the proposition that "one man's vulgarity is another's lyric." If it was true, as the Court here taught, that "all political doctrines are be tolerated because all are equal and none is erroneous, this in large part deprives the citizenry of the ability to evaluate regimes and serves to undermine their attachment to republican government."[56] Another critic urged advocates of judicial statesmanship, including Straussian confrères, to better appreciate that the line distinguishing "statesmanship and partisanship in judicial matters was no more precise than in other political matters." The whole enterprise of judicial statesmanship ought to be abandoned because it came "dangerously close to the full-blown ideological commitment to a living Constitution" as defined by judges.[57]

A lengthy attack on judicial statesmanship noted that it had been encouraged by Straussians as well as liberal theoreticians. To the extent the idea had derived from Tocqueville, argued Matthew J. Franck, it ought to be abandoned in favor of closer adherence to the constitutional text as delineated by Justice Joseph Story's originalist rules of interpretation. Franck's reading of *The Federalist* similarly found no invitation to judges to act as statesmen in ways that might usurp the constitutional authority of the executive or legislative branches. In fact, Publius issued a dire warning to judges in recommending impeachment as the remedy for any such overreach.[58]

Franck subsequently distinguished between prudence as found in Aristotle and jurisprudence as related to a written constitution featuring the separation of powers. Prudence was the statesman's virtue and properly associated with the "deliberative" form of political rhetoric. Neither this virtue nor this rhetoric was appropriate to courts in the US system. Within Aristotle's categories, the opinions of American courts could be described as "forensic" rhetoric: they expressed judgment according to the standards of conventional justice established by the laws and the Constitution. Judicial opinions could even be described in Aristotle's terms as akin to "epideictic" rhetoric to the extent that judges could explicate, reaffirm, and laud the regime's principles so that citizens grew more attached to them and the regime. But American judges were not intended as true statesmen who used prudence and "deliberative" rhetoric to persuade the regime toward certain actions or choices as new circumstances arose. Based on these distinctions, it was possible to defend the Court as a "republican schoolmaster" only insofar as it reaffirmed constitutional principles, but not if it violated the separation of powers or confused its ambit with statesmanship in the deepest sense.[59]

While Franck's distinctions suggested that Straussian discourse on the judiciary had perhaps all along conflated concepts whose separation would have provided clearer criteria for evaluating judicial decisions, by the end of the 1990s few Straussians were sympathetic to judicial review. The Court might once have functioned properly as a "republican schoolmaster," but in recent decades it had become more of an "astigmatic schoolmarm." Now it saw the constitutional order only from its own limited perspective, which tended toward judicial supremacy and which derogated the other branches and the well-formed citizen's capacity to affirm the constitutional order.[60] Ralph Rossum concluded more bluntly that Straussians had shown for decades that the Court had "failed abysmally" in its role as republican schoolmaster by routinely ignoring the original meaning of the Constitution and traducing the natural rights principles behind it.[61]

Responding to "Legal Liberal" Constitutional Theory

Straussians criticized liberal theorists who supported expansive judicial review. An early example was Robert K. Faulkner's critique of Alexander M. Bickel, the most significant heir of the Holmesian skeptical tradition of legal realism and pragmatic constitutional evolution.[62] Bickel's well-known early work had confidently posited judicial statesmen who vindicated the nation's deepest values in circumstances of their own prudential choice. But the excesses and errors of the Warren Court had convinced him that this approach was too easily corrupted by willful judges bent simply on achieving the results they wanted. His last book—*The Morality of Consent* (1975)—invoked Edmund Burke to affirm more gradual change and a deliberative process of constitutional colloquy in which the Court participated and by which society slowly adapted and improved. But there too he explicitly rejected the natural rights–social contract theory of the American founders, nor did his legal realist roots permit him to put much stock in the limits of a written constitution. His Constitution remained one of "open texture" and "evolving principle."[63] Faulkner judged that Bickel was unable to detach himself from the Holmesian legacy. He accepted "too easily the constitution of 'open texture,' traipsing abjectly after an open and indefinite historical process."[64] The result was a jurisprudence that tended "to replace the fixed rights and powers of constitutionalism not with other definite powers, but with an indefinite legal-intellectual colloquy by which principles (and thus principled powers) are evolved."[65] Thus Bickel ended very close to where he had begun: a cautious form of judicial statesmanship that underscored "how politic judgment should guide those who interpret the Constitution." But this now seemed inadequate in light of the vast reach of modern judicial review that had so appalled Bickel too. Bickel's cul-de-sac proved again the necessity of showing "both judges and political leaders the wisdom of abiding by the Constitution."[66]

If the cautious Bickel had come to this pass, what did Straussians make of later, pro-judicial liberal theories? Such "legal liberalism," they argued, was inconsistent with the founders' political philosophy of natural rights and irreconcilable to the republican political science of the Constitution. Such was the response, for example, to the work of John Hart Ely, who argued that the Court should elaborate the logic of *United States v. Carolene Products* by actively "clearing the channels of political representation" and "facilitating the representation of minorities." But along the way Ely rejected the founders' view of natural rights and justified the Court's controversial rulings on legislative apportionment, voting rights, and obscenity. For Straussians this vastly expanded conception of representation was well beyond the separation of powers and the limited textual meaning of the Constitution. The tenor of their response was well expressed by Lane V. Sunderland: Ely's theory "departs from the framers' constitutional theory" and in essence "asks the Court to act as a continuously functioning constitutional convention."[67]

Numerous other "legal liberal" justifications for modern judicial review emerged in the late 1970s and throughout the 1980s. Often they were intricately rendered, arcane, and abstract. We need not supply their details or fully reconstruct every response by Straussians, who consistently rejected liberals' too powerful role for the Court. One extensive analysis of this "tangled undergrowth of theory" found that its several varieties implored judges to effectuate "an unwritten but morally controlling Constitution, one that must take precedence over the written Constitution of 1787." This "'advocacy scholarship'" had only an attenuated and sometimes nonexistent connection to the actual Constitution, which served only as a site for the enactment of theorists' and judges' preferred political outcomes. "The result of their efforts has been the rise of a constitutionalism bereft of the Constitution."[68] Another study concluded that liberal theorists routinely premised the emancipation of judges from original constitutional meaning. Thus, in the terms of *Federalist* 78, they encouraged the judicial exercise of political will rather than legal judgment.[69] Law professors were telling the Court to "translate their ideas of what is good for the country into constitutional law."[70] Now far beyond the limited judicial role envisioned by the framers, the nation had endured "a generation of constitutional lawyers who feel obligated to spin out elegant (but obviously absurd) theories in the vain attempt to provide some valid textual basis for the Court's Fourteenth Amendment decisions."[71]

A frequent target of Straussian ire was Ronald Dworkin's influential call for a "fusion of constitutional law and moral theory."[72] Dworkin wrote that courts should protect the new über-right to "equal concern and respect" by applying their contemporary "conceptions" of the founders' basic "concepts." Liberated from time-bound textual restraints, judicial review could exercise "fresh moral insight," typically by vindicating rights, broadly defined, against the majority.[73]

Straussians routinely rejected Dworkin's theory, sometimes harshly, as utterly incompatible with the founders' constitutionalism and its concern to limit the power of all officials. Dworkin offered "judicial hegemony" by overconfidently privileging judges' capacity for moral reasoning.[74] Dworkin's elemental error was to think that judges were somehow immune from the natural human tendency "to confuse justice with one's perception of justice." To have asserted "that judges above all other mortals are capable of such virtue" was utterly unrealistic.[75] The founders' more sober estimation of human nature was less trustful of any official power. In practice Dworkin called for a "government of courts," ignoring "that the human propensity to overreach must be opposed not by exhortation to perfection but by limits on the power invested in any individual or group."[76]

To take only one more example, Dworkin's foundational concept-conception distinction fared poorly among Straussians. It was "a way of selectively ignoring original intent without blatantly appearing to do so." As a piece of intellectual legerdemain it enabled Dworkin to retain original intent as a term "while emptying it of any operational meaning."[77] Even if the distinction were conceded arguendo, why should judges rather than legislatures determine the present-day conception of a constitutional concept? Moral reasoning about a range of permissible but contestable constitutional meaning was not an inherently judicial task. In fact, the US system of representative government offered a strong argument for the courts deferring to legislatures in cases of arguable constitutional meaning.[78] Walter Berns accordingly concluded that Dworkin's "way of taking rights 'seriously' treats the Constitution frivolously and ultimately will undermine its structure."[79] Thomas Pangle was more derisive in an early review that later Straussians frequently cited. While Dworkin was often elusive and imprecise, he wrote, it was clear enough that he would supplant the actual constitutional order with one of his own imagining that enforced quintessentially liberal positions on a range of contemporary policy issues. Disjoined from the American regime, Dworkin offered as a serious philosophical inquiry about rights and constitutionalism what was merely "a systematic account of his personal conception of fairness and his own policy preferences as a conforming liberal professor of the 1970's."[80]

Straussians knew that Dworkin built on John Rawls. The latter's famously abstruse and complicated theory, modified over the years, sought initially to displace utilitarianism with a form of social contract theory that could generate a rationally defensible concept of justice independent of putatively transhistorical natural rights. Rawls said that rational individuals in an imagined "original position," placed behind a "veil of ignorance" about their station in a future society, would avoid risk in constructing the principles of government. Consequently, they would agree to a contract of equal liberties for all, and, more controversially, this contract would specify that any social or economic inequalities (a) be of the greatest benefit to the least advantaged and (b) be attached to offices and positions that remained open to all on the basis of equal opportunity. The overall gist of the system, to summarize somewhat crudely, was to guarantee both a large sphere of individual liberty as autonomous choice and a method for improving the condition of the worst off. This conception of "justice as fairness" could then be implemented and regulated by a sequenced movement from the original position through constitution making, legislation, and rule application (adjudication). Rawls reworked his original effort, eventually attempting to ground and justify contemporary liberalism amid the modern conditions of philosophical pluralism and disagreement. This revision made it clearer that courts would play a substantial role. As "exemplars of public reason," they could advance Rawls's conception of justice without recourse to older, exclusionary "comprehensive doctrines" that rested on inadmissible claims about religion, nature, or truth.[81]

Straussians found Rawls's theory massively misconceived. Its analytic abstractions slighted the considerations of human nature and political life that had accrued in the canonical texts of Western political thought, while its political prescriptions ignored the American founding, the doctrine of natural rights in the Declaration of Independence, and the political theory of the Constitution.[82] These initial criticisms treated Rawls's relation (or lack of it) to the political tradition leading to the Constitution, rather than the institutions the Constitution itself created.

As Rawls's theory developed, more Straussian attention focused on its proposed role for the judiciary. One careful analysis concluded that the judiciary was subtly and somewhat evasively cast as an ongoing constitutional convention. Judges were to guard the principles of justice expressed in the sequence of agreements that followed from the original position, recapitulating the reasoning of people along the way, and bringing Rawls's constitutive principles of justice to bear as adjudications arose. The rationality of legal argumentation and courts' characteristic orientation to procedure and detachment made them the institution best suited to this task. Thus, despite his hesitations and qualifications, Rawls's theory "opens the door for an expansive use of judicial power in the service of justice as he defines it."[83] Courts that could overturn statutes based on Rawls's principles of justice "would be both the architect of the constitutional framework and a part of that framework; they would define their own function, which is practically to say they would be without limits" other than their own acceptance and articulation of those principles.[84] This was a powerful judiciary indeed, so much so that "it is hard to see how the concept of a judiciary that sets its own limits is compatible with any definition of constitutionalism as limited government," or with adequate room for majority rule.[85]

The role of "public reason" in Rawls's emended theory clarified that judges would not be overly constrained by the constitutional text or other traditional legal materials. Michael P. Zuckert saw "a judicial approach with much activist bite," despite Rawls's heightened concern for constitutional interpretations that could be regarded as legitimate. Rawls had at last encountered, but not solved, a problem coeval with constitutionalism: authoritative law required a moral justification, yet law cannot simply be collapsed into the moral pronouncements of those who make and apply it. There was no eluding the "question of *whose* moral conceptions are to judge and justify positive law." Constitutional legitimacy demanded that a political program or concrete adjudication be linked to and justified in terms of the received meaning of the actual Constitution.[86]

A book by David Lewis Schaefer (his second on Rawls) more harshly stated a similar conclusion, declaring that "the effectual truth of Rawls's doctrine is a recipe for irresponsible government-by-judiciary."[87] "Public reason" seemed designed particularly for courts to effectuate Rawls's philosophy rather than abide by the original design of the Constitution. Rawlsian judges, who "impos[ed] a 'higher' vision of justice on a recalcitrant, because insufficiently enlightened, citizenry," were not likely to "be deterred by counsels of moderation and respect for the constitutional text."[88] Judges' moral-cum-constitutional pronouncements would govern the benighted masses, and when necessary, new rights would be invented and original constitutional meaning ignored. "Our judges are encouraged by Rawls and his cohorts to contemn the supposed moral immaturity of their fellow citizens and to rewrite our Constitution in a way that undermines the people's right of self-government."[89] On this view, it was unsurprising that Rawls's theory attracted liberal law professors who wanted to displace the older natural rights constitutionalism of the founders that obstructed their goals.[90]

The Turn to Textualist-Restraintist Originalism

Criticism of both liberals' pro-judicial constitutional theory and the earlier schoolmaster-statesmanship approach implied a more textualist and judicial restraintist form of originalism. In many respects this shift grew logically from the orientation that Diamond and Storing had given Straussian constitutional thought. Indeed, Straussian analysts of the judiciary had always understood themselves as abiding by and preserving the original Constitution—even within the schoolmaster-statesmanship view. Likewise, from Berns and Clor onward, the many Straussian studies of the First Amendment premised that "recovering the original meaning" of the founders' text was the "first task of constitutional scholarship."[91] This context led some (but of course not all) Straussians comfortably to include themselves in the developing discourse of originalism that in the 1970s began to call for a more restrained judiciary.

In 1976 Walter Berns was once again likely the first Straussian to use the originalist idiom in criticizing modern judicial review, though he did not make elaborate distinctions among associated concepts. He wrote variously of "the original understanding of the [First] Amendment" and "what the Founders understood to be the purpose of the provisions respecting religion," and that the amendment "was not intended to require government to be neutral between religion and irreligion."[92] His indictment, of course, was that "the Court doesn't care what the original intention was."[93]

Berns influenced Gary L. McDowell, as had Raoul Berger. McDowell was thinking in originalist terms while critiquing both judicial statesmanship and liberal theory, as he had both before and after his advancement of originalism in the Reagan Justice Department (as noted in the introduction to part IV). The best response to modern judicial review was a recovery of "the idea that the Constitution was intended to be a permanent means, a fixed arrangement of institutions and processes that will issue in safe popular government." Interpretation began with the text of the document. If it was unclear, "the first place to look is to the Founders: what was their intention?"[94] McDowell's seminal book on equity jurisprudence (1982) embodied the originalist idea. It argued that changes in the rules of civil procedure, combined with the Warren Court's reformist impulse, had resulted in equitable remedies that made social policy which positioned the judiciary well beyond the originally intended separation of powers. Equity was understood at the founding "to offer relief to individuals from 'hard bargains'" but had become "the asserted judicial power to draw the line between governmental powers and the rights of 'discrete and insular minorities' and to create remedies for past encroachments against whole classes of people."[95] Close examination of even this somewhat arcane jurisprudential topic revealed that the Court had dangerously accrued political power beyond the original Constitution.

As originalism gained force in the 1990s, it informed two extended Straussian rejoinders to modern judicial review. Matthew Franck opposed the "imperial judiciary," wherein judges as pseudo-statesmen announced new rights according to their own conceptions of justice or natural law. His book proposed that "the text of the Constitution and its meaning as originally understood provided durable standards for a critique of present-day judicial behavior."[96] Lane Sunderland less directly invoked originalist terminology in condemning the modern combination of judicial supremacy and judicial rights creation, but agreed that "the historical record and theory of the Constitution are consistent with a judicial power narrower than that of setting forth absolute rules for all branches of government and deciding cases on the basis of unenumerated rights."[97] The actual, original Constitution was cast aside when contemporary theorists invited the Court "to enforce rights that they see as missing in our system of government."[98]

Such studies were cast in terms of the limited role originally intended for the

Court, as measured by the political theory of the founders and the thinkers who influenced them. Straussians did not often undertake empirical historical research on the original meaning of particular constitutional provisions. When they did, however, it was clear that they thought original meaning could be recovered and should inform and limit judicial interpretation.[99]

Straussians paid particular attention to Thomas Hobbes. His founding of liberalism on natural rights and consent was convincing, though Straussians agreed that the American founders had properly replaced his absolute sovereign with constitutionally limited government. Several analyses underscored Hobbes's strict enforcement of the contract by which individuals relinquished their unlimited natural right of self-preservation upon leaving his posited state of nature. Each individual gave up his "private judgment" of what was good or bad and agreed to create a sovereign authority that enforced peace by holding all equally to the same rules. People could agree on the need for individual security through civil peace, though less often on ultimate questions of good and bad.[100] The founders adapted this general view, as refined especially by Locke, by insisting that sovereign authority should be limited by established law, as opposed to the unlimited commands of Hobbes's Leviathan.

As in Hobbes, truly constitutional limits did not permit appeals to truth or justice to redefine the original terms of the social contract. That would be to reintroduce "private judgment" as the basis for rule (or exemption from rule) against what people had previously consented to. Several Straussian analysts worked this view of Hobbes into their originalist or quasi-originalist defenses of the written Constitution. As Hobbes had made clear, and because of his influence on the Constitution, judges were subordinate to the sovereign will. Their purpose was to apply what that will intended, not to invoke their own sense of justice or right.[101]

Some Straussians' move toward originalism carried a jurisprudential claim about the nature and object of interpretation as such. Most of the writers analyzed above did not treat this subject in great detail. Usually they cited the rules of interpretation in the treatises of the English jurist William Blackstone (1765–69) or Supreme Court justice Joseph Story (1833), or both. Both of them had delineated methods for discerning the lawgiver's intent and overall purpose, which they understood as the content and limit of the law.[102] So too did Christopher Wolfe, whose work stood as the most developed Straussian intervention in the jurisprudential debate about originalism in the 1980s.[103]

Wolfe, who began writing about the topic at that time, had by the mid-1990s produced three books, plus a revised edition of his major work, *The Rise of Mod-*

ern Judicial Review.[104] He studied how the founders had understood the nature of interpretation and argued that by the mid-twentieth century it had been transformed into a discretionary act that was nearly indistinguishable from legislation. At the founding there was "general agreement that existed on the question of *how* to go about interpreting the Constitution, what the rules of interpretation were." This underlying agreement did not produce unanimity on questions of interpretation but rather the acknowledged criteria for resolving them. "The most fundamental assumption shared by all was that the Constitution did have an ascertainable meaning—one given by its authors—and that that 'original intention' was the end or object of constitutional interpretation—it was authoritative."[105] Interpretation properly understood, "traditional" interpretation, was originalism: the discernment of the original meaning of a text that had been ratified by the sovereign act of consent. Modern faux interpretation was an act of juro-legislation that first abstracted the terms of the text from the underlying political theory of the Constitution, then raised them to a high level of generality beyond anything contemplated by their creators, and finally gave them specific content to resolve cases according to what the judge thought was right or just.[106]

Wolfe showed how the concept of interpretation linked directly to the characteristic Straussian concern with the Court's capacity to preserve or undermine American constitutionalism. Like other Straussian originalists, he judged that the new form of judicial review was overly assertive and ultimately illegitimate. It undermined and even displaced the polity's capacity for self-government. The truth was that original constitutional meaning could be known; that to interpret was to ascertain it; and that at times it would run out or be indeterminate. Accordingly, "judicial review should not be very common under a proper standard of review." When there was interpretive uncertainty, "constitutional disputes ought to be worked out in the ordinary political process. There is no sound reason for delegating the decision of such issues (i.e., where there is not clear constitutional mandate) to the least democratic branch of our government."[107] Wolfe thus encapsulated the movement of many Straussians toward a conception of originalism that sought to restrain the Court more than had the older understanding of it as a statesmanlike republican schoolmaster.

Attacks on Originalism as Vulgar Positivism

The textualist-restraintist form of originalism thus attracted Straussian support, but it also raised another set of concerns that were central to the overall Straussian perspective. As defended most prominently by Raoul Berger, Robert

Bork, William Rehnquist, Edwin Meese, and Antonin Scalia, originalism denied that legitimate judicial decisions could be based on appeals to natural law or natural rights that went beyond the constitutional text as originally understood. In this lawyerly and positivist form of originalism, judges should defer to legislative majorities; they should not appeal to transhistorical standards of nature not delineated in the positive law of the Constitution's text. As discussed earlier, some Straussians affirmed this view. But was this kind of originalism divorced from—or ignorant of—the doctrine of natural rights contained in the Declaration of Independence? And what role should that doctrine have in any form of originalism that offered itself as the voice of constitutional conservatism?

These questions were asked and answered in forceful attacks on positivist originalism by Harry V. Jaffa, the leader of "West Coast" Straussians. He condemned at length every figure listed above (excepting only Berger).[108] Originalism came to Jaffa's attention because it had successfully linked constitutionalism with conservatism, challenging his long-standing goal of basing conservatism on natural rights and consent as announced in the Declaration and explicated by Abraham Lincoln. Jaffa repeatedly professed himself a loyal originalist, but insisted that positivism was wrong about what the founders originally intended and, consequently, that conservatism was ceding to liberalism the language of humanity and justice.

Positivist originalism was philosophically impoverished because, despite its majoritarianism, it lacked an account of what originally made consent, and with it *limits* on majority rule, the basis of legitimate government. Bereft of this base, originalism merely accepted the subjective values that a majority happened to prefer. Jaffa countered that, according to the logic of the Declaration that informed the Constitution, only human beings as natural equals, who were not rationally justified in ruling anyone but themselves, could consent to the creation of a government. And no rational person would consent to a government that was empowered to treat him or her despotically as if they were an unequal or less than human.[109] In sum, then, "the government cannot derive from the people powers that individuals did not consent should be exercised on their behalf."[110]

It was in this sense that the principles of the Declaration grounded the positive law of the Constitution, and thus that the "natural law principles are present *within* the Constitution, as elements of the *positive law* of the Constitution, and in accordance with the *original understanding* of those who framed and those who ratified the Constitution."[111] Jaffa advanced this view with relentless explications of the infamous decision in *Dred Scott v. Sandford* (1857). Only through the Declaration properly understood—and not from within the text of the Constitution—could the Court have reached the morally correct conclusion that a slave of African descent was a human being entitled to his liberty under the Due Process Clause of the Fifth Amendment. That Chief Justice Roger Taney had not done so, and that Lincoln would have, made Jaffa's point (and Lincoln's) that the Declaration was the necessary key to interpreting the Constitution.

Jaffa was far more concerned to reorient conservatism toward his version of originalism than to critique Supreme Court decision making.[112] Nonetheless, he said that *Brown v. Board of Education* would more properly have been decided in terms of the Fourteenth Amendment's overcoming of *Dred Scott* by the constitutionalization of the concept of human equality.[113] He likewise let it be known, though usually in passing, that neither *Roe v. Wade* nor any legal approbation of homosexuality could be reconciled with natural law and natural human equality as he understood them.[114]

As noted above, Jaffa extensively elaborated his position against prominent lawyerly originalists. He similarly did so in his decades-long public argument—some would call it a feud—with Walter Berns, his erstwhile friend who had moved closer to positivist originalism.[115] Several of Jaffa's fellow West Coast Straussians, while always respectful of his learning and fully endorsing the Declaration as the basis of American political life, remained leery of the potential for judicial abuse in his approach. It could liberate judges to invoke the laws and rights of nature as a way of eluding constitutional limits: there was simply no way of guaranteeing that Jaffa's more circumspect view would prevail. As Ralph Rossum put it, "In our law schools today, there is at work a version of Gresham's Law: bad natural rights teachings have all but forced out good natural rights teachings." At the time of the founding the positivism of an Antonin Scalia would have endangered constitutionalism and individual rights, but now it was preservative because "the principal threat to democracy is not majority rule trampling on the rights of minorities, but the Court itself threatening the right of the majority to rule itself."[116] Michael M. Uhlmann agreed with Jaffa that "the world would undoubtedly be a better place if federal judges were sympathetic to Abraham Lincoln's arguments about natural right and the American founding," but then asked, "How comfortable would [Jaffa] be vesting modern judges with the authority to interpret the meaning, say, of 'the pursuit of happiness'?"[117]

Hadley Arkes agreed with Jaffa that legal positivist originalists had mistakenly dismissed authentic reasoning based on the first principles of the regime in their zeal to reject specious modern claims about "human dignity" or "equal concern and respect" by such figures as William Brennan and Ronald Dworkin. These claims had the form of an appeal to what was right by nature but bore no relation to the substance of the founders' political science or the limits it imposed on courts.[118] The positivist originalists' conjunctive dismissal of both bodies of thought had cut off judges from a true jurisprudence of natural right, which Arkes saw best represented in the twentieth century by Justice George Sutherland.[119] Without a retrieval of Sutherland's kind of thinking, Arkes concurred with Jaffa, American conservatism was hitched to a positivist-majoritarian constitutional discourse that slipped inevitably into moral relativism. As such it would be unable philosophically to defend the transhistorical moral basis of the United States as a regime.

Again like Jaffa, Arkes was not immune to the concern of fellow Straussians that judicial recourse to precepts "beyond the Constitution" was both irreconcilable to the founders' conception of the judiciary and ill-advised amid the era of modern judicial power.[120] Nevertheless, Arkes participated in the *First Things* symposium analyzed in the previous chapter, agreeing that the modern Court was reaching momentous decisions with little guidance from the original meaning of the Constitution. Legislative authority had "been withdrawn from the people themselves, or the 'consent of the governed,' and transferred by the judges to their own hands."[121] Arkes correctly predicted that the acceptance of homosexuality as a legally protected category in *Romer v. Evans* (1996) would become the predicate for the Court's creation of a constitutional right to gay marriage.

He was similarly concerned that America's supposedly religious culture seemed unperturbed that the beliefs of conscientious Christians and Jews were increasingly subject to legal proscription. Quiescent public opinion might be jolted awake and then moved to political deliberation if it understood that *Roe v. Wade* mirrored *Dred Scott*. Notably, he called on Jaffa's analysis of Lincoln to make this point: both decisions had contravened the principles of the Declaration by misinterpreting the Constitution to allow one class of people to control and tyrannize another. *Dred Scott* had held that white people could enslave descendants of Africans because they were lesser beings without rights; *Roe v. Wade* had created a legal "private right to kill" the unborn. In both cases, the Court had not applied the idea of a right as something equally held by all, but instead allowed a "right to do wrong" (in Lincoln's words). Both slavery and abortion were crises of the regime in that judges had appealed to the idea of a right in a way that allowed some people to crush the rights of others. Accordingly, Arkes urged (again with Lincoln) that the time had come for citizens and the other branches of government to realize that the Court had never been intended as the only or supreme arbiter of constitutional meaning (judicial supremacy). It had always been perfectly legitimate for others to interpret the meaning of the Constitution and to deliberate about matters of moral consequence.[122] Arkes even thought that a certain rapprochement with legal positivism could advance this goal. A rigorously positivist approach could detect when a legal text failed to justify a decision that was demanded by deeper constitutional principles. That revelation could either compel judges carefully to construct a principled argument beyond the strict limits of the text, or apprise citizens and legislators that their own deliberation and action were required because the text and its fair implications had run out.[123] Arkes hoped that in this way both courts and politics in general might be brought more fully within the discipline of the nation's founding principles.

Conclusion

By the end of the twentieth century there was no general accord about judicial review among Straussians. They disagreed about whether a legal positivist form of originalism could be reconciled with a different form that more directly acknowledged the preexisting principles of natural right underlying the Constitution. Nevertheless, as this chapter shows, Straussians consistently understood themselves as originalists of one kind or another, even as they argued among themselves. This was true of the schoolmaster-statesmanship approach insofar as it was plausible to argue that the founders' had originally intended some version of it. There was a closer link to jurisprudential originalism in the work of textualist-restraintists, who found no justification in the founders' text or political science for the modern Court's wide-ranging role. The Straussians who attacked the positivism of textualist-restraintist originalism similarly claimed the mantle of original meaning, insisting that the principles of natural law and natural right should always inform judicial decision making. Accordingly, a brief but invaluable study correctly concluded that Straussians were originalists who, amid their varying specialties and disagreements, sought to "to identify and preserve the Constitution's original meaning" even though it might not accord with contemporary judicial decisions—or with the views of other Straussians.[124] The definitive Straussian focus on political founding and regime principles ensured that claims about the proper role and extent of judicial authority would necessarily be expressed in terms of original constitutional meaning. Straussians knew that, in the United States, political acceptability and constitutional legitimacy usually mandated this kind of argument.

CHAPTER TEN

Libertarians and Modern Judicial Review

Toward the Imperative of Litigation

Major figures brought libertarian constitutional theory to increased prominence in American law schools in the last few decades of the twentieth century. Libertarians typically claimed that the original meaning of the Constitution justified assertive judicial protection of individual rights, and they usually rejected classic notions of "judicial restraint" associated with other forms of conservatism and originalism. Libertarians also readily participated in litigation that advanced their conception of rights, and by the end of the century most other types of conservatives, whatever their ultimate stance on the legitimacy of modern judicial review, also felt compelled to litigate in defense of their views.

Precursors: Before the Mainstreaming of the Libertarian Legal Movement

Libertarian constitutional thought was relegated to "fringe obscurity" in the decades immediately after the Great Depression.[1] As we have seen, general libertarian ideas did endure in criticism of the New Deal order. Only in the 1970s did distinctly libertarian analysis of judicial review coalesce; it then emerged more distinctly in the 1980s.[2] Before focusing on that process, it is worth a brief glance further back to consider earlier libertarian responses to the momentous constitutional changes of the New Deal. Although such efforts were isolated (and sometimes obscure), they did anticipate the direction of several later theoretical developments.

One reliable barometer was the second series of *The Freeman*, a small libertarian journal that began publishing in 1950. Several articles from that era considered the New Deal's victory over the old constitutional order with a sense of loss and dismay. The Constitution had been "mutilated" and "twisted and bent to serve the purposes of collectivism."[3] Yet these libertarians urged a rally to the original Constitution, which was authentically if not wholly libertarian, rather than capitulation to the New Deal order. From their perspective it was the people of the current age who had failed the Constitution. A more libertarian future required that the Constitution "be restored to its original purity and strength."[4] This basic and quasi-originalist idea was never wholly absent from libertarian thought.

A more learned presentation was Friedrich A. Hayek's major work from this time, *The Constitution of Liberty* (1960). While conceding that the pre–New Deal Supreme Court had sometimes overstepped its bounds, Hayek still affirmed judicial review. American courts could restrain legislatures by ensuring that they acted on principles that were generalizable in future circumstances. It was this conception of law and government that had motivated opponents of Franklin Roosevelt's "court packing" plan of 1937. Thus the pre–New Deal form of liberalism, whatever the errors of the old Court, had enabled Americans "to defend freedom by defending their Constitution."[5] Hayek also forecast, though only briefly, the direction of much later libertarian theory in highlighting both the Ninth Amendment and the Privileges or Immunities Clause of the Fourteenth Amendment. Despite both having sadly lapsed into desuetude, he argued that they had been originally intended to empower courts to vindicate rights and limit legislation without having to rely on a specific portion of the constitutional text.[6]

Robert Bork advanced a similar line of thought in 1968, just before his shift from libertarianism to a more traditionalist and conservative originalism. He attacked the Warren Court's opinions as sloppily reasoned and unconvincing and, therefore, as posing a threat to the rule of law and the Court's legitimacy. Yet the traditional guides of constitutional text, history, and precedent appeared unable to restrain the Court. Needed was a theory congruent with the basics of the constitutional order that could both discipline and justify the Court's actions. Bork argued that the Court normally should keep to monitoring the processes by which representative institutions made law, but should intervene actively when individual rights were violated. Nor should such "legitimate activism" be bound by the text of the Constitution. Bork buttressed this proposition with Justice Arthur Goldberg's use of the Ninth Amendment in his concurrence in *Griswold v. Connecticut* (1965). Although Justice William O. Douglas's majority opinion was disappointingly "shallow, murky, and rhetorical" in deriving a constitutional right of privacy from the supposed "penumbras" and "emanations" of the Bill of Rights, Bork nevertheless agreed that judges trained in the common law could "construct principles that explain existing constitutional rights and extrapolate from them to define new natural rights." This approach had the potential to "radically" reshape judicial review as new rights proliferated and, perhaps, to reverse the New Deal's demotion of economic and property rights to second-class status. Anticipating later libertarian theorists, Bork suggested that "the new concept of rights becomes, indeed, something roughly describable as a presumption in favor of human autonomy." He cautioned that his theory might prove impracticable and that in cases of deep uncertainty democratic norms still required judicial deference to the legislature. But at this point his libertarian instincts allowed for far more judicial innovation and assertiveness than what he later supported.[7] Nevertheless, Bork's attempt to derive a libertarian theory of judicial review from decisions of the Warren Court was merciless in criticizing its actual reasoning.

Likewise, one of Richard Epstein's first published articles attacked *Roe v. Wade* for its notoriously imprecise justification of a constitutional right to abortion. The decision was "symptomatic of the analytical poverty possible in constitutional litigation."[8] Moreover, while the Court had ostensibly declined to define when life began, it nevertheless insisted that the state had an interest in protecting the "potential life" of the fetus in the first trimester of pregnancy. In logic and practice this move appeared to be an admission of the personhood of the fetus. It thus raised for Epstein the likelihood that abortion violated the "harm" principle of John Stuart Mill that was so dear to libertarians: the state should not restrict someone's liberty unless its action prevented harm to others.[9] Eschewing any such inquiry, the Court had simply enacted its own views into law and truncated the states' varying attempts to wrestle with the abortion issue on their own.[10] Epstein concluded that the Court had dealt a severe blow to the right to life, its own legitimacy, and the constitutional order.

Murray Rothbard offered a more fundamental and radical rejection of the Court and the Constitution, as was his wont. Even the continual judicial invention of new rights did not prevent his declaration that both judicial review and constitutionalism more generally had failed to stop the growth of government. He agreed with John C. Calhoun's conclusion that the Court was an agent of central state power and thus fated inevitably to ratify the expansion of that power, not its limitation. Rothbard's own preferred solution, as in so many others areas, was abolition of the government monopoly on law in favor of a system of custom and competition among private courts or all-purpose "legal services" firms.[11]

That view was too radically utopian for libertarians who hoped to advance their principles through judicial review in the extant constitutional order. This goal came to define most libertarian constitutional theory and was clearly indicated by a conference on the philosophical basis of rights held in 1979.[12] It was organized by Roger Pilon, who subsequently held posts in the Reagan administration and founded the libertarian Cato Institute's Center for Constitutional Studies in 1989 (the institute itself was founded in 1977). His basic aim for the conference was to advance libertarianism via the "'rights explosion'" then evident in both judicial decisions and academic philosophy. His own contribution sought to firm up the moral rationalist and Lockean foundations of rights understood as the property of human individuals. Rights so conceived were "intended precisely to stand athwart the utilitarian calculus, to brake the democratic engine" for the sake of individual autonomy. Here Pilon did not directly focus on legal issues, but he intended his description as "a model for legislators, and in particular for jurists; it is the 'higher law' background to the positive law."[13]

Specific attention to judicial review came from Edwin Vieira Jr., who condemned post–New Deal jurisprudence for validating the legislative omnipotence that inevitably overwhelmed the natural rights of individuals. Far preferable was the activist and more antistatist judicial review of the old Court. It is telling that at this early date the response to Vieira's staunchly libertarian approach anticipated later criticisms from more traditional and originalist critics of modern judicial review. Thus David F. Forte argued that Vieira's "vision of the Supreme Court rigorously enforcing an ideology of natural rights" would subject a "massive amount of legislation [to] judicial annihilation." Such governance was "as far removed from the intentions of the framers as one can imagine." The solution to excessive government, said Forte, was "the wisdom and experience of a free people in the exercise of their democratic prerogatives," not "activist judges."[14] Prominent libertarians were undaunted by the intensification of such criticism as they elaborated their defenses of judicial review over the following two decades.

Three Leading Advocates of Judicial Review:
Siegan, Epstein, and Barnett

Bernard H. Siegan (1924–2006) wrote the first major work of modern libertarian constitutional analysis, *Economic Liberties and the Constitution* (1980), which influenced numerous later commentators. Before becoming a law professor, Siegan had practiced in Chicago. From that experience he wrote *Land Use without Zoning* (1972), which challenged municipal regulations in favor of market ordering. He held several advisory posts in the Reagan administration and was nominated for a seat on the Circuit Court of Appeals for the Ninth Circuit, but the Senate Judiciary Committee voted against him along party lines in 1988.[15]

Siegan did nothing less than attack the fundamental constitutional settlement of the New Deal, rejecting both judicial deference to economic regulation and the displacement of the old Court's substantive due process, liberty of contract jurisprudence. The New Deal Court had improperly endorsed a bifurcated system of review as expressed most famously in *United States v. Carolene Products* (1938). The new jurisprudence treated regulations of economic rights as presumptively valid so long as they had some rational basis, but held to a higher standard any laws touching personal rights, including those it had begun to create. Siegan condemned this development as "judicial abdication" of the traditional duty "to protect economic liberties."[16] Property rights were personal rights, and the New Deal had wrongly demoted them.

Siegan argued in self-consciously and insistently originalist terms.[17] He examined the centrality of property rights and limited government in the Anglo-American tradition, the natural rights–social contract basis of the American founding, and the judicial development of due process protections for property and economic rights before the New Deal.[18] On his reading, the Progressive bogey of *Lochner v. New York* (1905) was rightly decided and consistent with the foundational principles of the constitutional order.[19] Moreover, in a subsequent study of the Fourteenth Amendment, he argued that its original meaning sustained *Lochner*'s derivation of liberty of contract from the antebellum doctrine of vested property rights. The time had come to "rehabilitate" this once infamous decision, which for Siegan was an originalist effort that required use of historical evidence beyond the bare text of the Constitution.[20]

Siegan's forthright originalism governed his understanding of interpretation itself. While accepting that textual meaning might run out and that interpretation could be indeterminate and even subjective, the aim of the interpretive enterprise was always to discern original meaning, to fulfill "the will of the authors of the fundamental document and of its amendments without damaging the fabric of society."[21] Abiding by the framers "intent and purpose" in novel circumstances was difficult but not impossible, nor did a good faith attempt to do so mandate "reversal of all judicial decisions contrary to original meaning and understanding."[22] Rather, a court's attempt to link its decision to original meaning was a way of limiting its own discretion and achieving the rule of law. "A meaningful legal system cannot exist if those who follow recognized procedures in putting their intentions in writing cannot expect that those intentions will be honored and observed."[23] There was no mistaking Siegan's commitment to originalism as traditionally understood, even as he ran together concepts and methods that its later developers would minutely parse.

Siegan's originalism dictated the Court's true and proper role, he said, while modern judicial power in its full extent was beyond what the founders had intended. The Court was not designed to affirmatively legislate and thereby accrue governing authority, or to redistribute private property and public resources. Nor should judges make up new rights whose limits they determined, as in the case of abortion. On the contrary, "the Framers' generation viewed the judiciary as another means for achieving libertarian objectives of government. The Framers surely never would have accepted judicial review if they thought it would have been used in an antilibertarian fashion."[24] The modern Court had mistakenly "wandered from its mission" to undertake "departures from original design."[25]

While seeking to cabin modern judicial review, Siegan nevertheless proposed standards that would reverse the New Deal's presumption of constitutionality for regulations of property, occupations, and contractual relationships. The government should have the burden of proof for justifying interference in these areas, while courts should have substantial leeway to consider the motivations and justifications offered by a legislature for any such action (as they did in the *Lochner* era). Only this form of judicial review could again give economic and property rights the same protection as other rights. Summarizing his position in true libertarian fashion, Siegan concluded that "the presumption that the state is correct in curtailing people's activities can only be accepted in societies where restraint is normal—those which, unlike ours, equate government direction and control with the public interest."[26]

Siegan had only briefly noted the expansion of the government's power of eminent domain under the Takings Clause of the Fifth Amendment ("nor shall private property be taken for public use without just compensation"). Soon thereafter Richard Epstein argued in *Takings* (1985) that courts should reinvigorate property rights to restrict the post–New Deal state, which he too judged to be unconstitutional.[27] More comfortable with describing himself as a "classical liberal" than as a libertarian (whose intense individualism he regarded as unrealistically extreme), Epstein always appealed to the principles underlying the Constitution and to the logic of originalism. He became probably the nation's most influential libertarian-cum–classical liberal theorist, treating at length widespread topics in private law, constitutional law, and legal philosophy. This chapter concentrates on his attempt to link the idea of takings to both originalism and to increased judicial intervention. These were his core positions as libertarians assessed modern judicial power in the 1980s and 1990s.

Takings placed the Constitution in the tradition of Anglophone liberal, rule of law constitutionalism. Beginning with Hobbes's conception of human nature and the consequent imperative of order for the security of rights, Epstein then followed the modifications wrought by Locke's conception of property and social contract. The latter was expressed especially well in William Blackstone's famously expansive legal definition of property: it was "that sole and despotic dominion which one man claims and exercises over the external things of the world, in total exclusion of the right of any other individual in the universe." It directly implied "the free use, enjoyment, and disposal of all his acquisitions, without any control or diminution, save only by the laws of the land." From this broad base, Epstein expanded the definition of a taking by a long list of compensable harms, so that individuals could be shielded from government's reach.[28] A taking should no longer be narrowly restricted to the classic case of land taken for a public road or building. Now it should include a variety of regulations and other government actions. For example, regulations that required access or entry to an owner's property, limitations or prohibitions on the use of land, neighborhood requirements for lot size or boundary setbacks, landmark designations, control of the sale of certain goods or their prices—"these protean forms of regulation all amount to partial takings of private property."[29] Further, Epstein found "constitutionally infirm or suspect many of the heralded reforms and institutions of the twentieth century: zoning, rent control, workers' compensation laws, transfer payments, progressive taxation."[30] With a broad enough definition of takings, these actions too could be seen as benefits or wealth transfers that government extracted from private individuals who deserved compensation.

On the other side of the ledger, as it were, Epstein held that while seemingly any and all takings were compensable, government should be held to a strict definition of "public use." It should not be expanded to include a mere public "benefit" or "good," by which courts had validated urban development programs and economic growth plans that first condemned private property and then transferred it from the unwilling original owners to someone else.[31] This trend had only worsened by the time of the infamous twenty-first-century case of *Kelo v. City of New London* (2005). It was only the latest in a long line of abuses of eminent domain that highlighted the "imperative to keep a tight rein on public uses lest government power be used to move resources from A to B in ways that heighten the level of political intrigue, as particular groups vie to have the state exercise its condemnation power in their own direction."[32]

Epstein consistently related the takings project to the originalist conception of constitutional authority and interpretation. He claimed the mantle of originalism for its capacity to limit government by the rule of law while also holding that constitutional meaning could not be reduced to the subjective intentions or concrete expected applications of framers or ratifiers at the time of the founding. So, on one hand, he adopted the traditional, originalist view about the nature of a written constitution: "In order for judges to make principled interpretations, the language of the Constitution must be clear and precise enough to bind even those who disagree with what it says"; otherwise constitutionalism was impossible.[33] "If one assumes that all doctrines are mushy, intellectually open, politically adaptable, and morally contestable, then any effort to formulate a constitution is in vain."[34] On the other hand, it was "the integrity of constitutional text," one written in designedly general terms, that was to be accepted and guarded, not necessarily extrinsic historical evidence about its meaning or what its authors might have expected.[35] An overly constraining view of textual meaning would make it impossible to apply the Constitution to circumstances unforeseen by the founders—as they intended it to be. Nor did Epstein accept that this more general or abstract treatment of the text "was necessarily a rejection of the framers' intention." They might have endorsed or expected certain policies that were not delineated in the text or that actually conflicted with it. In which case "their explicit choice takes precedence over their silent one. Suppose the framers believed both A and X, when A entails not-X. If A is in the constitutional text then X is not allowed."[36] Historical evidence was always relevant and helpful as far as it went, but it could not relieve later generations of the burden of applying general principles to unforeseen circumstances. Epstein consistently retained this understanding of the validity, necessity, and limitations of originalism.[37] Despite its imperfections, no convincing and sustainable form of jurisprudence could dispense with it.

Like Siegan, Epstein rejected the traditional conservative presumption of judicial restraint and called for more active judicial intervention on behalf of property and economic rights: it should be "far greater than we now have, and indeed far greater than we have ever had."[38] But this was not because he supported judicial activism as a principled claim about the proper judicial role as such. The old "activism versus restraint" debate could be put aside if the question of judicial role was reconceived as a quest for more specific knowledge about the constitutional text. The more that was attained, the clearer would be the duty of courts to apply it. Courts should decide cases based on the "necessary implications derived from the constitutional text and the underlying theory of the state that it embodies."[39] Epstein wanted to provide courts with this kind of knowledge. Then they could more confidently and dependably protect property and economic liberty under the original and classically liberal Constitution the New Deal had displaced. Epstein held steadfastly that "it is not possible to marry any conception of limited constitutional governance with large doses of judicial passivity."[40]

A retrieval of neglected constitutional provisions, a version of originalism, and a defense of judicial intervention similarly cohered in the work of Randy E. Barnett—another libertarian law professor and a leading theorist. Barnett's initial goal was to resurrect the all but forgotten Ninth Amendment as the basis for stronger judicial protection of individual rights. Eventually he undertook historical studies of other constitutional provisions, defended originalism, and participated in several constitutional cases (including opposition to the Affordable Care Act). Rather than treating comprehensively this large corpus, the focus here, as with Siegan and Epstein, is Barnett's effort to advance the libertarian conception of rights and limited government amid the debate about modern judicial power in the 1980s and 1990s.

Barnett turned to the Ninth Amendment just as Robert Bork's controversial nomination to the Supreme Court and his subsequent best-selling book brought attention to the topic. Bork the erstwhile libertarian now argued that the amendment's terms ("The enumeration in the Constitution of certain rights shall not be construed to deny or disparage others retained by the people") were nonjusticiable: the words provided courts no guidance about how to resolve a legal dispute. In words Barnett often quoted, Bork went so far as to liken the amendment to an "inkblot" whose meaning judges could not adequately discern. No respectable originalist would invoke it as the basis for judicial review, he insisted. Indeed, Bork held that judges overstepped their own constitutional bounds if they attempted to give it substantive content, and he now condemned earlier such attempts he had once sought to elaborate.

Barnett probed the historical evidence of the amendment's creation and linked his findings to the natural rights principles of the founding. It was not difficult for him to show that John Locke's conception of natural rights influenced the founders and, likewise, that the Ninth Amendment was created to defeat the implication that the enumeration of some rights elsewhere in the Constitution left unprotected those not enumerated. His innovation as a constitutional theorist was to argue that the intrusive modern Leviathan made it necessary for courts to redeploy the amendment to protect individual rights in circumstances the founders could not have foreseen. He urged greater judicial skepticism (and accordingly less deference) toward laws that, in the age of big government, infringed on rights not listed in the Constitution.[41]

A crucial element of his theory was the "presumption of liberty." Building on the natural rights doctrine of Lockean liberalism and the traditional common law protections for the individual, Barnett argued that people had a "sphere of moral jurisdiction" over themselves and their actions. "Rights" were in principle innumerable, extending to all "the various acts we may perform within our respective jurisdictions."[42] The presumption of liberty was that all such conduct was allowable absent some countervailing set of constitutionally legitimate reasons, including the rights of others, which could be adjudicated in the traditional common law fashion. In a concrete sense, then, "common law principles of property, contract, tort, restitution, and agency (this list is not exhaustive of potential categories) provide the basic legal definitions of these natural rights."[43] Thus could the Ninth Amendment serve as the constitutional basis for judicial protection of the natural rights traditionally secured in the common law, making "the freedom to act within the boundaries provided by one's common law rights a central background presumption of the Constitution."[44] This presumption of liberty aimed to displace the *Carolene Products* presumption of constitutionality for government action, which Siegan too had opposed, and thereby put the burden of proof on the government to justify its action, not on the individual to justify his or her liberties.[45] Barnett eventually made a similar historical argument about the Privileges or Immunities Clause of the Fourteenth Amendment: it too was intended to shield unenumerated rights from state government interference, and the federal judiciary also should use it rigorously to scrutinize state laws.[46]

Barnett's theory emerged alongside the ascendance of originalism. Until well into the 1990s, however, he understood himself as a nonoriginalist. But even in this period his immersion in the history of the Ninth Amendment forced him to wrestle with originalism—and aspects of his argument were cast in quasi-originalist terms. Some equivocation resulted. If James Madison had intended the Ninth Amendment to play a significant role in protecting unenumerated rights, "it will be quite difficult to sustain an objection to such a theory on the ground that it violates original intent."[47] Rather, it was the continual modern erosion of individual liberty that contravened the framers' intent. "It does not follow that such judicial review [based on the Ninth Amendment] is not a legitimate constitutional device from the perspective of the original scheme. For these Framers also did not contemplate that the structure they designed would fail to constrain the power of government as they hoped it would." The Ninth Amendment was the fallback mechanism of the original Constitution that now must be used.[48] Nevertheless, Barnett also protested that originalism approached the framers as "wardens" whose commands must be obeyed, even though people today had not consented to them. It was equally unsatisfying for originalists to hypothesize how the framers might have resolved issues unknown to them, which required "a type of constitutional 'channeling' in which originalist clairvoyants ask: 'Oh Framers, tell us what would you think about the following law?'"[49] Rather, the framers might be affirmed as good constitutional "designers" who offered sound principles that could claim assent in the present. We today are not "bound by their intentions as such, but [rather] we today share their intentions to limit the power of government in a way that enhances and protects the liberty of the people."[50]

What Barnett subsequently described as originalism's "gravitational force" persuaded him to accommodate his project to a version of it.[51] He accepted the shift from a focus on the founders' "intent" or expectations, or both, to the definition of interpretation as finding the Constitution's "original public meaning." Unlike the attempt to recover the mental states of past historical actors that was associated with the concept of intent, the public meaning of words was often readily available through historical research. Barnett's originalism, then, was a defense of the writtenness of a text whose original public meaning could be restated in the present as a restraint on government. He still rejected the related claim of some originalists that ratification was the sovereign act of consent that legally obligated present-day citizens who had not formally consented. Rather, people in the present could give good reasons to abide by the original meaning of the Constitution as law, reasons best served by abiding by the Constitution's original public meaning. Barnett was now convinced that a version of originalism was intellectually and philosophically correct, and that it could advance libertarian ends. "Putting a constitution in writing is conducive to preserving the rights of the people from infringement by government officials, but only if its original meaning is not contradicted or altered without adhering to formal amendment procedures." Today's citizens too could regard the original Constitution as legitimate, but the advantages of writtenness "can only be obtained if the meaning of the constitution does not change by mere judicial interpretation."[52] Barnett had the intellectual courage to write about why he came to take originalism more seriously and the theoretical ambition to link it more strongly to libertarian principles.[53]

Barnett's originalism went beyond abstract argument about the nature of a written text and the meaning of interpretation. He undertook sustained historical investigation of the original public meaning of various constitutional clauses. His most extensive effort was a study of the Commerce Clause (Article I, section 8). It was inspired by Rehnquist Court decisions that had halted the expansion of the clause for the first time since the New Deal—especially Clarence Thomas's concurrence in *United States v. Lopez* (1995)—and by Richard Epstein's earlier conclusion that the New Deal interpretation of the clause was beyond the "original constitutional understanding."[54] In one article, Barnett examined every use of the word "commerce" in the Philadelphia convention, the ratification debates, and *The Federalist* papers. Every such usage involved trade, exchange, or transportation—as distinguished from manufacture or agriculture. Not once was "commerce" used broadly to mean any and all economic activity. "To regulate" was similarly used narrowly to mean "make regular" in the rules or manner of conducting commercial activity. To regulate included the broader power of outright prohibition only with respect to foreign trade, but not domestic trade. Another article used an online archive of the *Pennsylvania Gazette* to survey its every use of "commerce" from 1728 to 1800. Here too Barnett found overwhelmingly consistent usage of the narrow meaning, along with very few broad uses of "to regulate" or its cognates.[55]

Given this move to originalism, what was the role of courts in Barnett's theory? Support for robust judicial review marked his early work and did so as well after his originalist turn. He urged courts to examine intently laws suspected of infringing on individual rights—whether enumerated in the Constitution or not. Courts should place on government officials the burden of justifying new restraints on liberty. Any tendency toward judicial overreach was reliably disciplined by the incremental and precedential reasoning of the common law and through the Anglo-American moral and legal tradition that judges could not legitimately create new entitlements or "positive" rights to public resources. In fact, the modern interventionist-regulatory state undertook "legislative activism [that] gives rise to a need for a principled judicial activism."[56] At its extreme this position had no particular allegiance to the Constitution, which Barnett said "only has authority to the extent that it comports with our best moral knowledge[, if] the framework it establishes generally fits our best conception of individual rights."[57] Moreover, it was merely a pragmatic consideration to determine whether the assertion of judicial authority, or instead judicial deference to the legislature, better protected rights in a particular circumstance. Deference was sometimes appropriate, but "a judge should 'make' new law when the preexisting law inadequately respects or protects these individual rights. In no event where well-defined rights of an individual are at stake should a judge yield in the defense of these rights to the will of the legislature." The credo for those who supported this view was "Judicial activism in pursuit of liberty is no vice; judicial restraint in pursuit of justice is no virtue."[58]

Barnett's embrace of public-meaning originalism somewhat altered his description of the traditional problem of activism-versus-restraint, but not his overall approach. Somewhat like Epstein, Barnett thought the old dichotomy could be dissolved by redescribing the proper judicial role: judges should apprehend and then apply the text's original public meaning. "Unless one abandons judicial review entirely, one simply cannot know whether a court is being activist unless one also knows what the text means. The epithet 'activism' provides no escape from the need to take a stance on how the critic thinks the Constitution should be interpreted."[59] To recover and enforce the original public meaning of the Constitution was neither activism nor restraint but rather the proper judicial role. "It is not activist (if one insists on using that term) for a court to strike down legislation that violates the original meaning of the text."[60] By this measure, the Rehnquist Court's federalism decisions could not be deemed illegitimate activism. Rather, they overturned congressional legislation in accordance with the original meaning of the Commerce Clause (even though the opinions other than Thomas's concurrence in *Lopez* remained within the New Deal order's expansive conception of commerce).

Barnett regarded the older tradition of judicial deference to legislative majorities as a corruption of American constitutionalism. The original, animating purpose of the text and the surrounding universe of jurisprudence had been emphatically to protect the rights of individuals. A probing and assertive judiciary was required to that end. In the era of modern statism, however, rights would continue to erode if courts deferred to legislatures when they violated the Constitution. Barnett now found that originalism properly understood justified judicial intervention for the sake of rights, including reconsideration of wrongly decided precedents. There was hope for a return to the proper judicial role, because "the original meaning of the entire Constitution, as amended, is much more libertarian than the one selectively enforced by the Supreme Court."[61]

Against Judicial Restraint

Siegan, Epstein, and Barnett all claimed originalist fidelity to the Constitution. They were thus similar to the other kinds of conservatives analyzed in part IV: each theory responded to modern judicial review by orienting itself around the basic originalist idea. But libertarians stood apart in consistently seeing courts as the institution best able to advance their basic political philosophy. This view abided from libertarians' first foothold in law schools in the 1980s to their growing presence in constitutional theory and Supreme Court litigation in the twenty-first century. Accordingly, libertarians openly rejected judicial "restraint" and "deference" to legislatures as originalism emerged among traditionalists and Straussians in the 1980s (and thereafter).[62]

One example of this clash was a noted debate between Antonin Scalia, then a federal circuit court judge, and Richard Epstein at the Cato Institute in October 1984. Against the libertarian call for judicial intervention on behalf of economic liberties, Scalia observed that he had "little hope that judicial and lawyerly attitudes can be coaxed back to a more restricted view of the courts' role in a democratic society at the same time that we are charging forward on an entirely new front." Even more fundamentally, he said, "this issue presents the moment of truth for many conservatives who have been criticizing the courts in recent years. They must decide whether they really believe, as they have been saying, that the courts are doing too much, or whether they are actually nursing only the less principled grievance that the courts have not been doing what *they* want."[63] Epstein responded that the constitutionality of legislation affecting economic liberties could not be settled merely by a presumption of judicial restraint, as had been happening since the New Deal. That approach had "courts simply give up before they try." Judges should intervene "when there is strong textual authority and constitutional theory" and not permit legislatures to determine the extent of their own power in a way that "totally subverts the original constitutional arrangement of limited government." Epstein condemned the Supreme Court's jurisprudence on economic liberties and property rights as "intellectually incoherent." The remedy was "some movement in the direction of judicial activism," and "the only sensible disagreement is over the nature, the intensity, and the duration of the shift."[64]

Libertarians attacked other leading conservative originalist restraintists, especially Robert Bork. Additional targets included Lino Graglia and various members of Reagan's Department of Justice.[65] As in Epstein's response to Scalia, libertarians at this time accepted the label of judicial "activism." Judicial restraint, they said, too readily allowed derogation of rights. And it further calcified the post–New Deal regulatory-welfare state, which they accused conservatives of too readily accepting. Needed was a "principled judicial activism" in defense of rights.[66] Roger Pilon of the Cato Institute, who had served in the Reagan administration, had since the early 1980s urged conservatives to drop their automatic obeisance to judicial restraint and recognize the benefits of a more interventionist judiciary. Deference to the political branches in the name of self-government should be replaced with "strict constitutional scrutiny" of their actions. "There is no place for 'restraint'" in the proper judicial role any more than for anticonstitutional "activism." Rather, the Constitution "is rich enough to enable the judge to discover the rights that are there to be discovered." In instances of textual unclarity judges should return to the original understanding, "including the theory of natural rights that informed that understanding, [and give] meaning to the text and legitimacy to the document as a whole. This is not unwarranted 'activism.' It is what judges are appointed to do."[67]

This consistent libertarian theme was expressed early in the new century by Clint Bolick, a longtime libertarian activist and litigator. Judges "should see themselves," Bolick wrote, "as what they were intended to be: fearless guardians of individual liberty." He warned that "by emasculating judicial power, as some conservatives urge, we remove the ultimate protection against abuse of rights by the other branches of government." He wrote a book that aimed "to help remove judicial activism from the realm of the epithet" by showing that it was compatible with the original rights-protecting purpose of the Constitution and was sorely needed in the age of overly intrusive government.[68]

The libertarian wedding of originalism to assertive judicial review found expression in another important context. Michael S. Greve, a leading theorist of competitive federalism (treated in chapter 4), also sought to rework originalism and strengthen judicial review.[69] Dominant versions of conservative originalist restraint, he argued, were too narrowly clause bound, positivist, and deferential to legislatures. The originalist drive to constrain judicial adventurism had focused so much on the original public meaning of the text that its practitioners mistakenly eschewed any normative appeals, which were treated as a dangerous entrée into "the unbounded terrain of natural law sophistry."[70] Nevertheless, the older restraintist mode of originalism had not slowed judicial rights creation. Instead it had cast doubt on judicial doctrines that Greve saw as central to refurbishing competitive federalism and a truly open national market, such as the dormant Commerce Clause and the implied federal preemption of state laws. He concluded that an originalist "jurisprudence that cannot contain rights proliferation while emboldening the institutional and regulatory agenda of the political Left is not a sustainable basis for a conservative political force."[71]

A more expansive originalism and stronger judicial review would better advance Greve's core claims: that the Constitution's structure instituted competitive federalism *avant la lettre*, and that courts should actively enforce it. To these ends he also invoked the idea of constitutional "construction" as the deliberative process by which, over time, the polity settled unclear constitutional meaning. Courts practiced such construction by reasoning like good common lawyers, gradually developing doctrines that more fully specified concepts not exhaustively expressed in the original Constitution's text, structure, and institutional relationships. This loosening of the originalist approach could avoid collapsing into the bad old days of unchecked judicial rights creation, said Greve. It was safe because federalism was fundamentally about structure and limitation, not rights. Competitive federalism was thus a construction derivable from the Constitution's overall structure as expressed in its text and logic. Although "competition" was not in the text, this "construction makes sense *of* the text, leaves none of it out, and insists that each clause must be given its full and fair meaning."[72] Therefore, Greve argued, judicially enforced competitive federalism did not "invite, but rather helps to forestall" appeals to "constitutionally unhinged metaprinciples. The point is not to unleash judicial federalism but to reground and discipline it."[73] Other leading libertarians pushed in this direction, though without Greve's attempt to reconcile it with originalism. For example, support for competition and for the mobility of people and capital was paired with insistence that a central authority, typically the federal judiciary, must protect basic rights (especially immobile property) from oppressive local majorities.[74] A similar argument for assertive judicial power held that only courts stood a chance of limiting the federal subsidies to states that so corrupted competitive federalism and the national market.[75] As in the area of individual rights, an assertive judiciary was the preferred libertarian way to advance deregulation and market competition.

Judicial Engagement: Activism Redux?

This enduring libertarian commitment to judicial review is the proper context for considering the emergence of "judicial engagement." In 2005 this term was first coined by Chip Mellor of the Institute for Justice, a libertarian litigation firm founded in 1991. As suggested in the discussion this chapter recounts, judicial engagement too aimed to hurdle or dissolve the older activism-restraint dichotomy. Libertarians thought that the earlier rubric had hindered both liberals and conservatives from adequately defending economic liberty and property rights. The remedy was "consistent and principled judicial engagement [to] rehabilitate them."[76] In practice, said Mellor, this meant persuading liberals to drop the *Carolene Products* presumption of constitutionality for any and all regulations of economic and property rights, and persuading conservatives to drop the aversion to judicial power they had developed in response to the rights revolution of the Warren Court and *Roe v. Wade.*

This understanding informed the Institute for Justice's creation of a Center for Judicial Engagement as part of its litigation efforts. The idea was further developed by its director, Clark M. Neily III, in *Terms of Engagement* (2013). Randy Barnett likewise adopted the term to describe the basic position he had been advocating for years.[77] Neily described judicial engagement as "deciding cases on the basis of actual facts, without bent or bias in favor of government. It means ensuring that the government has a valid reason for restricting people's freedom."[78] Barnett's laudatory review of Neily's book added that "this modest degree of judicial skepticism isn't activism." Rather it was "the simple duty" of judges who had taken an oath to uphold the Constitution.[79] Judicial engagement, like judicial activism before it, would advance core libertarian principles by reviving constitutional limits on government and maximizing individuals' ability to live as they chose. "Government would shrink considerably if it were required to give an honest account of its actions in court and restricted to pursuing genuinely public-spirited ends when making policy."[80] After all, as Barnett pointed out, it was because of judicial restraint rather than engagement that the Affordable Care Act's mandate to buy insurance had survived in *National Federation of Independent Business v. Sebelius* (2012). Chief Justice John Roberts, a supposed conservative, wanted so badly to defer to Congress that he redefined the mandate as a tax, though plainly it was not. Judicial engagement opposed "judges closing their eyes—or rewriting statutes such as the Affordable Care Act—so they may 'defer' to legislative will and uphold legislation without assessing whether the legislation is properly within the power of Congress or state legislatures to enact." Barnett hoped that perhaps now conservatives would rethink their reflexive commitment to the outdated doctrine of judicial restraint.[81]

The new nomenclature of engagement continued libertarians' decades-long endorsement of vigorous judicial review—or activism as some had previously called it. The label had changed but the thrust of the core argument had not. Although there was no consensus definition of judicial activism, libertarians recognized that originalist attacks on modern judicial review had given the term a deeply negative connotation. Clint Bolick's attempt in 2007 had failed to make judicial activism something other than an epithet. Libertarians' terminological shift to engagement thus contained an element of rhetorical strategy. Denying that activism and engagement were wholly convertible, Barnett wanted judges to focus on conserving constitutional limits by requiring them to abide by the original meaning of the Constitution when it could be known. " 'Judicial engagement' is both a less pejorative and more accurate label for how a constitutionally conservative judge should act."[82] Neily proposed that activism-versus-restraint be replaced with engagement-versus-abdication. The negative connotation would now fall on the other side. It was unwarranted "abdication" for courts "simply [to] refuse to enforce [constitutional limits] in any meaningful way, deferring instead to public officials at the expense of liberty." (Earlier libertarians had suggested judicial "passivism" or "abstinence.")[83]

The growing libertarian acceptance of originalism worked with judicial engagement to erode the activist-restraint dichotomy. As previously suggested, the claim that courts were obligated to enforce the original public meaning of the Constitution tended to reposition the entire argument about judicial review away from the judicially self-chosen role of activism or restraint. Libertarian defenders of judicial engagement saw the power in insisting that a judge could not legitimately decline to enforce the recoverable meaning of the Constitution. Courts should abide by it, and as Barnett put it, debates about original meaning should be resolved by "evidence, not label-mongering." Since to interpret was to recover and apply the original meaning as law, "every justice appointed to the Supreme Court must publicly commit to the principle that judges have no power to amend or modify the Constitution of the United States by 'interpretation.' "[84] Enforcement of the known meaning of the Constitution was not judicial activism but rather judicial duty.[85]

Libertarians yet again stood apart from more traditionally conservative and originalist views about the proper limits of the judiciary. In many respects this disagreement replayed the libertarian-versus-conservative debates about activism-versus-restraint from the late twentieth century. For example, one conservative critic doubted that judicial engagement was "anything more than camouflage for libertarian judicial activism—an effort to smuggle in the back door what can't be formally established by straightforward and persuasive arguments about original meaning."[86] In practice, said conservatives, this newly relabeled approach only further undermined republican self-government by magnifying the judicial role beyond what the founders intended. Courts should not be deciding the nation's most serious social and political issues and did not merit libertarians' trust that they would stay within the bounds of the Constitution. Judicial engagement elevated the libertarian beau ideal of the unencumbered sovereign individual against the menacing state, but the theory had no real place for self-governing communities that wanted to safeguard their principles in law. As all public questions were increasingly distorted into a conflict between individual rights and state power and were left to judges to resolve, eventually political deliberation about the common good would become impossible.[87] The turn to judicial engagement again highlighted the old tension between libertarians' antistatist individualism and other forms of conservatism that emphasized community, locality, and moral restraint.

Conclusion: The Imperative of Litigation in the Age of Modern Judicial Review

The major varieties of conservatism wanted their respective conceptions of original constitutional meaning to discipline and direct the Court toward their preferred ends. Their contending forms of constitutional commentary and theory grew alongside the birth and maturation of conservative and libertarian public interest litigation, which began in the 1970s. There is now a substantial and growing scholarly literature on this subject. Consideration of some of its major themes is necessary to appreciate how modern judicial review drew conservatives and libertarians beyond intellectual criticism and into courtrooms.[88]

Decades of successful liberal litigation campaigns convinced conservatives and libertarians that they simply had to undertake their own such efforts to advance their goals. To fight fire with fire was a quite logical response. Moreover, new conservative and libertarian public interest law firms quite self-consciously modeled their organization and sometimes their strategy on their liberal counterparts. The newcomers well understood that they were attempting to beat liberals at their own game.

While there had been a few precursors, such as the National Right to Work Legal Defense Fund (founded in 1968), the key turning point came in 1973 when veterans of the administration of then California governor Ronald Reagan created the Pacific Legal Foundation. In the next few years similar groups replicated in other regions of the country. Typically they focused on defending property rights and challenging new government regulations. Others issues were added as a wide variety of conservative and libertarian public interest law firms proliferated. Some specialized in attacking abortion or affirmative action, others in defending home schooling and school choice, and still others in defending religious liberty. Libertarian and religiously rooted traditionalist organizations became particularly well established. In 1999 West Coast Straussians created the Claremont Center for Constitutional Jurisprudence.

Especially in the early days, many of these firms were limited to filing amicus curiae briefs—a practice of indeterminate efficacy that left firms' financial donors increasingly dissatisfied. Such filings of course continued, but over time more firms directly sponsored cases and represented clients in the attempt to establish new precedents. An early galvanizing victory was *Nollan v. California Coastal Commission* (1987), in which the Supreme Court held that the state's conditioning of a building permit on property owners' granting of an easement across their land amounted to an uncompensated taking under the Fifth Amendment.[89] Another landmark was *Rosenberger v. University of Virginia* (1995), which held that the denial of funding to a student organization with a religious viewpoint violated the Free Speech Clause of the First Amendment.[90] Congress was prevented from using the Commerce Clause to extend federal criminal law to sex-based violence in *United States v. Morrison* (2000).[91] In *Zelman v. Simmons-Harris* (2002) the Court held that a state-financed school voucher program that allowed parents to send their children to religious schools was not an establishment of religion under the First Amendment.[92]

Conservatives and libertarians sometimes took opposed positions, as in cases about homosexual rights or the treatment of detainees in the War on Terror. Sometimes too they lost cases or won only split decisions, as in the areas of eminent domain and affirmative action. But collectively and over time their litigation helped shift constitutional discourse in favor of once marginal ideas. Their efforts also had considerable staying power. Conservative and libertarian public interest litigation now appears to be a permanent feature of the constitutional landscape.[93]

Scholars have observed that litigation often drew its practitioners into the discourse of "rights" that legal liberals had long dominated. Now conservatives and libertarians sued on behalf of the right to property, the right of free speech, the right to equal protection, the right to life, and the right to free association. As one study concluded, "Conservatives could not turn back the clock on the rights revolution. But they could make a rights revolution of their own."[94] This dynamic tended to push their public interest litigation in a more libertarian direction, and prominent libertarian theorists such as Richard Epstein and Randy Barnett contributed to briefs in cases dealing with property rights, gun rights, and the Commerce Clause. Libertarian firms like the Institute for Justice and the Center for Individual Rights were among the most active and successful. Moreover, a detailed study of litigation by religious conservatives traced how the unfavorable landscape of the Court's establishment and free exercise jurisprudence compelled them to pursue their goals through free speech arguments. Signal cases such as *Rosenberger* were won, but the overall logic tended to displace religion from its historic position as the foundation of American culture to merely another choice from the buffet of postmodern value relativism.[95]

Challenges to liberal governance via judicial protection of new "counter-rights" also could complicate the issues of judicial restraint and originalism.[96] To be sure, conservative public interest law firms signed on to the concept of originalism as it ascended in conservative legal discourse, typically styling their litigation as an effort to retrieve some of the original limits on the reach of government. But there was disagreement about how actively courts should overturn old precedents in order to do so, as there always had been among originalist commentators and theorists. Nor did litigation firms agree on how much judicial intervention could be justified by the original meaning of the Constitution. And of course conservatives and libertarians could not avoid originalist critiques of their own originalist arguments. For example, in property rights and gun rights litigation they were accused of merely reading their preferred contemporary version of economic theory or individual liberty back onto the past.[97]

The move into public interest litigation thus reflected yet again both the principles of the various elements of conservatism and the tensions among them. Each variety gravitated to originalism while finding its own path and emphasis amid the terrain of modern judicial review. That terrain was no more conducive to unanimity or wholesale intellectual consistency than was the broader realm of constitutional commentary and theory. But as courts and the discourse of rights claimed an ever more consequential role in American constitutionalism, conservatives could not afford to stay on the sidelines, and they did not.

Conclusion

Conservatives, Congress, and the Future
of American Constitutionalism

Different kinds of conservatives varied in their relation to the constitutional changes first charted in Progressivism and then advanced in the New Deal and the 1960s. Their responses included condemnation, penetrating critique, adaptation, and attempts at steering the debate—and ultimately political results— in their favored direction. Conservatives criticized the propriety and sometimes even the legitimacy of the institutional structures and relationships they confronted, yet few serious thinkers held that the New Deal order could be somehow undone. Calls to "redeem" or "restore" the old order might have been useful in mobilizing some strata of political opinion, but from the perspective of the early twenty-first century it is clear that the New Deal and then the Great Society pulled the nation's political spectrum permanently to the Left in a way that conservatives could bemoan but not reverse. The redirection of government's overall purpose, and the kinds of policies it pursued, confirmed that the conservative renaissance had produced only "an attenuated reconstruction, one far more equivocal than the insurgents' rhetorical repudiation of the liberal regime might lead us to expect."[1] Indeed, a notable recent call for rooting "constitutional conservatism" in both political moderation and accommodation of conservatives' diversity counseled that both the New Deal order and the sexual revolution are irreversible.[2]

While a true counterrevolution or restoration was never in the offing, the preceding chapters show that conservative ideas did help shape constitutional discourse and decision making. The power of the administrative state grew apace, but conservatives spearheaded an ongoing reevaluation of its legitimacy, and the subject has likewise garnered renewed attention on the Supreme Court.[3] The Court also revisited federalism. Decades of conservative criticism encouraged its limitation of the Commerce Clause in the 1990s and again in *National Federation of Independent Business v. Sebelius* (2012). Yet, as with the federalism decisions of the Rehnquist era, the Court was "feeling its way toward a distinctly post–New Deal decentralization of the federal system."[4] Conservatives were ambivalent about both the modern presidency and how far the theory of the unitary executive could be legitimately extended. The relentless expansion of the office has once again induced some conservative-leaning thinkers to call for the reinvigoration of constitutional limitations.[5] Intense conservative resistance to modern judicial review helped curtail its reach, but neither originalist jurisprudence nor originalist justices on the Court guaranteed the results that conservatives wanted. Nor did originalism always result in the more limited and restrained role for the Court that its initial advocates had urged.[6]

Post–New Deal conservatives thus advanced a discourse of constitutional maintenance or preservation amid constantly shifting political circumstances that were still housed within the New Deal order. Such discourse is good for a healthy constitutional system. Times change and constitutions change. Serious and informed debate about what is to be adapted or cast off, and what must never be violated or forgotten, is itself a crucial way that constitutionalism as a form of political order is conserved. A self-governing people will always need this dialogue about its constitutional principles and their concrete expression in politics, and should always welcome it. But today there are increasingly grave concerns about the health of American constitutionalism—likely more than for the past few generations. Figures from the major schools of American conservatism concur that the Progressive theoretical and political project severely distorted American constitutionalism. Several now think that the constitutional system may be at—or beyond—a tipping point at which basic reform is necessary if a recognizably constitutional regime is to endure.[7] Simultaneously, notable liberal and Progressive theorists increasingly pronounce the Constitution a failure that should be changed wholesale, or disobeyed, or radically democratized.[8]

Does America's constitutionally limited republican government under the rule of law remain to be conserved? That momentous question has to some extent been implicated throughout this study. Certainly we have seen that

American conservatives defended their understanding of the nation's constitutionalism as if it truly existed and could be reasserted as the nation's definitive expression of self-government. Yet we come to the conclusion of this book without having directly considered conservatives' assessment of Congress—in large measure because they gave it so little sustained attention. Conservatives did not completely ignore Congress, nor did they address it as thoroughly or frequently as the topics in the foregoing chapters. The reader is owed some consideration of this issue.

There is no shortage of scholarship on Congress from the mostly progressive-liberal and behavioralist perspective of the academic mainstream. Moreover, whatever their intellectual-political orientation, both canonical and recent studies usually agree that Congress is not all that it might be. Even many of its defenders criticize it as complicit in its own decline, while its detractors portray it as a failing institution that is increasingly irrelevant when it is not actively pathological. Congress is said to be so riddled by obstruction and inaction that it constitutes the "deadlock of democracy." It is the "broken branch" by any number of metrics. It long ago committed "legiscide" by delegating its authority in vague terms to the bureaucracies of the administrative state, preferring instead to blame them for unpopular regulations, take credit for popular programs, and act as ombudsmen for constituents who run afoul of bureaucrats. Congress likewise "abdicated" its responsibilities with respect to the spending and war powers. Instead it obscures its various modes of taxation and the continual growth of the national debt, preferring to enact last-minute omnibus appropriations. It capitulates to nearly any imaginable presidential military adventure, and then sometimes impotently sues the executive branch over foreign policy disagreements. Finally, Congress has long enervated the independent governing authority of the states through conditional grants-in-aid and unfunded mandates.[9] One could continue with some profit down this well-trod analytic path. Serious questions of constitutional authority and responsibility are involved, though a leading scholar rightly cautions that the steady stream of "critique literature" has, since Woodrow Wilson, been part of the ongoing political debate that always penetrates academic social science. No one will be consistently satisfied by the partisan conflict and intentional inaction naturally exhibited by a democratic assembly in a large and heterogeneous society.[10]

As previous chapters show, conservatives also intimated similar views of Congress. Today's ongoing and seemingly intensifying concern about the health of both American constitutionalism in general and Congress in particular make it appropriate to consider conservatives' relatively sparse attention to the institution. Despite this paucity, telling in its own right, conservative assessments were in general consistent with the core principles and approaches of each type. This overview prepares us to conclude that no conservative defense of American constitutionalism can forsake Congress.

Traditionalists

Prominent traditionalists were decidedly pro-Congress in the 1950s and 1960s. James Burnham initially articulated this position in his seminal *Congress and the American Tradition* (1959). It developed further in the various writings of Willmoore Kendall (sometimes with George W. Carey). Congress was the central representative and deliberative institution of the constitutional system, designed to legislate in light of the diverse and shared beliefs and customs of Americans as one people. For traditionalists, to defend this conception of Congress was to conserve the Constitution. As noted in chapters 1 and 6, traditionalists arrayed Congress against the modern presidency and the administrative state, rejecting the latter two as the visionary-plebiscitary and managerial-bureaucratic forms of governance that had evolved with mass democracy.

Burnham maintained that the founders had always intended a government based on consent—and therefore the primacy of the legislature. Congress was a locally rooted institution whose members were tied by sympathy and interest to the people of their particular districts or states, which were organically rooted and not mere quantitative entities.[11] A majority formed in this assembly would be a rough consensus of the nation's diffuse and diverse subdivisions. Members negotiated and compromised among numerous crosscutting and frequently incommensurate imperatives, laboriously fashioning accords and accommodations from shared principles and mores. This kind of deliberation was slow and often cumbersome. Much of it occurred beneath the surface of floor debates and usually for longer than could be captured in a vote tally. And this process was the proper way of democratic consensus building in a large and diverse nation—messy and dilatory as it was.[12]

Burnham addressed the looming question of whether Congress could last in the age of the modern presidency, the administrative state, and the accompanying decline of federalism. He cautioned that the fall of Congress would spell "a constitutional revolution in the American political system" whereby liberty and self-government would lose to "plebiscitary despotism." For the moment, however, Congress remained "the prime intermediary institution, the chief political organ of the people as distinguished from the masses."[13] The capacity of a properly functioning Congress to resist the anticonstitutional program of progressive liberalism properly oriented midcentury conservatives to its defense. "Conservatives tend to be *for* Congress—for Congress as an institution, that is, not necessarily for each of its actions; to wish to defend, strengthen and preserve it."[14] But Burnham severely doubted that Congress could survive in the new order.

Kendall (sometimes with Carey) deepened several of Burnham's key points, often with detailed attention to the founders' political science in *The Federalist*. Voters in local communities chose representatives who could embody their generally culturally conservative virtues and mores. These representatives were dispatched to the capital not with specific binding instructions or to realize a program but rather to deliberate with their constituency in mind. They met with others in Congress to discern the "deliberate sense" of the majority in light of the views of the various local districts that constituted it. The founders' political science, said Kendall, held that "the way to handle diversity is to represent it and let it talk itself through to agreement."[15] Accordingly, Congress, along with the constitutional system more generally, was structured to frustrate and moderate intense but short-lived or destructive majoritarian impulses. This result was "deadlock" or "obstruction" only if the desideratum was the immediate realization of mass democratic opinion. Instead, the structured, somewhat plodding methods of Congress aimed at as much consensus as possible and at accommodating minorities as much as possible. The founders' Constitution "treats *deliberation*, that is, dialogue back and forth among members of the assembly and among the 'branches' of the government, as the be-all-end-all of the democratic process, and claims for it that it will produce the 'sense' (*not* the will) of the people as a whole."[16] Kendall's "deliberate sense" of the people was established over time, often in fits and starts, and could include what Congress resolutely declined to do as much as what it formally legislated.

Given these bases, purposes, and methods, Kendall described Congress as typically conservative. It was anti-ideological, sometimes provincial, and "nationalistic" on most issues. Its conservatism was apparent in matters ranging from immigration and internal security to civil rights and international affairs (he listed several more topics). This conservative-tending majority was the local, communal one that Kendall favored. But as in Burham's analysis, it confronted the rise of progressive liberal egalitarianism that was so often advanced via the modern presidency (or the courts). Kendall (with Carey) counseled that "we must learn, we conservatives, that the issue is *not* whether the American system is or is not 'democratic,' but which of two competing versions of 'democracy'—that which equates it with government by the 'deliberate sense' of the people, acting through their elected representatives, and that which equates it with direct majority rule and equality—should prevail."[17]

The most prominent traditionalist to carry forward Kendall's basic position was his sometime coauthor George W. Carey.[18] Building on his and Kendall's *Basic Symbols of the American Political Tradition* (1970), Carey argued that the deepest expression of American civilization was deliberative self-government in accord with the morality of the Western natural law tradition. From this perspective, the Declaration of Independence was not "revolutionary" in any fundamental sense. Its purpose was "establishing popular self-government in which majorities rule," and, if natural law so required, rights could be "modified or altered by deliberative majorities for society's well-being." Nor did the Constitution break from this view. On the contrary, its forms and mechanisms structured majoritarian deliberation.[19] Carey wanted students to know that Congress was the "mainspring of the constitutional system" and that the framers had accorded it a "predominant position" over the other branches. It most directly represented the people and had been given superior power to legislate and to govern.[20] Carey's extensive study of *The Federalist* held that Congress's basis in sober realism, combined with its capacity for reason, deliberation, and compromise, were always to be defended against progressive liberal calls for "participatory" or populist direct democracy.[21] But again the modern presidency, recently so warmly embraced by the Republican Party, necessitated modification of Kendall's earlier conclusion about Congress. It was inherently the more conservative branch only if "party differences enable it to exercise a truly independent will, to demonstrate some institutional pride and backbone along the lines that the framers envisioned."[22]

Both Burnham and Kendall had been important early figures at *National Review.* For most of its history the magazine supported the democratic "deliberate sense" of the American people against a reformist Supreme Court and an imperial presidency.[23] Editor William F. Buckley Jr. maintained this view, having been taught at Yale by Kendall and subsequently mentored by Burnham. Buckley urged conservatives to revisit Burnham's book during the reconsideration of institutional loyalties that occurred immediately after Watergate. A primary principle for conservatives was that "the natural answer to an irresponsible Congress is—a responsible Congress." Conservatives erred if they too willingly and fundamentally cast their lot with a powerful executive. "Nothing is achieved by congressional irresponsibility except the loss of freedom and stability."[24] Fifteen years later (in 1990) Buckley again reiterated what by then was becoming a minority view: "In a federal republic, Congress is the likeliest repository of conservative affinity. . . . The inertial domination of Congress by the Democratic Party has done much to confuse conservative thought, causing it to be spastically pro-executive, which is a misdirection of energy that should be going into electoral reform and a vigorous loyalty to sound congressional representation of conservative views and analyses."[25]

As Buckley illustrated, the waning of the Cold War presented the diminishing band of traditionalist conservatives with a brief moment to reassert the primacy of Congress. For example, Mickey Edwards, then a well-known figure, resoundingly agreed with Buckley. He noted especially the perpetual struggle between Congress and the president for control of foreign policy and the spending power.[26] Samuel Francis, a nationally syndicated columnist at the *Washington Times*, in turn praised Edwards and invoked both Burnham and Kendall. Burnham's prophecy about the plebiscitary presidency's domination of Congress in the managerial-administrative state appeared increasingly accurate. Still, though Francis affirmed the Reagan administration's confrontation with communism, conservatives were mistaken to abandon what he called, paraphrasing Kendall, the "powers of Congress as the representative of state and local communities, the expression of the deliberate sense of the American people."[27] Francis had earlier lauded Kendall as the "prophet of the heartland" whose thought was "indispensable for the resurgence of a militant popular conservatism."[28] Francis's prescriptions ultimately took a more pessimistic and sinister turn— part of which entailed giving up entirely on Congress. By the late 1990s his judgment was that it "no longer checks and balances the executive branch and in fact has become largely an extension of it." Congress had become not merely the executive's partner but "more often its lackey."[29]

Francis aside, the long-standing pro-Congress view echoed among traditionalists in the early twenty-first century, despite their small presence in constitutional discourse. For example, while George Carey and Bruce Frohnen described Congress as "the great enabler" that fostered the constitutional deformations of the administrative state and the modern presidency, they still thought the legislature the most representative and most powerful branch.[30] Congress was mostly supine, but it retained the power to effectuate real change.[31] It would act more responsibly if communities and citizens concerned about self-government demanded more of it. Peter Lawler and Richard Reinsch sounded similar themes, invoking Kendall to argue that constitutional majorities—the "deliberate sense of the community"—would produce not mob rule but, rather, limited, moderate, and truly representative government. It was possible to have a more modest and deliberative politics of dialogue and compromise structured by constitutional forms. And this politics would have legislatures doing more—and courts, bureaucracies, and heroic presidents doing less.[32] Even though traditionalist influence lessened over time, its spokesmen never wavered in understanding Congress as the primary institution of republican self-government, albeit one that would require substantial revitalization and reform if American constitutionalism was to flourish. Traditionalists' own doubts that Congress had withstood the New Deal transformation contributed to the ebbing of particularly traditionalist constitutional discourse at the end of the twentieth century.

Libertarians

Libertarians' valorization of the unencumbered individual produced an abiding suspicion of collective action, including majority rule and legislation as such. This posture attenuated the libertarian attachment to American constitutionalism, a limitation that was apparent even in the rather moderate classical liberalism of Friedrich Hayek. The more extreme rational egoism and antistatism of public choice analysis dismissed as fantasy any notion of the public good or shared deliberation, let alone national interest. Hence the project of "constitutional political economy" inaugurated by James Buchanan was a libertarian form of public choice that called for a theoretical refounding of the constitutional order based on the self-interest of the rationally calculating individual. This new departure was a remedy for the putative failure of the founders' original constitutionalism to adequately shield individuals and their property from the grasping hand of government in general and legislative majorities in particular. Likewise, influential libertarian constitutional scholars, as exemplified by both Bernard H. Siegan in the 1980s and Randy Barnett in the twenty-first century, had little patience with majority rule and sought always to limit the legislature's reach. A brief review of these ideas shows why, for libertarians, Congress could not be a potential source of reform of post–New Deal constitutionalism. Libertarians' sovereign, self-defining individual required iron limits on self-serving and redistributionist legislation that was undertaken for the supposed "public good."

Hayek held that the original Constitution had appropriately recognized the basis of legitimate legislation in generally applicable rules: a particular command addressed to the immediate demands of the moment was not truly law. But he warned that modern democracy was undermining this crucial conception of the rule of law. Now current majority opinion, or whatever ad hoc policy issued from the legislature, was being equated with law itself.[33] As limits on legislatures eroded, they took on the characteristics of what Hayek called a "bargaining democracy." Lawmakers used the power of government to serve their interests and those of the constituencies that kept them in power. The democratic ideal had thus "miscarried." An "omnipotent democratic government" with no real limits was incapable of effectuating the majority principle. Rather, it "will be forced to bring together and keep together a majority by satisfying the demands of a multitude of special interests, each of which will consent to the special benefits granted to other groups only at the price of their own special interests being equally considered."[34] Legislators in this circumstance had no incentive to limit their ability to dole out special privileges; consequently they would corrupt the rule of law. The results for constitutionalism were dire. "Because of this defect in the construction of our supposedly constitutional democracies we have in fact again got that unlimited power which the eighteenth century Whigs represented as 'so wild and monstrous a thing that however natural it be to desire it, it is as natural to oppose it.'"[35]

Although his judgment involved some circumlocution, Hayek concluded that the US Constitution had indeed failed in this way. The American attempt to limit the legislature constitutionally "in fact did no more to prevent Congress from becoming primarily a governmental rather than a truly legislative institution and from developing in consequence all the characteristics which this chief preoccupation is apt to impress on an assembly."[36] The way forward was fundamental constitutional reform that corrected the "wrong turn taken by the development of representative institutions." Needed now was a new "model constitution" that separated and limited power better than the 1787 Constitution, which had failed "effectively [to] limit the powers of government."[37] Thus did Hayek the great classical liberal defender of limited constitutional government quit the American project.

Hayek had clearly deployed (and occasionally cited) aspects of the public choice approach that was ascending in economics and political science. In turn, the libertarian version of public choice subsequently elaborated and intensified Hayek's basic critique of both legislatures and American constitutionalism.[38] Most fundamentally, libertarian public choice saw politics as a process of exchange based on individuals' rational calculation of their self-interest. Collective action, labeled the "common good" or what have you, was merely a set of constraints cast around the pursuit of individual preferences. Any actual majority position was usually impossible. Studies of voting, for example, showed that deadlock or minority preferences frequently resulted when individuals made joint decisions among ranked alternatives (e.g., Kenneth J. Arrow's "impossibility theorem"). Collective decisions about public policy usually favored small, well-organized groups with intense interests, frequently at the expense of broadly diffused interests with little incentive to concert themselves (e.g., Mancur Olson's logic of collective action). The legislature was merely a forum for "rent-seeking," the use of government's rule-making power to benefit favored officials, constituencies, or businesses. The characteristic legislative activity was "logrolling," whereby representatives traded votes with colleagues to realize reciprocally one another's rent-seeking objectives.

Starting with *The Calculus of Consent*, James Buchanan (often collaborating with Gordon Tullock or others) led the libertarian development of this complex of ideas. *The Calculus* asked what constitutional rules of interaction and exchange self-interested, rational individuals would unanimously consent to before being bound by them in society. Without rehearsing the minutiae, the proffered answer was a system in which any conception of "the public" had no place, and majority rule precious little. The aim was "explicitly and deliberately [to defend] constitutional limits on majority voting" and to justify "bounds on the exercise of majoritarian democracy."[39] Later public choice scholars also typically viewed Congress as a den of self-serving rent seekers, concluding that a "bias toward government growth seems to be an inherent characteristic of representative government."[40]

The American founders certainly wanted limits on legislative majorities, but Buchanan wanted constitutional change to create more. His drive to constrict democratic will and legislative action was proper to a theory of constitutional refounding—or revolution—and not to constitutional conservatism as such. Although *The Calculus of Consent* lauded James Madison's view that political factions necessitated constitutional limits on the majority, it also hinted that a "better understanding" would have to wait until American democracy could reach a "point of mutual recognition of the advantages to be secured from the requisite constitutional changes."[41] Buchanan thus agreed with Hayek about the United States' fate and reflected that *The Limits of Liberty* (1975) had been "a diagnosis of this constitutional failure." It was now a "certainty" that in America "the Leviathan state is the reality of our time."[42] Accordingly, pragmatic or policy reforms were inadequate: "Basic constitutional reform, even revolution, may be needed." The clock was ticking because the current order was quickly becoming economically and politically unsustainable. "Genuine constitutional change" must aim, as Buchanan always did, to better secure individual rights by reducing "the scope for collectively determined coercive activity."[43]

The name given to this theoretical reconstruction was "constitutional economics," now more commonly called "constitutional political economy." Charting its direction in a new journal devoted to the cause, Buchanan emphasized that "critics who call upon extraindividual sources of value cannot participate in the ongoing dialogue, nor can those skeptics who refuse to apply models of rational choice to the behavior of individuals as autonomous actors."[44] This pronouncement, admirably self-conscious in its exclusion, clarified how the new Atlantis would constrain majorities by reducing constitutionalism to merely the rule-following of self-interested utility maximizers.[45]

While Hayek and Buchanan responded to supposedly inevitable legislative corruption by calling for a new constitutionalism, if only at the level of theory, the more practical and immediate solution was valorization of assertive judicial review. As noted in chapter 10, one of the first legal academics to stake out a thoroughly libertarian position was Bernard Siegan. He did not go as deep theoretically as the public choice critique of majorities and legislatures, though he cited and restated some of its key claims as outlined above (and similarly acknowledged Hayek).[46] The upshot was that "the legislative process is seriously flawed in important respects."[47] Beyond all the ignorance and irrationality involved in voting and elections, the problem with legislation most fundamentally was that terms such as " 'over-all good,' " " 'public interest,' " and " 'general welfare' " had "no precise meaning." Instead, Siegan said derisively, the compromise, trade-offs, and special interests involved in legislating made the result comparable "to surgery conducted by a team composed of Christian scientists, exorcists, and surgeons."[48] The libertarian remedy for inevitable legislative corruption was thorough judicial supervision of legislators in the name of individual rights.

The general libertarian hostility to legislative majorities continued as the perspective's presence in constitutional discourse grew. Several additional examples might be adduced, but one more of prominence must suffice. Randy Barnett, like Siegan, was not a public choice theorist, but he was likewise a forceful exponent of individual rights and similarly wanted assertive courts to defend them. Thus legislative majorities were inherently suspect. In fact, argued Barnett, the problem of "too much democracy" was the primary motivation for creating the Constitution. The original document had been decidedly libertarian, but now a judicially led project of originalist reclamation must reorient the post–New Deal system away from the "majoritarian pressures" that induced the "politically popular growth of government."[49]

Barnett even rejected the orthodox view that the Constitution rested on the contractarian foundation of popular sovereignty and consent. Those were mere fictions, he held, and dangerous ones to the extent that they encouraged majority rule and legislative dominance. Rather, it was individuals who were "sovereign" over themselves. Since it was impossible for each individual to give explicit consent, the "presumption of liberty" at the center of Barnett's theory meant that the Constitution or a statute was legitimate only if it did not violate individual rights very broadly construed. Sovereign individuals could never be merely presumed to have consented to majority control over their inalienable rights to life, liberty, and property.[50] Moreover, contemporary analysis of the legislative process revealed that both majorities and minorities frequently manipulated it in their own interests. Therefore, neither citizens nor courts should automatically accept the legitimacy of legislation. Statutes did not "create a duty of obedience in the citizenry simply because they are enacted," and likewise "the fact that such legislation reflects a majority preference is insufficient to overcome the presumption [of unenumerated rights] established by the Ninth Amendment."[51] Rather, democratic majorities and legislation, and thus Congress too, were the source of the problem. As Barnett exemplified, libertarians simply denied that representative institutions expressed the deliberative capacity of a political community. Nor were legislators thought able to limit and moderate themselves apart from assertive judicial supervision that tended toward judicial supremacy.[52] Congress was all but a lost cause from the libertarian point of view.

Straussians

Legislatures received a more positive evaluation in the relatively few Straussian analyses of Congress.[53] These efforts were characteristically Straussian insofar as they contextualized the Constitution within the history of political thought and defended the role of Congress in the founders' political science. Nevertheless, Straussians concurred that much was wrong with Congress, including in ways highlighted by public choice. Abject corruption did occur. Legislation too often merely agglomerated benefits to special interests, while legislators fixated on their reelection or else exploited the perquisites of office and incumbency for personal and political gain. But the appropriate response, said Straussians, was to return Congress to its constitutionally proper dimensions and purposes, and likewise to accept the inevitable imperfections of legislation in a society that had always been diverse, pluralistic, and competitive. Thus the Straussian approach was authentically constitutionally conservative—a realistic yet encouraging defense of Congress as the representative and deliberative assembly it could and should be—rather than a call to superintend or remake it.

Before considering Congress proper, it is relevant that early students of Strauss, irrespective of their disagreements, emphasized the importance of popular sovereignty and majority rule. For example, Martin Diamond defended the democratic bona fides of the Constitution from the Progressive charge that it was an oligarchic reaction to the American Revolution. Rather, the Constitution aimed to moderate and enlighten popular government because the founders were irrevocably committed to it. As Diamond put it, "the constitutional devices and arrangements do not derogate from the legal power of majorities to rule." Americans understood that "they were not founding any other kind of government; they were establishing a democratic form, and it was the dangers peculiar to it against which all their efforts had to be bent."[54] Although Harry Jaffa disagreed with Diamond about the relationship between the Constitution and the Declaration of Independence, he similarly insisted that America's foundation in natural rights made consent the basis of legitimate government—and thus justified democratic-majoritarian decision making. "That the will of the majority should prevail is a 'sacred principle' because the authority of the majority is derived from those natural rights with which all men have been equally 'endowed by their Creator.'" Of course, on this same principle, majorities could not justly violate the rights of minorities. With that important caveat, Jaffa willingly accepted that "the doctrine of legislative supremacy, so fundamental to the American Revolution, is a direct inference from the doctrine of natural equality."[55]

The smattering of Straussian studies of Congress built on these views. Typically they highlighted how in Congress the founders had accounted for natural human self-interest, political ambition, and the propensity for factions to form in a free society. Congress represented the people in their variability, registering both their more immediate opinions and their longer-term considerations. Particularly in the House of Representatives, the interaction of the many factions derived from such a large and diverse nation was inevitably conflictual and somewhat raucous, and its horizon often shortsighted. Moreover, in this environment the process of coalition building and legislation itself necessarily involved bargaining and compromise. There was no denying that sometimes the purity of principle would suffer. Straussians thus counseled, along with the founders, a certain hardheaded realism about what could be expected from democratic politics among a free people. Reformist critics who demanded constant rectitude were reminded that "one cannot take the politics out of politics. . . . Confrontational partisanship is part and parcel of a democratic people governing themselves. While not always pretty, it is in its own way a wonder to behold." Moreover, condemnation of Congress for not meeting impossible standards undermined the respect that representative institutions needed if they were to have even a chance at cohering or leading America's democratic pluralism.[56]

While Straussians accepted that any enduring form of democratic politics must acknowledge the realities of self-interest and popular opinion, another hallmark of their attention to Congress was insistence that the institution was designed for—and could achieve—reasoned deliberation about the public good.[57] Joseph M. Bessette led the way in reconstructing the founders' philosophical and institutional logic in creating Congress to filter, moderate, and broaden interests and opinions that originated in the local and short-term. Representatives engaged in this process could shape legislation in the national interest. Congress was the "conjunction of deliberation and democracy," thereby allowing reason and public spirit to rise above passion and self-interest. Nor was this conception of legislative deliberation some bygone relic of the eighteenth century, as Bessette illustrated through several detailed case studies of twentieth-century legislators and legislation.[58]

Congress could deliberate about the public good, but it could not be expected wholly to transcend the context of public opinion in a vast and thoroughly commercial society. Typically it would register that opinion in all its diversity, complexity, and conflict as representatives sought to "refine and enlarge the public views." Although Congress's aim was to elevate democratic will through deliberation—to put reason above passion—the aim did not guarantee the result. Consequently, if political opinion was fundamentally unresolved on a pressing national issue, or polarized on a variety of issues, it was to be expected that Congress usually would reflect such realities. The institution simply was not constituted to impose consensus where none existed. Nor could it routinely create fully coherent legislation that thoroughly integrated policies across a wide domain.[59]

Congress thus embodied for Straussians the truth that self-government was a fragile enterprise in need of constant care. A danger inherent in the American system was that democratic leaders would merely reflect or pander to public opinion, rather than making it more moderate, deliberative, and rational. Great statesman-presidents such as Abraham Lincoln could sometimes lead common opinion toward justice, but "there is nothing in human nature or in how deliberative democracy is structured to guarantee the wisdom of popular deliberations."[60] Nor, as the founders well understood, would great statesmen or presidents always be available when they were most needed, or even frequently. Congress was thus a fundamental expression of the American experiment in self-government. That experiment would fail if enough people came to believe that the national legislature was useless or beyond repair. As one Straussian concluded upon reviewing the subject, neither the presidency nor anything else could substitute for self-governing citizens who demanded integrity from their representatives. "However parochial and irresponsible Congress may sometimes be, . . . the republican remedy is a more disciplined and responsible Congress demanded by a more disciplined and responsible people."[61]

As noted above, Straussians acknowledged that the modern Congress had serious shortcomings. They frequently accepted recommendations from the large critical literature that called for procedural and technical reforms, such as reinvigorating the committee system or allowing more open rules of debate on the floor of the House. Congress was to be thoughtfully and faithfully reformed in line with the founders' political science, not written off. Accordingly, such a seemingly mundane development as the rapid growth in the size and activity of congressional staff had to be measured by its effects on the ability of representatives to understand and deliberate about legislation.[62] A similar continuity of perspective was apparent among the several Straussian contributions to two books published nearly three decades apart, *The Imperial Congress* (1988) and *Is Congress Broken?* (2017).[63] A recurring point in each was that the administrative state, with its basis in early-twentieth-century Progressivism, had deranged the separation of powers and cast Congress in roles and activities for which it was not constituted and not effective. The more Congress delegated power to the bureaucracy and then conducted oversight that hobbled executive branch administration, the less it was able to fulfill its core functions. In the 1980s it was thought that a sharp reassertion of presidential power might force basic changes in Congress and the bureaucracy. Decades later it had not happened. Congress would have to heal itself, in part by confronting the presidency and the bureaucracy more directly and politically.[64]

Deeper beneath both Congress's frequent ineptitude and irresponsibility and the public's dissatisfaction with it stood the enormous power of modern government. The Constitution was originally designed for limited government, but "expecting a restricted structure to support a government whose ends now seem unlimited is to require that government to perform its role in a way that will inevitably lead the population to frustration, a sense that the system is broken, and distrust of the institutions themselves." Reestablishment of the proper constitutional perspective would have Congress thinking anew about retrenchment of its responsibilities to the range of their effective prosecution. In sum, then, Straussians argued that Congress was more overextended and misunderstood than broken. A revitalization of the original constitutional design, not its rejection, was the proper remedy. "We can improve Congress by returning to a constitutional Congress, complete with proposed reforms premised on an appreciation for constitutional context."[65]

While properly accounting for the varying critiques of the post–New Deal order, American conservatives, and citizens in general, must again see that their ability to be a self-governing people is tied to the fate of Congress. Its shortcomings are real, as all the major schools of conservatism accept, but it must be reengaged and reinvigorated if the republic is to endure. So perhaps it is necessary again to state the obvious in relation to the developments traced in this book that so animated conservative critics. By the intentional design of the founders of the republic, Congress has the constitutional authority to address them all. If conservatives remain interested in conserving the Constitution, their intellectuals should give more sustained attention to Congress and how it might be improved, and their activists should put in the grassroots work required to change political opinions and win elections. In the long run, irresponsible bureaucracy, centralized governance that destroys federalism, a plebiscitary and imperial presidency, and modern judicial review cannot sustain republican self-government. In fact, they all undermine it. Congress's singular capacity to address each of these problems still places it at the center of American constitutionalism, even though it has been too often neglected and more frequently maligned.

None of the foregoing is to claim that Congress is somehow "supreme" over the other branches of government. Nor is it to deny that Congress too is properly limited, balanced, and moderated in dialogue with the executive and the judiciary—as the first principles of the US Constitution require. As a society and as citizens, we need to relearn and rededicate ourselves to those principles, which entails asking and expecting better of Congress and ourselves and accepting that government cannot be expected to solve all social problems. In turn, these goals require the revitalization of authentic civic education and the engaged citizenship it promotes. Constitutionalism, republican self-government, and human liberty hang in the balance—as they always have.

Introduction

1. As in Ken I. Kersch, *Conservatives and the Constitution: Imagining Constitutional Restoration in the Heyday of American Liberalism* (New York: Cambridge University Press, 2019). Kersch explicitly eschews consideration of conservatives' response to the reigning institutional order of New Deal constitutionalism. Ibid., xvii–xviii, 81. Instead he studies the "constitutional consciousness" of different kinds of conservative identity groups, tracing their various tropes, or "constitutive stories." His focus is on conservative narratives, often by popularizers, in the realms of markets, communism, and Christianity, showing how in each area the stories said to be embedded in conservative political culture condemned liberal policies and presumptions.

2. Alan Brinkley, "The Problem of American Conservatism," *American Historical Review* 99 (1994): 409–29; Leo P. Ribuffo, "Why Is There So Much Conservatism in the United States and Why Do So Few Historians Know Anything about It?" *American Historical Review* 99 (1994): 438–49. The ensuing historiographical wave is assessed in Kim Phillips-Fein, "Conservatism: A State of the Field," *Journal of American History* 98 (2011): 723–43; and Julian E. Zelizer, "Reflections: Rethinking the History of American Conservatism," *Reviews in American History* 38 (2010): 367–92.

3. There were constitutionally informed critics of Progressivism, too often overlooked, prior to the New Deal. See Joseph Postell and Johnathan O'Neill, eds., *Toward an American Conservatism: Constitutional Conservatism during the Progressive Era* (New York: Palgrave Macmillan, 2013); and Joseph Postell and Johnathan O'Neill, eds., *American Conservatism, 1900–1930: A Reader* (Lanham, MD: Lexington Books, 2019).

4. For two major works among many that elaborate these themes, see Paul D. Moreno, *The American State from the Civil War to the New Deal: The Twilight of Constitutionalism and the Triumph of Progressivism* (New York: Cambridge University Press, 2013); and G. Edward White, *The Constitution and the New Deal* (Cambridge, MA: Harvard University Press, 2000).

5. Karen Orren and Stephen Skowronek, "Institutions and Intercurrence: Theory Building in the Fullness of Time," in *Nomos XXXVIII: Political Order*, ed. Ian Shapiro and Russell Hardin (New York: New York University Press, 1996), 111–46, quote on 112. See also Karen Orren and Stephen Skowronek, *The Search for American Political Development* (New York: Cambridge University Press, 2004).

6. Steven M. Teles, *The Rise of the Conservative Legal Movement: The Battle for Control of the Law* (Princeton, NJ: Princeton University Press, 2008); Amanda Hollis-Brusky, *Ideas with Consequences: The Federalist Society and the Conservative Counterrevolution* (New York: Oxford University Press, 2015); Jefferson Decker, *The Other Rights Revolution: Conservative Lawyers and the Remaking of American Government* (New York: Oxford University Press, 2016); Daniel Bennett, *Defending Faith: The Politics of the Christian Conservative Legal Movement* (Lawrence: University Press of Kansas, 2017); Johnathan O'Neill, *Originalism in American Law and Politics: A Constitutional History* (Baltimore: Johns Hopkins University Press, 2005).

7. The locus classicus for understanding the intellectual-political principles of the varieties of American conservatism is George H. Nash, *The Conservative Intellectual Movement in America since 1945* (1976; reprint, Wilmington, DE: ISI, 1996), which treats traditionalists, libertarians, Straussians, and (briefly) neoconservatives. I adopt this basic categorization but do not treat anticommunism separately. Also helpful as exercises in definition and distinction from within the conservative ambit are Peter Berkowitz, ed., *Varieties of American Conservatism* (Stanford, CA: Hoover Institution Press, 2004); Charles W. Dunn and J. David Woodward, *American Conservatism from Burke to Bush: An Introduction* (Lanham, MD: Madison Books, 1991). Helpful and more critical is Kersch, *Conservatives and the Constitution*, 9–22, 38–49, 72–81, 103–19, 308–25. Issues of definition and fault lines are also well treated in George Hawley, *Right-Wing Critics of American Conservatism* (Lawrence: University Press of Kansas, 2016).

8. Russell Kirk, *The Conservative Mind: From Burke to Santayana* (Chicago: Regnery, 1953); Russell Kirk, *Rights and Duties: Reflections on Our Conservative Constitution* (Dallas: Spence, 1997).

9. Two histories from the traditionalist perspective are Paul Edward Gottfried, *Conservatism in America: Making Sense of the American Right* (New York: Palgrave Macmillan, 2007); and Joseph Scotchie, *Revolt from the Heartland: The Struggle for an Authentic Conservatism* (New Brunswick, NJ: Transaction, 2002).

10. Russell Kirk, *The Roots of American Order*, 4th ed. (Wilmington, DE: ISI, 2003).

11. For example, Kirk, *Rights and Duties*, 95–109, 119–20; Bruce P. Frohnen, "George Carey on Constitutions, Constitutionalism, and Tradition," in *Defending the Republic: Constitutional Morality in a Time of Crisis*, ed. Bruce P. Frohnen and Kenneth L. Grasso (Wilmington, DE: ISI, 2008), 27, 28; M. E. Bradford, *Remembering Who We Are: Observations of a Southern Conservative* (Athens: University of Georgia Press, 1985), 41–42.

12. M. E. Bradford, "The Heresy of Equality: Bradford Replies to Jaffa," *Modern Age* 20 (Winter 1976): 62–77; Willmoore Kendall and George W. Carey, *The Basic Symbols of the American Political Tradition* (1970; reprint, Washington, DC: Catholic University Press, 1995), generally; Bruce P. Frohnen and Kenneth L. Grasso, "Editors' Introduction," in *Defending the Republic*, xi–xii, xxi–xxii.

13. Willmoore Kendall and George W. Carey, "Preface," in *Basic Symbols of the American Political Tradition*, xxii–xxiii; M. E. Bradford *Original Intentions: On the Making and Ratification of the United States Constitution* (Athens: University of Georgia Press, 1993), 33, 104–105; Frohnen, "George Carey on Constitutions," 19–20.

14. This same basic idea, sans the reference to Oakeshott, was central to Kirk's understanding of American constitutionalism. See, for example, Kirk, *Rights and Duties*, 15–16.

15. For example, Frohnen, "George Carey on Constitutions," 34–35.

16. This is a primary theme of Kendall and Carey, *Basic Symbols of the American Political Tradition*.

17. Mark C. Henrie, "Traditionalism," in *American Conservatism: An Encyclopedia*, ed. Bruce Frohnen, Jeremy Beer, and Jeffrey O. Nelson (Wilmington, DE: ISI, 2006), 873.

18. Bruce P. Frohnen, "Law's Culture: Conservatism and the American Constitutional Order," *Harvard Journal of Law and Public Policy* 27 (Spring 2004): 459–88.

19. Helpful overviews of American libertarianism called on in the following two paragraphs are David Boaz, *Libertarianism: A Primer* (New York: Free Press, 1997); and Charles Murray, *What It Means to Be a Libertarian: A Personal Interpretation* (New York: Broadway Books, 1997). For a history, see Brian Doherty, *Radicals for Capitalism: A Freewheeling History of the Modern Libertarian Movement* (New York: PublicAffairs, 2007).

20. Ronald Hamowy, "Editor's Introduction," in *The Encyclopedia of Libertarianism*, ed. Ronald Hamowy et al., (Thousand Oaks, CA: Sage, 2008), xxi–xxiii.

21. Albert Jay Nock, *Our Enemy, The State* (New York: Morrow, 1935). See also Michael Wreszin, *The Superfluous Anarchist: Albert Jay Nock* (Providence: Brown University Press, 1971).

22. Murray N. Rothbard, *The Betrayal of the American Right* (Auburn, AL: Ludwig von Mises Institute, 2007), xii.

23. Friedrich A. Hayek, *The Constitution of Liberty* (Chicago: University of Chicago Press, 1960), 182, 192.

24. Randy E. Barnett, *Restoring the Lost Constitution: The Presumption of Liberty* (Princeton, NJ: Princeton University Press, 2004); Randy E. Barnett, "Is the Constitution Libertarian?" *Cato Supreme Court Review* 2008–9 (July 2009): 9–33.

25. Two helpful overviews are Thomas L. Pangle, *Leo Strauss: An Introduction to His Thought and Intellectual Legacy* (Baltimore: Johns Hopkins University Press, 2006); and Catherine and Michael Zuckert, *The Truth about Leo Strauss: Political Philosophy and American Democracy* (Chicago: University of Chicago Press, 2006). See also Kenneth L. Deutsch and John A. Murley, ed., *Leo Strauss, the Straussians, and the American Regime* (Lanham, MD: Rowman and Littlefield, 1999).

26. Hilail Gildin, ed., *An Introduction to Political Philosophy: Ten Essays by Leo Strauss* (Detroit: Wayne State University Press, 1989), 81.

27. Leo Strauss, *Natural Right and History* (Chicago: University of Chicago Press, 1953).

28. Gildin, *Introduction to Political Philosophy*, 81–98.

29. William A. Galston, "Leo Strauss's Qualified Embrace of Liberal Democracy," in *The Cambridge Companion to Leo Strauss*, ed. Steven B. Smith (Cambridge: Cambridge University Press, 2009), 193–214.

30. Leo Strauss, *Liberalism, Ancient and Modern* (New York: Basic Books, 1968), 24.

31. Zuckert and Zuckert, *The Truth about Strauss*, 58–79, 197–202.

32. James W. Ceaser, *Designing a Polity: America's Constitution in Theory and Practice* (Lanham, MD: Rowman and Littlefield, 2011), 49.

33. Charles R. Kesler, "A New Birth of Freedom: Harry V. Jaffa and the Study of America," in *Leo Strauss, the Straussians, and the American Regime*, 276–77.

34. Zuckert and Zuckert, *The Truth about Leo Strauss*, 239–52, quote at 251.

35. Michael P. Zuckert, "Straussians," in *Cambridge Companion*, 280–86.

36. Ceaser, *Designing a Polity*, 47–48, 50.

37. Thomas L. Pangle, *The Ennobling of Democracy: The Challenge of the Postmodern Age* (Baltimore: Johns Hopkins University Press, 1992), 216.

38. Pangle, *Ennobling of Democracy*, 148–54. See also Lorraine Smith Pangle and Thomas L. Pangle, *The Learning of Liberty: The Educational Ideas of the American Founders* (Lawrence: University Press of Kansas, 1993).

39. Ceaser also observes the eastern emphasis on Tocqueville. Ceaser, *Designing a Polity*, 50. See also Pangle, *Ennobling of Democracy*, 206, 213–16; Harvey C. Mansfield Jr., *America's Constitutional Soul* (Baltimore: Johns Hopkins University Press, 1991), 177–92; Robert P. Kraynak, "Tocqueville's Constitutionalism," *American Political Science Review* 81 (1987): 1175–95; and James W. Ceaser, *Liberal Democracy and Political Science* (Baltimore: Johns Hopkins University Press, 1990).

40. Mansfield, *America's Constitutional Soul*, 215, 16.

41. Strauss, *Liberalism*, 24.

42. Ceaser, *Designing a Polity*, 50.

43. Peter Steinfels, *The Neoconservatives: The Men Who Are Changing America's Politics* (New York: Simon and Schuster, 1979); Justin Vaïsse, *Neoconservatism: The Biography of a Movement* (Cambridge, MA: Belknap Press of Harvard University Press, 2010); Gary J. Dorrien, *The Neoconservative Mind: Politics, Culture, and the War of Ideology* (Philadelphia: Temple University Press, 1993). See also John Ehrman, "Neoconservatism," in *American Conservatism*, 610–14. A helpful early assessment is Amitai Etzioni, "The Neoconservatives," *Partisan Review* 44 (1977): 431–37.

44. Frohnen, Beer, and Nelson, *American Conservatism*; Hamowy, *Encyclopedia of Libertarianism*; John A. Murley, ed., *Leo Strauss and His Legacy: A Bibliography* (Lanham, MD: Lexington, 2005). There is also an extensive bibliography in Pangle, *Leo Strauss*.

45. See, generally, Hawley, *Right-Wing Critics*; and Nash, *Conservative Intellectual Movement*. Jaffa had an ongoing dispute with fellow Straussian Walter Berns. Steven F. Hayward, *Patriotism Is Not Enough: Harry Jaffa, Walter Berns, and the Arguments That Redefined American Conservatism* (New York: Encounter, 2017). He also frequently attacked traditionalists M. E. Bradford and Willmoore Kendall (continuing long after Kendall's death). John McKee Barr, *Loathing Lincoln: An American Tradition from the Civil War to the Present* (Baton Rouge: Louisiana State University Press, 2014), 231–36, 239, 213–18; Joseph Postell, "Philosopher-Kings or the Sense of the Community? Jaffa, Kendall, and the Problem of Majority Rule," *Anamnesis* 7 (2018): 50–69. See also Kersch, *Conservatives and the Constitution*, 49–68.

Part I · The Administrative State: An Overview

1. Leading critical works by conservative-leaning scholars are Philip Hamburger, *Is Administrative Law Unlawful?* (Chicago: University of Chicago Press, 2014); Joseph Postell, *Bureaucracy in America: The Administrative State's Challenge to Constitutional Government* (Columbia: University of Missouri Press, 2017); and Paul D. Moreno, *The Bureaucrat Kings: The Origins and Underpinnings of America's Bureaucratic State* (Santa Barbara, CA: ABC-CLIO/Praeger, 2017). More sympathetic, liberal treatments are Daniel R. Ernst, *Tocqueville's Nightmare: The Administrative State Emerges in America, 1900–1940* (New York: Oxford University Press, 2014); and Joanna L. Grisinger, *The Unwieldy American State: Administrative Politics since the New Deal* (New York: Cambridge University Press, 2012).

2. Herman Belz, *A Living Constitution or Fundamental Law?* (Lanham, MD: Rowman and Littlefield, 1998), 159–60. See also R. Shep Melnick, "Constitutional Bureaucracy," in *Educating the Prince: Essays in Honor of Harvey Mansfield*, ed. Mark Blitz and William Kristol (Lanham, MD: Rowman and Littlefield, 2000), 246–63.

3. Ernst, *Tocqueville's Nightmare*, and Grisinger, *Unwieldly American State*, treat this theme. See also William Novak, "The Myth of the 'Weak' American State," *American Historical Review* 113 (2008): 752–72, esp. 763, 767.

4. Barry D. Karl, *The Uneasy State: The United States from 1915 to 1945* (Chicago: University of Chicago Press, 1985).

5. Nicholas S. Zeppos, rev. by Richard J. Pierce, "Administrative State," in *The Oxford Companion to the Supreme Court of the United States*, 2nd ed., ed. Kermit L. Hall (New York: Oxford University Press, 2005), 12.

6. See, generally, Peri E. Arnold, *Making the Managerial Presidency: Comprehensive Reorganization Planning, 1905–1996*, 2nd rev. ed. (Lawrence: University Press of Kansas, 1998); Phillip J. Cooper, *The War against Regulation: From Jimmy Carter to George W. Bush* (Lawrence: University Press of Kansas, 2009); David H. Rosenbloom, *Building a Legislative-Centered Public Administration: Congress and the Administrative State, 1946–1999* (Tuscaloosa: University of Alabama Press, 2000); and Kenneth F. Warren, *Administrative Law in the Political System*, 5th ed. (Boulder, CO: Westview Press, 2010). A major recent overview focused on the tension between constitutionalism and the administrative state is Postell, *Bureaucracy in America*. See also Robert L. Rabin, "Federal Regulation in Historical Perspective," *Stanford Law Review* 38 (1986): 1189–1326.

7. J. David Alvis, Jeremy D. Bailey, and F. Flagg Taylor IV, *The Contested Removal Power, 1789–2010* (Lawrence: University Press of Kansas, 2013).

8. John A. Rohr, *To Run a Constitution: The Legitimacy of the Administrative State* (Lawrence: University Press of Kansas, 1986); Anthony M. Bertelli and Laurence E. Lynn Jr., *Madison's Managers: Public Administration and the Constitution* (Baltimore: Johns Hopkins University Press, 2006); Brian J. Cook, *Bureaucracy and Self-Government: Reconsidering the Role of Public Administration in American* Politics, 2nd ed. (Baltimore: Johns Hopkins University Press, 2014).

9. Anne M. Kornhauser, *Debating the American State: Liberal Anxieties and the New Leviathan, 1930–1970* (Philadelphia: University of Pennsylvania Press, 2015). Two enduring works that present the basic issues are Theodore J. Lowi, *The End of Liberalism: Ideology, Policy, and the Crisis of Public Authority* (New York: W. W. Norton, 1969); and James O. Freedman, *Crisis and Legitimacy: The Administrative Process and American Government* (Cambridge: Cambridge University Press, 1978). Hamburger, *Is Administrative Law Lawful?* and Postell, *Bureaucracy in America*, conclude that the crisis of legitimacy is ongoing.

10. Chevron USA, Inc. v. Natural Resources Defense Council, Inc., 467 U.S. 837 (1984).

11. Warren, *Administrative Law*, 70.

12. Warren, 62.

13. Sidney M. Milkis, *The President and the Parties: The Transformation of the American Party System since the New Deal* (New York: Oxford University Press, 1993), 8, 9, 11.

14. R. Shep Melnick, "The Courts, Congress, and Programmatic Rights," in *Remaking American Politics*, ed. Richard A. Harris and Sidney M. Milkis, (Boulder, CO: Westview Press, 1989), 188–212; Milkis, *President and the Parties*, 240–50, 303, 305; Sidney M. Milkis,

"Remaking Government Institutions in the 1970s: Participatory Democracy and the Triumph of Administrative Politics," *Journal of Policy History* 10 (1998): 51–74; Cook, *Bureaucracy and Self-Government*, 167–71; Postell, *Bureaucracy in America*, 247–79.

Chapter 1 · *Traditionalists, Neoconservatives, Libertarians, and the Administrative State*

1. Nash, in *Conservative Intellectual Movement*, 191–93, 203, briefly attends to these themes. Kirk did not use the term "administrative state."

2. Kirk, *Conservative Mind*, 414, 409, 407, 413.

3. Kirk, 414, 410–11.

4. Kirk, 445–46. See also Russell Kirk, *The American Cause* (Chicago: Regnery, 1957), 106, 110.

5. Kirk, *Conservative Mind*, 439, 400.

6. Kirk, *Conservative Mind*, 407.

7. Matthew Mancini, *Alexis de Tocqueville and American Intellectuals: From His Times to Ours* (Lanham, MD: Rowman and Littlefield, 2006), 191. Mancini properly notes that Kirk wrongly assimilated Tocqueville to Burke.

8. Kirk, *Conservative Mind*, 183.

9. Robert A. Nisbet, *The Quest for Community* (New York: Oxford University Press, 1953); Kirk, *Conservative Mind*, 430.

10. Nisbet, *Quest for Community*, 252–53, 255, 282; Robert Nisbet, *The Present Age: Progress and Anarchy in Modern America* (New York: Harper and Row, 1988), 57–58.

11. Robert Nisbet, *Prejudices: A Philosophical Dictionary* (Cambridge, MA: Harvard University Press, 1982), 28.

12. Nisbet, *Quest for Community*, 33, 252–53, 256–57, 268 (quote), 282. See also Brad Lowell Stone, *Robert Nisbet: Communitarian Traditionalist* (Wilmington, DE: ISI, 2000), 27–29, 37–38.

13. Nisbet, *Present Age*, 40–42, 50–51; Robert Nisbet, *Twilight of Authority* (1975; reprint, Indianapolis: Liberty Fund, 2000), 47–48, 50; Nisbet, *Prejudices*, 58 (quote), 214–16.

14. Nisbet, *Quest for Community*, 254. See also Nisbet, *Prejudices*, 34.

15. Nisbet, *Present Age*, 68–69; Nisbet, *Quest for Community*, 260–63.

16. Nisbet, *Prejudices*, 60 (quote); Nisbet, *Present Age*, 59 (quote), 60 (quote), 133.

17. Nisbet, *Prejudices*, 59. For a similar formulation, see ibid., 55; see also Robert Nisbet, *Conservatism: Dream and Reality* (Minneapolis: University of Minnesota Press, 1986).

18. Nisbet, *Prejudices*, 55.

19. Nisbet, *Conservatism*, 40, 40–41 (quote).

20. Nisbet, *Conservatism*, 41; Nisbet, *Prejudices*, 59–61.

21. Ivan Szelenyi and Bill Martin, "Three Waves of New Class Theories," *Theory and Society* 17 (1988): 645–67; Garry Dorrien, *The Neoconservative Mind: Politics, Culture, and the War of Ideology* (Philadelphia: Temple University Press, 1993), 30–34.

22. Kirk, *Conservative Mind*, 407; Nisbet, *Present Age*, 65–66; Samuel T. Francis, *Thinkers of Our Time: James Burnham* (1984; reprint, London: Claridge, 1999), 27–30.

23. Francis, *Thinkers of Our Time*, 6, 76–77, 86 (quote), 87, 134, 144–45. Francis provides a fuller explication of Burnham; here I focus on his ideas most germane to the administrative state.

24. This exposition has been aided by Francis, *Thinkers of Our Time*, chap. 1. See also Dorrien, *Neoconservative Mind*, 34–44.

25. James Burnham, *Congress and the American Tradition* (Chicago: Regnery, 1959).

26. Burnham, 336, 298, 337.

27. Nisbet, *Prejudices*, 31–32, 34 (quote); Nisbet, *Twilight of Authority*, 47.

28. Nisbet, *Present Age*, 64, 65–66.

29. Nisbet, *Twilight of Authority*, 177–209.

30. Samuel Francis, *Beautiful Losers: Essays on the Failure of American Conservatism* (Columbia: University of Missouri Press, 1993.)

31. Francis, 225.

32. Francis, 98–99.

33. Francis, 225, 63.

34. Francis, 225 (quotes), 3–4, 11, 16–17, 226.

35. Francis, 231. "Political action in a cultural power vacuum will be largely futile." Ibid.

36. Francis, 61–62, 77, 230.

37. Francis, 230.

38. Samuel T. Francis, *Leviathan and Its Enemies* (Arlington, VA: Radix/Washington Summit, 2016). See Johnathan O'Neill, "Traditionalist Conservatism and the Administrative State: The Diagnosis of a New Social Form," *Political Science Reviewer* 42 (2018): 398–430; and Matthew Rose, "The Outsider," *First Things* 296 (October 2019): 33–42.

39. Paul Edward Gottfried, *After Liberalism: Mass Democracy in the Managerial State* (Princeton, NJ: Princeton University Press, 1999).

40. Gottfried, xi.

41. Gottfried, 91, 141.

42. Gottfried, 85, 91, 95, 99, 109.

43. Gottfried, 134, 140 (quote).

44. Gottfried, 139. This judgment was central to Paul Gottfried, *Conservatism in America: Making Sense of the American Right* (New York: Palgrave Macmillan, 2007), which argued that this development helped neoconservatism to displace traditionalism.

45. Gottfried, *After Liberalism*, 103, 139 (quote), 141.

46. Kendall and Carey, *Basic Symbols of the American Political Tradition*.

47. Kendall and Carey, 105.

48. Kendall and Carey, xxii.

49. Kendall and Carey, 84–95.

50. Kendall and Carey, xxi, xix.

51. Bruce Frohnen and George W. Carey, *Constitutional Morality and the Rise of Quasi-law* (Cambridge, MA: Harvard University Press, 2016).

52. Frohnen and Carey, 12 and chap. 6.

53. Frohnen and Carey, 86–90, 232–33.

54. Frohnen and Carey, 18. See also ibid., 159–60, 218–19, 236, 238, 240–41.

55. Frohnen and Carey, 18.

56. Frohnen and Carey, 14, 52.

57. Frohnen and Carey, 221, 240, 110–14, 10.

58. Frohnen and Carey, 150–151, 162, 166, 181, 8.

59. Frohnen and Carey, 230.

60. Frohnen and Carey, 18 (quote), 239.

61. Frohnen and Carey, 241.

62. Steinfels, *Neoconservatives*, 58–65; Vaïsse, *Neoconservatism*, 53–58, 78.

63. Neoconservatives often cited Nisbet, and occasionally he published in their journals. Early assessments labeled him a neoconservative. Amitai Etzioni, "The Neoconservatives," *Partisan Review* 44 (1977): 431–37, 431; Steinfels, *Neoconservatives*, 5, 11, 54, 243, 284.

64. Vaïsse, *Neoconservatism*, 54–55.

65. Office of Policy Planning and Research, United States Department of Labor, "The Negro Family: The Case for National Action" (Washington, DC: Government Printing Office, 1965); Greg Weiner, *American Burke: The Uncommon Liberalism of Daniel Patrick Moynihan* (Lawrence: University Press of Kansas, 2015), 67–68, 76, 80. See also Nathan Glazer, "The Limits of Social Policy," *Commentary* (September 1971), 51–58; Irving Kristol, "Welfare: The Best of Intentions, the Worst of Results" in *Neoconservatism: The Autobiography of an Idea* (New York: Free Press, 1995), 43–49.

66. Ken I. Kersch, "Neoconservatives and the Courts: *The Public Interest*, 1965–1980," in *Ourselves and Our Posterity: Essays in Constitutional Originalism*, ed. Bradley C. S. Watson (Lanham, MD: Lexington, 2009), 249.

67. Vaïsse, *Neoconservatism*, 54, 55 (quote), 78. See also Steinfels, *Neoconservatives*, 65.

68. Irving Kristol, "Skepticism, Meliorism, and *The Public Interest*," *Public Interest* 81 (Fall 1985): 31–41, 32.

69. James Q. Wilson, "A Life in the Public Interest," *Wall Street Journal*, Sept. 21, 2009, www.wsj.com.

70. James Q. Wilson, "The Rise of the Bureaucratic State," *The Public Interest* 41 (Fall 1975): 77–103, 80.

71. Wilson, 100–101.

72. Wilson, 96–97, 93–94, 102–3.

73. Wilson, 103.

74. James Q. Wilson, *Bureaucracy: What Government Agencies Do and Why They Do It* (New York: Basic Books, 1989), 376.

75. James Q. Wilson, "The Bureaucracy Problem," *The Public Interest* 6 (Winter 1967): 3–9, 6 (italics removed).

76. Wilson, "Bureaucracy Problem," 6

77. James Q. Wilson, "Foreword," in *The Essential Neoconservative Reader*, ed. Mark Gerson (Reading, MA: Addison Wesley, 1996), viii.

78. Wilson, *Bureaucracy*.

79. Wilson's scholarship on bureaucracy is treated insightfully in an online forum at www.lawliberty.org (November 2014), and in Jeremy Rozansky and Josh Lerner, "The Political Science of James Q. Wilson," *New Atlantis* 35 (Spring 2012): 84–98.

80. John O. McGinnis, "How to Make Bureaucracy More Accountable," *Law & Liberty*, November 7, 2014, https://lawliberty.org/forum/how-to-make-the-bureaucracy-more-accountable/; and Georg Vanberg, "When They're Too Good at Their Job . . . ," *Law & Liberty*, November 20, 2014, https://lawliberty.org/forum/when-theyre-too-good-at-their-job/.

81. Kimberley Hendrickson, "Bureaucracy and Some Bureaucracy Problems," *Law &*

Liberty, November 14, 2014, https://lawliberty.org/forum/bureaucracy-and-some-bureau cracy-problems/.

82. Wilson, "Bureaucracy Problem," 8.

83. Wilson, *Bureaucracy*, 377, 378. See also Wilson, "Bureaucracy Problem," 9; Wilson, "Rise of the Bureaucratic State," 102–3.

84. James Q. Wilson, "Does the Separation of Powers Still Work?" *The Public Interest* 86 (Winter 1987): 36–52, 39, 50 (quote).

85. Wilson, "Does the Separation of Powers Still Work?" 50, 52 (quote).

86. Scholars of neoconservatism have accorded substantial attention to the "new class" theme. See Vaïsse, *Neoconservatism*, 77–78; Steinfels, *Neoconservatives*, 56–58, 188–213, 279–91; Dorrien, *Neoconservative Mind*, 13–17, 95–98, 217–22, 381–85.

87. Francis, *James Burnham*, 27–30, Dorrien, *Neoconservative Mind*, 63; Vaïsse, *Neoconservatism*, 26.

88. David Bazelon, *Power in America: The Politics of the New Class* (New York: New American Library, 1967), 331–32, 367–76.

89. Michael Harrington, *Toward a Democratic Left: A Radical Program for a New Majority* (New York: Macmillan, 1968), 288, 290, 291. See also Dorrien, *Neoconservative Mind*, 14–15. Moynihan was initially cautiously optimistic that a combination of affluence and expertise was inaugurating a new era of professionally directed and effective social reform. Moynihan, "The Professionalization of Reform," *The Public Interest* 1 (Fall 1965): 6–16.

90. Norman Podhoretz, "The Adversary Culture and the New Class," in *The New Class?* ed. B. Bruce-Briggs (New Brunswick, NJ: Transaction, 1979), 19–31; Jeanne J. Kirkpatrick, "Politics and the New Class," ibid., 33–48.

91. Irving Kristol, *Two Cheers for Capitalism* (New York: Basic Books, 1978), 183, 177 (emphasis in orig.).

92. Nathan Glazer, "Lawyers and the New Class," in *The New Class?* 97–100; Podhoretz, "Adversary Culture," 30; Kirkpatrick, "Politics and the New Class," 45–46; Robert L. Bartley, "Business and the New Class," in *The New Class?* 59, 64, 66. See also Steinfels, *Neoconservatives*, 287; Dorrien, *Neoconservative Mind*, 94–97, 102, 221; Weiner, *American Burke*, 25–26, 65–66.

93. Daniel Bell, "The New Class: A Muddled Concept," in *The New Class?* 169–90; Steinfels, *Neoconservatives*, 57 (second quote); Bruce-Briggs, "Introduction," in *The New Class?* 1–18; Dorrien, *Neoconservative Mind*, 382.

94. This is a theme in Steinfels, *Neoconservatives*.

95. Quoted in Dorrien, *Neoconservative Mind*, 102.

96. This judgment accords with Daniel T. Rodgers, *Age of Fracture* (Cambridge, MA: Belknap Press of Harvard University Press, 2011), 85; and Vaïsse, *Neoconservatism*, 77.

97. Kristol, *Two Cheers for Capitalism*, 145; Steinfels, *Neoconservatives*, 189 (quote), 289–91; Dorrien, *Neoconservative Mind*, 100–103, 385.

98. Francis, *Beautiful Losers*, 93 (quote), 110–11, 116.

99. Francis, 114. See also Burnham, "What New Class?" *National Review*, January 20, 1978, 98–99.

100. Francis, *Beautiful Losers*, 12–13, 117, 223–24, 204, 229.

101. Gottfried, *After Liberalism*, 72–74; Gottfried, *Conservatism in America*, 70–73.

102. Friedrich A. Hayek, *The Road to Serfdom* (Chicago: University of Chicago Press, 1944), chaps. 5 and 6; Hayek, *Constitution of Liberty*, part 2; Friedrich A. Hayek, "The Use

of Knowledge in Society" (1945) in *The Libertarian Reader*, ed. David Boaz (New York: Free Press, 1997), 215–24.

103. Hayek, *Road to Serfdom*, 83.

104. Hayek, *Road to Serfdom*, 82.

105. Friedrich A. Hayek, *Law, Legislation, and Liberty: A New Statement of the Liberal Principles of Justice and Political Economy*, 3 volumes in 1 (London: Routledge, 1982), 2:87, 85.

106. Hayek, *Law, Legislation, and Liberty*, 2:86.

107. Hayek, *Law, Legislation, and Liberty*, 3:30.

108. Hayek, *Constitution of Liberty*, 202.

109. Hayek, *Constitution of Liberty*, 200–201.

110. Hayek, *Constitution of Liberty*, 201.

111. Hayek, *Constitution of Liberty*, 245.

112. Hayek, *Constitution of Liberty*, 246, 247.

113. Hayek, *Constitution of Liberty*, 247. See also Joseph Postell, "The Anti–New Deal Progressive: Roscoe Pound's Alternative Administrative State," *Review of Politics* 74 (2012): 53–85.

114. Hayek, *Constitution of Liberty*, 261 (quote), 262 (citing Pound); see also ibid., 215.

115. Hayek, *Constitution of Liberty*, 262 (italics removed). Hayek was of course aware of the ultimately Tocquevillian provenance of this argument. Ibid., 251.

116. Hayek, *Law, Legislation, Liberty*, 3:100.

117. Hayek, *Law, Legislation, and Liberty*, 3:35.

118. Hayek, *Law, Legislation, and Liberty*, 3:27–29. This question is taken up in relation to legislatures in the present book's conclusion.

119. Hayek, *Law, Legislation, and Liberty*, 3:30.

120. Hayek, *Law, Legislation, and Liberty*, 3:105. See also ibid., 3:35.

121. Hayek, *Law, Legislation, and Liberty*, 3:115.

122. Ludwig von Mises, *Bureaucracy* (New Haven, CT: Yale University Press, 1944).

123. Mises, 7, 44 (quote).

124. Mises, 89–92.

125. Mises, 5–7.

126. Mises, 9.

127. Mises, 9.

128. Mises, 120.

129. Helpful overviews of what quickly became a large field are Ronald Wintrobe, "Modern Bureaucratic Theory," in *Perspectives on Public Choice: A Handbook*, ed. Dennis C. Mueller (New York: Cambridge University Press, 1997), 429–54; and Terry M. Moe, "The Positive Theory of Public Bureaucracy," ibid., 455–80. See, generally, Charles K. Rowley and Friedrich Schneider, ed., *The Encyclopedia of Public Choice*, 2 vols. (New York: Kluwer/Springer, 2004).

130. Peter Boettke and Peter Leeson, "An 'Austrian" Perspective on Public Choice," in *Encyclopedia of Public Choice*, 2:27–31, 28–29.

131. Dennis C. Mueller, "Public Choice, Social Choice, and Political Economy," *Public Choice* 163 (2015): 379–87. See also Patrick Dunleavy, *Democracy, Bureaucracy, and Public Choice: Economic Explanations in Political Science* (Hemel Hempstead, UK: Harvester Wheatsheaf, 1991), 5.

132. Canonical works include Anthony Downs, *An Economic Theory of Democracy* (New

York: Harper and Row, 1957); James M. Buchanan and Gordon Tullock, *The Calculus of Consent* (Ann Arbor: University of Michigan Press, 1962); William H. Riker, *The Theory of Political Coalitions* (New Haven, CT: Yale University Press, 1962); and Mancur Olson Jr., *The Logic of Collective Action* (Cambridge, MA: Harvard University Press, 1965). A helpful historical overview is William C. Mitchell, "Virginia, Rochester, and Bloomington: Twenty-Five Years of Public Choice and Political Science," *Public Choice* 56 (1988): 101–19.

133. William A. Niskanen, "Gordon Tullock's Contribution to Bureaucracy," *Public Choice* 152 (2012): 97–101, 97. To them this perspective was "inordinately naïve." William F. Shugart II, "James Buchanan and Gordon Tullock: A Half-Century On," in *Public Choice, Past and Present: The Legacy of James M. Buchanan and Gordon Tullock*, ed. Dwight R. Lee (New York: Springer, 2013), 101–23, 112.

134. Gordon Tullock, *The Politics of Bureaucracy* (Washington, DC: PublicAffairs, 1965). On Tullock's analysis of bureaucracy, see Christopher J. Coyne, "*The Politics of Bureaucracy* and the Failure of Post-War Reconstruction," *Public Choice* 135 (2008): 11–22; Niskanen, "Gordon Tullock's Contribution"; and James M. Buchanan, "Foreword," in Tullock, *Politics of Bureaucracy*, 1–9.

135. Tullock, *Politics of Bureaucracy*, 137–41, 73, 167–68.

136. Tullock, 176, 177 (quote), 186.

137. Anthony Downs, *Inside Bureaucracy* (Boston: Little, Brown, 1967), 259–60. Mueller, in "Public Choice, Social Choice," 386, describes him (and others) as a liberal "in the American sense of the term."

138. Downs, *Inside Bureaucracy*, 88.

139. Downs, 87.

140. Dunleavy, *Democracy, Bureaucracy*, 147–54, 154 (quote). See also Larry D. Terry, *Leadership of Public Bureaucracies: The Administrator as Conservator* (Thousand Oaks, CA: Sage, 1995), 39–40.

141. Moe, "Positive Theory of Public Bureaucracy," in *Perspectives on Public Choice*, 457.

142. William A. Niskanen Jr., *Bureaucracy and Representative Government* (Chicago: Aldine-Atherton, 1971).

143. Thomas E. Borcherding and Portia D. Besocke, "The Contemporary Political Economy Approach to Bureaucracy," in *Encyclopedia of Public Choice*, 2:116–21, 117 (quote); Michelle A. Vachris, "Principal-Agent Relationships in the Theory of Bureaucracy," in *Encyclopedia of Public Choice*, 433–36. See also Moe, "Positive Theory"; and Wintrobe, "Modern Bureaucratic Theory."

144. Shugart, "James Buchanan and Gordon Tullock," 115–16. For a similarly fundamental summary statement, see Gordon Tullock, Arthur Seldon, and Gordon L. Brady, *Government Failure: A Primer in Public Choice* (Washington, DC: Cato Institute, 2002), 62.

145. Rodgers, *Age of Fracture*, 85–89.

146. Roger Pilon, "On the Origins of the Modern Libertarian Legal Movement," *Chapman Law Review* 16 (2013): 255–68, 257.

147. Richard A. Epstein, *Takings: Private Property and the Power of Eminent Domain* (Cambridge, MA: Harvard University Press, 1985), x, 281; Richard A. Epstein, "Why the Modern Administrative State Is Inconsistent with the Rule of Law," *NYU Journal of Law and Liberty* 3 (2008): 491–515, 495–96; Gary Lawson, "The Rise and Rise of the Administrative State," *Harvard Law Review* 107 (1994): 1231–54, 1231 (quote).

148. Richard A. Epstein, "Self-Interest and the Constitution," *Journal of Legal Education* 37 (1987): 153–61, 156.

149. Lawson, "Rise and Rise of the Administrative State," 1248.

150. A. L. A. Schecter Poultry Corp. v. United States, 295 U.S. 495 (1935); Panama Refining Co v. Ryan, 293 U.S. 388 (1935). Richard A. Epstein, *Design for Liberty: Private Property, Public Administration, and the Rule of Law* (Cambridge, MA: Harvard University Press, 2011), 3, 6–7, 28, 151–52, 176–79, 191–92; Richard A. Epstein, *The Classical Liberal Constitution: The Uncertain Quest for Limited Government* (Cambridge, MA: Harvard University Press, 2014), 39, 267–84; Lawson, "Rise and Rise of the Administrative State," 1237–41; Gary Lawson, "Delegation and the Constitution," *Regulation* 22 (Summer 1999): 23–29, the argument of which is elaborated in Gary Lawson, "Delegation and Original Meaning," *Virginia Law Review* 88 (2002): 327–404.

151. Epstein, *Design for Liberty*, 151; Epstein, *Classical Liberal Constitution*, 39 (quote), 276; Lawson, "Rise and Rise of the Administrative State," 1248.

152. Chevron USA, Inc. v. Natural Resources Defense Council, Inc., 467 U.S. 837 (1984); Epstein, *Design for Liberty*, 7, 153–54, 156–59; Epstein, "Why the Modern Administrative State Is Inconsistent with the Rule of Law," 505, 508–10, 514–15; Lawson, "Rise and Rise of the Administrative State," 1247–48.

153. A libertarian defense of the strong version of the removal power, which particularly disagrees with Lawson, is Neomi Rao, "Removal: Necessary and Sufficient for Presidential Control," *Alabama Law Review* 65 (2014): 1205–76.

154. Lawson, "Rise and Rise of the Administrative State," 1243–46.

155. Epstein, *Classical Liberal Constitution*, 276 (italics removed). See also Epstein, "Modern Administrative State," 499–503.

156. Epstein, *Classical Liberal Constitution*, 278.

Chapter 2 · Straussians, the Administrative State, and the Rise of the Unitary Executive

1. Leo Strauss, "An Epilogue," in *Essays on the Scientific Study of Politics*, ed. Herbert J. Storing (New York: Holt, Rinehart, and Winston, 1962), 311.

2. Strauss offered a litany of Weber's self-contradictions. Strauss, *Natural Right and History*, 49–62.

3. Strauss, "An Epilogue"; Leo Strauss, *On Tyranny*, revised and enlarged ed. (New York: Free Press, 1963), 189; Strauss, *Natural Right and History*, 1–5; Nasser Behnegar, *Leo Strauss, Max Weber, and the Scientific Study of Politics* (Chicago: University of Chicago Press, 2003), 187, 189–94, 199–206.

4. A helpful overview is Kent Aiken Kirwan, "Herbert J. Storing and the Study of Public Administration," *Political Science Reviewer* 11 (1981): 193–219, 201–9.

5. Herbert J. Storing, "The Science of Administration: Herbert A. Simon," in *Essays on the Scientific Study of Politics*, 85, 86, 128, 76, 77.

6. Storing, 144–47, 150 (quote).

7. Storing, 126, Strauss, "An Epilogue," 317–18.

8. Herbert J. Storing, "The Problem of Big Government" (1963), in *Toward a More Perfect Union: Writings of Herbert J. Storing*, ed. Joseph M. Bessette (Washington, DC: AEI, 1995), 305.

9. Storing, "The Problem of Big Government," 304. My analysis is informed by Kirwan,

"Herber J. Storing and the Study of Public Administration," 210–20; and Douglas Morgan et al., "Recovering, Restoring, and Renewing the Foundations of American Public Administration: The Contributions of Herbert J. Storing," *Public Administration Review* 70 (2010): 621–33.

10. Woodrow Wilson, "The Study of Administration," *Political Science Quarterly* 2 (1887): 197–222. The process of abandonment is well traced in Kent Aiken Kirwan, "The Crisis of Identity in the Study of Public Administration: Woodrow Wilson," *Polity* 9 (1977): 321–43, 323–26.

11. Herbert J. Storing, "Leonard D. White and the Study of Public Administration" (1965), in *Toward a More Perfect Union*, 345.

12. Storing, "Political Parties and Bureaucracy" (1964), in *Toward a More Perfect Union*, 312–14; Storing, "American Statesmanship: Old and New" (1980), ibid., 411–18; Morgan et al., "Recovering, Restoring, and Renewing," 625.

13. Storing, "The Crucial Link: Public Administration, Public Responsibility, and the Public Interest" (1964), in *Toward a More Perfect Union*, 282.

14. Storing, "Political Parties and Bureaucracy," 314–24. Paul O. Carrese, in "Constitutionalist Political Science: Rediscovering Storing's Philosophical Moderation," *American Political Thought* 4 (Spring 2015): 259–88, emphasizes the centrality of moderation in Storing's thought but does not analyze bureaucracy in this context.

15. Storing, "The Problem of Big Government"; Storing, "American Statesmanship," 419.

16. Storing, "The Problem of Big Government," 302–3.

17. Storing, "Political Parties and Bureaucracy," 320.

18. Storing, "Political Parties and Bureaucracy," 322.

19. Storing, "Political Parties and Bureaucracy," 320.

20. Storing, "Political Parties and Bureaucracy," 322 (emphasis in orig.).

21. Morgan et al., "Recovering, Restoring, and Renewing," 628; Stephanie P. Newbold, "Toward a Constitutional School for American Public Administration," *Public Administration Review* 70 (July–August 2010): 538–46, 543; Terry, *Leadership of Public Bureaucracies*, 16–19; Pangle, *Leo Strauss*, 115–17. See also Peter Augustine Lawler, Robert Martin Schaefer, and David Lewis Schaefer, *Active Duty: Public Administration as Democratic Statesmanship* (Lanham, MD: Rowman and Littlefield, 1998).

22. John A. Rohr, *To Run a Constitution: The Legitimacy of the Administrative State* (Lawrence: University Press of Kansas, 1986), 4–5, 11, 56, 73–75, 171.

23. Rohr, "Toward a More Perfect Union," *Public Administration Review* 53 (1993): 246–49; Rohr, *To Run a Constitution*, 5–9, ix–xii.

24. Rohr, *To Run a Constitution*, xii, xiii.

25. Rohr, *To Run a Constitution*, 18.

26. Rohr, *To Run a Constitution*, 18 (quoting *Federalist* 47, Rohr's emphasis).

27. Rohr, *To Run a Constitution*, 19 (quoting *Federalist* 66).

28. Rohr, *To Run a Constitution*, 27.

29. Rohr, *To Run a Constitution*, 28–39.

30. Rohr, *To Run a Constitution*, 40–53.

31. John Uhr, "John Rohr's Concept of Regime Values: Locating Theory in Public Administration," *Administration & Society* 46 (2014): 141–52, 143, 146–47, 150.

32. John A. Rohr, *Ethics for Bureaucrats: An Essay on Law and Values* (New York: Marcel Dekker, 1978), 2.

33. Rohr, *Ethics for Bureaucrats*, 2 (quote), 59, 81–82n33.

34. Rohr, *Ethics for Bureaucrats*, 237 (quote; emphasis in orig.), 238, 59–86.

35. Rohr, *Ethics for Bureaucrats*; Rohr, *To Run a Constitution*, xii–xiii, 184, 192–93, 181.

36. Rohr, *To Run a Constitution*, 193 (emphasis in orig.).

37. Rohr, *To Run a Constitution*, 186–92, 193 (quote).

38. Rohr, *To Run a Constitution*, 180 (quote), 172, 117.

39. Rohr, *To Run a Constitution*, 157.

40. John A. Rohr, "Constitutional Legitimacy and the Administrative State: A Reading of the Brownlow Commission Report," in *The New Deal and Its Legacy: Critique and Reappraisal*, ed. Robert Eden (New York: Greenwood Press, 1989), 116, 117 (quote). See also Rohr, *To Run a Constitution*, x–xiii.

41. Ralph A. Rossum, "Herbert J. Storing's Constitutionalism," *Political Science Reviewer* 29 (2000): 39–69, 54–55; John Marini, "Bureaucracy and America: Leo Strauss on Constitutionalism, the State, and Tyranny," in *Leo Strauss, the Straussians, and the American Regime*, 384, 397–98, 402–3n35; Ronald J. Pestritto, *Woodrow Wilson and the Roots of Modern Liberalism* (Lanham, MD: Rowman and Littlefield, 2005), 235–37, 249–50n49. See also Charles R. Kesler, "Woodrow Wilson and the Statesmanship of Progress," in *Natural Right and Political Right: Essays in Honor of Harry V. Jaffa*, ed. Thomas B. Silver and Peter W. Schramm (Durham, NC: Carolina Academic Press, 1984), 125n13.

42. Martin Diamond, "Democracy and *The Federalist*: A Reconsideration of the Framers' Intent" (1959), in Martin Diamond, *As Far as Republican Principles Will Admit*, ed. William A. Schambra (Washington, DC: AEI, 1992), 17–36; Martin Diamond, "Conservatives, Liberals, and the Constitution" (1967), ibid., 70–73; Michael P. Zuckert, "Refinding the Founding: Martin Diamond, Leo Strauss, and the American Regime," in *Leo Strauss, the Straussians, and the American Regime*, 239.

43. It is worth noting that the general idea of a "German connection" in Progressivism was not solely a Straussian interpretation. See Robert D. Miewald, "The Origins of Wilson's Thought: The German Tradition and the Organic State," in *Politics and Administration: Woodrow Wilson and American Public Administration*, ed. Jack Rabin and James S. Bowman (New York: Marcel Dekker, 1984), 17–30; and Christian Rosser, "Woodrow Wilson's Administrative Thought and German Political Theory," *Public Administration Review* 70 (2010): 547–56. Philip Hamburger, in *Is Administrative Law Unlawful?* (Chicago: University of Chicago Press, 2014), 447–53, 462–78, emphasizes that German thought transmitted older civilian absolutist administrative concepts as well as historicism.

44. Paul Eidelberg, *A Discourse on Statesmanship: The Design and Transformation of the American Polity* (Urbana: University of Illinois Press, 1974), 358 (quoting Wilson), 359 (quoting Wilson; emphasis in orig.), 360.

45. Eidelberg, 295–302. Will Morrissey has observed that Eidelberg's "argument on Wilson's project has been seminal, at least among Strauss-influenced scholars." Will Morrissey, "Paul Eidelberg: The Mixed Regime and the American Regime," in *Leo Strauss, the Straussians, and the American Regime*, 253–63, quote at 262.

46. Kirwan, "Crisis of Identity," 326 (quote), 327–30, 341 (quote).

47. Kent Aiken Kirwan, "Historicism and Statesmanship in the Reform Argument of Woodrow Wilson," *Interpretation* 9 (1981): 339–51, 350. Another assessment that empha-

sized Darwinian evolution more than historicism is Christopher Wolfe, "Woodrow Wilson: Interpreting the Founding," *Review of Politics* 41 (1979): 121–42.

48. Pestritto, *Woodrow Wilson*; Ronald J. Pestritto, "The Progressive Origins of the Administrative State: Wilson, Goodnow, and Landis," *Social Philosophy and Policy* 24 (2007): 16–54; Ronald J. Pestritto, "The Birth of the Administrative State: Where It Came From and What It Means for Limited Government," Heritage Foundation, November 20, 2007, https://www.heritage.org/political-process/report/the-birth-the-administrative-state -where-it-came-and-what-it-means-limited; John Marini, *The Politics of Budget Control: Congress, the Presidency, and the Growth of the Administrative State* (Washington, DC: Crane Russak, 1992); Marini, "Bureaucracy and America"; John Marini, *Unmasking the Administrative State: The Crisis of American Politics in the Twenty-First Century* (New York: Encounter, 2019). See also John Marini and Ken Masugi, eds., *The Progressive Revolution in Politics and Political Science* (Lanham, MD: Rowman and Littlefield, 2005); Charles R. Kesler, "Separation of Powers and the Administrative State," in *The Imperial Congress: Crisis in the Separation of Powers*, ed. Gordon S. Jones and John A. Marini (New York: Pharos, 1988), 20–40; Kesler, "Woodrow Wilson and the Statesmanship of Progress"; Bradley C. S. Watson, *Living Constitution, Dying Faith: Progressivism and the New Science of Jurisprudence* (Wilmington, DE: ISI, 2009), esp. 12, 88, 90, 94–105.

49. James W. Ceaser, Glen E. Thurow, Jeffrey Tulis, and Joseph M. Bessette, "The Rise of the Rhetorical Presidency," *Presidential Studies Quarterly* 11 (1981): 158–71.

50. The connection between Wilson's leadership doctrine, the historicist conception of progress, and the purpose of the administrative state is perhaps most explicitly drawn in Kesler, "Separation of Powers and the Administrative State," 31–39; Marini, *Politics of Budget Control*, 41–48, 184–89; and Pestritto, *Woodrow Wilson*, 204–16, 221–46.

51. Bernard Crick, *The American Science of Politics: Its Origins and Conditions* (Berkeley: University of California Press, 1959).

52. John Marini, "Progressivism, Modern Political Science, and the Transformation of American Constitutionalism," in *Progressive Revolution*, 221–51, quotes at 233, 234.

53. Marini, "Bureaucracy and America," 385–89; Marini, "Progressivism, Modern Political Science, and the Transformation of American Constitutionalism," 235–42; Dennis J. Mahoney "A Newer Science of Politics: *The Federalist* and American Political Science in the Progressive Era," in *Saving the Revolution:* The Federalist *Papers and the American Founding* (New York: Free Press, 1989), 250–64. See also Dennis J. Mahoney, *Politics and Progress: The Emergence of American Political Science* (Lanham, MD: Lexington, 2004).

54. Marini, "Progressivism, Modern Political Science, and the Transformation of American Constitutionalism," quotes at 234, 235.

55. A good summary statement of this view is Kesler, "Separation of Powers and the Administrative State." My treatment of this theme in this and the following paragraph presents a composite as expressed in the various works of Marini cited above, as well as Jeremy Rabkin, *Judicial Compulsions: How Public Law Distorts Public Policy* (New York: Basic Books, 1989); Melnick, "The Courts, Congress, and Programmatic Rights"; John Adams Wettergreen, "The Regulatory Revolution and the New Bureaucratic State," Heritage Lectures 153, Heritage Foundation, April 2, 1988, https://www.heritage.org/political -process/report/the-regulatory-revolution-and-the-new-bureaucratic-state; and John Adams Wettergreen, "The Regulatory Revolution and the New Bureaucratic State, Part II," Heritage Lectures 181, Heritage Foundation, February 1, 1989, https://www.heritage.org/government

-regulation/report/the-regulatory-revolution-and-the-new-bureaucratic-state-part-ii. See also Mansfield, 75, 160, 186–88.

56. Rabkin, *Judicial Compulsions*, 39.

57. Melnick, "Constitutional Bureaucracy."

58. Mancini, *Alexis de Tocqueville and American Intellectuals*, 203.

59. Mancini, *Alexis de Tocqueville and American Intellectuals*, 210 (quote; italics removed). See also Peter Augustine Lawler, *The Restless Mind: Alexis de Tocqueville on the Origin and Perpetuation of Human Liberty* (Lanham, MD: Rowman and Littlefield, 1993), 101–2, 179n16.

60. Paul A. Rahe, *Soft Despotism, Democracy's Drift: Montesquieu, Rousseau, Tocqueville, and the Modern Prospect* (New Haven, CT: Yale University Press, 2009), 242–70; John Marini, "Centralized Administration and the 'New Despotism,'" in *Interpreting Tocqueville's Democracy in America*, ed. Ken Masugi (Lanham, MD: Rowman and Littlefield, 1991), 255–86; Marini, *Politics of Budget Control*, 167, 185–86, 193; Wettergreen, "Regulatory Revolution," 12; Wettergreen, "Regulatory Revolution, Part II," 3, 6.

61. Arnold, *Making the Managerial Presidency*; Grisinger, *Unwieldy American State*.

62. Developments prior to Reagan can be traced in George C. Eads and Michael Fix, *Relief or Reform? Reagan's Regulatory Dilemma* (Washington, DC: Urban Institute Press, 1984), 45–67; Cooper, *War against Regulation*, 14–28; Barry D. Friedman, *Regulation in the Reagan-Bush Era: The Eruption of Presidential Influence* (Pittsburgh: University of Pittsburgh Press, 1995), 27–32; Melanie Marlowe, "The Unitary Executive and Review of Agency Rulemaking," in *The Unitary Executive and the Modern Presidency*, ed. Ryan J. Barilleaux and Christopher S. Kelley (College Station: Texas A&M University Press, 2010), 81–85.

63. Friedman, *Regulation in the Reagan-Bush Era*, 5, 178.

64. Reuel Schiller, "An Unexpected Antagonist: Courts, Deregulation, and Conservative Judicial Ideology, 1980–94," in *Making Legal History: Essays in Honor of William E. Nelson*, ed. Daniel J. Hulsebosch and R. B. Bernstein (New York: New York University Press, 2013), 264–92.

65. The most detailed study is Amanda Hollis-Brusky, "Helping Ideas Have Consequences: Political and Intellectual Investment in the Unitary Executive Theory, 1981–2000," *Denver University Law Review* 89 (2011): 197–244.

66. Executive Order 12,291, 46 *Federal Register* 13193 (February 17, 1981).

67. "Proposed Executive Order Entitled 'Federal Regulation,'" 5 *Opinions of the Office of Legal Counsel* 59, 60 (February 13, 1981), quoting Myers v. United States, 272 US 52, 135 (1926).

68. "Proposed Executive Order Entitled 'Federal Regulation,'" 60.

69. "Proposed Executive Order Entitled 'Federal Regulation,'" 61–62, 62n4, citing Myers, 272 US 135.

70. Marshall J. Breger and Gary J. Edles, *Independent Agencies in the United States: Law, Structure, and Politics* (New York: Oxford University Press, 2015), 183–84.

71. Hollis-Brusky, "Helping Ideas Have Consequences," 205–6; "Statute Limiting the President's Authority to Supervise the Director of the Centers for Disease Control in the Distribution of an AIDS Pamphlet," 12 *Opinions of the Office of Legal Counsel* 47, 49–52, (March 11, 1988).

72. "Statute Limiting," 48 (emphasis in orig.).

73. Steven Teles, "Transformative Bureaucracy: Reagan's Lawyers and the Dynamics of Political Investment," *Studies in American Political Development* 23 (2009): 61–83.

74. Teles, 75–82. See also Johnathan O'Neill, *Originalism in American Law and Politics: A Constitutional History* (Baltimore: Johns Hopkins University Press, 2005), 153–59.

75. Teles, "Transformative Bureaucracy," 79, 80; Hollis-Brusky, "Helping Ideas Have Consequences," 207.

76. "Address of the Honorable Edwin Meese III, Attorney General of the United States, before the Federal Bar Association," September 13, 1985, US Department of Justice, accessed December 28, 2021, www.justice.gov/sites/default/files/ag/legacy/2011/08/23/09-13 -1985.pdf.

77. "Address of the Honorable Edwin Meese III," 3, 5, 9, 10.

78. "Address of the Honorable Edwin Meese III," 9.

79. Brief for the United States, Bowsher v. Synar, April 9, 1986, 1986 WL 728082 (U.S.) (Appellate Brief), Supreme Court of the United States, 10.

80. Brief for the United States, Bowsher v. Synar, 46n32.

81. Oral argument, April 23, 1986, in *Bowsher v. Synar, Oyez*, accessed December 28, 2021, https://www.oyez.org/cases/1985/85-1377, at 01:01:45.

82. Bowsher v. Synar, 478 US 714, 724, 725n4 (1986). See also Alvis, Bailey, and Taylor, *Contested Removal Power*, 191–96; Breger and Edles, *Independent Agencies*, 65; and Bernard Schwartz, "An Administrative Law 'Might Have Been': Chief Justice Burger's *Bowsher v. Synar* Draft," *Administrative Law Review* 42 (Spring 1990): 221–49.

83. *In re Sealed Case*, 838 F.2d 476 (D.C. Cir. 1988).

84. Brief for the United States as Amicus Curiae Supporting Appellees, Morrison v. Olson, April 8, 1988, 1988 WL 1031600 (U.S.) (Appellate Brief), Supreme Court of the United States, 6–9.

85. Brief for the United States as Amicus Curiae, 29.

86. Morrison v. Olson, 487 US 654, 705 (1988) (emphasis in orig.).

87. Morrison v. Olson, 487 US 706 (quote), 726.

88. Katy J. Harriger, *The Special Prosecutor in American Politics*, 2nd rev. ed. (Lawrence: University Press of Kansas, 2000), 113–15, 117, 119.

89. Phillip J. Cooper, *By Order of the President: The Use and Abuse of Executive Direct Action*, 2nd rev. ed. (Lawrence: University Press of Kansas, 2014), 326–30.

90. Hollis-Brusky, "Helping Ideas Have Consequences," 211.

91. Ronald Reagan, "Statement on Signing the Bill Increasing the Public Debt Limit and Enacting the Balanced Budget and Emergency Deficit Control Act of 1985," December 12, 1985, *The American Presidency Project*, accessed December 28, 2021, http://www .presidency.ucsb.edu/node/259393.

92. Bowsher v. Synar, 478 US 719n1.

93. Ronald Reagan, "Statement on Signing the Independent Counsel Reauthorization Act of 1987," December 15, 1987, *The American Presidency Project*, accessed December 28, 2021, http://www.presidency.ucsb.edu/node/252254.

94. Christopher S. Kelley, "A Matter of Direction: The Reagan Administration, the Signing Statement, and the 1986 *Westlaw* Decision," *William & Mary Bill of Rights Journal* 16 (2007): 283–306. See also Douglas W. Kmiec, "OLC's Opinion Writing Function: The Legal Adhesive for a Unitary Executive," *Cardozo Law Review* 15 (1993): 337–74, 352.

95. Ralph W. Tarr, Acting Assistant Attorney General, Office of Legal Counsel, Mem-

orandum for T. Kenneth Cribb, Counselor to the Attorney General, Re: Presidential Signing Statements, October 28, 1985, 6, National Archives, https://www.archives.gov/files/news/samuel-alito/accession-060-89-269/Acc060-89-269-box3-SG-ChronologicalFile.pdf. See also Kelley, "A Matter of Direction," 303–4; Cooper, *By Order of the President,* 328–29.

96. Steven G. Calabresi and Daniel Lev, "The Legal Significance of Presidential Signing Statements," *Forum* 4 (2006): 1–9.

97. Hollis-Brusky, "Helping Ideas Have Consequences," 213–15, 219–23.

98. Leading contributions include Geoffrey P. Miller, "Independent Agencies," *Supreme Court Review* 1986: 41–97; Steven G. Calabresi and Kevin H. Rhodes, "The Structural Constitution: Unitary Executive, Plural Judiciary," *Harvard Law Review* 105 (1992): 1153–1216; Steven G. Calabresi, "Some Normative Arguments for the Unitary Executive," *Arkansas Law Review* 48 (1995): 23–104; Steven G. Calabresi and Saikrishna B. Prakash, "The President's Power to Execute the Laws," *Yale Law Journal* 104 (1994): 541–665.

99. These efforts culminated in Steven G. Calabresi and Christopher S. Yoo, *The Unitary Executive: Presidential Power from Washington to Bush* (New Haven, CT: Yale University Press, 2008).

100. Calabresi and Rhodes, "Structural Constitution," 1165–66 (citation omitted).

101. Hollis-Brusky, "Helping Ideas Have Consequences," 227, 213. See also Mark Tushnet, "A Political Perspective on the Theory of the Unitary Executive," *Journal of Constitutional Law* 12 (2010): 313–29.

102. Hollis-Brusky, "Helping Ideas Have Consequences," 224.

103. Marlowe, "The Unitary Executive and Review of Agency Rulemaking," 81–85, 89–97; Ryan J. Barilleaux and David Zellers, "Executive Unilateralism in the Ford and Carter Presidencies," in *Unitary Executive and the Modern Presidency,* 41–76; Christopher S. Kelley, "The Unitary Executive in the Clinton Administration," ibid., 107–22.

104. Ryan J. Barilleaux and Christopher S. Kelley, "Going Forward," in *Unitary Executive and the Modern Presidency,* 221.

105. Calabresi and Yoo, *Unitary Executive,* 18–21, 429–30.

106. Peter M. Shane, *Madison's Nightmare: How Executive Power Threatens American Democracy* (Chicago: University of Chicago Press, 2009), 31.

107. Excellent treatments include Richard A. Brisbin Jr., "'Administrative Law Is Not for Sissies': Justice Antonin Scalia's Challenge to American Administrative Law," *Administrative Law Review* 44 (1992): 107–29; and James B. Staab, *The Political Thought of Justice Antonin Scalia: A Hamiltonian on the Supreme Court* (Lanham, MD: Rowman and Littlefield, 2006), 137–67, 59–87.

108. Antonin Scalia, "Regulatory Reform—The Game Has Changed," *Regulation* (January–February 1981): 13–15; Antonin Scalia, "Regulation—The First Year: Regulatory Review and Management," *Regulation* (January–February 1982): 19–21.

109. Antonin Scalia, "Historical Anomalies in Administrative Law," *Supreme Court Historical Society Yearbook 1985:* 103–11, 110; Synar v. United States, 626 F.Supp. 1374, 1403 (D. D.C. 1986).

110. Mistretta v. United States, 488 US 361, 416 (Scalia dissenting) (1989).

111. Mistretta v. United States, 488 US 416. See also Whitman v. American Trucking Assns., Inc., 531 US 457, 474 (2001); and Staab, *Political Thought of Justice Antonin Scalia,* 74–77, 161.

112. Antonin Scalia, "Rulemaking as Politics," *Administrative Law Review* 34 (1982): v–xi, quotes at x, vi

113. Chevron USA, Inc. v Natural Resources Defense Council, Inc., 467 US 837, 865 (1984).

114. Antonin Scalia, "Judicial Deference to Administrative Interpretations of Law," *Duke Law Journal* (1989): 511–21, 518.

115. The two best studies of Scalia's administrative law jurisprudence clearly emphasize the connection between deference and the unitary executive. Brisbin, "'Administrative Law Is Not for Sissies,'" 109, 115–19, 127–29; Staab, *Political Thought of Justice Antonin Scalia*, 160–61. See also Peter M. Shane, "Legislative Delegation, the Unitary Executive, and the Legitimacy of the Administrative State," *Harvard Journal of Law and Public Policy* 33 (2010): 103–10.

116. Stephen Skowronek, "The Conservative Insurgency and Presidential Power: A Developmental Perspective on the Unitary Executive," *Harvard Law Review* 122 (2009): 2070–103, 2098.

117. Skowronek, 2097–2100.

118. Skowronek, 2103.

119. Gillian E. Metzger, "1930s Redux: The Administrative State under Siege," *Harvard Law Review* 131 (2017): 1–95; Philip Wallach, "The Administrative State's Legitimacy Crisis," Center for Effective Public Management at Brookings, April 2016, https://www.brookings.edu/wp-content/uploads/2016/07/Administrative-state-legitimacy-crisis_FINAL.pdf.

120. Ernst, *Tocqueville's Nightmare*; Grisinger, *Unwieldy American State*; Kornhauser, *Debating the American State*.

121. Postell, *Bureaucracy in America*; Moreno, *Bureaucrat Kings*; Christophe DeMuth, "Can the Administrative State Be Tamed?" *Journal of Legal Analysis* 8 (2016): 121–90.

122. John J. DiIulio Jr., *Bring Back the Bureaucrats: Why More Federal Workers Will Lead to Better (and Smaller!) Government* (West Conshohocken, PA: Templeton Press, 2014).

123. Eric A. Posner and Adrian Vermeule, *The Executive Unbound: After the Madisonian Republic* (New York: Oxford University Press, 2011); Adrian Vermeule, *Law's Abnegation: From Law's Empire to the Administrative State* (Cambridge, MA: Harvard University Press, 2016).

124. Hamburger, *Is Administrative Law Unlawful?*

125. Charles Murray, *By the People: Rebuilding Liberty without Permission* (New York: Crown Forum, 2015).

126. Free Enterprise Fund v. Public Company Accounting Oversight Board, 561 US 477 (2010).

127. U.S. Department of Transportation v. Association of American Railroads, 575 US __ (2015) (Justice Thomas citing Hamburger, *Is Administrative Law Unlawful?* slip opinion at 5, 6, 8); B&B Hardware v. Hargis Industries, 575 US __ (2015).

128. Perez v. Mortgage Bankers Association, 575 US __ (2015).

129. Michigan v. Environmental Protection Agency, 576 US __ (2015). Several of Thomas's opinions are analyzed in Charles J. Cooper, "Confronting the Administrative State," *National Affairs* 25 (Fall 2015): 96–108. See also George F. Will, "Battling the Modern Administrative State," *Washington Post*, November 27, 2015, www.washingtonpost.com.

130. City of Arlington v. FCC, 569 US 290 (2013) (slip opinion 4).

131. King v. Burwell, 576 US __ (2015).

132. On this point, see Adam J. White, "Scalia and Chevron: Not Drawing Lines, but Resolving Tensions," *Notice and Comment* (blog), February 23, 2016, www.yalejreg.com /blog.

133. Hamburger, *Is Administrative Law Unlawful?* 309–21; Murray, *By the People*, 69–71, 185–86, 189; "The Administrative State and Congressional Abrogation of the *Chevron* and *Seminole Rock* Doctrines," Testimony of Charles J. Cooper before the Homeland Security and Governmental Affairs Committee, U.S. Senate Subcommittee on Regulatory Affairs and Federal Management, March 17, 2016, https://www.hsgac.senate.gov/; Joseph Postell, *From Administrative State to Constitutional Government* (Washington, DC: Heritage Foundation, 2012), 30. Postell also suggests several other reforms.

134. DeMuth, "Can the Administrative State Be Tamed?" 178–83.

Part II · The Erosion of Federalism: An Overview

1. Alfred H. Kelly, Winfrid A. Harbison, and Herman Belz, *The American Constitution: Its Origins and Development*, 7th ed., 2 vols. (New York: W. W. Norton, 1991), 2:500–503.

2. David Brian Robertson, *Federalism and the Making of America* (New York: Routledge, 2012), 112, 118–20; David B. Walker, *The Rebirth of Federalism: Slouching toward Washington* (Chatham, NJ: Chatham House, 1995), 101–3, 107–10; Kelly, Harbison, and Belz, *American Constitution*, 2:502–3.

3. Particularly helpful here are Martha Derthick, *Keeping the Compound Republic: Essays on American Federalism* (Washington, DC: Brookings Institution Press, 2001); Walker, *Rebirth of Federalism*, 130–34; Martha Derthick, "Federalism," in *Understanding America: The Anatomy of an Exceptional Nation*, ed. Peter H. Schuck and James Q. Wilson (New York: PublicAffairs, 2008), 121–45.

4. In addition to the sources cited in note 3, see Harry N. Scheiber, "Federalism," in *Oxford Companion to the Supreme Court of the United States*, 321–32, 328–29.

5. Kelly, Harbison, and Belz, *American Constitution*, 2:611. The cases and doctrines are explicated in ibid., 612–38. The most detailed study of the Warren Court is Lucas A. Powe Jr., *The Warren Court and American Politics* (Cambridge, MA: Belknap Press of Harvard University Press, 2000).

6. Tim Conlan, "From Cooperative to Opportunistic Federalism: Reflections on the Half-Century Anniversary of the Commission on Intergovernmental Relations," *Public Administration Review* 66 (2006): 663–76, 663–66; Mortin Grodzins and Daniel Elazar, "Centralization and Decentralization in the American Federal System," in *A Nation of States: Essays on the American Federal System*, 2nd ed., ed. Robert A. Goldwin (Chicago: Rand McNally, 1974), 1–24, 5–6; Walker, *Rebirth of Federalism*, 103.

7. Timothy Conlan, *From New Federalism to Devolution: Twenty-five Years of Intergovernmental Reform* (Washington, DC: Brookings Institution, 1998); Walker, *Rebirth of Federalism*, 135–41; Robertson, *Federalism and the Making of America*, 135–36.

8. Ronald Reagan, "Executive Order 12,612—Federalism," October 26, 1987, *The American Presidency Project*, accessed December 29, 2021, http://www.presidency.ucsb.edu/node /251147.

9. Walker, *Rebirth of Federalism*, 151–62, quote at 161; Robertson, *Federalism and the Making of America*, 148–52; Conlan, *From New Federalism to Devolution*, 93–211. See also

Andrew E. Busch, *Ronald Reagan and the Politics of Freedom* (Lanham, MD: Rowman and Littlefield, 2001), 33–40, 255.

10. Conlan, *From New Federalism to Devolution*, 257–72; Tim Conlan and John Dinan, "Federalism, the Bush Administration, and the Transformation of American Conservatism," *Publius: The Journal of Federalism* 37 (2007): 279–303.

11. National League of Cities v. Usery, 426 U.S. 833 (1976), overruled by Garcia v. San Antonio Metropolitan Transit Authority, 469 U.S. 528 (1985).

12. These four categories are delineated in Scheiber, "Federalism," 329–31. There are numerous studies of these and other federalism decisions of the Rehnquist Court. A particularly helpful overview of the federalism cases (including others not discussed here) is Ralph A. Rossum, *Federalism, the Supreme Court, and the Seventeenth Amendment: The Irony of Constitutional Democracy* (Lanham, MD: Lexington Books, 2001). A more technical treatment is Christopher P. Banks and John C. Blakeman, *The U.S. Supreme Court and the New Federalism: From the Rehnquist to the Roberts Court* (Lanham, MD: Rowman and Littlefield, 2012). A good overview of the Rehnquist Court more generally is Earl M. Maltz, ed., *Rehnquist Justice: Understanding the Court Dynamic* (Lawrence: University Press of Kansas, 2003).

13. New York v. United States, 505 U.S. 144 (1992); Printz v. United States, 521 U.S. 898 (1997). In *Printz* Justice Scalia's majority opinion appealed to "state sovereignty" and quoted the Tenth Amendment but also relied on the separation of powers insofar as only the president was formally responsible for enforcement of federal law.

14. Seminole Tribe v. Florida, 517 U.S. 44 (1996).

15. Alden v. Maine, 527 U.S. 706 (1999). The line of sovereign immunity decisions extended into several other regulatory contexts that cannot be pursued here.

16. United States v. Lopez, 514 U.S. 549 (1995).

17. United States v. Morrison, 529 U.S. 598 (2000).

18. City of Boerne v. Flores, 521 U.S. 507 (1997).

19. William Leuchtenberg, "The Tenth Amendment over Two Centuries: More than a Truism," in *The Tenth Amendment and State Sovereignty: Constitutional History and Contemporary Issues*, ed. Mark R. Killenbeck (Lanham, MD: Rowman and Littlefield, 2002), 41–105, 99; Mark R. Killenbeck, "Revolution or Retreat," in ibid., 181–89, 187, 182; Maltz, "Introduction," in *Rehnquist Justice*, 3.

20. Stephen Skowronek, "Afterword: An Attenuated Reconstruction; The Conservative Turn in American Political Development," in *Conservatism and American Political Development*, ed. Brian J. Glenn and Steven M. Teles (New York: Oxford University Press, 2009), 348–63; Robert F. Nagel, *The Implosion of American Federalism* (New York: Oxford University Press, 2001), 11, 30, 47; Keith E. Whittington, "Taking What They Give Us: Explaining the Court's Federalism Offensive," *Duke Law Journal* 51 (2001): 477–520, 515, 519–20, quote at 519.

21. Derthick, "Federalism," 138–42.

22. Keith E. Whittington, "Dismantling the Modern State? The Changing Structural Foundations of Federalism," *Hastings Constitutional Law Quarterly* 25 (1998): 483–527, 520–22; Walker, *Rebirth of Federalism*, 249–83; Robertson, *Federalism and the Making of America*, 154–56; Richard S. Williamson, *Reagan's Federalism: His Efforts to Decentralize Government* (Lanham, MD: University Press of America, 1990), 27–37.

23. Compare Richard A. Epstein and Michael S. Greve, ed., *Federal Preemption: States'*

Powers, National Interests (Washington, DC: AEI, 2007), with Thomas O. McGarity, *The Preemption War: When Federal Bureaucracies Trump Local Juries* (New Haven, CT: Yale University Press, 2008).

24. Jack P. Greene, *Peripheries and Center: Constitutional Development in the Extended Polities of the British Empire and the United States, 1607–1788* (Athens: University of Georgia Press, 1986); Allison L. LaCroix, *The Ideological Origins of American Federalism* (Cambridge, MA: Harvard University Press, 2010); Edward A. Purcell Jr., *Originalism, Federalism, and the American Constitutional Enterprise: A Historical Inquiry* (New Have, CT: Yale University Press, 2007); David L. Shapiro, *Federalism: A Dialogue* (Evanston, IL: North western University Press, 1995); Erin Ryan, *Federalism and the Tug of War Within* (New York: Oxford University Press, 2011).

25. Compare Samuel H. Beer, *To Make a Nation: The Rediscovery of American Federalism* (Cambridge, MA: Belknap Press of Harvard University Press, 1993), with Forrest McDonald, *States' Rights and the Union: Imperium in Imperio, 1776–1876* (Lawrence: University Press of Kansas, 2000).

26. Derthick, "Federalism," 142–45; Ernest A. Young, "The Conservative Case for Federalism," *George Washington Law Review* 74 (2006): 874–87; Robertson, *Federalism and the Making of America*, 4–6, 171–78; Ryan, *Federalism and the Tug of War Within*, 34–67; Eugene W. Hickock, *Why States? The Challenge of Federalism* (Washington, DC: Heritage Foundation, 2007), 83–91.

Chapter 3 · Traditionalists, Neoconservatives, and the Erosion of Federalism

1. John Kyle Day, *The Southern Manifesto: Massive Resistance and the Fight to Preserve Segregation* (Jackson: University Press of Mississippi, 2014).

2. Day, *Southern Manifesto*, 95–96.

3. The Manifesto is reprinted in Day, *Southern Manifesto*, 160–62.

4. Day, *The Southern Manifesto*, 13–15.

5. James Jackson Kilpatrick, *The Sovereign States: Notes of a Citizen of Virginia* (Chicago: Regnery, 1957), 17, 146–47; James Jackson Kilpatrick, "Conservatism and the South," in *The Lasting South: Fourteen Southerners Look at Their Home*, ed. Louis D. Rubin Jr. and James Jackson Kilpatrick (Chicago: Regnery, 1957), 188–205, 196–98; James Jackson Kilpatrick, "The Case for States' Rights" (1963), in *Nation of States*, 91–107, 95–99. See also William P. Hustwit, *James J. Kilpatrick: Salesman for Segregation* (Chapel Hill: University of North Carolina Press, 2013), 49–54.

6. Hustwit, *James J. Kilpatrick*, 55–56; Joseph J. Thorndike, "'The Sometimes Sordid Level of Race and Segregation': James J. Kilpatrick and the Virginia Campaign against *Brown*," in *The Moderates' Dilemma: Massive Resistance to School Desegregation in Virginia*, ed. Matthew D. Lassiter and Andrew B. Lewis (Charlottesville: University of Virginia Press, 1998), 51–71, 57, 61, 71.

7. Hustwit, *James J. Kilpatrick*, 90–106, 124–40.

8. Hustwit, 73–75, 134, 66, 141–42, 219, 221–22. See also Nash, *Conservative Intellectual Movement*, 186–87.

9. Kilpatrick, "Conservatism and the South," 204, 205, 195. See also Thorndike, "'The Sometimes Sordid Level of Race and Segregation,'" 65–67.

10. Hustwit, *James J. Kilpatrick*, 184–85, 187.

11. My understanding of this strain of southern traditionalism has been informed by

Michael O'Brien, *The Idea of the American South, 1920–1971* (Baltimore: Johns Hopkins University Press, 1979); Paul Conkin, *The Southern Agrarians* (Knoxville: University of Tennessee Press, 1988); Mark G. Malvasi, *The Unregenerate South: The Agrarian Thought of John Crow Ransome, Allen Tate, and Donald Davidson* (Baton Rouge: Louisiana State University Press, 1997); and Paul V. Murphy, *The Rebuke of History: The Southern Agrarians and American Conservative Thought* (Chapel Hill: University of North Carolina Press, 2001).

12. Twelve Southerners, *I'll Take My Stand: The South and the Agrarian Tradition* (New York: Harper, 1930), x–xi, 15–19, 193–94, 202–6.

13. Hustwit, *James J. Kilpatrick*, 190–94, 219, 78. Hustwit observes that Kilpatrick accepted as a matter of course, like nearly all other conservatives, the modern capitalist economy that the original Agrarians had pointedly criticized.

14. Hustwit, *James J. Kilpatrick*, 203–12.

15. Murphy, *Rebuke of History*, 177–78; Murphy does not make the point explicitly in terms of natural rights.

16. George M. Curtis III and James J. Thompson Jr., eds., *The Southern Essays of Richard M. Weaver* (Indianapolis: Liberty Fund, 1987), 250, 251.

17. Curtis and Thompson, 253.

18. Curtis and Thompson, 254. My analysis generally accords with the more extensive treatment in Jeremy David Bailey, "Richard Weaver's Untraditional Case for Federalism," *Publius* 34 (2004): 33–50.

19. Murphy, *Rebuke of History*, 202–5; Hustwit, *James J. Kilpatrick*, 75, 184.

20. M. E. Bradford, "Not in Memoriam, but in Affirmation," in Fifteen Southerners, *Why the South Will Survive* (Athens: University of Georgia Press, 1981), 222.

21. M. E. Bradford, *Remembering Who We Are: Observations of a Southern Conservative* (Athens: University of Georgia Press, 1985), 70.

22. This point is emphasized in James McClellan, "Walking the Levee with Mel Bradford," in *A Defender of Southern Conservatism: M. E. Bradford and His Achievements*, ed. Clyde N. Wilson (Columbia: University of Missouri Press, 1999), 35–57. See also Malvasi, *Unregenerate South*, 232–50; Murphy, *Rebuke of History*, 227–34, 244–45, 251–52.

23. Marshall L. De Rosa, "M. E. Bradford's Constitutional Theory: A Southern Reactionary's Affirmation of the Rule of Law," in *Defender of Southern Conservatism*, 92–129.

24. M. E. Bradford, "The Heresy of Equality: Bradford Replies to Jaffa," *Modern Age* 20 (1976): 62–77, 68.

25. M. E. Bradford, *Original Intentions: On the Making and Ratification of the United States Constitution* (Athens: University of Georgia Press, 1993), 13 (citation omitted).

26. Kendall and Carey, *Basic Symbols of the American Political Tradition*, xxii–xxiii; Bradford, *Original Intentions*, 33, 104–5; Bradford, "Not in Memoriam," 220.

27. Bradford, "Heresy of Equality"; Bradford, *Remembering Who We Are*, 143–56. See also Kendall and Carey, *Basic Symbols of the American Political Tradition*.

28. Malvasi, *Unregenerate South*, 245–47; Elizabeth Fox Genovese and Eugene D. Genovese, "M. E. Bradford's Historical Vision," in *Southern Conservatism*, 84–85; Eugene D. Genovese, *The Southern Tradition: The Achievement and Limitations of an American Conservatism* (Cambridge, MA: Harvard University Press, 1994), 79–80; Murphy, *Rebuke of History*, 261–62.

29. Genovese and Genovese, "M. E. Bradford's Historical Vision," 82–83.

30. Nancy Maclean, "Neo-Confederacy versus the New Deal: The Regional Utopia of

the Modern American Right," in *The Myth of Southern Exceptionalism*, ed. Matthew D. Lassiter and Joseph Crespino (New York: Oxford University Press, 2009), 308–29.

31. Nisbet, *Prejudices*, 55. See also Hawley, *Right-Wing Critics*, 82–85.

32. Robert F. Nagel, "States and Localities: A Comment on Robert Nisbet's Communitarianism," *Publius: The Journal of Federalism* 34 (2004): 125–38.

33. Nagel, 131 and passim.

34. Kirk, *Conservative Mind*, 429.

35. Russell Kirk, *A Program for Conservatives* (Chicago: Regnery, 1954), 42.

36. Kirk, *Program for Conservatives*, 258.

37. Gerald J. Russello, "Russell Kirk and Territorial Democracy," *Publius: The Journal of Federalism* 34 (2004): 109–24, 118.

38. Russell Kirk, "The Prospects for Territorial Democracy in America" (1963), in *A Nation of States*, 47. See also Kirk, *Roots of American Order*, 447, 463.

39. Kirk, *Roots of American Order*, 419.

40. Kirk, *Roots of American Order*, 422.

41. Kirk, *Roots of American Order*, 423, 422.

42. Kirk, *Roots of American Order*, 423.

43. Kirk, *Roots of American Order*, 419.

44. Kirk, *Roots of American Order*, 426 (quote), 427.

45. Kirk, *Roots of American Order*, 467–68; Russell Kirk, *The American Cause* (1957), ed. Gleaves Whitney (Wilmington, DE: ISI, 2002), 83 (quote); Gleaves Whitney, "Editor's Introduction," in ibid., xiv–xvi. See also Bradley J. Birzer, *Russell Kirk: American Conservative* (Lexington: University Press of Kentucky, 2015), 269–70.

46. Kirk, "Prospects for Territorial Democracy," 53. See also Kirk, *Roots of American Order*, 463–64.

47. Kirk, "Prospects for Territorial Democracy," 60.

48. Kirk, 56–60.

49. Kirk, 54.

50. Kirk, 62.

51. Kirk, 60–63, quote at 63.

52. Kirk, 65.

53. Kirk, 66.

54. Kirk, *Rights and Duties*, 29.

55. Kirk, *Rights and Duties*, 135–38, quote at 135; Russell Hittinger, "Introduction," in ibid., xxvi–xxix.

56. Kirk, *Rights and Duties*, 138; see also 256.

57. Kirk, *Rights and Duties*, 207.

58. Kirk, 208.

59. Kirk, 208.

60. For an overview of Carey's work, see *Defending the Republic*, ed. Frohnen and Grasso. Especially helpful therein are Frohnen and Grasso, "Editors' Introduction," vii–xxx; and Frohnen, "George Carey on Constitutions," 17–35.

61. Kendall and Carey, *Basic Symbols of the American Political Tradition*. See also George W. Carey, "The Constitution and Community," in *Community and Tradition: Conservative Perspectives on the American Experience*, ed. George W. Carey and Bruce Frohnen (Lanham, MD: Rowman and Littlefield, 1998), 63–84, 64–68.

62. Kendall and Carey, *Basic Symbols of the American Political Tradition*, 138.

63. Kendall and Carey, 105.

64. George W. Carey, "Preface to This Edition," in Kendall and Carey, xxii.

65. George W. Carey, *The Federalist: Design for a Constitutional Republic* (Urbana: University of Illinois Press, 1989), 160 (quote); Carey, "The Constitution and Community," 75–78; George W. Carey, *A Student's Guide to American Political Thought* (Wilmington, DE: ISI 2004), 98–100.

66. Carey, "The Constitution and Community," 63.

67. Carey, "The Constitution and Community," 64.

68. Carey, 68–73.

69. Carey's analysis of federalism at the founding can be traced in George Carey, "Federalism: Historic Questions and Contemporary Meanings: A Defense of Political Process," in *Federalism: Infinite Variety in Theory and Practice*, ed. Valerie Earle (Itasca, IL: Peacock, 1968), 42–61; Carey, *The Federalist*, 96–127; George W. Carey, *In Defense of the Constitution*, revised and expanded ed. (Indianapolis: Liberty Fund, 1995), 77–121.

70. George W. Carey, "Conservatism, Centralization, and Constitutional Federalism," *Modern Age* 46 (Winter/Spring, 2004): 48–59, 50–53.

71. *Federalist* 46 (quotes); Carey, *The Federalist*, 109–15, 121, 123; Carey, "Federalism," 54–56, 60, 51; Carey, *In Defense of the Constitution*, 116–19, 79.

72. Carey, *The Federalist*, 124.

73. Carey, *In Defense of the Constitution*, 102–5, quote at 104.

74. Carey, "Conservatism, Centralization, and Constitutional Federalism," 48–50; Carey, *Student's Guide to American Political Thought*, 71–75.

75. Carey, *In Defense of the Constitution*, 119–20.

76. Kendall and Carey, *Basic Symbols of the American Political Tradition*, 84–95.

77. Carey, "Preface," in Kendall and Carey, *Basic Symbols of the American Political Tradition*, xxi, xix.

78. Carey, *In Defense of the Constitution*, 9–16; George W. Carey, "Who or What Killed the Philadelphia Constitution?" *Tulsa Law Journal* 36 (2001): 621–40, 632–37; Carey, *Student's Guide to American Political Thought*, 73–75.

79. Carey, "Who or What Killed the Philadelphia Constitution?" 632, 633, 635.

80. Carey, "Who or What Killed the Philadelphia Constitution?" 637–38; Carey, "The Constitution and Community," 78–83; Carey, "Preface," in Kendall and Carey, *Basic Symbols of the American Political Tradition*, x–xxi.

81. Carey, "The Constitution and Community," 81, 82 (quote); Carey, "Conservatism, Centralization, and Constitutional Federalism," 58.

82. Carey, "The Constitution and Community," 83.

83. Carey, "The Constitution and Community," 78.

84. Carey, *In Defense of the Constitution*, 79.

85. Carey, "Conservatism, Centralization, and Constitutional Federalism," 53, 54–55; Carey, *Student's Guide to American Political Thought*, 75–77.

86. Carey, "Conservatism, Centralization, and Constitutional Federalism," 56–57.

87. Carey, "Conservatism, Centralization, and Constitutional Federalism," 57–59; Carey, "The Constitution and Community," 73–75.

88. Carey, "Conservatism, Centralization, and Constitutional Federalism," 57.

89. Carey, "The Constitution and Community," 84.

90. Frohnen and Carey, *Constitutional Morality*, 18.

91. Frohnen and Carey, *Constitutional Morality*, 18. See also ibid., 218–19, 236, 238, 240–41, 159–60.

92. Frohnen and Carey, 240.

93. Frohnen and Carey, 241.

94. For a somewhat idiosyncratic but still useful treatment of this general theme, see Jeff Taylor, *Politics on a Human Scale: The American Tradition of Decentralism* (Lanham, MD: Lexington Books, 2013).

95. Allan Carlson, "Wendell Berry and the Twentieth-Century Agrarian 'Series,'" in *Wendell Berry: Life and Work*, ed. Jason Peters (Lexington: University Press of Kentucky, 2007), 96–111; Patrick J. Deneen, "Wendell Berry and the Alternative Tradition in American Political Thought," ibid., 300–315. See also Hawley, *Right-Wing Critics*, 80–82.

96. Rod Dreher, *Crunchy Cons* (New York: Crown Forum, 2006), 26 (quote). See also ibid., xi, 245–46; and Hawley, *Right-Wing Critics*, 95–97.

97. Dreher, *Crunchy Cons*, 2.

98. Dorrien, *Neoconservative Mind*, 16. See also Peter Steinfels, *The Neoconservatives: The Origins of a Movement, from Dissent to Political Power* (1979; reprint, New York: Simon and Schuster, 2013), xi–xii; and Irving Kristol, "A Conservative Welfare State" (1993), in *The Neocon Reader*, ed. Irwin Stelzer (New York: Grove, 2004), 145–48.

99. Irving Kristol, "Urban Civilization and Its Discontents" (1970), in *Reflections of a Neoconservative: Looking Back, Looking Ahead* (New York: Basic Books, 1983), 55–69, 69.

100. Vaïsse, *Neoconservatism*, 78, 53–55.

101. Steinfels, *Neoconservatives*, 68; Wilson, "Bureaucracy Problem."

102. Daniel Patrick Moynihan, *Coping: Essays on the Practice of Government* (New York: Random House, 1973), 188 (italics removed), 190.

103. As quoted in Weiner, *American Burke*, 23.

104. Weiner, 23–24, 27, 29, 34, 36, 135, 137, 17.

105. Banfield was a subtle thinker who deserves more attention from scholars. His approach to federalism is helpfully placed in the context of his broader views in Kimberly Hendrickson, "Edward Banfield on the Promise of Politics and the Limits of Federalism," *Publius* 34 (2004): 139–52, which I rely on here.

106. Edward C. Banfield, "Federalism and the Dilemma of Popular Government," in *How Federal Is the Constitution?* ed. Robert A. Goldwin and William A. Schambra (Washington, DC: AEI, 1987), 1–15, 13.

107. Banfield, 13.

108. Banfield, 2.

109. Banfield, 1, 2 (quote).

110. Edward C. Banfield, "Revenue Sharing in Theory and Practice," *Public Interest* 23 (Spring 1971): 33–45; and Hendrickson, "Edward Banfield on the Promise of Politics," 144–46.

Chapter 4 · Libertarians and the Erosion of Federalism

1. A good overview of its development is Ilya Somin, "Libertarianism and Federalism," *Cato Institute Policy Analysis*, no. 751 (June 2014): 1–17, www.cato.org.

2. Jonathan H. Adler, "Frank Meyer: The Fusionist as Federalist," *Publius: The Journal of Federalism* 34 (2004): 51–67.

3. Friedrich A. Hayek, "The Economic Conditions of Interstate Federalism" (1939), in Hayek, *Individualism and the Economic Order* (Chicago: University of Chicago Press, 1948), 255–72; Hayek, *Constitution of Liberty*, 184–85, 263–64. See also Francesco Violi, "Federalist Thought in Friedrich von Hayek," *The Federalist: A Political Review* 52 (2015): 159, http://www.thefederalist.eu/site/.

4. Charles M. Tiebout, "A Pure Theory of Local Expenditures," *Journal of Political Economy* 64 (1956): 415–24.

5. Albert O. Hirschman, *Exit, Voice, and Loyalty* (Cambridge, MA: Harvard University Press, 1970).

6. An early application of public choice economics to federalism that was often used to support the libertarian position was Thomas R. Dye, *American Federalism: Competition among Governments* (Lexington, MA: Lexington Books, 1990). For another early effort, see Robert L. Bish, "Federalism: A Market Economics Perspective," *Cato Journal* 7 (1987): 377–96.

7. For an overview, see Roderick M. Hills Jr., "Federalism and Public Choice," in *Research Handbook on Public Choice and Public Law*, ed. Daniel A. Farber and Anne Joseph O'Connell (Cheltenham, UK: Edward Elgar, 2010), 207–33. See also Gordon Tullock, *The New Federalist* (Vancouver, British Columbia: Fraser Institute, 1994); and Ilya Somin, "Foot Voting, Federalism, and Political Freedom," in *Nomos LV: Federalism and Subsidiarity*, ed. James E. Fleming and Jacob T. Levy (New York: New York University Press, 2014), 83–119.

8. Robert P. Inman and Daniel L. Rubinfeld, "The Political Economy of Federalism," in *Perspectives on Public Choice*, 73–105. See also John Ferejohn and Barry R. Weingast, eds., *The New Federalism: Can the States be Trusted?* (Stanford, CA: Hoover Institution Press, 1997).

9. For an overview of the historical context, see John Kincaid, "From Cooperative to Coercive Federalism," *Annals of the American Academy of Political and Social Science* 509 (1990); 139–52. A fine treatment of Buchanan is G. Patrick Lynch, "Protecting Individual Rights through a Federal System: James Buchanan's View of Federalism," *Publius: The Journal of Federalism* 34 (2004): 153–67.

10. Geoffrey Brennan and James M. Buchanan, *The Power to Tax: Analytical Foundations of a Fiscal Constitution* (Cambridge: Cambridge University Press, 1980), 171–75, 184–86.

11. James M. Buchanan, "Federalism as an Ideal Political Order and an Objective for Constitutional Reform," *Publius: The Journal of Federalism* 25 (1995): 19–27, quote at 21; James M. Buchanan, *The Collected Works of James M. Buchanan*, Vol. 18: *Federalism, Liberty, and the Law* (Indianapolis: Liberty Fund, 2001), 92 (quote), 93.

12. Buchanan, "Federalism as an Ideal Political Order," 19–23.

13. New York v. United States, 505 U.S. 144, 182 (1992), quoted in John O. McGinnis and Ilya Somin, "Federalism vs. States' Rights: A Defense of Judicial Review in a Federal System," *Northwestern University Law Review* 99 (2004): 89–130, 105.

14. McGinnis and Somin, 112–15.

15. McGinnis and Somin, 122–26.

16. McGinnis and Somin, 127, 90.

17. Michael S. Greve, *Real Federalism: Why It Matters, How It Could Happen* (Washington, DC: AEI, 1999), 23 (both quotes).

18. Greve, 80–81.

19. Michael S. Greve, *The Upside-Down Constitution* (Cambridge, MA: Harvard University Press, 2012). See also Ilya Somin "Turning Federalism Right-Side Up," *Constitutional Commentary* 82 (2012): 303–23; Michael S. Greve, *Federalism and the Constitution: Competition versus Cartels* (Arlington, VA: Mercatus Center, George Mason University), 2015.

20. Greve, *Upside-Down Constitution*, 178, 384–85; Greve, *Federalism and the Constitution*, 23–24, quote at 24 (emphasis in orig.).

21. Greve, *Upside-Down Constitution*, 3–4, 20–22, 72–75. See also 261–63, 309, 314–18, 388–89.

22. Greve, *Upside-Down Constitution*, 389 (quote), 63–86.

23. Greve, *Upside-Down Constitution*, 380–85; Greve, *Federalism and the Constitution*, 31–48, 55–60.

24. For earlier arguments in this vein, see Brennan and Buchanan, *Power to Tax*, 180–83, 85; Dye, *American Federalism*, 99–115, 181; Ilya Somin, "Closing the Pandora's Box of Federalism: The Case for Judicial Restriction of Federal Subsidies to State Governments," *Georgetown Law Journal* 90 (2002): 461–502, esp. 464–473; and McGinnis and Somin, "Federalism vs. States' Rights," 115–18.

25. For pre–New Deal opponents of subsidies, see Albert C. Ritchie [governor of Maryland], "Back to States' Rights," *World's Work* (March 1924): 525–29; Albert C. Ritchie, "Federal Subsidies to the States," in *Selected Articles on States Rights*, ed. Lamar T. Beman (New York: H. W. Wilson, 1926), 294–311; James W. Wadsworth [US senator from New York], "Let's Stop This 'Fifty-Fifty' Business," *Nation's Business* (March 1926): 23–24; and Charles Warren, *Congress as Santa Claus: National Donations and the General Welfare Clause of the Constitution* (Charlottesville, VA: Michie, 1932), 95–106. For post–New Deal opposition, see Barry M. Goldwater, *The Conscience of a Conservative* (Shepherdsville, KY: Victor, 1960), 25–27; and Sam J. Ervin Jr. [US senator from North Carolina], "Federalism and Federal Grants-in-Aid," *North Carolina Law Review* 43 (1965): 487–501. Republican senator Robert Taft, however, advocated federal subsidies to states in some areas. Russell Kirk and James McClellan, *The Political Principles of Robert A. Taft* (1967; reprint, New Brunswick, NJ: Transaction, 2010), 139, 148–49. And even southern proponents of "states' rights" also sometimes supported them. J. Richard Piper, *Ideologies and Institutions: American Conservative and Liberal Governance Prescriptions since 1933* (Lanham, MD: Rowman and Littlefield, 1997), 192.

26. Greve, *Federalism and the Constitution*, 21 (quote), 31–39, quote at 35.

27. Greve, *Federalism and the Constitution*, 62–63 (emphasis in orig.); Greve, *Upside-Down Constitution*, 8, 243–58, 381–82. See also Richard E. Wagner, "A Competitive Federalism for the New Century," *Madison Review* (Fall 1995): 34–40, 38.

28. A prominent recent example that incorporates this view is Randy E. Barnett, *Our Republican Constitution: Securing the Liberty and Sovereignty of We the People* (New York: Broadside, 2016), 175–84, which cites both Somin and Greve.

29. See, for example, Gordon Tullock, "Federalism: Problems of Scale," *Public Choice* 6 (1969): 19–29, 22; Kincaid, "From Cooperative to Coercive Federalism," 152; James M. Buchanan, "Federalism and Individual Sovereignty," *Cato Journal* 15 (1995–96): 259–68, 262–64; Somin, "Closing the Pandora's Box," 464–65; Barnett, *Our Republican Constitution*, 167–74, 178–80.

30. William H. Riker, *Federalism: Origin, Operation, Significance* (Boston: Little, Brown, 1964), 152, 155. Riker later became more sympathetic to federalism as a possible means of checking centralizing statism but ultimately regarded it as not very successful. See Craig Volden, "Origin, Operation, and Significance: The Federalism of William H. Riker," *Publius: The Journal of Federalism* 34 (2004): 89–107.

31. Somin, "Libertarianism and Federalism," 9–11; Clint Bolick, *Grassroots Tyranny: The Limits of Federalism* (Washington, DC: Cato Institute, 1993).

32. Somin, "Libertarianism and Federalism," 11–12; Ilya Somin, "Federalism and Property Rights," *University of Chicago Legal Forum* 2011: 53–88; Richard A. Epstein, "Exit Rights under Federalism," *Law and Contemporary Problems* 55 (1992): 147–165, 154–58.

33. Somin, "Federalism and Property Rights," 56–57, 87–88; Barnett, *Our Republican Constitution*, 162–63, 224–25, 232–33, 243–45; Epstein, "Exit Rights," 165. It is notable in this regard that in a generally appreciative assessment of Greve's *Upside-Down Constitution* Somin thought it had slighted the importance of judicial protection of property rights and economic liberties from state legislation. Somin, "Federalism Right-Side Up," 316–17.

34. The fullest treatment of this school of thought is Paul Dragos Aligica and Peter J. Boettke, *Challenging Institutional Analysis and Development: The Bloomington School* (New York: Routledge, 2009).

35. Vincent Ostrom, Charles M. Tiebout, and Robert Warren, "The Organization of Government in Metropolitan Areas: A Theoretical Inquiry," *American Political Science Review* 55 (1961): 831–42, reprinted in Vincent Ostrom, *The Meaning of American Federalism: Constituting a Self-Governing Society* (San Francisco: Institute for Contemporary Studies, 1991), 137–61, quote at 137.

36. Ostrom, Tiebout, and Warren, 138.

37. Michael D. McGinnis and Elinor Ostrom, "Reflections on Vincent Ostrom, Public Administration, and Polycentricity," *Public Administration Review* 72 (2011): 15–25, 16.

38. Ostrom, *Meaning of American Federalism*, 144, 153 (quote), 155 (quote), 152; Aligica and Bottke, *Challenging Institutional Analysis*, 36–46.

39. Ostrom, *Meaning of American Federalism*, 153–54; McGinnis and Ostrom, "Reflections on Vincent Ostrom," 17.

40. Vincent Ostrom, *The Political Theory of a Compound Republic: Designing the American Experiment*, 3rd ed. (Lanham, MD: Lexington, 2008), 19 (quote), 57, 71. See also Ostrom, *Meaning of American Federalism*, 29–52; Aligica and Bottke, *Challenging Institutional Analysis*, 23.

41. Ostrom, *Political Theory of a Compound Republic*, 83–84 (quote), 103–9; Vincent Ostrom, *The Intellectual Crisis in American Public Administration*, 3rd ed. (Tuscaloosa: University of Alabama Press, 2008), 72–80, 137–38, 147–49, 153–54; Ostrom, *Meaning of American Federalism*, 89.

42. Ostrom, *Intellectual Crisis*, 80–86; Ostrom, *Meaning of American Federalism*, 11–15, 200–203, 212–17. Much but not all of that latter work is duplicated in Vincent Ostrom, "Federalism, Polycentricity, and *Res Publica*: Some Reflections on the American Experiments in Republican Government," in *The Practice of Constitutional Development: Vincent Ostrom's Quest to Understand Human Affairs*, ed. Filippo Sabetti, Barbara Allen, and Mark Sproule-Jones (Lanham, MD: Lexington Books, 2009), 31–57. Attention to Tocqueville ran throughout Ostrom's work. See, especially, Vincent Ostrom, *The Meaning of Democracy and Vulnerability of Democracies: A Response to Tocqueville's Challenge* (Ann Arbor: Univer-

sity of Michigan Press, 1997). See also Michael A. Fotos III, "Vincent Ostrom's Revolutionary Science of Association," *Public Choice* 163 (2015): 67–83, esp. 77–78.

43. Ostrom, *Intellectual Crisis*, 86. See also Ostrom, *Meaning of Democracy*, 280.

44. Ostrom, *Intellectual Crisis*, 153–63; Ostrom, *Political Theory of a Compound Republic*, 219–22; Ostrom, *Meaning of American Federalism*, 163–97, 231–32; Aligica and Bottke, *Challenging Institutional Analysis*, 36–46; Richard E. Wagner, "Self-Governance, Polycentrism, and Federalism: Recurring Themes in Vincent Ostrom's Scholarly Oeuvre," *Journal of Economic Behavior and Organization* 57 (2005): 173–88, 179–84, quote at 180.

45. Ostrom, *Meaning of American Federalism*, 8 (quote), 51.

46. Ostrom, *Intellectual Crisis*, 156. See also Wagner, "Self-Governance," 184–86; and Aligica and Bottke, *Challenging Institutional Analysis*, 138–40.

47. Ostrom, *Meaning of American Federalism*, 17, 23, 97; Ostrom, *Political Theory of a Compound Republic*, 19–20, 129.

48. "Ostrom, Vincent and Elinor (1919– and 1933–)," in *Encyclopedia of Libertarianism*, 368.

49. Ostrom, *Meaning of American Federalism*, 93. Ostrom's book reprinted his earlier "The Meaning of Federalism in *The Federalist*: A Critical Examination of the Diamond Thesis," *Publius: The Journal of Federalism* 15 (1985): 1–21.

50. Ostrom, *Meaning of American Federalism*, 94–95 (quote).

51. Ostrom, *Meaning of American Federalism*, 80–81.

52. This point is emphasized in Jean Yarbrough, "Rethinking '*The Federalist*'s View of Federalism,'" *Publius: The Journal of Federalism* 15 (1985): 31–53, 52.

53. Ostrom, *Meaning of American Federalism*, 80–81, 88–89, 94–97.

54. Ostrom, *Meaning of American Federalism*, 97.

55. Vincent Ostrom, "Historical Circumstances and Theoretical Structures as Sources of Meaning: A Response," *Publius: The Journal of Federalism* 15 (1985): 55–64, 61.

56. Ostrom, "Historical Circumstances and Theoretical Structures," 62 (quote), 63.

57. Ostrom, *Intellectual Crisis*, 20–30, 42, 65–66, 87–90, 97; Ostrom, *Political Theory of a Compound Republic*, 181–87, 212–13; Ostrom, *Meaning of American Federalism*, 30, 131.

58. Ostrom, *Intellectual Crisis*, 164.

59. Ostrom, *Intellectual Crisis*, 69–71, 112–15, 146–48, 152–54.

60. Ostrom, *Intellectual Crisis*, 147.

61. Ostrom, *Political Theory of a Compound Republic*, 188–92; Ostrom, *Intellectual Crisis*, 129–32; Ostrom, *Meaning of American Federalism*, 114–16.

62. Ostrom, *Meaning of American Federalism*, 101 (quote), 129–32.

63. Ostrom, *Intellectual Crisis*, 30.

64. Ostrom, *Intellectual Crisis*, 33–36, 108–11, 117–20; Ostrom, *Political Theory of a Compound Republic*, 192–94.

65. Ostrom, *Intellectual Crisis*, 120–27; Ostrom, *Meaning of American Federalism*, 116–19. See also Ostrom, *Political Theory of a Compound Republic*, 187.

66. See, generally, Aligica and Bottke, *Challenging Institutional Analysis*, 137–41.

Chapter 5 · *Straussians and the Erosion of Federalism*

1. Many of Diamond's essays are collected in Diamond, *As Far as Republican Principles Will Admit*. Helpful studies include Richard G. Stevens, ed. "Martin Diamond's Contri-

bution to American Political Thought: A Symposium," *Political Science Reviewer* 28 (1999): 3–120; Daniel J. Elazar, ed., "Dimensions of the Democratic Republic: A Memorial to Martin Diamond," *Publius: The Journal of Federalism* 8 (1978): 1–218; Zuckert, "Refinding the Founding," 235–51.

2. Martin Diamond, "What the Framers Meant by Federalism" (1963), in *As Far as Republican Principles Will Admit*, 94–98; Martin Diamond, "On the Relationship of Federalism and Decentralization," in *Cooperation and Conflict: Readings in American Federalism*, ed. Daniel J. Elazar et al. (Itasca, IL: Peacock, 1969), 81 (quote).

3. Diamond, "What the Framers Meant," 98–107.

4. Diamond, "What the Framers Meant," 100.

5. Martin Diamond, "*The Federalist*'s View of Federalism" (1961), in *As Far as Republican Principles Will Admit*, 113–18, quote at 113.

6. Diamond, "*The Federalist*'s View of Federalism," 117–18.

7. Diamond, 125.

8. Diamond, 133, 132.

9. Diamond, 126–33, quote at 133.

10. Diamond, 138–43.

11. Zuckert, "Refinding the Founding," 243.

12. Robert A. Goldwin, ed., *A Nation of States: Essays on American Federalism* (Chicago: Rand McNally, 1963).

13. As earlier noted by Nash in *Conservative Intellectual Movement*, 207.

14. Storing's major essays are collected in *Toward a More Perfect Union*, ed. Bessette. Storing, "Problem of Big Government," 288 (quote), 292–95. See also Storing, "The Constitutional Convention: Toward a More Perfect Union" (1983), in *Toward a More Perfect Union*, 36.

15. Herbert Storing, "The Role of Government in Society" (speech delivered in 1967), in *Toward a More Perfect Union*, 352.

16. Storing, "Problem of Big Government," 290 (quote), 300.

17. Storing, "Role of Government in Society," 354 (quote), 361.

18. Storing, "Problem of Big Government," 297, 300. See also Storing, "Role of Government in Society," 361.

19. Storing, "Problem of Big Government," 297, 305; Storing, "Role of Government in Society," 360–66.

20. Storing, "Role of Government in Society," 359.

21. Storing, "Problem of Big Government," 298.

22. Storing, "Problem of Big Government," 306.

23. Storing, "Problem of Big Government," 295 (quotes), 296–97.

24. Storing, "Problem of Big Government," 296–97, 298 (quote).

25. See, generally, Carrese, "Constitutionalist Political Science."

26. Storing, "Problem of Big Government," 296, 297.

27. Storing, "Role of Government in Society," 366.

28. Storing, "Problem of Big Government," 305.

29. Storing, "Problem of Big Government," 305 (quote), 306.

30. Harry V. Jaffa, "The Case for a Stronger National Government," in *A Nation of States*, 1st ed., 106–25, quote at 123 (emphasis in orig.).

31. Jaffa, 125.

32. This essay was also reprinted in the second edition; see Walter Berns, "The Meaning of the Tenth Amendment," in *Nation of States*, 2nd ed., 143.

33. Berns, 145 (quote), 144 (quote), 158.

34. Berns, 147–51.

35. Berns, 158–60.

36. Frank S. Meyer, "Lincoln without Rhetoric," *National Review*, August 24, 1965, 725; Frank S. Meyer, "Again on Lincoln," *National Review*, January 25, 1966, 71, 85.

37. Harry V. Jaffa, "Lincoln and the Cause of Freedom," *National Review*, September 21, 1965, 828.

38. Jaffa, "Lincoln and the Cause of Freedom," 828 (emphasis in orig.).

39. Jaffa amplified this last point in the second edition of *A Nation of States* (1974), arguing in "'Partly Federal, Partly National': The Political Theory of the Civil War," that John C. Calhoun's justification for secession by reference to the Virginia and Kentucky Resolutions could not be sustained and, therefore, that Lincoln was correct in dismissing it as an "ingenious sophism" that had rightly failed to dislodge the orthodox view of perpetual union (109–37, 110).

40. Harry V. Jaffa, *A New Birth of Freedom: Abraham Lincoln and the Coming of the Civil War* (Lanham, MD: Rowman and Littlefield, 2000), 191–92, 515n45 (citing Diamond, *"Federalist's* View of Federalism"), 375–79, 464–65.

41. Barr, *Loathing Lincoln*, 216–17, 219–22, 226. Jaffa's well-known conflict with Willmoore Kendall similarly involved Lincoln and the tension between consent, majority rule, and natural rights, but it did not engage federalism as explicitly as the debate with Meyer. See Barr, *Loathing Lincoln*, 214–18; and Nash, *Conservative Intellectual Movement*, 207–10.

42. Hayward, *Patriotism Is Not Enough*, 112–14.

43. Barr, *Loathing Lincoln*, 226, 229–30, quote at 230.

44. Nash, *Conservative Intellectual Movement*, 209–10.

45. Gottfried, *Conservatism in America*, 20–21; Barr, *Loathing Lincoln*, 230.

46. Michael Zuckert, "Herbert J. Storing's Turn to the Founding," *Political Science Reviewer* 28 (1999): 9, 28 (first and fourth quotes); Rossum, "Herbert J. Storing's Constitutionalism," 40, 56 (second and third quotes); Richard G. Stevens, "Martin Diamond's Contribution to American Political Thought: Editor's Preface," *Political Science Reviewer* 29 (2000): 3, 13 (fifth quote, emphasis removed).

47. Morton J. Frisch, *Franklin D. Roosevelt: The Contribution of the New Deal to American Political Thought and Practice* (New York: Twayne, 1975), 114 (emphasis in orig.).

48. Frisch, 117.

49. Frisch, 66.

50. Frisch reached this judgment even though he saw the potential for Tocqueville's "soft despotism" as "perhaps the greatest difficulty underlying the New Deal." Frisch, 117. See also Morton J. Frisch, "The Welfare State as a Departure from the Older Liberalism," in *The Thirties: A Reconsideration in Light of the American Political Tradition*, ed. Morton J. Frisch and Martin Diamond (DeKalb: Northern Illinois University Press, 1968), 68–83; Morton J. Frisch, "Franklin Delano Roosevelt," in *American Political Thought: The Philosophic Dimension of American Statesmanship*, ed. Morton J. Frisch and Richard G. Stevens (New York: Charles Scribner's Sons, 1971), 219–35.

51. Herbert J. Storing, *What the Anti-Federalists Were For* (Chicago: University of Chicago Press, 1981), 15–23.

52. Storing, *What the Anti-Federalists Were For*, 76, citation omitted.

53. Storing, 15.

54. Storing, 24.

55. See Carrese, "Storing's Philosophical Moderation," esp. 265, 275. See also Harry M. Clor, "Our Problem of Moral Community: Lessons from the Teaching of Herbert Storing," *Political Science Reviewer* 29 (2000): 94–120.

56. Storing, "Role of Government in Society," 355.

57. Storing, "Role of Government in Society," 366.

58. On this point, see, especially, William A. Schambra, "Martin Diamond's Doctrine of the American Regime," *Publius: The Journal of Federalism* 8 (1978): 213–18; Zuckert, "Refinding the Founding," 242–43.

59. Diamond, "*The Federalist* on Federalism" (1977), in *As Far as Republican Principles Will Admit*, 176. See also Martin Diamond, *The Founding of the Democratic Republic* (Itasca, IL: Peacock, 1981), 130–32.

60. Diamond, "*Federalist* on Federalism," 176.

61. Diamond, "The Forgotten Doctrine of Enumerated Powers" (1976), in *As Far as Republican Principles Will Admit*, 184–85.

62. Diamond, "The Electoral College and the American Idea of Democracy" (1977), in *As Far as Republican Principles Will Admit*, 186–205.

63. Diamond, "The Ends of Federalism" (1973), in *As Far as Republican Principles Will Admit*, 160, 162.

64. Diamond, "Ethics and Politics: The American Way" (1977), in *As Far as Republican Principles Will Admit*, 361–66. See also Zuckert and Zuckert, *The Truth about Leo Strauss*, 257–58.

65. Gary L. McDowell, "Were the Anti-Federalists Right? Judicial Activism and the Problem of Consolidated Government," *Publius: The Journal of Federalism* 12 (1982): 99–108; Gary L. McDowell, "The Losers' Legacy," *Virginia Quarterly Review* 60 (1984): 550–61; Gary L. McDowell, "Federalism and Civic Virtue: The Antifederalists and the Constitution," in *How Federal Is the Constitution?* 122–44. Other examples from this period include Jean Yarbrough, "Federalism in the Foundation and Preservation of the American Republic," *Publius: The Journal of Federalism* 6 (1976): 43–60; Yarbrough, "Rethinking '*The Federalist*'s View of Federalism'"; Jean Yarbrough, "Madison and Modern Federalism," in *How Federal Is the Constitution?* 84–108; Michael P. Zuckert, "Federalism and the Founding: Toward a Reinterpretation of the Constitutional Convention," *Review of Politics* 48 (1986): 166–210.

66. McDowell, "Federalism and Civic Virtue," 140.

67. McDowell, "Losers' Legacy," 559; McDowell, "Were the Anti-Federalists Right?" 108. Saul Cornell notes the connection between Straussian influence, the Reagan DOJ, and McDowell specifically, in *The Other Founders: Anti-Federalism and the Dissenting Tradition in America, 1788–1828* (Chapel Hill: University of North Carolina Press, 1999), 305, 305n4.

68. Teles, "Transformative Bureaucracy."

69. Working Group on Federalism, *The Status of Federalism in America* (Washington, DC: Domestic Policy Council, November 1986), 61–70.

70. Working Group on Federalism, 2–4 (executive summary), 61, 18–51; McDowell, "Were the Anti-Federalists Right?" See also Gary L. McDowell, *Curbing the Courts: The*

Constitution and the Limits of Judicial Power (Baton Rouge: Louisiana State University Press, 1988).

71. Keith E. Whittington, *Political Foundations of Judicial Supremacy: The Presidency, the Supreme Court, and Constitutional Leadership in U.S. History* (Princeton, NJ: Princeton University Press, 2007), 275–78; Robertson, *Federalism and the Making of America*, 151–54.

72. Hollis-Brusky, *Ideas with Consequences*, 93–143.

73. Rossum, *Federalism, the Supreme Court, and the Seventeenth Amendment*, 285.

74. Rossum, 3.

75. Rossum criticized Storing for failing to consider adequately the importance of the Senate as the structural protection for the states in the founders' original understanding of federalism. Rossum, "Herbert Storing's Constitutionalism," 57.

76. Hayward, *Patriotism Is Not Enough*, 191–92.

77. Eidelberg, *Discourse on Statesmanship*, 331, 363n2.

78. Pestritto, *Woodrow Wilson*, 112–17, 175, 182, quote at 114.

79. Wettergreen, "The Regulatory Revolution and the New Bureaucratic State," 12; Wettergreen, "The Regulatory Revolution and the New Bureaucratic State, Part II," 3; John Adams Wettergreen, "Bureaucratizing the American Government," in *Imperial Congress*, 74–79; Marini, *Politics of Budget Control*, 166–67, 185, 191; Rahe, *Soft Despotism, Democracy's Drift*, 276–80, 257–58. See also Marini, "Centralized Administration and the 'New Despotism,'" 255–86.

80. Rahe, *Soft Despotism, Democracy's Drift*, 278, 279. See also Rahe's frequent use of Tocqueville to emphasize the importance of federalism, in Paul Rahe, James Ceaser, and Thomas West, *Soft Despotism, Democracy's Drift: What Tocqueville Teaches Today* (Washington, DC: Heritage Foundation, 2009).

Part III · The Modern Presidency: An Overview

1. Sidney M. Milkis and Michael Nelson, *The American Presidency: Origins and Development, 1776–2011*, 6th ed. (Washington, DC: CQ Press, 2012), 289, 307.

2. Kelly, Harbison, and Belz, *American Constitution*, 2:640 (quote), 658. For an influential delineation of the characteristics of the modern presidency, see Fred I. Greenstein, "Change and Continuity in the Modern Presidency," in *The New American Political System*, ed. Anthony King (Washington, DC: AEI, 1978), 45–85.

3. The developments related in this and the following paragraph are treated in more detail in Louis Fisher, *Presidential War Power*, 3rd ed., rev. (Lawrence: University Press of Kansas, 2013). See also Stephen M. Griffin, *Long Wars and the Constitution* (Cambridge, MA: Harvard University Press, 2013).

4. 343 US 579.

5. Thomas E. Cronin, *The State of the Presidency* (Boston: Little, Brown, 1975), 23–51, quotes at 33, 23.

6. Fisher, *Presidential War Power*, 101–3. As Fisher notes, both Commager and Schlesinger later came publicly to regret their encouragement of presidential power.

7. Clinton Rossiter, *The American Presidency* (New York: Harcourt Brace, 1956).

8. Richard Neustadt, *Presidential Power: The Politics of Leadership* (New York: Wiley, 1960).

9. Neustadt, quoted in Louis Fisher, "The Law: Scholarly Support for Presidential Wars," *Presidential Studies Quarterly* 35 (2005): 590–607, 598.

10. Edward S. Corwin, *The President: Office and Powers; History and Analysis of Practice and Opinion* (New York: New York University Press, 1940), 29 (quote); Andrew Rudalevige, *The New Imperial Presidency: Renewing Presidential Power after Watergate* (Ann Arbor: University of Michigan Press, 2005), 53–56, quote at 55–56.

11. Rudalevige, *New Imperial Presidency*, 101–38.

12. Rudalevige, 101–38. Rudalevige traces this development as much in the domestic realm as in the international one.

13. Fisher, *Presidential War Power*, 185–91, 197–200.

Chapter 6 · *Traditionalists, the Modern Presidency, and the Rise of the Unitary Executive*

1. David E. Kyvig, *Explicit and Authentic Acts: Amending the U.S. Constitution, 1776–1995* (Lawrence: University Press of Kansas, 1996), 333, 327.

2. C. Perry Patterson, *Presidential Government in the United States: The Unwritten Constitution* (Chapel Hill: University of North Carolina Press, 1947). Patterson is treated in Raymond Tatalovich and Steven E. Schier, *The Presidency and Political Science: Paradigms of Presidential Power from the Founding to the Present*, 2nd ed. (Armonk, NY: M. E. Sharpe, 2014), 126–30. See also "Patterson, Caleb Perry," *Handbook of Texas Online*, updated May 1, 1995, https://tshaonline.org/handbook/entries/patterson-caleb-perry.

3. Patterson, *Presidential Government*, 38 (quote), 137–42, 234–38.

4. Patterson, 150 (quotes), 237.

5. Patterson, 142.

6. Patterson, 56–62, 65–69. As proposed by Edward Corwin (1945) and earlier by Henry Campbell Black (1914), Patterson recommended a modified form of cabinet government as the way to make the president more politically accountable to Congress.

7. Statement of Robert A. Taft, June 28, 1950, Cong. Rec., 81st Cong., 2nd sess., 9323. See also Ronald Radosh, *Prophets on the Right: Profiles of Conservative Critics of American Globalism* (New York: Simon and Schuster, 1975), 174.

8. The best overview is David R. Kepley, *The Collapse of the Middle Way: Senate Republicans and the Bipartisan Foreign Policy, 1948–1952* (Westport, CT: Greenwood, 1988), 101–16.

9. Statement of Robert A. Taft, March 29, 1951, Cong. Rec., 82nd Cong., 1st sess., 2987.

10. "Powers of the President to Send the Armed Forces outside the United States," US Senate, Joint Committee of Committees on Foreign Affairs and Armed Services, 82nd Cong., 1st sess., February 28, 1951, quotes at 1, 27.

11. Robert A. Taft, *A Foreign Policy for Americans* (Garden City, NY: Doubleday, 1951), 24.

12. Taft, 24.

13. Taft, 25.

14. Taft, 26–27.

15. Taft, 23.

16. Kepley, *Collapse of the Middle Way*, 115–16; Fisher, *Presidential War Power*, 112; Geoffrey Matthews, "Robert A. Taft, the Constitution, and American Foreign Policy," *Journal of Contemporary History* 17 (1982): 507–22, 518–19.

17. "Speech on the Seizure of the Steel Industry," April 15, 1952, Pittsburgh, PA, in *The*

Papers of Robert A. Taft, vol. 4 (Kent, OH: Kent State University Press, 2006), 368–73, quotes at 368, 369, 372, 373. See also Kirk and McClellan, *Political Principles of Robert A. Taft*, 97.

18. Youngstown Sheet & Tube Co. v. Sawyer, 343 U.S. 579 (1952).

19. See, generally, Duane Tananbaum, *The Bricker Amendment Controversy: A Test of Eisenhower's Political Leadership* (Ithaca, NY: Cornell University Press, 1988).

20. Tananbaum, *Bricker Amendment Controversy*, 44; Kyvig, *Explicit and Authentic Acts*, 340–47; Justin Raimondo, *Reclaiming the American Right: The Lost Legacy of the Conservative Movement* (1993; reprint, Wilmington, DE: ISI, 2008), 180–82; Griffin, *Long Wars and the Constitution*, 108.

21. James Burnham, "The Bricker Amendment: Its Background and Meaning," *National Review*, April 4, 1956, 9–12, 10 (quote); Frank S. Meyer, "The Revolt against Congress," *National Review*, May 30, 1956, 9–10, 9 (quote).

22. Clinton Rossiter, *Conservatism in America* (London: Heinemann, 1955), 198.

23. Burnham, *Congress and the American Tradition*.

24. Burnham, 322. Theodore J. Lowi stated that "The Plebiscitary Presidency" was the original title of his book *The Personal President: Power Invested, Promise Unfulfilled* (Ithaca, NY: Cornell University Press, 1985); Theodore J. Lowi, "Foreword: The End of Presidential Power," in Tatalovich and Schier, *Presidency and Political Science*, xiii.

25. Burnham, *Congress and the American Tradition*, 325.

26. Burnham, 326.

27. Burnham 326.

28. Burnham, 144.

29. Burnham, 255.

30. Burnham, 187–93.

31. Burnham, 192.

32. Burnham, 304 (quote), 149–50.

33. As offered in Kendall and Carey, *Basic Symbols of the American Political Tradition*. A good introduction is John A. Murley and John E. Alvis, eds., *Willmoore Kendall: Maverick of American Conservatives* (Lanham, MD: Lexington, 2002). George H. Nash, in *Conservative Intellectual Movement*, 210–32, observes that "long before it became fashionable, Kendall was a critic of the 'imperial presidency'" (222).

34. Willmoore Kendall, "The Two Majorities," *Midwest Journal of Political Science* 4 (1960): 317–45, reprinted in Willmoore Kendall, *Willmoore Kendall Contra Mundum*, ed. Nellie D. Kendall (New Rochelle, NY: Arlington House, 1971), 202–27.

35. Kendall, "Two Majorities," 205 (italics omitted), 206.

36. Kendall, "Two Majorities," 208 (italics omitted).

37. Kendall, 208.

38. Kendall, 225.

39. Kendall, 225.

40. Kendall, 207.

41. Steve Allen et al., *Dialogues in Americanism* (Chicago: Regnery, 1964), 120–24; Willmoore Kendall and George W. Carey, eds., *Liberalism versus Conservatism: The Continuing Debate in American Government* (Princeton, NJ: Van Nostrand, 1966), 389–402, quotes at 399 (italics removed), 400; Kendall, *Willmoore Kendall Contra Mundum*, 282–89; Tatalovich and Scheier, *Presidency and Political Science*, 3–15.

42. Willmoore Kendall, *The Conservative Affirmation in America* (1963; reprint, Chicago: Regnery Gateway, 1985), 252. This review originally appeared in *National Review*, November 7, 1959.

43. Kendall, *Conservative Affirmation*, 252. The importance of the dispute with Jaffa in relation to Kendall's affirmation of Congress over the statesmanship of powerful presidents is treated most extensively in Postell, "Philosopher-Kings or the Sense of the Community?" See also John A. Murley, "On the 'Calhounism' of Willmoore Kendall," in *Willmoore Kendall*, 99–139, esp. 107. For the argument that Kendall's critique was sufficiently deep to influence Jaffa's thought, see Zuckert and Zuckert, *The Truth about Leo Strauss*, 240–41.

44. Amaury de Riencourt, *The Coming Caesars* (New York: Coward McCann, 1957); Burnham, *Congress and the American Tradition*, 298–99; Kendall and Carey, *Liberalism versus Conservatism*, 241–58. See also J. Richard Piper, "Presidential-Congressional Power Prescriptions in Conservative Political Thought since 1933," *Presidential Studies Quarterly* 21 (1991): 35–54, 38.

45. Alfred de Grazia, *Republic in Crisis: Congress against the Executive Force* (New York: Federal Legal Publications, 1965).

46. Arthur M. Schlesinger Jr. and Alfred de Grazia, *Congress and the Presidency: Their Roles in Modern Times* (Washington, DC: AEI, 1967), 65–69, 88–89.

47. Schlesinger and de Grazia, 77, 79.

48. Schlesinger and de Grazia, 88. See also Tatalovich and Scheier, *Presidency and Political Science*, 130–31.

49. Kendall and Carey, *Liberalism versus Conservatism*, 224, 225.

50. Charlie Savage, *Takeover: The Return of the Imperial Presidency and the Subversion of American Democracy* (New York: Little, Brown, 2007; paperback, New York: Back Bay, 2008), 29; Julian Zelizer, "How Conservatives Learned to Stop Worrying and Love Presidential Power," in *The Presidency of George W. Bush: A First Historical Assessment*, ed. Julian Zelizer (Princeton, NJ: Princeton University Press, 2010), 22.

51. Savage, *Takeover*, 31–33, 40–42; Barilleaux and Zellers, "Executive Unilateralism in the Ford and Carter Presidencies."

52. Marjorie Hunter, "Ford Says That Congress Hobbles President by Foreign Policy Action," *New York Times*, December 14, 1978, A22.

53. Zelizer, "How Conservatives Learned to Stop Worrying," 23–25. See also David J. Barron and Martin S. Lederman, "The Commander in Chief at the Lowest Ebb: A Constitutional History," *Harvard Law Review* 121 (2008): 941–1111, 1076–78; Savage, *Takeover*, 36–37.

54. As quoted in Savage, *Takeover*, 43. I have emended the abbreviated words reported by Savage.

55. The most detailed study is Malcolm Byrne, *Iran-Contra: Reagan's Scandal and the Unchecked Abuse of Presidential Power* (Lawrence: University Press of Kansas, 2014).

56. United States v. Curtiss-Wright Export Corp., 299 U.S. 304 (1936).

57. Charles J. Cooper, "Memorandum for the Attorney General: The President's Compliance with the 'Timely Notification' Requirement of Section 501(b) of the National Security Act," December 17, 1986, reprinted in U.S. Senate Select Committee on Secret Military Assistance to Iran and the Nicaraguan Opposition, and House Select Committee to Investigate Covert Arms Transactions with Iran, *Iran-Contra Investigation: Joint Hearings*, 100th Cong., 1st sess., 1987, vol. 100-9, pp. 1546–72, 1547 (capitalization removed), 1569,

1563. See also Louis Fisher, "Investigating Iran-Contra," in *When Congress Comes Calling: A Study on the Principles, Practices, and Pragmatics of Legislative Inquiry*, ed. Morton Rosenberg (Washington, DC: Constitution Project, 2017), 280–81; Barron and Lederman, "Commander in Chief at the Lowest Ebb," 1081–83. This memorandum was published with the same title in US Department of Justice, 10 *Opinions of the Office of Legal Counsel* 159 (1986).

58. US Senate Select Committee on Secret Military Assistance to Iran and the Nicaraguan Opposition, and House Select Committee to Investigate Covert Arms Transactions with Iran, *Report of the Congressional Committees Investigating the Iran-Contra Affair, with Supplemental, Minority, and Additional Views*, 100th Cong., 1st sess., 1987, Minority Report, 431–586 (hereafter cited as Minority Report). The committee included Dick Cheney as a US representative from Wyoming and David Addington as a staff researcher, both of whom later played central roles in advancing presidential war making under the rubric of the unitary executive after 9/11.

59. Minority Report, 457 (quote), 458, 466.

60. Minority Report, 459–60, 469, 478.

61. Minority Report, 469; Cooper, "Memorandum for the Attorney General," 1547.

62. Memorandum of Law of the United States Filed by the Department of Justice as *Amicus Curiae* with Respect to the Independent Counsel's Opposition to the Defendant's Motions to Dismiss or Limit Count One, United States v. Oliver L. North, U.S.D.C. (D.C. Crim. No. 88-0080-02-GAG) (filed November 18, 1988), quoted in both Harold Hongju Koh, *The National Security Constitution: Sharing Power after the Iran-Contra Affair* (New Haven, CT: Yale University Press, 1990), 28; and Griffin, *Long Wars and the Constitution*, 190.

63. Dick Cheney, "Congressional Overreaching in Foreign Policy," in *Foreign Policy and the Constitution*, ed. Robert A. Goldwin and Robert A. Licht (Washington, DC: AEI, 1990), 101–22, 112.

64. Cheney, 102.

65. Jack N. Rakove, "Making Foreign Policy—the View from 1787," in *Foreign Policy and the Constitution*, 16, 13.

66. Bruce E. Fein, "The Constitution and Covert Action," *Houston Journal of International Law* 11 (1988): 53–68, 60.

67. Charles Bennett, Arthur B. Culvahouse, Jr., Geoffrey P. Miller, William Bradford Reynolds, and William Van Alstyne, "The President's Powers as Commander-in-Chief versus Congress' War Power and Appropriations Power," *University of Miami Law Review* 43 (1988): 17–59, 32 (citations omitted).

68. Hollis-Brusky, "Helping Ideas Have Consequences," 224–26.

69. Theodore B. Olson, "The Impetuous Vortex: Congressional Erosion of Presidential Authority," in *The Fettered Presidency: Legal Constraints on the Executive Branch*, ed. L. Gordon Crovitz and Jeremy Rabkin (Washington, DC: AEI, 1989), 225–44, 226–31.

70. Gary J. Schmitt and Abram N. Shulsky, "The Theory and Practice of Separation of Powers: The Case of Covert Action," in *Fettered Presidency*, 59–81, 61 (citation omitted). This essay also cites Montesquieu's *Spirit of the Laws* (1748) as rejecting "a legislative check on the executive that impairs the functional advantages of a unified executive office" (61).

71. Terry Eastland, *Energy in the Executive: The Case for the Strong Presidency* (New York: Free Press, 1992), 13 (emphasis in orig.).

72. Jeffrey Rosen, "Power of One: Bush's Leviathan State," *New Republic*, July 24, 2006, 8–10, 9.

73. Eastland, *Energy in the Executive*, 123.

74. Eastland, 123.

75. Eastland, 123.

76. Barron and Lederman, "Commander in Chief at the Lowest Ebb," 1083–87. See also Charles Tiefer, *The Semi-sovereign Presidency: The Bush Administration's Strategy for Governing without Congress* (Boulder, CO: Westview Press, 1994).

77. Griffin, *Long Wars and the Constitution*, 174–81; Eastland, *Energy in the Executive*, 119–20, 125–35.

78. William Thomas Allison, *The Gulf War, 1990–91* (New York: Palgrave Macmillan, 2012), 78–83, 88–95.

79. "Crisis in the Persian Gulf Region: U.S. Policy Options and Implications," *Hearings before the Committee on Armed Services*, US Senate, 101st Cong., 2nd sess., 1990, 701–702.

80. George Bush, "Statement on Signing the Resolution Authorizing the Use of Military Force Against Iraq," January 14, 1991, *The American Presidency Project*, accessed January 8, 2022, http://www.presidency.ucsb.edu/node/265739.

81. Fisher, *Presidential War Power*, 174–200; Kelley, "Unitary Executive in the Clinton Administration"; Savage, *Takeover*, 63–67. See also Rosen, "Power of One," 9.

82. Calabresi, "Some Normative Arguments for the Unitary Executive," 89.

83. Calabresi, 90.

84. John C. Yoo, "The Continuation of Politics by Other Means: The Original Understanding of War Powers" *California Law Review* 84 (1996): 167–305, 230.

85. Yoo, 174.

86. Yoo, 299.

87. John C. Yoo, "Kosovo, War Powers, and the Multilateral Future," *University of Pennsylvania Law Review* 148 (2000): 1673–1731. See also John C. Yoo, "UN Wars, US War Powers," *Chicago Journal of International Law* 1 (2000): 355–73.

88. Jane E. Stromseth, "Understanding Constitutional War Powers Today: Why Methodology Matters," *Yale Law Journal* 106 (1996): 845–915; Louis Fisher, "Unchecked Presidential Wars," *University of Pennsylvania Law Review* 148 (2000): 1637–72; Yoo, "Kosovo, War Powers, and the Multilateral Future," 1693–95; John C. Yoo, "Clio at War: The Misuse of History in the War Powers Debate," *University of Colorado Law Review* 70 (1999): 1169–1222.

89. Hollis-Brusky, "Helping Ideas Have Consequences," 231–36.

90. Robert J. Spitzer, *Saving the Constitution from Lawyers: How Legal Training and Law Reviews Distort Constitutional Meaning* (New York: Cambridge University Press, 2008), 103–109; Janet Cooper Alexander, "John Yoo's *War Powers*: The Law Review and the World," *California Law Review* 100 (2012): 331–64.

91. Barilleaux and Kelley, "Going Forward," 228.

92. Hollis-Brusky, "Helping Ideas Have Consequences," 227.

93. Benjamin A. Kleinerman, *The Discretionary President: The Promise and Peril of Executive Power* (Lawrence: University Press of Kansas, 2009). For a probing philosophical treatment, see Harvey C. Mansfield Jr., *Taming the Prince: The Ambivalence of Modern Executive Power* (Baltimore: Johns Hopkins University Press, 1989). Mansfield's analysis is taken up in chapter 7 of this book.

94. Stephen J. Markman, Assistant Attorney General, Office of Legal Policy, to Edwin Meese, Attorney General, April 30, 1986, 8, 9, available at National Security Archive, https://nsarchive.gwu.edu (accessed January 24, 2019) (cited hereafter as Markman memo).

95. Minority Report, 449 (all quotes).

96. Savage, *Takeover*, 8–9, 28, 39–40, 50–57.

97. Cheney, "Congressional Overreaching in Foreign Policy," 103.

98. Cheney, 121.

99. See, for example, L. Gordon Crovitz and Jeremy Rabkin, "Introduction," in *Fettered Presidency*, 8; C. Boyden Gray, "Special Interests, Regulation, and the Separation of Powers," in ibid., 211–14. This literature is treated most extensively in Tatalovich and Schier, *Presidency and Political Science*, 174–84.

100. Thomas G. West, "Restoring the Separation of Powers," in *Imperial Congress*, 309–29, 320. West and Marini were Straussians but neither advanced the theory of the unitary executive as such.

101. Calabresi, "Some Normative Arguments for the Unitary Executive," 34.

102. Jeffrey Hart, "The Presidency: Shifting Conservative Perspectives?" *National Review*, November 22, 1974, 1351–55, quotes at 1355, 1353.

103. William F. Buckley Jr., "And Now Legislative Supremacy," *National Review*, June 6, 1975, 630–31, quotes at 631.

104. See, generally, Milkis and Nelson, *American Presidency*, 377–80. See also Tatalovich and Schier, *Presidency and Political Science*, 174–84. This concept is applied to Reagan by one of its key originators, Jeffrey K. Tulis, in *The Rhetorical Presidency* (Princeton, NJ: Princeton University Press, 1987), 189–202. Its importance in Straussian approaches to the presidency is treated in chapter 7 of the present volume.

105. Markman memo, 36 (quote), 37.

106. Minority Report, 450.

107. Minority Report, 450.

108. Gordon S. Jones and John A. Marini, "General Introduction," in *Imperial Congress*, 12. See also West, "Restoring the Separation of Powers," 318–19; and "Recommendations," in *Imperial Congress*, 357–58.

109. Eastland, *Energy in the Executive*, 22, 328n11, 56 (quote) 280 (quote).

110. Eastland, 24–41, 279–80.

111. Ryan J. Barilleaux, "Conservatives and the Presidency," in *Contending Approaches to the American Presidency*, ed. Michael A. Genovese (Washington, DC: Congressional Quarterly, 2012), 30–49, 36–38; Zelizer, "How Conservatives Learned to Stop Worrying," 15–17; Piper, "Presidential-Congressional Power Prescriptions," 43–46; Theodore J. Lowi, "Afterword: Presidential Power and the Ideological Struggle over Its Interpretation," in *The Constitution and the American Presidency*, ed. Martin L. Fausold and Alan Shank (Albany: State University of New York Press, 1991), 227–44, 235–36. See also M. Stanton Evans, *Clear and Present Dangers: A Conservative View of America's Government* (New York: Harcourt Brace Jovanovich, 1975), 51–72.

112. Skowronek, "Conservative Insurgency and Presidential Power," 2100–2101; Hollis-Brusky, "Helping Ideas Have Consequences," 200–201.

113. This is also the general conclusion of Piper, "Presidential-Congressional Power Prescriptions," 46.

114. Nisbet, *Present Age*, 1–2, 40, 69, 76–83.

115. Nisbet, 79, 80.

116. Claes G. Ryn, *The New Jacobinism: Can Democracy Survive?* (Washington, DC: National Humanities Institute, 1991), 13. Ryn later elaborated this study after 9/11 in *America the Virtuous: The Crisis of Democracy and the Quest for Empire* (New Brunswick, NJ: Transaction, 2003).

117. Ryn, *New Jacobinism*, 14, 13.

118. Ryn, *New Jacobinism*, 67 (quote), 19 (quote), 33–35, 41.

119. Ryn, 72–73.

120. Ryn, 73.

121. Ryan J. Barilleaux, "Liberals, Conservatives, and the Presidency," *Congress and the Presidency* 20 (1993): 75–82, 79. Barilleaux elaborated on these views after 9/11 in "Conservatives and the Presidency."

122. Barilleaux, "Liberals, Conservatives, and the Presidency," 77, 81.

123. Carey, "Who or What Killed the Philadelphia Constitution?" 626–28.

124. George W. Carey, "Willmoore Kendall and the Doctrine of Majority Rule," in *Willmoore Kendall*, 42.

125. George W. Carey, "The Irony of Conservative Success," in *The Future of Conservatism: Conflict and Consensus in the Post-Reagan Era*, ed. Charles W. Dunn (Wilmington, DE: ISI, 2007), 31–41, 34, 33.

126. Gary L. Gregg II, *The Presidential Republic: Executive Representation and Deliberative Democracy* (Lanham, MD: Rowman and Littlefield, 1997). Gregg treats foreign policy at 167–71 and 175–78.

127. Gregg, 112.

128. Gregg, 209.

129. Gregg, 215.

130. Mickey Edwards, "Of Conservatives and Kings: The New Monarchism Is an Abdication of Our Principles," *Policy Review* (Spring 1989): 24–30, 30.

131. Edwards, 25 (quote), 27–28.

132. Edwards, 26.

133. Edwards, 27.

134. Edwards, 28.

135. Edwards, 30 (quote), 25.

136. William F. Buckley Jr., "Agenda for the Nineties," *National Review*, February 19, 1990, 34–40, quotes at 39, 39–40.

137. Samuel Francis, "Imperial Conservatives?" *National Review*, August 4, 1989, 37–38, quote at 38.

138. Francis, 38.

139. Samuel Francis, "Message from Mars" (1982), in Francis, *Beautiful Losers*, 75–76, 77.

140. Samuel Francis, "Who's in Charge Here?" (1988), in Francis, *Beautiful Losers*, 164 (quote), 165–68.

141. Samuel Francis, "Caesar's Column," *Chronicles* (October 1997), 23–26, 26.

142. For an early statement, see Patrick J. Buchanan, "America First—and Second and Third," in *America's Purpose: New Visions of U.S. Foreign Policy*, ed. Owen Harries (San Francisco: ICS Press, 1991), 23–34. Buchanan offered a lengthy treatment of the noninterventionist tradition in US history in *A Republic Not an Empire: Reclaiming America's Destiny* (Chicago: Regnery, 1999).

143. Samuel Francis, "Principalities and Powers," *Chronicles* (December 1991), 9–11, 11.

144. Thomas Fleming, "America First: 1941/1991," *Chronicles* (December 1991), 12–14, 13.

145. Bill Kauffman, *America First! Its History, Culture, and Politics* (Amherst, NY: Prometheus, 1995), 252.

Chapter 7 · *Straussians, Neoconservatives, Libertarians, and the Modern Presidency*

1. The few scholars to examine synthetically the Straussian view of the presidency include Robert Devigne, *Recasting Conservatism: Oakeshott, Strauss, and the Response to Postmodernism* (New Haven, CT: Yale University Press, 1994), 51–53, 56–58, 69–77; and Pangle, *Leo Strauss*, 112–15. Robert Eden, "Executive Power and the Presidency," in *Leo Strauss, the Straussians, and the American Regime*, 351–61, is in its entirety a study of Harvey C. Mansfield Jr.'s *Taming the Prince: The Ambivalence of Modern Executive Power* (1989), which is treated below.

2. For a brief discussion, see Galston, "Leo Strauss's Qualified Embrace of Liberal Democracy," 211–12.

3. Strauss, *Natural Right and History*, 160; Galston, "Leo Strauss's Qualified Embrace of Liberal Democracy," 209–10.

4. Strauss, *Natural Right and History*, 160.

5. Strauss, 162.

6. Richard H. Cox, *Locke on War and Peace* (Oxford: Clarendon Press, 1960); Robert A. Goldwin, "John Locke," in *History of Political Philosophy*, 3rd ed., ed. Leo Strauss and Joseph Cropsey (Chicago: University of Chicago Press, 1987), 476–512 (1st ed., 1963); John Locke, *Two Treatises of Government*, student edition, ed. Peter Laslett (Cambridge: Cambridge University Press, 1988). All references to this edition of Locke are by treatise and section number; spelling and italicization have been modernized.

7. Locke, *Two Treatises*, II: 147; Cox, *Locke on War and Peace*, 126; Goldwin, "John Locke," 501–2.

8. Locke, *Two Treatises*, II: 147.

9. Cox, *Locke on War and Peace*, 194.

10. Cox, 195.

11. Locke, *Two Treatises*, II: 144.

12. Locke, II: 159.

13. Locke, II: 160.

14. Locke, II: 160.

15. Locke, II: 166.

16. My treatment is informed by Murray Dry, "Herbert Storing: The American Founding and the American Regime," in *Leo Strauss, the Straussians, and the American Regime*, 305–28; and Ralph A. Rossum, "Herbert Storing's Constitutionalism," *Political Science Reviewer* 29 (2000): 39–69.

17. Herbert J. Storing, "Introduction," in Charles C. Thach Jr., *The Creation of the American Presidency, 1775–1789: A Study in Constitutional History* (1923; reprint, Indianapolis: Liberty Fund, 2007), 166. Storing's introduction is also reprinted in *Toward a More Perfect Union*, 369–76.

18. Storing, "Problem of Big Government," 301 (quote); Storing "Introduction," esp. 163, 171.

19. Storing, "Role of Government in Society," 354 (quote); Storing, "The Presidency and the Constitution" (speech originally given in 1974), in *Toward a More Perfect Union*, 379, 381.

20. Storing, "The Presidency and the Constitution," 380–81.

21. Storing, "The Presidency and the Constitution," 381.

22. Storing, 381.

23. Storing, 382.

24. Storing, 383.

25. Storing, 382.

26. Storing, 384.

27. Harvey C. Mansfield Jr., *Taming the Prince: The Ambivalence of Modern Executive Power* (Baltimore: Johns Hopkins University Press, 1989; paperback ed., 1993), xx.

28. Mansfield, 257, quoting *Federalist 72*.

29. Mansfield, 284, 287.

30. Mansfield, 17–19.

31. Mansfield, xxiii. See also, Eden, "Executive Power and the Presidency," 358.

32. Mansfield, *Taming the Prince*, xv–xvii.

33. Mansfield, 255, 255–56.

34. Mansfield, 269, 270 (internal quotes from *Federalist 72*).

35. Mansfield, xvii (quote); Harvey C. Mansfield Jr., "The Revival of Constitutionalism," in *The Revival of Constitutionalism*, ed. James W. Muller (Lincoln: University of Nebraska Press, 1988), 214–27, 223.

36. Mansfield, *Taming the Prince*, 297. See also ibid., 263–64, 278; Mansfield, *America's Constitutional Soul*, 148, 215–16.

37. Mansfield, *Taming the Prince*, 291–92; Mansfield, *America's Constitutional Soul*, 216–19. See also, Eden, "Executive Power and the Presidency," 359.

38. Mansfield, *Taming the Prince*, 278.

39. Morton J. Frisch, "Executive Power and Republican Government—1787," *Presidential Studies Quarterly* 17 (1987): 281–91, 289, 290. See also Larry Arnhart, "'The God-Like Prince': John Locke, Executive Prerogative, and the American Presidency," *Presidential Studies Quarterly* 9 (Spring 1979): 121–30; Werner J. Dannhauser, "Reflections on Statesmanship and Bureaucracy," in *Bureaucrats, Policy Analysts, Statesmen: Who Leads?* ed. Robert A. Goldwin (Washington, DC: AEI, 1980), 114–32, 118–19, 121–22; Joseph M. Bessette and Jeffrey Tulis, "The Constitution, Politics, and the Presidency," in *The Presidency in the Constitutional Order*, ed. Joseph M. Bessette and Jeffrey Tulis (Baton Rouge: Louisiana State University Press, 1981), 3–29, 19–29 (this volume is dedicated to Herbert J. Storing); Thomas L. Pangle, "Executive Energy and Popular Spirit in Lockean Constitutionalism," *Presidential Studies Quarterly* 17 (1987): 253–65; Ralph Ketcham, "Executive Leadership, Citizenship, and Good Government," *Presidential Studies Quarterly* 17 (1987): 267–79; Douglas A. Jeffrey, "Executive Authority under the Separation of Powers," in *Imperial Congress*, 41–67, 44, 48–50; Robert Scigliano, "The President's 'Prerogative Power,'" in *Inventing the American Presidency*, ed. Thomas E. Cronin (Lawrence: University Press of Kansas, 1989), 236–56.

40. Nathan Tarcov, "Principle, Prudence, and the Constitutional Division of Foreign Policy," in *Foreign Policy and the Constitution*, 21–39, 35–38; Mark Blitz, "The Problem of Practice: Foreign Policy and the Constitution," ibid., 72–89, 82, 83, 84; L. Peter Schultz, "The Separation of Power and Foreign Affairs," in *Separation of Powers—Does It Still Work?* ed. Robert A. Goldwin and Art Kaufman (Washington, DC: AEI, 1986), 118–37, 128, 129, 130, 133.

41. Richard H. Cox, "Executive and Prerogative: A Problem for Adherents of Constitutional Government," in *E Pluribus Unum: Constitutional Principles and the Institutions of Government*, ed. Sarah Baumgartner Thurow (Lanham, MD: University Press of America, 1988), 102–22, 111.

42. Robert J. Scigliano, "The War Powers Resolution and the War Powers," in *Presidency in the Constitutional Order*, 115–53, esp., 138–49.

43. Jeffrey, "Executive Authority under the Separation of Powers," 53.

44. Gary J. Schmitt, "Executive Privilege: Presidential Power to Withhold Information from Congress," *Presidency in the Constitutional Order*, 154–94, 175–76, 182 (quote), 183. Schmitt responded in this chapter to Raoul Berger, *Executive Privilege: A Constitutional Myth* (1974), which opponents of Richard Nixon lauded as bolstering the case for his impeachment.

45. Schmitt and Shulsky, "Theory and Practice of Separation of Powers," 74–75.

46. Schmitt and Shulsky, 75. See also Gary J. Schmitt and Abram N. Shulsky, "Leo Strauss and the World of Intelligence (by Which We Do Not Mean *Nous*)," in *Leo Strauss, the Straussians, and the American Regime*, 407–12.

47. Carnes Lord, *The Presidency and the Management of National Security* (New York: Free Press, 1988).

48. Lord, 12.

49. Walter Berns, "In Times of Crisis, How Much Power Does a President Have?" (orig. pub. *Washington Times*, June 3, 1987), *World and I* (August 1987): 555–60, 560.

50. Walter Berns, "Constitutional Power and the Defense of Free Government," in *Terrorism: How the West Can Win*, ed. Benjamin Netanyahu (New York: Farrar, Strauss, and Giroux, 1986), 149–54, 152.

51. Storing, "In Defense of the Electoral College," in *Toward a More Perfect Union*, 395, 396 (statement to the Senate Judiciary Committee, 1977).

52. Storing, 400; Diamond, "Electoral College and the American Idea of Democracy," 187–93.

53. Diamond, "Electoral College and the American Idea of Democracy," 204.

54. James W. Ceaser, *Presidential Selection: Theory and Development* (Princeton, NJ: Princeton University Press, 1979).

55. Ceaser, 5 (quote), 258.

56. Ceaser, 318–27.

57. Ceaser, 339.

58. Ceaser et al., "Rise of the Rhetorical Presidency."

59. Tulis, *Rhetorical Presidency*.

60. Ceaser, *Presidential Selection*, 318–27, 54–61; Tulis, *Rhetorical Presidency*, 27–31, 119, 130–32. See also James W. Ceaser, "Demagoguery, Statesmanship, and Presidential Politics," in *The Constitutional Presidency*, ed. Joseph M. Bessette and Jeffrey K. Tulis (Baltimore: Johns Hopkins University Press, 2009), 247–88.

61. Ceaser et al., "Rise of the Rhetorical Presidency," 161.

62. Ceaser et al., 163.

63. Jeffrey K. Tulis, "The Constitutional Presidency in American Political Development," in *Constitution and the American Presidency*, 133–46, 140.

64. Ceaser, *Presidential Selection*, 324–26, quote at 325; Tulis, *Rhetorical Presidency*, 176, 181, 202–204, quote at 202.

65. Ceaser et al., "Rise of the Rhetorical Presidency," 161.

66. Ceaser, *Presidential Selection*, 349.

67. Tulis, *Rhetorical Presidency*, 181 (quote); Ceaser, *Presidential Selection*, 349–50; Ceaser et al., "Rise of the Rhetorical Presidency," 169, 170.

68. Ceaser, *Liberal Democracy and Political Science* , 183, 182, 184, 189.

69. Ceaser, *Liberal Democracy and Political Science*, 195.

70. Ceaser, 196, 209–10. See also Tulis, *Rhetorical Presidency*, 22.

71. James W. Ceaser, "The Rhetorical Presidency Revisited," in *Modern Presidents and the Presidency*, ed. Marc Landy (Lexington, MA: Lexington Books, 1985), 19–20, 21–22, quote at 22.

72. Ceaser et al., "Rise of the Rhetorical Presidency," 170.

73. Jeffrey K. Tulis, "Revising the Rhetorical Presidency," in *Beyond the Rhetorical Presidency*, ed. Martin J. Medhurst (College Station: Texas A&M University Press, 1996), 3–14, 7; Ceaser, "Rhetorical Presidency Revisited," 23–24, 31–33.

74. Tulis, "Revising the Rhetorical Presidency," 6.

75. Tulis, "Revising the Rhetorical Presidency," 11.

76. Tulis, 13.

77. David K. Nichols, *The Myth of the Modern Presidency* (University Park: Pennsylvania State University Press, 1994).

78. Nichols, 62.

79. Nichols, 170.

80. Nichols, 172.

81. Nichols, 173 (quote), 10.

82. Nichols, 172.

83. Pangle, *Leo Strauss*, 113

84. Jeffrey K. Tulis, "Reflections on the Rhetorical Presidency in American Political Development," in *Speaking to the People: The Rhetorical Presidency in Historical Perspective*, ed. Richard J. Ellis (Amherst: University of Massachusetts Press, 1998), 214 (quote, citation omitted); Ceaser, "Rhetorical Presidency Revisited," 22.

85. Tulis, "Constitutional Presidency," 140 (quote), 290n2. Tulis here acknowledged the influence of Storing, "Problem of Big Government." See also Pangle, *Leo Strauss*, 113–14.

86. Skowronek, "Conservative Insurgency and Presidential Power," 2093. See also Lowi, "Afterword," 236.

87. A leading statement of this position was William Kristol and Robert Kagan, "Toward a Neo-Reaganite Foreign Policy," *Foreign Affairs* 75 (1996): 18–32. A detailed and generally fair-minded study is Gary Dorrien, *Imperial Designs: Neoconservatism and the New Pax Americana* (New York: Routledge, 2004).

88. Kristol and Kagan, "Toward a Neo-Reaganite Foreign Policy," 31.

89. Kristol and Kagan, 20 (quote), 31.

90. William Kristol and Robert Kagan, "Introduction: National Interest and Global Responsibility," in *Present Dangers: Crisis and Opportunity in American Foreign and Defense Policy*, ed. Robert Kagan and William Kristol (San Francisco: Encounter, 2000), 17.

91. Kristol and Kagan, "Toward a Neo-Reaganite Foreign Policy," 31, 32.

92. Kristol and Kagan, "Introduction," 23; Kristol and Kagan, "Toward a Neo-Reaganite Foreign Policy," 27.

93. Kristol and Kagan, "Introduction," 19, 7; Dorrien, *Imperial Designs*, 65–70, 92–96.

94. Kristol and Kagan, "Introduction," 24, 23. See also James W. Ceaser, "The Great Divide: American Internationalism and Its Opponents," in *Present Dangers*, 38–40.

95. Harvey C. Mansfield Jr., "The Law and the President: In a National Emergency, Who You Gonna Call?" *Weekly Standard*, January 16, 2006, archived at www.washington examiner.com.

96. Harvey C. Mansfield Jr., "The Case for the Strong Executive," *Claremont Review of Books* 7 (Spring 2007): 21–24, 24.

97. Mansfield, "The Case for the Strong Executive," 24.

98. James W. Ceaser, "The Presidency and the New 'Bully Pulpit,'" in *The Imperial Presidency and the Constitution*, ed. Gary J. Schmitt, Joseph M. Bessette, and Andrew E. Busch (Lanham, MD: Rowman and Littlefield, 2017), 125–44, 140 (citation omitted).

99. Ceaser, "Presidency and the New 'Bully Pulpit,'" 140.

100. Steinfels, *Neoconservatives*; Vaïsse, *Neoconservatism*, 271 (quote).

101. Kersch, "Neoconservatives and the Courts," esp. 292.

102. Including the leading Straussian effort, Zuckert and Zuckert, *The Truth about Leo Strauss*, 263–64.

103. Ceaser, *Designing a Polity*, 45–46, 51, 49, 143.

104. As exemplified by Paul Gottfried's insightful intellectual biography, *Leo Strauss and the Conservative Movement in America: A Critical Appraisal* (New York: Cambridge University Press, 2012), 123, 128–29, 125–26; and Dorrien, *Imperial Designs*, 132, 44.

105. Zuckert and Zuckert, *The Truth about Leo Strauss*, 266.

106. C. Bradley Thompson, with Yaron Brook, *Neoconservatism: An Obituary for an Idea* (Boulder, CO: Paradigm, 2010).

107. Irving Kristol, *On the Democratic Idea in America* (New York: Harper and Row, 1972), ix, vii (quote).

108. Ceaser, *Designing a Polity*, 49, 143–44.

109. Kristol, quoted in Vaïsse, *Neoconservatism*, 5. See also ibid., 272; Justin Vaïsse, "Was Irving Kristol a Neoconservative?," *Foreign Policy*, September 23, 2009, www.foreign policy.com; Zuckert and Zuckert, *The Truth about Leo Strauss*, 263–66.

110. Nathan Tarcov, "If This Long War Is Over," in *America's Purpose: New Visions of U.S. Foreign Policy*, ed. Owen Harries (San Francisco: ICS, 1991), 15–22, 17.

111. Tarcov, 20.

112. Nathan Tarcov, "Will the Real Leo Strauss Please Stand Up?" *American Interest* (Autumn 2006): 120–28, 120. See also, Julie Englander, "Defending Strauss," *Chicago Reader*, August 23, 2007, www.chicagoreader.com.

113. Tarcov, "Will the Real Leo Strauss Please Stand Up?" 128.

114. Nathan Tarcov and Thomas L. Pangle, "Leo Strauss and the History of Political Philosophy," in *History of Political Philosophy*, 907–38.

115. Steven Lenzner and William Kristol, "What Was Leo Strauss Up To?" *Public Interest* 153 (Fall 2003): 19–39, 38. See also Kristol and Kagan, "Introduction," 17.

116. Vaïsse too notes the idea of "regime" in both Strauss and neoconservatism, but concludes nevertheless that "nothing was more foreign to [Strauss's] thinking than the idea of global promotion of democracy by the United States." Vaïsse, *Neoconservatism*, 272 (quote), 233–34. When William Kristol was twice asked directly about Strauss's influence on him, he spoke in general terms and did not invoke Strauss as an authority for any particular neoconservative policy position. Ibid., 272; Dorrien, *Imperial Designs*, 132.

117. Kenneth R. Weinstein, "Philosophic Roots, the Role of Leo Strauss, and the War in Iraq," in *Neocon Reader*, 203–12, 207.

118. Charles R. Kesler, "Iraq and the Neoconservatives," *Claremont Review of Books* 7 (Summer 2007): 8–13, quotes at 12, 13.

119. Thomas G. West, "Leo Strauss and American Foreign Policy," in *Life, Liberty, and the Pursuit of Happiness: Ten Years of the* Claremont Review of Books, ed. Charles R. Kesler and John B. Kienker (Lanham, MD: Rowman and Littlefield, 2012), 158–66. For a detailed explication (by a non-Straussian) of Strauss's views on foreign policy that is consonant with this interpretation, see Robert Howse, *Leo Strauss: Man of Peace* (New York: Cambridge University Press, 2014).

120. West, "Leo Strauss and American Foreign Policy," 163.

121. West, 163.

122. West, 163.

123. George H. Nash, "The Uneasy Future of American Conservatism," in *Future of Conservatism*, 15–16; Vaïsse, *Neoconservatism*, 278; Gottfried, *Leo Strauss and the Conservative Movement*, 129–30; Walter A. McDougall, "Editor's Column," *Orbis* 42 (Winter 1998): 1–6, 3–6.

124. Kesler, "Iraq and the Neoconservatives," 12.

125. West, "Leo Strauss and American Foreign Policy," 162 (emphasis in orig.).

126. West, 163.

127. Robert D. Tollison, "Voting in U.S. Presidential Elections," in *Encyclopedia of Public Choice*, 2:596–99, quote at 598.

128. "Powers of the President to Send the Armed Forces outside the United States"; Garet Garrett, *The People's Pottage* (Caldwell, ID: Caxton, 1953), 55. See also Raimondo, *Reclaiming the American Right*, 93–103. For an overview of Garrett's work, see Carl Ryant, *Profit's Prophet: Garet Garrett (1878–1954)* (Selinsgrove, PA: Susquehanna University Press, 1989).

129. Garrett, *People's Pottage*, 73, 53 (quote).

130. Garrett, 57

131. Justus D. Doenecke, *Not to the Swift: The Old Isolationists in the Cold War Era* (Lewisburg, PA: Bucknell University Press, 1979), 86, 79, 91.

132. Felix Morley, *Freedom and Federalism* (Chicago: Regnery, 1959), 107–10, 96, 155.

133. Raimondo, *Reclaiming the American Right*, 180–83; Rothbard, *Betrayal of the American Right*, 139–41.

134. William F. Buckley Jr., "A Young Republican's View: The Party and the Deep Blue Sea," *Commonweal* 55 (January 25, 1952): 391–93, quote at 392–93.

135. Raimondo, *Reclaiming the American Right*, 146–47; Rothbard, *Betrayal of the American Right*, 159.

136. Lawrence V. Cott, "Cato Institute and the Invisible Finger," *National Review*, June 8, 1979, 740–42.

137. Raimondo, *Reclaiming the American Right*, 106, 296; Rothbard, *Betrayal of the American Right*, 172, 170, 161.

138. Murray Rothbard, *For a New Liberty* (New York: Macmillan, 1973), 76.

139. Thomas E. Woods Jr., "Introduction," in Rothbard, *Betrayal of the American Right*, xviii–xix; Raimondo, *Reclaiming the American Right*, 258–68; Scotchie, *Revolt from the Heartland*, 81–91.

140. Doherty, *Radicals for Capitalism*, 609.

141. Llewellyn H. Rockwell Jr., "Down with the Presidency," *Chronicles* (October 1997): 27–32, quotes at 28, 32.

142. John V. Denson, ed., *Reassessing the Presidency: The Rise of the Executive State and the Decline of Freedom* (Auburn, AL: Ludwig von Mises Institute, 2001). See also the insightful review by Herman Belz in *Independent Review: A Journal of Political Economy* 7 (Spring 2003): 607–11.

143. Clyde N. Wilson, "The American President: From Cincinnatus to Caesar," in Denson, *Reassessing the Presidency*, 697–710, 710.

144. Hans-Hermann Hoppe, "On the Impossibility of Limited Government and the Prospects for a Second American Revolution," in Denson, *Reassessing the Presidency*, 667–96, 671 (quote), 681.

145. Hoppe, 682–96.

146. Doherty, *Radicals for Capitalism*, 610–12.

147. Gene Healy, *The Cult of the Presidency: America's Dangerous Devotion to Executive Power* (Washington, DC: Cato Institute, 2008).

148. Healy, 28.

149. Healy, 312.

150. Healy, 298.

151. Healy, 312.

152. Epstein, *Classical Liberal Constitution*, 293, 293–94.

Part IV · Modern Judicial Review: An Overview

1. The literature on this topic is immense, but here and in the following two paragraphs I have found particularly helpful Moreno, *American State from the Civil War to the New Deal*; Patrick M. Garry, *An Entrenched Legacy: How the New Deal Constitutional Revolution Continues to Shape the Role of the Supreme Court* (University Park: Pennsylvania State University Press, 2008); White, *Constitution and the New Deal*; Howard Gillman, "The Collapse of Constitutional Originalism and the Rise of the Notion of the 'Living Constitution' in the Course of American State-Building," *Studies in American Political Development* 11 (1997): 191–247; Christopher Wolfe, *The Rise of Modern Judicial Review: From Constitutional Interpretation to Judge-Made Law*, rev. ed. (Lanham, MD: Rowman and Littlefield, 1994).

2. 304 U.S. 144 (1938).

3. Palko v. Connecticut, 302 U.S. 319, 325, 328 (1937).

4. United States v. Darby, 312 U.S. 100, 124 (1941).

5. Here and in the following paragraph I draw on Neil Duxbury, *Patterns of American Jurisprudence* (New York: Oxford University Press, 1995), chapter 4; Laura Kalman, *The Strange Career of Legal Liberalism* (New Haven, CT: Yale University Press, 1996), 19–42;

and Brian Z. Tamanaha, *Law as a Means to an End: Threat to the Rule of Law* (New York: Cambridge University Press, 2006), 102–11. See also Gary Peller, "Neutral Principles in the 1950's," *University of Michigan Journal of Law Reform* 21 (1988): 561–622; and O'Neill, *Originalism in American Law and Politics*, chapter 2.

6. Alexander M. Bickel, *The Least Dangerous Branch: The Supreme Court at the Bar of Politics* (New York: Bobbs-Merrill, 1962). See also Herbert Wechsler, "Toward Neutral Principles of Constitutional Law," *Harvard Law Review* 73 (1959): 1–35.

7. A highly sympathetic synoptic account is Morton J. Horowitz, *The Warren Court and the Pursuit of Justice* (New York: Hill and Wang, 1998). Also sympathetic and written for nonspecialists is Melvin I. Urofsky, *The Warren Court: Justices, Rulings, and Legacy* (Santa Barbara, CA: ABC-CLIO, 2001). More detailed and moderate treatments are Lucas A. Powe Jr., *The Warren Court and American Politics* (Cambridge, MA: Belknap Press of Harvard University Press, 2000); and Michael R. Belknap, *The Supreme Court under Earl Warren, 1953–1969* (Columbia: University of South Carolina Press, 2005).

8. Cooper v. Aaron, 358 U.S. 1 (1958).

9. Baker v. Carr, 369 U.S. 186 (1962). For a history of the political question doctrine in relation to judicial supremacy, see Rachel E. Barkow, "More Supreme than Court? The Fall of the Political Question Doctrine and the Rise of Judicial Supremacy," *Columbia Law Review* 102 (2002): 237–336. See also Jared P. Cole, "The Political Question Doctrine: Justiciability and the Separation of Powers," Congressional Research Service, December 23, 2014, www.crs.gov.

10. Miranda v. Arizona, 384 U.S. 436 (1966).

11. The leading cases in each area are New York Times v. Sullivan, 376 U.S. 254 (1964); Memoirs v. Massachusetts, 383 U.S. 413 (1966); Engel v. Vitale, 370 U.S. 421 (1962); and Griswold v. Connecticut, 381 U.S. 479 (1965).

12. Philip B. Kurland, *Politics, the Constitution, and the Warren Court* (Chicago: University of Chicago Press, 1970), 90–91.

13. Powe, *Warren Court and American Politics*, 496.

14. Nathan Glazer, "Towards an Imperial Judiciary?" *Public Interest* 41 (1975): 104–23, 106. Glazer is treated below in chapter 8.

15. Vincent Blasi, ed., *The Burger Court: The Counter-Revolution That Wasn't* (New Haven, CT: Yale University Press, 1983). The best study of the Burger Court emphasizes its continuity and extension of Warren Court liberalism. Earl M. Maltz, *The Chief Justiceship of Warren Burger, 1969–1986* (Columbia: University of South Carolina Press, 2000).

16. Swann v. Charlotte-Mecklenburg Board of Education, 402 U.S. 1 (1971).

17. Regents of the University of California v. Bakke, 438 U.S. 265 (1978); United Steelworkers of America v. Weber, 443 U.S. 193 (1979); Fullilove v. Klutznick, 448 U.S. 448 (1980).

18. Roe v. Wade, 410 U.S. 113 (1973).

19. The complicated issue of standing in relation to the administrative state and the growth of judicial power is well explicated in Postell, *Bureaucracy in America*, 260–65, 274–78, 286–88. See also Moreno, *The Bureaucrat Kings*, 124–25.

20. Nollan v. California Coastal Commission, 483 U.S. 825 (1987); Dolan v. City of Tigard, 512 U.S. 374 (1994); Lucas v. South Carolina Coast Council, 505 U.S. 1003 (1992).

21. Wards Cove Packing Company, Inc. v. Atonio, 490 U.S. 642 (1989); Adarand Constructors, Inc. v. Peña, 515 U.S. 200 (1995); Shaw v. Reno, 509 U.S. 630 (1993); Gratz v. Bollinger, 539 U.S. 244 (2003).

22. City of Boerne v. Flores, 521 U.S. 507, 536 (1997).

23. Planned Parenthood of Southeastern Pa. v. Casey, 505 U.S. 833, 868, 851 (1992).

24. Stenberg v. Carhart, 530 U.S. 914 (2000).

25. Lawrence v. Texas, 539 U.S. 558 (2003).

26. For similar judgments, see, for example, Tinsley E. Yarbrough, *The Rehnquist Court and the Constitution* (New York: Oxford University Press, 2000), xi; and Lawrence Friedman, "The Rehnquist Court: Some More or Less Historical Comments," in *The Rehnquist Court: A Retrospective*, ed. Martin H. Belsky (New York: Oxford University Press, 2002), 143–58, 146, 151–54.

27. Earl M. Maltz, "Introduction," in Maltz, *Rehnquist Justice*, 1–7, quote at 4. See also Lino A. Graglia, "The Rehnquist Court and Economic Rights," in *Rehnquist Court*, 116–40, 120–23.

28. Christopher Wolfe, "The Rehnquist Court and 'Conservative Judicial Activism,'" in *That Eminent Tribunal: Judicial Supremacy and the Constitution*, ed. Christopher Wolfe (Princeton, NJ: Princeton University Press, 2004), 199–224; Michael W. McConnell, "Toward a More Balanced History of the Supreme Court," in ibid., 141–58.

29. See, generally, O'Neill, *Originalism in American Law and Politics*.

30. In addition to O'Neill, *Originalism in American Law and Politics*, see Teles, "Transformative Bureaucracy"; Ralph A. Rossum, "James McClellan, *Benchmark*, and an Informed Public," *Modern Age* 54 (Winter/Fall 2012): 7–16; and Hollis-Brusky, *Ideas with Consequences*. Several of Meese's speeches are collected in *Major Policy Statements of the Attorney General: Edwin Meese III, 1985–1988* (Washington, DC: Government Printing Office, 1989). See also US Department of Justice, Office of Legal Policy, *Original Meaning Jurisprudence: A Sourcebook*, March 12, 1987; and US Department of Justice, Office of Legal Policy, *The Constitution in the Year 2000: Choices Ahead in Constitutional Interpretation*, October 11, 1988.

31. See Kalman, *Strange Career of Legal Liberalism*, 132–63; and O'Neill, *Originalism in American Law and Politics*, 190–216. See also Logan E. Sawyer III, "Principle and Politics in the New History of Originalism," *American Journal of Legal History* 57 (2017): 198–222.

32. The best sources for understanding the new originalism are Keith E. Whittington, "The New Originalism," *Georgetown Journal of Law and Public Policy* 2 (2004): 599–613; Robert W. Bennett and Lawrence B. Solum, *Constitutional Originalism: A Debate* (Ithaca, NY: Cornell University Press, 2011); Grant Huscroft and Bradley W. Miller, ed., *The Challenge of Originalism: Essays in Constitutional Theory* (New York: Cambridge University Press, 2011); Thomas B. Colby and Peter J. Smith, "Living Originalism," *Duke Law Journal* 59 (2009): 239–307; and Keith E. Whittington, "Originalism: A Critical Introduction," *Fordham Law Review* 82 (2013): 375–409. See also Lawrence B. Solum, "Originalist Methodology," *University of Chicago Law Review* 84 (2017): 269–95; and Lee J. Strang, *Originalism's Promise: A Natural Law Account of the American Constitution* (Cambridge: Cambridge University Press, 2019).

Chapter 8 · *Traditionalists, Neoconservatives, and Modern Judicial Review*

1. Richard Weaver, "The South and the American Union" (1957), in Curtis and Thompson, *Southern Essays of Richard M. Weaver*, 253, 254 (quote). See also Richard M. Weaver, "Integration Is Communization," *National Review*, July 13, 1957, 67–68.

2. Frank Lawrence Owsley, "Democracy Unlimited," in *The South: Old and New Fron-*

tiers; Selected Essays of Frank Lawrence Owsley, ed. Harriet Fason Chappell Owsley (Athens: University of Georgia Press, 1969), 201 (both quotes).

3. Donald Davidson, "The New South and the Conservative Tradition," *National Review*, September 10, 1960, 141–46, quotes at 145, 146. Davidson was a leader in the Tennessee massive resistance movement. See Murphy, *Rebuke of History*, 202–5.

4. The Southern Manifesto is reprinted in Day, *Southern Manifesto*, 160–62. See also ibid., 27, 80.

5. *A Question of Intent: The States, Their Schools, and the 14th Amendment* (Richmond: Virginia Commission on Constitutional Government, 1959), i, 16.

6. Speech originally delivered February 9, 1957, in Leon I. Salomon, ed., *The Supreme Court* (New York: H. W. Wilson, 1961), 158.

7. Kilpatrick, *Sovereign States*, 263.

8. Kilpatrick, 263.

9. Kilpatrick, 262, 276. See also ibid., 277, 258, 261–62, 272–76, 286, 304; and Kilpatrick, "Conservatism and the South," 188–205, 201–04.

10. Ken I. Kersch, "Ecumenicalism through Constitutionalism: The Discursive Development of Constitutional Conservatism in *National Review*, 1955–1980," *Studies in American Political Development* 25 (2011): 1–31, 19, 20.

11. Hustwit, *James J. Kilpatrick*, 90–106; Gregory L. Schneider, *The Conservative Century: From Reaction to Revolution* (Lanham, MD: Rowman and Littlefield, 2009), 82–86; James R. Sweeney, ed., *Race, Reason, and Massive Resistance: The Diary of David J. Mays, 1954–1959* (Athens: University of Georgia Press, 2008), 215–16, 279.

12. David Lawrence, *The Editorials of David Lawrence*, 6 vols. (Washington, DC: U.S. New & World Report, 1970), 5:182.

13. Lawrence, *Editorials*, 5:282.

14. Lawrence, *Editorials*, 5:358. See also ibid., 6:98, 5:211–17, 230–31, 281–82, 291, 293–94, 300, 342, 347, 348–49, 354–55.

15. For a figure who was once so prominent, Manion is understudied. See Donald T. Critchlow, *The Conservative Ascendency: How the Republican Right Rose to Power in Modern America*, 2nd ed. (Lawrence: University Press of Kansas, 2011), 44–48, 52; Kersch, *Conservatives and the Constitution*, 343–45.

16. Michael Bauman, ed. and comp., *The Best of the* Manion Forum*: A Conservative and Free Market Sourcebook* (San Francisco: Mellen Research University Press, 1990), 352–59, 337–45, 106, 107, 113, 115, 43–57, 16–18.

17. Bauman, *Best of the* Manion Forum, 343–44. See also Clarence Manion, *The Conservative American: His Fight for National Independence and Constitutional Government* (New York: Devin-Adair, 1964), 150–60, 182–89.

18. Barry Goldwater, *The Conscience of a Conservative* (Sheperdsville, KY: Victor, 1960), 16.

19. Goldwater, *Conscience of a Conservative*, 34.

20. Goldwater, *Conscience of a Conservative*, 36. See also ibid., 15–23, 29, 32–37, 40, 60–61, 77.

21. Dean Smith, *Conservatism: A Guide to Its Past, Present, and Future in American Politics* (New York: Avon, 1963), 174 (quote), 164–65, 168–71.

22. Charles Hyneman, *The Supreme Court on Trial* (New York: Atherton, 1963), 207.

23. Hyneman, *Supreme Court on Trial*, 198, 199.

24. Hyneman, *Supreme Court on Trial*, 274.

25. Charles E. Rice, *The Supreme Court and Public Prayer: The Need for Restraint* (New York: Fordham University Press, 1964). Rice also eventually took aim at *Roe v. Wade* (1973), as discussed later in this chapter.

26. Rice, *Supreme Court and Public Prayer*, 40, 42, 45–49, 67.

27. Rice, *Supreme Court and Public Prayer*, 157.

28. Kendall, *Willmoore Kendall Contra Mundum*, 370, 363–64, 376.

29. Kendall, *Willmoore Kendall Contra Mundum*, 337, 338.

30. L. Brent Bozell, *The Warren Revolution: Reflections on the Consensus Society* (New Rochelle, NY: Arlington House, 1966), 28, 27.

31. Bozell, *Warren Revolution*, 42 (emphasis omitted).

32. Bozell, *Warren Revolution*, 112.

33. Bozell, *Warren Revolution*, 339.

34. Nash, *Conservative Intellectual Movement*, 186–87; Schneider, *Conservative Century*, 84–86; Hustwit, *James J. Kilpatrick*, 73–74; Jeffrey Hart, *The Making of the American Conservative Mind: National Review and Its Times* (Wilmington, DE: ISI, 2005), 101–5, 107–9, 312, 371. See also Murphy, *Rebuke of History*, 174–75.

35. Kersch, in "Ecumenicalism through Constitutionalism," 18–28, makes this point about *National Review*'s treatment of constitutional issues.

36. Nash, *Conservative Intellectual Movement*, 199–204.

37. John Hart Ely, "The Wages of Crying Wolf: A Comment on *Roe v. Wade*," *Yale Law Journal* 82 (1973): 920–49.

38. Patrick Allitt, *The Conservatives: Ideas and Personalities throughout American History* (New Haven, CT: Yale University Press, 2009), 217, 218.

39. For a collection of citations of law review articles critical of the decision, see David J. Garrow, *Liberty and Sexuality: The Right to Privacy and the Making of* Roe v. Wade (New York: Macmillan, 1994), 875–76nn16–17.

40. Robert M. Byrn, "An American Tragedy: The Supreme Court on Abortion," *Fordham Law Review* 41 (1973): 807–62, 842. See also ibid., 813, 837, 838, 850, 851.

41. Joseph O'Meara, "Abortion: The Court Decides a Non-case," *Supreme Court Review* (1974): 337–360, quotes at 352, 337–38, 341. See also Patrick T. Conley and Robert J. McKenna, "The Supreme Court on Abortion—A Dissenting Opinion," *Catholic Lawyer* 19 (1973): 19–28, 22, 25.

42. John T. Noonan Jr., *A Private Choice: Abortion in America in the Seventies* (New York: Free Press, 1979), 182 (quote), 8 (quote), 5–9, 189.

43. Charles E. Rice, "The Dred Scott Case of the Twentieth Century," *Houston Law Review* 10 (1973): 1059–86, 1067–68.

44. Rice, "Dred Scott Case of the Twentieth Century," 1074.

45. Rice, "Dred Scott Case of the Twentieth Century," 1068, 1071.

46. Rice, "Dred Scott Case of the Twentieth Century," 1084.

47. Charles E. Rice, *Beyond Abortion: The Theory and Practice of the Secular State* (Chicago: Franciscan Herald Press, 1979), 37–45, 49 (quote) 51 (quote), 54–56.

48. Rice, *Beyond Abortion*, 102–11; Noonan, *Private Choice*, 178–88.

49. Evans, *Clear and Present Dangers*, 19–49, quotes at 21, 46.

50. Evans, *Clear and Present Dangers*, 263–77, 350, 44–49.

51. Evans, *Clear and Present Dangers*, 400.

52. George W. Carey, "The Supreme Court, Judicial Review, and Federalist Seventy-Eight," *Modern Age* 18 (Fall 1974): 356–68; George W. Carey, "Abortion and the American Political Crisis," *Human Life Review* 3 (Winter 1977): 39–54. Both articles are collected in Carey, *In Defense of the Constitution*.

53. Kendall and Carey, *Basic Symbols of the American Political Tradition*, 143–44.

54. Carey, *In Defense of the Constitution*, 136.

55. Carey, *In Defense of the Constitution*, 137–38, 184 (quote).

56. Carey, *In Defense of the Constitution*, 191–94.

57. Kersch, "Ecumenicalism through Constitutionalism."

58. "Government by Judiciary," *Firing Line* transcript for telecast of October 28, 1977, available at Hoover Institution Library and Archives, https://digitalcollections.hoover.org; William F. Buckley Jr., "Berger's Big Book," *National Review*, November 11, 1977, 1320.

59. Berger's central role in early originalist jurisprudence is detailed in O'Neill, *Originalism in American Law and Politics*, 111–32.

60. M. J. Sobran, "Taking the Fourteenth," *National Review*, March 2, 1978, 283–84, 286; Raoul Berger, "Academe vs. the Founding Fathers," *National Review*, April 14, 1978, 468–71.

61. Berger, "Academe vs. the Founding Fathers," 469–70.

62. Raoul Berger, "Judicial Government vs. Self-Government," *National Review*, April 4, 1980, 402.

63. Rice, *Beyond Abortion*, 52 (quote), 142n15.

64. Noonan, *Private Choice*, 31 (quote), 197n50.

65. Robert A. Destro, "Some Fresh Perspectives on the Abortion Controversy," *Human Life Review* 4 (Spring 1978): 22–32, 24.

66. This view generally accords with Kersch, "Neoconservatives and the Courts," 247–96. Stephen M. Feldman makes a strained attempt to attribute some recent decisions to neoconservatism in *Neoconservative Politics and the Supreme Court: Law, Power, and Democracy* (New York: New York University Press, 2013). For the several problems with this interpretation, see reviews by J. Mitchell Pickerill, in *Perspectives on Politics* 13 (2015): 864–66; and Haydn Davies, in *Journal of Law and Society* 41 (2014): 315–22.

67. Glazer, "Towards an Imperial Judiciary?"

68. Nathan Glazer, "Should Judges Administer Social Services?" *Public Interest* 50 (1978): 64–80, 66.

69. Daniel Patrick Moynihan, "Social Science and the Courts," *Public Interest* 54 (1979): 12–31, 18.

70. Moynihan, 19, 20 (quote).

71. Moynihan, 22–23.

72. Glazer, "Towards an Imperial Judiciary?" 118.

73. Glazer, "Towards an Imperial Judiciary?" 119. See also Glazer, "Social Services and the Courts," 79.

74. Nathan Glazer, "Lawyers and the New Class," in *The New Class?* 89–100, 97 (citation omitted).

75. Glazer, "Lawyers and the New Class," 99, 99–100.

76. Nathan Glazer, *Affirmative Discrimination: Ethnic Inequality and Public Policy* (New York: Basic Books, 1975; paperback ed., 1978), 218 (quote), 219, 209, xvi.

77. This distinction is emphasized in Kersch, "Neoconservatives and the Courts."

78. Glazer, *Affirmative Discrimination*, 220.

79. Glazer, 221.

80. Terry Eastland and William J. Bennett, *Counting by Race: Equality from the Founding Fathers to* Bakke *and* Weber (New York: Basic Books, 1979), vii.

81. Daniel Patrick Moynihan, "What Do You Do When the Supreme Court Is Wrong?" *Public Interest* 57 (1979): 3–24.

82. Moynihan, 13–14.

83. Richard E. Morgan, *Disabling America: The "Rights Industry" in Our Time* (New York: Basic Books, 1984), 194.

84. Morgan, 195.

85. Morgan, 166.

86. Morgan, 191–99. In an obituary Michael M. Uhlmann, who served in the Reagan administration, said that Morgan was "an originalist before that term became popular. That's a pertinent and interesting point of view that really deserves to be heard and [Morgan] was among the very first in his own quiet way to do that." "Remembering Professor Richard Morgan '59," *Bowdoin Orient*, November 21, 2014, https://bowdoinorient.com /bonus/article/9783.

87. Robert H. Bork, *A Time to Speak: Selected Writings and Arguments* (Wilmington, DE: ISI, 2008), 280.

88. Bork, 400.

89. Bork, 402, 282.

90. George Carey, "The Popular Roots of Conservatism," *Intercollegiate Review* 21 (Spring 1986): 12–14, 14.

91. M. E. Bradford, "On Being a Conservative in a Post-liberal Era," *Intercollegiate Review* 21 (Spring 1986): 15–18, 17–18.

92. The most extensive study of originalism and the Bork nomination is O'Neill, *Originalism in American Law and Politics*, 175–86, which I follow here.

93. Henry Regnery, "The Bork Case in Perspective—An Editorial," *Modern Age* 31 (Spring 1987): 98–100.

94. Hart, *Making of the Conservative Mind*, 310–15.

95. Robert H. Bork, *The Tempting of America: The Political Seduction of the Law* (New York: Free Press, 1990), 7.

96. Bork, 8–9, 12, 249–50, 258–59.

97. Scholars closely attuned to the traditionalist perspective affirmed this view. Charles W. Dunn and J. David Woodward emphasize the Court's egalitarianism in *American Conservatism from Burke to Bush*, 161, 163–64.

98. Robert Nisbet, "Judicial Activism," in *Prejudices*, 205–10.

99. Nisbet, *Present Age*, 1, 40, 133.

100. Nisbet, *Present Age*, 66, 67 (quote), 68.

101. Nisbet, *Prejudices*, 209.

102. Bradford, *Original Intentions*, xx (quote), 15–16, 87, 101, 119, 120–21, 125, 128–31. See also Marshall L. DeRosa, "M. E. Bradford's Constitutional Theory: A Southern Reactionary's Affirmation of the Rule of Law," in *Defender of Southern Conservatism*, 92–129.

103. Gerald J. Russello, *The Postmodern Imagination of Russell Kirk* (Columbia: University of Missouri Press, 2007), 154–55. Russello's chapter 4, "The Jurisprudence of Russell Kirk," is helpful, as is Hittinger's "Introduction" to Kirk, *Rights and Duties*.

104. Kirk, *Rights and Duties*, 18, 20.

105. Kirk, 29–30.

106. Kirk, 256, 16.

107. O'Neill, *Originalism in American Law and Politics*, 176, 177; Bork, *Tempting of America*, 66–67, 241–50.

108. O'Neill, *Originalism in American Law and Politics*, 192–93, 188–89.

109. Robert H. Bork, "Natural Law and the Constitution," *First Things* 21 (March 1992): 16–20, 19.

110. Bork, "Natural Law and the Constitution," 20.

111. Robert H. Bork, "Natural Law and the Law: An Exchange," *First Things* 23 (May 1992): 45–54, 52.

112. Bork, "Natural Law and the Law," 52.

113. Russell Hittinger, "Natural Law in the Positive Laws: A Legislative or Adjudicative Issue?" *Review of Politics* 55 (1993): 5–34, 27.

114. Robert P. George, "Natural Law, the Constitution, and the Theory and Practice of Judicial Review," *Fordham Law Review* 69 (2001): 2269–83, 2282.

115. Robert P. George, *In Defense of Natural Law* (Oxford, UK: Clarendon, 1999) 110 (quote), 111.

116. Bork, *Tempting of America*, 66; George, *In Defense of Natural Law*, 111; Robert P. George, "Natural Law and the Constitution Revisited," *Fordham Law Review* 70 (2001): 273–82, 280.

117. Hittinger, "Natural Law in the Positive Laws," 30, 30n62 (quote), 34.

118. Kirk, *Rights and Duties*, 135–38, quote at 135; Hittinger "Introduction," xxvi–xxix.

119. Kirk, *Rights and Duties*, 138. See also ibid., 256.

120. The symposium and responses are collected in two volumes, Mitchell S. Muncy, ed., *The End of Democracy? The Judicial Usurpation of Politics* (Dallas, TX: Spence, 1997) (hereafter cited as *End of Democracy* I); and Mitchell S. Muncy, ed., *The End of Democracy? II: A Crisis of Legitimacy* (Dallas, TX: Spence, 1999) (hereafter cited as *End of Democracy* II). Participants in the original symposium were Robert H. Bork, Russell Hittinger, Hadley Arkes, Charles Colson, and Robert P. George.

121. Editors of *First Things*, "Introduction," in *End of Democracy* I, 6.

122. Editors of *First Things*, "Introduction," 8.

123. Planned Parenthood v. Casey, 505 U.S. 833, 851, 868 (1992); Romer v. Evans, 517 U.S. 620, 634 (1996); Lee v. Weisman, 505 U.S. 577, 589 (1992).

124. Editors of *First Things*, "Part II: Questions of Legitimacy," in *End of Democracy* I, 116.

125. Richard John Neuhaus, "Rebuilding the Civil Public Square," in *End of Democracy* II, 8, 18. See also, Russell Hittinger, "A Crisis of Legitimacy," in *End of Democracy* I, 18–20.

126. Richard John Neuhaus, "Democracy Restored?" in *End of Democracy* I, 240.

127. Robert H. Bork, "Our Judicial Oligarchy," in *End of Democracy* I, 14.

128. Robert P. George, "Justice, Legitimacy, and Allegiance," in *End of Democracy* II, 104 (citation omitted).

129. Robert H. Bork, *Slouching towards Gomorrah: Modern Liberalism and American Decline* (New York: HarperCollins, 1996), xiii.

130. Bork, 98–99, 140, 147–49, 289–90.

131. Neuhaus, "Rebuilding the Civil Public Square," 20.

132. Editors of *First Things*, "Part II: Questions of Legitimacy," 121; Neuhaus, "Democracy Restored?" 265–66.

133. Bork, "Our Judicial Oligarchy," 17; William J. Bennett, [Questions of Legitimacy], in *End of Democracy* I, 65–69; Mary Ann Glendon, [Questions of Legitimacy], ibid., 84–87; Editors of *First Things*, "Part II: Questions of Legitimacy," 116. For an excellent treatment of this issue based on Tocqueville's insistence on the necessity of religion for the moderation of democracy, see Carson Holloway, "Democracy in America," in *End of Democracy* II, 134–60.

134. Carey, "Preface," in *Basic Symbols of the American Political Tradition*, xxiii. See also Carey, *The Federalist*, 169–70.

135. George W. Carey, "Judicial Activism and Regime Change," in *A Moral Enterprise: Politics, Reason, and the Human Good: Essays in Honor of Francis Canavan*, ed. Kenneth L. Grasso and Robert P. Hunt (Wilmington, DE: ISI, 2002), 305–19, 309.

136. Carey, "Judicial Activism and Regime Change," 319 (quote), 317.

137. George W. Carey, "The Philadelphia Constitution: Dead or Alive?" in *End of Democracy* II, 229–51.

138. Carey, "Who or What Killed the Philadelphia Constitution?" 622.

139. Carey, "The Philadelphia Constitution," 250.

140. Carey, "The Philadelphia Constitution," 245–51, quote at 251. See also Carey, "Judicial Activism and Regime Change," 317–19; and Carey, "Who or What Killed the Philadelphia Constitution?" 640.

Chapter 9 · Straussians and Modern Judicial Review

1. Zuckert, "Herbert J. Storing's Turn to the Founding," 16–18, 11–12; Zuckert and Zuckert, *The Truth about Leo Strauss*, 215–16; Hayward, *Patriotism Is Not Enough*, 160.

2. Storing, "In Defense of the Electoral College," 396, 398.

3. Storing, "Problem of Big Government," 287.

4. Martin Diamond, "Democracy and *The Federalist*," 18.

5. Diamond, "Conservatives, Liberals, and the Constitution," 68.

6. Diamond, "Conservatives, Liberals, and the Constitution," 80.

7. Diamond, "Forgotten Doctrine of Enumerated Powers," 182.

8. Walter Berns, *Freedom, Virtue, and the First Amendment* (1957; reprint, Chicago: Regnery, 1965). See Zuckert and Zuckert, *The Truth about Leo Strauss*, 202–9; and Gary D. Glenn, "Walter Berns: The Constitution and American Liberal Democracy," in Deutsch and Murley, *Leo Strauss, the Straussians, and the American Regime*, 193–204.

9. Berns, *Freedom, Virtue, and the First Amendment*, 46.

10. Berns, 250 (quote), 126–27.

11. Berns, 161–62.

12. Berns, 162 (square brackets in orig.).

13. Berns, 254 (both quotes).

14. Berns's concern with the relation between the original meaning of the First Amendment and republican government attracted numerous other Straussian analysts and was developed in Berns's own later work. See Ralph Rossum, "The Supreme Court: Republican Schoolmaster," in Deutsch and Murley, *Leo Strauss, the Straussians, and the American Regime*, 369–74.

15. Leo Strauss and Joseph Cropsey, eds., *History of Political Philosophy*, 628 (Herbert J. Storing on Blackstone), 774 (Marvin Zetterbaum on Tocqueville). Montesquieu's thought on this subject was treated only glancingly in this volume by David Lowenthal, ibid., 524. The contribution of all three of these thinkers to a conception of American judicial statesmanship is considered at length in Paul O. Carrese, *The Cloaking of Power: Montesquieu, Blackstone, and the Rise of Judicial Activism* (Chicago: University of Chicago Press, 2003), which is treated below.

16. Tocqueville quoted in Ralph Lerner, "The Supreme Court as Republican Schoolmaster," *Supreme Court Review* 1967: 127–80, 127–28.

17. Lerner, 128.

18. Lerner, 166.

19. Lerner, 180.

20. Paul Eidelberg, *The Philosophy of the American Constitution: A Reinterpretation of the Intentions of the Founding Fathers* (New York: Free Press, 1968), 223–25, 242–46. See also Morrissey, "Paul Eidelberg," 253–63.

21. Robert Kenneth Faulkner, *The Jurisprudence of John Marshall* (Princeton, NJ: Princeton University Press, 1968), xv (quote).

22. Faulkner, 217.

23. Faulkner, 212 (quote), 216, 219 (quote), 233.

24. Harry M. Clor, *Obscenity and Public Morality: Censorship in Liberal Society* (1969; reprint, Chicago: University of Chicago Press, 1985).

25. Clor, 202.

26. Clor, 278. Another Straussian who generally agreed with Clor was Lane V. Sunderland, in *Obscenity: The Court, the Congress, and the President's Commission* (Washington, DC: AEI, 1974), 63–64, 79–82.

27. Clor, *Obscenity*, 204 (both quotes).

28. Gary J. Jacobsohn, *Pragmatism, Statesmanship, and the Supreme Court* (Ithaca, NY: Cornell University Press, 1977).

29. Jacobsohn, 164.

30. Jacobsohn, 183.

31. Jacobsohn, 196 (quote), 195.

32. Home Building and Loan Association v. Blaisdell, 290 U.S. 398, 439 (1934).

33. Jacobsohn, *Pragmatism, Statesmanship, and the Supreme Court*, 190.

34. Blaisdell, 290 U.S. 453.

35. Howard Gilman, "The Collapse of Constitutional Originalism and the Rise of the Notion of the 'Living Constitution' in the Course of American State-Building," *Studies in American Political Development* 11 (1997): 191–247, 223–25, 234, 235, 237; Charles A. Miller, *The Supreme Court and the Uses of History* (Cambridge, MA: Belknap Press of Harvard University Press, 1969), 39–51; Raoul Berger, *Government by Judiciary: The Transformation of the Fourteenth Amendment*, 2nd ed. (Indianapolis: Liberty Fund, 1997), 429n6.

36. Hadley Arkes, *The Return of George Sutherland: Restoring a Jurisprudence of Natural Rights* (Princeton, NJ: Princeton University Press, 1994), 243–50; Matthew J. Franck, "Statesmanship and the Judiciary," *Review of Politics* 51 (1989): 510–32, 512, 529n8; Wolfe, *Rise of Modern Judicial Review*, 219–21.

37. John Agresto, *The Supreme Court and Constitutional Democracy* (Ithaca, NY: Cornell University Press, 1984), 144, 143–44.

38. Harry M. Clor, "Judicial Statesmanship and Constitutional Interpretation," *South Texas Law Journal* 26 (1985): 397–433.

39. Sotirios A. Barber, *The Constitution of Judicial Power* (Baltimore: Johns Hopkins University Press, 1993), 54.

40. Barber, *Constitution of Judicial Power*, 57, 65.

41. Barber, 176 (quote), 234–35.

42. Sotirios A. Barber, *On What the Constitution Means* (Baltimore: Johns Hopkins University Press, 1984), 218–20.

43. Barber, *Constitution of Judicial Power*, 66.

44. Pangle, *Leo Strauss*, 110, 111.

45. Carrese, *Cloaking of Power*, 205, 224.

46. Carrese, 254.

47. Carrese, 261.

48. Carrese, 254.

49. For a history of the explosion of such liberal theories to defend and advance modern judicial power as exercised by the Warren Court, see Kalman, *Strange Career of Legal Liberalism*.

50. Zuckert and Zuckert, *The Truth about Leo Strauss*, 203; Hayward, *Patriotism Is Not Enough*, 157–58.

51. Walter Berns, *The First Amendment and the Future of American Democracy* (New York: Basic Books, 1976), 235–36.

52. Berns, *First Amendment and the Future of American Democracy*, 233.

53. Walter Berns, *Taking the Constitution Seriously* (New York: Simon and Schuster, 1987), 214, 241.

54. Walter Berns, "The Supreme Court as Republican Schoolmaster: Constitutional Interpretation and the 'Genius of the People,'" in *The Supreme Court and American Constitutionalism*, ed. Bradford P. Wilson and Ken Masugi (Lanham, MD: Rowman and Littlefield, 1998), 3–15, 13, 15.

55. Ralph Rossum, "The Supreme Court as Republican Schoolmaster: Freedom of Speech, Political Equality, and the Teaching of Political Responsibility," in *Taking the Constitution Seriously: Essays on the Constitution and Constitutional Law*, ed. Gary L. McDowell (Dubuque, IA: Kendall Hunt, 1981), 125–38, 125.

56. Rossum, 129.

57. Gary L. McDowell, *The Constitution and Contemporary Constitutional Theory* (Cumberland, VA: Center for Judicial Studies, 1985), 39 (quote), 37 (quote), 40.

58. Franck, "Statesmanship and the Judiciary."

59. Matthew J. Franck, *Against the Imperial Judiciary: The Supreme Court vs. the Sovereignty of the People* (Lawrence: University Press of Kansas, 1996), 21–28, 104–5, 107–8, 213.

60. Stanley C. Brubaker, "The Court as Astigmatic Schoolmarm: A Case for the Clear-Sighted Citizen," in *Supreme Court and American Constitutionalism*, 69–91.

61. Rossum, "Supreme Court as Republican Schoolmaster," 374.

62. Robert K. Faulkner, "Bickel's Constitution: The Problem of Moderate Liberalism," *American Political Science Review* 72 (1978): 925–40.

63. Alexander M. Bickel, *The Morality of Consent* (New Haven, CT: Yale University Press, 1975), 29, 25.

64. Faulkner, "Bickel's Constitution," 936.

65. Faulkner, 935.

66. Faulkner, 940. On Bickel, see also McDowell, in *Constitution and Contemporary Constitutional Theory*, 2–5, who generally follows Faulkner. This study was incorporated into McDowell's *Curbing the Courts: The Constitution and the Limits of Judicial Power* (Baton Rouge: Louisiana State University Press, 1988).

67. Lane V. Sunderland, "Constitutional Theory and the Role of the Court: An Analysis of Contemporary Constitutional Commentators," *Wake Forest Law Review* 21(1986): 855–900, 898. This article was incorporated into Sunderland's *Popular Government and the Supreme Court: Securing the Public Good and Private Rights* (Lawrence: University Press of Kansas, 1996). For additional Straussian criticism of Ely (along with other liberal theorists), see McDowell, *Constitution and Contemporary Constitutional Theory*, 14–16; Walter Berns, "Judicial Review and the Rights and Laws of Nature," *Supreme Court Review* (1982): 49–83, 54–56; Wolfe, *Rise of Modern Judicial Review*, 343–52; Gary J. Jacobsohn, *The Supreme Court and the Decline of Constitutional Aspiration* (Totowa, NJ: Rowman and Littlefield, 1986), 100–107, 127–29; Clor, "Judicial Statesmanship and Constitutional Interpretation," 419–20.

68. McDowell, *Constitution and Contemporary Constitutional Theory*, 2, 28, 35.

69. Wolfe, *Rise of Modern Judicial Review*, 329–52.

70. Berns, "Judicial Review and the Rights and Laws of Nature," 83 (citation omitted).

71. Berns, "Judicial Review and the Rights and Laws of Nature," 51.

72. Ronald Dworkin, *Taking Rights Seriously* (Cambridge, MA: Harvard University Press, 1977), 149.

73. Dworkin, 180, 134–36, 137.

74. Sunderland, *Popular Government and the Supreme Court*, 99.

75. McDowell, *Constitution and Contemporary Constitutional Theory*, 7 (italics omitted).

76. Clifford Orwin and James R. Stoner Jr., "Neoconstitutionalism? Rawls, Dworkin, and Nozick," in *Confronting the Constitution*, ed. Allan Bloom (Washington, DC: AEI, 1990), 437–70, 456.

77. Jacobsohn, *Supreme Court and the Decline of Constitutional Aspiration*, 48, 49. See also Wolfe, *Rise of Modern Judicial Review*, 332.

78. Stanley C. Brubaker, "Reconsidering Dworkin's Case for Judicial Activism," *Journal of Politics* 46 (1984): 503–19; Wolfe, *Rise of Modern Judicial Review*, 333–36; Sunderland, *Popular Government and the Supreme Court*, 119–23.

79. Walter Berns, *In Defense of Liberal Democracy* (Chicago: Regnery Gateway, 1984), 22.

80. Thomas Pangle, "Rediscovering Rights," *Public Interest* 50 (Winter 1978): 157–60. Dworkin's deployment of his theory to reach consistently liberal outcomes is painstakingly contrasted with the founders' constitutionalism in Sunderland, *Popular Government and the Supreme Court*, 104–16.

81. John Rawls, *A Theory of Justice* (Cambridge, MA: Harvard University Press, 1971); John Rawls, *Political Liberalism* (New York: Columbia University Press, 1993).

82. Allan Bloom, "Justice: John Rawls vs. The Tradition of Political Philosophy," *American Political Science Review* 69 (1975): 648–62; Harvey C. Mansfield Jr., *The Spirit of Liberalism* (Cambridge, MA: Harvard University Press, 1978), 90–101; David Lewis Schaefer, *Justice or Tyranny? A Critique of John Rawls's* A Theory of Justice (Port Washington, NY: Kennikat, 1979). See also Michael Zuckert, "Justice Deserted: A Critique of Rawls' 'A Theory of Justice,'" *Polity* 13 (1981): 466–83.

83. Orwin and Stoner, "Neoconstitutionalism?" 452.

84. Orwin and Stoner, 447.

85. Orwin and Stoner, 447.

86. Michael P. Zuckert, "The New Rawls and Constitutional Theory: Does It Really Taste That Much Better?" *Constitutional Commentary* 11 (1994): 227–45, 239–45, quotes at 239, 244 (emphasis in orig.).

87. David Lewis Schaefer, *Illiberal Justice: John Rawls vs. the American Political Tradition* (Columbia: University of Missouri Press, 2007), 180–86, quote at 186. See also Schaefer, *Justice or Tyranny?*

88. Schaefer, *Illiberal Justice*, 254–57, 265–66, 186 (quote).

89. Schaefer, *Illiberal Justice*, 329.

90. Schaefer, 181–84, 327–30. See also Susan Shell, "'Kantianism' and Constitutional Rights," in *Old Rights and New*, ed. Robert A. Licht (Washington, DC: AEI, 1993), 148–63.

91. David Lowenthal, *No Liberty for License: The Forgotten Logic of the First Amendment* (Dallas, TX: Spence, 1997), xxii (quotes); Rossum, "Supreme Court as Republican Schoolmaster," 369–74.

92. Berns, *First Amendment and the Future of American Democracy*, x, 80, 70, 78 ("original intention"), 146 ("original understanding").

93. Berns, *First Amendment and the Future of American Democracy*, 237.

94. McDowell, *Taking the Constitution Seriously*, 1–4 (quotes at 4, 3), 141–43; McDowell, *Constitution and Contemporary Constitutional Theory*, 40–43; McDowell, *Curbing the Courts*, 105–113, 201–5.

95. Gary L. McDowell, *Equity and the Constitution: The Supreme Court, Equitable Relief, and Public Policy* (Chicago: University of Chicago Press, 1982), 132.

96. Franck, *Against the Imperial Judiciary*, 1.

97. Sunderland, *Popular Government and the Supreme Court*, 95.

98. Sunderland, 94.

99. See, for example, Michael P. Zuckert, "Congressional Power under the Fourteenth Amendment: The Original Understanding of Section Five," *Constitutional Commentary* 3 (1986): 123–55; and Michael P. Zuckert, "Completing the Constitution: The Thirteenth Amendment," *Constitutional Commentary* 4 (1987): 259–83. Gary L. McDowell evaluated the historical scholarship of others in "The Fourteenth Amendment: Should the Bill of Rights Apply to the States? The Disincorporation Debate," *Utah Law Review* (1987): 951–67. See also Eugene Hickok, ed., *The Bill of Rights: Original Meaning and Current Understanding* (Charlottesville: University of Virginia Press, 1991).

100. Several of the figures discussed in the following paragraph were influenced by the treatment if this idea in Harvey C. Mansfield Jr., "Hobbes and the Science of Indirect Government," *American Political Science Review* 65 (1971): 97–110.

101. Berns, "Judicial Review and the Rights and Laws of Nature," 58–62, 79–80, 83; McDowell, *Constitution and Contemporary Constitutional Theory*, 29; Gary L. McDowell, "Private Conscience and Public Order: Hobbes and *The Federalist*," *Polity* 25 (1993): 421–43; Franck, *Against the Imperial Judiciary*, 177–89; Sunderland, *Popular Government and the Supreme Court*, 12–15, 279.

102. McDowell, *Curbing the Courts*, 105–6; Franck, *Against the Imperial Judiciary*, 35, 207; Sunderland, *Popular Government and the Supreme Court*, 92–93

103. Christopher Wolfe, "A Theory of U.S. Constitutional History," *Journal of Politics* 43 (1981): 292–316, 294–95; Wolfe, *Rise of Modern Judicial Review*, 18–19.

104. In addition to the sources cited above, see also Christopher Wolfe, "John Marshall and Constitutional Law," *Polity* 15 (1982): 5–25; Christopher Wolfe, *Judicial Activism: Bulwark of Freedom or Precarious Security?* (Pacific Grove, CA: Brooks Cole, 1991); Christopher Wolfe, *How to Read the Constitution: Originalism, Constitutional Interpretation, and Judicial Power* (Lanham, MD: Rowman and Littlefield, 1996).

105. Wolfe, *How to Read the Constitution*, 12 (emphasis in orig.).

106. Wolfe, *Rise of Modern Judicial Review*; Wolfe, *How to Read the Constitution*, 85–103.

107. Wolfe, *Rise of Modern Judicial Review*, 399–400.

108. Harry V. Jaffa, *Original Intent and the Framers of the Constitution: A Disputed Question* (Washington, DC: Regnery Gateway, 1994); Harry V. Jaffa, *Storm over the Constitution* (Lanham, MD: Lexington, 1999). See also Charles R. Kesler, "The Higher Law and 'Original Intent': The Challenge for Conservatism," *Intercollegiate Review* 22 (Spring 1987): 9–13.

109. See, for example, Jaffa, *Original Intent and the Framers of the Constitution*, 19–20, 26; Jaffa, *Storm over the Constitution*, 100–102.

110. Jaffa, *Storm over the Constitution*, 42 (quote), 41.

111. Jaffa, *Storm over the Constitution*, 40 (emphasis in orig.).

112. Jaffa, *Original Intent and the Framers of the Constitution*, 238, 239.

113. Jaffa, *Original Intent and the Framers of the Constitution*, 259–60.

114. Jaffa, 249 (*Roe v. Wade*), 263–65 (homosexuality).

115. Hayward, *Patriotism Is Not Enough*, 147–49, 164–72.

116. Ralph A. Rossum, "A More Dependable Approach," *Claremont Review of Books* 6 (Winter 2005–6), www.claremont.org (first quote); Ralph A. Rossum, "Correspondence," *Claremont Review of Books* 5 (Fall 2005), www.claremont.org (second quote).

117. Michael M. Uhlmann, "A Response," *Claremont Review of Books* 7 (Winter 2006–7): 54. A similar thought is expressed in Hayward, *Patriotism Is Not Enough*, 170–71. See also Franck, *Against the Imperial Judiciary*, 31–32, 120.

118. Hadley Arkes, *Beyond the Constitution* (Princeton, NJ: Princeton University Press, 1990).

119. Arkes, *Return of George Sutherland*. See also John C. Eastman, with Harry V. Jaffa, "Understanding Justice Sutherland As He Understood Himself," *University of Chicago Law Review* 63 (1996): 1347–74.

120. Franck, *Against the Imperial Judiciary*, 172–75, 197, 211.

121. Hadley Arkes, "A Culture Corrupted," in *End of Democracy* I, 30–40, 32.

122. Hadley Arkes, "Prudent Warnings and Imprudent Reactions," in *End of Democracy* II, 44–85.

123. Hadley Arkes, "And Now for Something Different: A Good Word on Behalf of the Legal Positivists," in *Moral Enterprise*, 275–303, esp. 297–303.

124. Rossum, "Supreme Court as Republican Schoolmaster," 367 (quote, citations omitted), 363.

Chapter 10 · Libertarians and Modern Judicial Review

1. David E. Bernstein and Ilya Somin, "The Mainstreaming of Libertarian Constitutionalism," *Law and Contemporary Problems* 77 (2014): 43–70, 69.

2. Pilon, "On the Origins of the Modern Libertarian Legal Movement," 257.

3. Charles Wolfe, "Libertarians and the Constitution," *The Freeman*, September 1, 1956, archived at www.fee.org. See also "Twilight of the Republic?" editorial, *Palm Beach Post-Times*, April 13, 1958, reprinted in *The Freeman*, July 1, 1958, archived at www.fee.org.

4. Samuel B. Pettengill, "If I Were King," *The Freeman*, September 1, 1960, archived at www.fee.org; "Twilight of the Republic?" (quote).

5. Hayek, *Constitution of Liberty*, 190–92, 192 (quote).

6. Hayek, 188–89, 186.

7. Robert Bork, "The Supreme Court Needs a New Philosophy," *Fortune* (December 1968): 138, quotes at 170, 174.

8. Richard A. Epstein, "Substantive Due Process by Any Other Name: The Abortion Cases," *Supreme Court Review* (1973): 159–85, 184.

9. Epstein, 182, 176–77, 170–71.

10. Epstein, 180, 185. Epstein later reiterated this basic view of abortion as a violation of the harm principle. Epstein, *Classical Liberal Constitution*, 78, 372–75.

11. Rothbard, *For a New Liberty*, 50–51, 72–76, 219–47.

12. Contributions to the conference were published as "Perspectives on Rights," in *Georgia Law Review* 13 (1979): 1117–1510.

13. Roger Pilon, "Ordering Rights Consistently: Or What We Do and Do Not Have Rights To," *Georgia Law Review* 13 (1979): 1171–96, 1175, quote at 1174 (citation omitted).

14. Edwin Vieira Jr., "Rights and the United States Constitution: The Declension from Natural Law to Legal Positivism," *Georgia Law Review* 13 (1979): 1447–1500; David F. Forte, "Ideology and History," *Georgia Law Review* 13 (1979): 1501–10, 1509–10, 1510.

15. See Margalit Fox, "Bernard Siegan, 81, Legal Scholar and Reagan Nominee, Dies," *New York Times*, April 1, 2006, www.nytimes.com; Larry Alexander, "A Tribute to Bernard H. Siegan," *San Diego Law Review* 27 (1990): 275–77.

16. Bernard H. Siegan, *Economic Liberties and the Constitution* (Chicago: University of Chicago Press, 1980), 184–90, 83–108.

17. A point later noted by Richard A. Epstein, in "Property Rights, Public Use, and the Perfect Storm: An Essay in Honor of Bernard H. Siegan," *San Diego Law Review* 45 (2008): 609–32, 630.

18. Siegan, *Economic Liberties*, 24–59.

19. Siegan, *Economic Liberties*, 110–25.

20. Bernard H. Siegan, "Rehabilitating *Lochner*," *San Diego Law Review* 22 (1985): 453–97; this article was incorporated into Bernard H. Siegan, *The Supreme Court's Constitution: An Inquiry into Judicial Review and Its Impact on Society* (New Brunswick, NJ: Transaction, 1987), chapter 3. The later apogee of this theme in libertarian scholarship was David E. Bernstein, *Rehabilitating* Lochner: *Defending Individual Rights against Progressive Reform* (Chicago: University of Chicago Press, 2011).

21. Siegan, *Economic Liberties*, 7–14, 126–27, 10 (quote).

22. Siegan, *Economic Liberties*, 14, citing Raoul Berger, *Government by Judiciary* (1977).

23. Siegan, *Economic Liberties*, 13 (quote), 14.

24. Siegan, 107.

25. Siegan, 107.

26. Siegan, 324–27, quote at 325.

27. Epstein, *Takings*.

28. Epstein, *Takings*, 7–18, Blackstone quoted at 22.

29. Epstein, 101.

30. Epstein, x.

31. Epstein, 161–70.

32. Epstein, *Classical Liberal Constitution*, 358.

33. Epstein, *Takings*, 20.

34. Richard Epstein, "Self-Interest and the Constitution," *Journal of Legal Education* 37 (1987): 153–61, quote at 158.

35. Epstein, *Takings*, chapter 3.

36. Epstein, *Takings*, 28 (both quotes), 29.

37. Epstein, *Classical Liberal Constitution*, 46–56, 570–77.

38. Epstein, *Takings* 30–31.

39. Epstein, *Takings*, 31.

40. Richard A. Epstein, *How Progressives Rewrote the Constitution* (Washington, DC: Cato Institute, 2006), 83. See also Epstein, *Classical Liberal Constitution*, 570–72.

41. This position is laid out in Randy E. Barnett, "Introduction: James Madison's Ninth Amendment," in *The Rights Retained by the People: The History and Meaning of the Ninth Amendment* [vol. 1], ed. Randy E. Barnett (Fairfax, VA: George Mason University Press, 1989), 1–49; and in Randy E. Barnett, "Introduction: Implementing the Ninth Amendment," in *The Rights Retained by the People: The History and Meaning of the Ninth Amendment* [vol. 2], ed. Randy E. Barnett (Fairfax, VA: George Mason University Press, 1993), 6–31 (electronic book pagination). See also Randy E. Barnett, "The Ninth Amendment: It Means What It Says," *Texas Law Review* 85 (2006): 1–82; and Randy E. Barnett, "Kurt Lash's Majoritarian Difficulty: A Response to *A Textual-Historical Theory of the Ninth Amendment*," *Stanford Law Review* 60 (2008): 937–67.

42. Barnett, "Introduction," in *Rights Retained*, 1:40.

43. Randy E. Barnett, "The Intersection of Natural Rights and Positive Constitutional Law," *Connecticut Law Review* 25 (1993): 853–68, 863. See also Barnett, "Introduction," in *Rights Retained*, 2:9, 13 (electronic book pagination).

44. Barnett, "Introduction," in *Rights Retained*, 1:41. See also Barnett, "Intersection of Natural Rights and Positive Constitutional Law," 864.

45. Barnett, "Introduction," in *Rights Retained*, 2:10, 11, 15, 16, 240 (electronic book pagination). See also Barnett, *Restoring the Lost Constitution*, 224–34, 242, 254, 259–60.

46. Barnett, *Restoring the Lost Constitution*, 191–223.

47. Barnett, "Introduction," in *Rights Retained*, 1:4.

48. Barnett, "Introduction," 1:27 (quote), 30–31, 39. Barnett undertook historical analysis to dispute scholars who held more restrictive views of the amendment. Barnett, "Introduction," in *Rights Retained*, 2:17–22 (electronic book pagination).

49. Randy E. Barnett, "The Relevance of the Framers' Intent," *Harvard Journal of Law and Public Policy* 19 (1995): 403–10, 405.

50. Barnett, "Relevance of the Framers' Intent," 407, 410.

51. Randy E. Barnett, "Underlying Principles," *Constitutional Commentary* 24 (2007): 405–16, 405.

52. Randy E. Barnett, "An Originalism for Nonoriginalists," *Loyola Law Review* 45 (1999): 611–54, 654, 641.

53. Barnett, "Originalism for Nonoriginalists," 629; Barnett, *Restoring the Lost Constitution*, ix–xiv; Barnett, "Underlying Principles."

54. Richard A. Epstein, "The Proper Scope of the Commerce Power," *Virginia Law Review* 73 (1987): 1387–1455, quote at 1455. See also Epstein, *How Progressives Rewrote the Constitution*, 66–77.

55. Randy E. Barnett, "The Original Meaning of the Commerce Clause," *University of Chicago Law Review* 68 (2001): 101–47; Randy E. Barnett, "New Evidence of the Original Meaning of the Commerce Clause," *Arkansas Law Review* 55 (2003): 847–99. See also Barnett, *Restoring the Lost Constitution*, 274–318.

56. Barnett, "Introduction," in *Rights Retained*, 1:41–47; Barnett, "Introduction," in *Rights Retained*, 2:15–17 (electronic book pagination); Randy E. Barnett, "Judicial Conservatism v. Principled Judicial Activism," *Harvard Journal of Law and Public Policy* 10 (1987): 273–94, quote at 288. See also Barnett, *Restoring the Lost Constitution*, 259–69.

57. Barnett, "Judicial Conservatism v. Principled Judicial Activism," 290.

58. Randy E. Barnett, "Judicial Pragmactivism: A Definition," in *Economic Liberties and the Judiciary*, ed. James A. Dorn and Henry G. Manne (Fairfax, VA: George Mason University Press; Washington, DC: Cato Institute, 1987), 205–17, quotes at 208 and 217 (italics omitted).

59. Randy E. Barnett, "Is the Rehnquist Court an 'Activist' Court? The Commerce Clause Cases," *University of Colorado Law Review* 73 (2002): 1275–90, 1281.

60. Barnett, "Is the Rehnquist Court an 'Activist' Court?" 1280.

61. Barnett, *Restoring the Lost Constitution*, 266–69, 356 (quote); Barnett, *Our Republican Constitution*, 125–29, 160–63.

62. As the conclusion briefly notes, the libertarian embrace of judicial review was usually accompanied by a severe public choice critique of legislation and legislatures as such.

63. The Scalia-Epstein debate is reprinted in *Economic Liberties and the Judiciary*. Scalia's contribution is "Economic Affairs as Human Affairs," 31–37, both quotes at 35 (emphasis in orig.).

64. Ricard Epstein, "Judicial Review: Reckoning on Two Kinds of Error," in *Economic Liberties and the Judiciary*, 39–46, quotes at 42, 45, 43, 45–46.

65. Robert Bork criticized Epstein and Siegan in *Tempting of America*, 224–30. Siegan responded in "Majorities May Limit the People's Liberties Only When Authorized to Do So by the Constitution," *San Diego Law Review* 27 (1990): 309–58. See also Office of Legal Policy, US Department of Justice, *Report to the Attorney General: Wrong Turns on the Road to Judicial Activism; The Ninth Amendment and the Privileges or Immunities Clause*, September 25, 1987; Stephen Macedo, *The New Right v. the Constitution* (Washington, DC: Cato Institute, 1986).

66. Macedo, *New Right v. the Constitution*, 43–50; Barnett, "Judicial Conservatism v. Principled Judicial Activism." Another example from this period is Clint Bolick, "The Necessity of Judicial Action," chapter 7 in *Changing Course: Civil Rights at the Crossroads* (New Brunswick, NJ: Transaction, 1988).

67. Roger Pilon, "Rethinking Judicial Restraint," *Wall Street Journal*, February 1, 1991, www.wsj.com (quotes). See also Roger Pilon, "On the Foundations of Justice," *Intercollegiate Review* 17 (Fall–Winter 1981): 3–14; Roger Pilon, "Economic Liberty, the Constitution, and the Higher Law," *George Mason University Law Review* 11 (1988): 27–34.

68. Clint Bolick, *David's Hammer: The Case for an Activist Judiciary* (Washington, DC: Cato Institute, 2007), 159, 160, 164.

69. Greve, *Upside-Down Constitution*, 14–16, 390–96.

70. Greve, 14.

71. Greve, 393.

72. Greve, 390 (emphasis in orig.)

73. Greve, 396.

74. Somin, "Federalism and Property Rights," 56–57, 87–88; Epstein, "Exit Rights under Federalism," 150, 165.

75. Somin, "Closing the Pandora's Box of Federalism." See also Barnett, *Our Republican Constitution*, 224.

76. Chip Mellor, "Judicial Activism and Judicial Restraint: Two Paths to Bigger Government," *Liberty and Law* 14 (2005), 6–7, 10 (quote), available at Institute for Justice, www.ij.org (originally pub. in *American Lawyer*).

77. Clark M. Neily III, *Terms of Engagement: How Our Courts Should Enforce the Constitution's Promise of Limited Government* (New York: Encounter, 2013); Barnett, *Our Republican Constitution*, 225–45, 249, 163.

78. Neily, *Terms of Engagement*, 2.

79. Randy E. Barnett, "Book Review," *Wall Street Journal*, November, 19, 2013, www.wsj.com.

80. Neily, *Terms of Engagement*, 3.

81. Randy Barnett, "'Judicial Engagement' Is Not the Same as 'Judicial Activism,'" *Washington Post*, January 28, 2014, www.washingtonpost.com (quote); Barnett, *Our Republican Constitution*, 14–18, 201–2.

82. Barnett, "'Judicial Engagement.'"

83. Neilly, *Terms of Engagement*, 3 (quote), 10, and chapter 9, "From Abdication to Engagement"; Pilon, "On the Foundations of Justice," 5 (passivism); Bolick, *Changing Course*, 125 (abstinence).

84. Barnett, "'Judicial Engagement'" (quote); Barnett, *Our Republican Constitution*, 24, 257 (quote).

85. Chip Mellor, "Foreword," in Neily, *Terms of Engagement*, x–xi; Neily, *Terms of Engagement*, 10, 11; Evan Bernick, "The Supreme Court Needs a New Judicial Approach: The Case for Judicial Engagement," *Cato Unbound: A Journal of Debate*, September 12, 2016, www.cato-unbound.org.

86. Edward Whelan, "Let's Break Off the Engagement," *Cato Unbound: A Journal of Debate*, September 20, 2016, www.cato-unbound.org.

87. The most extensive conservative rejoinder is Greg Weiner, *The Political Constitution: The Case against Judicial Supremacy* (Lawrence: University Press of Kansas, 2019). See also Mark Pulliam, "The Libertarian Constitutional Fantasy," *Modern Age* 60 (Winter 2018): 13–22; Mark Pulliam, "Against 'Judicial Engagement,'" *City Journal*, February 8, 2017, www.city-journal.org.

88. Leading works are Steven P. Brown, *Trumping Religion: The New Christian Right, the Free Speech Clause, and the Courts* (Tuscaloosa: University of Alabama Press, 2002); Teles, *Rise of the Conservative Legal Movement*; Ann Southworth, *Lawyers of the Right: Professionalizing the Conservative Coalition* (Chicago: University of Chicago Press, 2008); Decker,

The Other Rights Revolution; and Bennett, *Defending Faith*. A helpful overview is Logan E. Sawyer III, "Why the Right Embraced Rights," *Harvard Journal of Law and Public Policy* 40 (2016): 729–57. For reflections by conservative and libertarian participants, see Lee Edwards, ed., *Bringing Justice to the People: The Story of the Freedom-Based Public Interest Law Movement* (Washington, DC: Heritage Foundation, 2004). For a treatment of the topic from a decidedly pro-libertarian perspective, see Damon Root, *Overruled: The Long War for Control of the U.S. Supreme Court* (New York: Palgrave Macmillan, 2014).

89. Nollan v. California Coastal Commission, 483 U.S. 825 (1987).

90. Rosenberger v. University of Virginia, 515 U.S. 819 (1995).

91. U.S. v. Morrison, 529 U.S. 598 (2000).

92. Zelman v. Simmons-Harris, 536 U.S. 639 (2002).

93. On these points see Southworth, *Lawyers of the Right*, 169–82.

94. Decker, *The Other Rights Revolution*, 227.

95. Brown, *Trumping Religion*, 141–45.

96. Decker, *The Other Rights Revolution*, 104.

97. O'Neill, *Originalism in American Law and Politics*, 203–4; Decker, *The Other Rights Revolution*, 2–3; Spitzer, *Saving the Constitution from Lawyers*, chapter 5.

Conclusion

1. "Redemption" and "restoration" are major themes in Kersch, *Conservatives and the Constitution*. Skowronek, "Afterword: An Attenuated Reconstruction," 348 (quote). See also Julian E. Zelizer, "Reflections," 371, 375–76, 379, 380, 388.

2. Peter Berkowitz, *Constitutional Conservatism: Liberty, Self-Government, and Political Moderation* (Stanford, CA: Hoover Institution Press, 2013), 114–15.

3. To cite a only a few of the most prominent and pointed recent efforts: Richard A. Epstein, *The Dubious Morality of Modern Administrative Law* (Lanham, MD: Rowman and Littlefield, 2020); Hamburger, *Is Administrative Law Unlawful?*; Murray, *By the People*; Marini, *Unmasking the Administrative State*. The most detailed history is Postell, *Bureaucracy in America*.

4. National Federation of Independent Business v. Sebelius, 567 US __ (2012); Whittington, "Taking What They Give Us," 519 (quote).

5. Jeffrey Crouch, Mark J. Rozell, and Mitchel A. Sollenberger, *The Unitary Executive Theory: A Danger to Constitutional Government* (Lawrence: University Press of Kansas, 2020); Saikrishna Bangalore Prakash, *The Living Presidency: An Originalist Argument against Its Ever-Expanding Powers* (Cambridge, MA: Belknap Press of Harvard University Press, 2020); Stephen F. Knott, *The Lost Soul of the American Presidency: The Decline into Demagoguery and the Prospects for Renewal* (Lawrence: University Press of Kansas, 2019).

6. Eric J. Segall, *Originalism as Faith* (New York: Cambridge University Press, 2018); Weiner, *Political Constitution*; Robert H. Bork, ed., *"A Country I Do Not Recognize": The Legal Assault on American Values* (Stanford, CA: Hoover Institution Press, 2005).

7. Peter Augustine Lawler and Richard M. Reinsch II, *A Constitution in Full: Recovering the Unwritten Foundation of American Liberty* (Lawrence: University Press of Kansas, 2019), 80, 95–98, 153–54; Frohnen and Carey, *Constitutional Morality*, 115–20, 129–82, 221–27, 233–34; Barnett, *Our Republican Constitution*, 81, 135–36, 247–58; Epstein, *How Progressives Rewrote the Constitution*; Charles R. Kesler, *Crisis of the Two Constitutions: The Rise, Decline, and Recovery of American Greatness* (New York: Encounter, 2021).

8. Stephen M. Griffin, *Broken Trust: Dysfunctional Government and Constitutional Reform* (Lawrence: University Press of Kansas, 2015); Louis Michael Seidman, *On Constitutional Disobedience* (New York: Oxford University Press, 2012); Sanford V. Levinson, *Our Undemocratic Constitution* (New York: Oxford University Press, 2006).

9. James MacGregor Burns, *The Deadlock of Democracy: Four-Party Politics in America* (Englewood Cliffs, NJ: Prentice Hall, 1963); Thomas E. Mann and Norman J. Ornstein, *The Broken Branch: How Congress Is Failing America and How to Get It Back on Track* (New York: Oxford University Press, 2006); Lowi, *End of Liberalism*, 297–303; Theodore J. Lowi, "Two Roads to Serfdom: Liberalism, Conservatism, and Administrative Power," *American University Law Review* 36 (1987): 295–322, 299 (defining "legiscide"); Morris P. Fiorina, *Congress: Keystone of the Washington Establishment*, 2nd ed. (New Haven, CT: Yale University Press, 1989); Louis Fisher, *Congressional Abdication on War and Spending* (College Station: Texas A&M University Press, 2000); Jasmine Farrier, *Constitutional Dysfunction on Trial: Congressional Lawsuits and the Separation of Powers* (Ithaca, NY: Cornell University Press, 2019); David Schoenbrod, *DC Confidential: Inside the Five Tricks of Washington* (New York: Encounter, 2017); James L. Buckley, *Saving Congress from Itself: Emancipating the States and Empowering Their People* (New York: Encounter, 2014).

10. David R. Mayhew, *The Imprint of Congress* (New Haven, CT: Yale University Press, 2017), 3 (quote), passim.

11. Burnham, *Congress and the American Tradition*, 93–100, 75–81.

12. Burnham, 327–32, 264–66.

13. Burnham, 352, 338.

14. Burnham, 123 (emphasis in orig.).

15. Kendall and Carey, *Liberalism versus Conservatism*, 133.

16. Kendall, *Willmoore Kendall Contra Mundum*, 500–501 (emphasis in orig.).

17. Kendall, 417.

18. Paul Edward Gottfried, "Making Sense of Majoritarianism," in *Defending the Republic*, 3–15; Carey, "Willmoore Kendall and the Doctrine of Majority Rule," 17–46.

19. George W. Carey, "Natural Rights, Equality, and the Declaration of Independence," *Ave Maria Law Review* 3 (2005): 45–68, 65, 67. See also Carey, *Student's Guide to American Political Thought*, 57, 63.

20. Carey, *Student's Guide to American Political Thought*, 77, 78.

21. Carey, *The Federalist*, 30–44; George W. Carey, "Majority Rule Revisited," *Modern Age* 16 (1972): 226–36.

22. Carey, "Irony of Conservative Success," 41 (quote), 144n21.

23. Hart, *Making of the American Conservative Mind*, 104, 109, 312, 315, 371.

24. Buckley, "And Now Legislative Supremacy," quotes at 631.

25. Buckley, "Agenda for the Nineties," 39.

26. Edwards, "Of Conservatives and Kings". As noted in chapter 6, Edwards was a noted conservative who had been a Republican member of Congress from Oklahoma, a founding trustee of the Heritage Foundation, and national chair of the American Conservative Union.

27. Francis, "Imperial Conservatives?" reprinted in Samuel Francis, *Beautiful Losers*, 174 (quote).

28. Francis, *Beautiful Losers*, 87. Francis also had earlier written a book on Burnham: *Thinkers of Our Time* (1984).

29. Francis, "Caesar's Column," 23. On Francis's turn to racism and anticonstitutionalism, see O'Neill, "Traditionalist Conservatism and the Administrative State," 417–23.

30. Frohnen and Carey, *Constitutional Morality*, 187 (quote), 178, 187–99.

31. Frohnen and Carey, 224, 236–37.

32. Lawler and Reinsch, *Constitution in Full*, 72–79, 151–52.

33. Hayek, *Constitution of Liberty*, 178–82, 192, 103–17. See also Hayek, *Law, Legislation, and Liberty*, 3:1–19, 20–31, 98–101.

34. Hayek, *Law, Legislation, and Liberty*, 3:99.

35. Hayek, *Law, Legislation, and Liberty*, 3:31. The internal quotation is from the eighteenth-century libertarian classic *Cato's Letters*.

36. Hayek, *Law, Legislation, and Liberty*, 3:21–22.

37. Hayek, *Law, Legislation, and Liberty*, 3:105 (italics omitted).

38. For critical historical and theoretical treatments, see S. M. Amadae, *Prisoners of Reason: Game Theory and Neoliberal Political Economy* (New York: Cambridge University Press, 2016); S. M. Amadae, *Rationalizing Capitalist Democracy: The Cold War Origins of Rational Choice Liberalism* (Chicago: University of Chicago Press, 2003); Donald P. Green and Ian Shapiro, *Pathologies of Rational Choice Theory: A Critique of Applications in Political Science* (New Haven, CT: Yale University Press, 1994); and Daniel A. Farber and Philip P. Frickey, *Law and Public Choice: A Critical Introduction* (Chicago: University of Chicago Press, 1991). See also Rodgers, *Age of Fracture*, 86–88.

39. Buchanan and Tullock, *Calculus of Consent*; James M. Buchanan, *Constitutional Economics* (Oxford: Basil Blackwell, 1991), 35–36. See also Amadae, *Rationalizing Capitalist Democracy*, 140, 142, 143, 145; Georg Vanberg, "Constitutional Political Economy, Democratic Theory, and Institutional Design," *Public Choice* 177 (2018): 199–216; James M. Buchanan, *The Limits of Liberty: Between Anarchy and Leviathan* (Chicago: University of Chicago Press, 1975), 151.

40. Glenn R. Parker, *Congress and the Rent-Seeking Society* (Ann Arbor: University of Michigan Press, 1996); Randall G. Holcombe, *An Economic Analysis of Democracy* (Carbondale: Southern Illinois University Press, 1985), 222 (quote). Two leading scholars delineated similar claims and likewise concluded that this kind of analysis "yields a series of disturbing propositions for democratic theory" and majority rule. William H. Riker and Barry R. Weingast, "Constitutional Regulation of Legislative Choice: The Political Consequences of Judicial Deference to Legislatures," *Virginia Law Review* 74 (1988): 373–401, quote at 374.

41. Buchanan and Tullock, *Calculus of Consent*, 25, 290.

42. Buchanan, *Constitutional Economics*, 41. For the public choice view of US history interpreted as a decline into Leviathan-democratic statism, see Randall G. Holcombe, *From Liberty to Democracy: The Transformation of American Government* (Ann Arbor: University of Michigan Press, 2002).

43. Buchanan, *Limits of Liberty*, 169, 179.

44. James M. Buchanan, "The Domain of Constitutional Economics," *Constitutional Political Economy* 1 (1990): 1–18, quote at 15.

45. Buchanan typically collapsed any distinction between rules and constitutionalism and wrote often of "generalized agreement on constitutional rules" (Buchanan, "Domain of Constitutional Economics," 9) and "the theory of rules, or of constitutions" (Buchanan, *Constitutional Economics*, 41).

46. Siegan, *Economic Liberties*, 265–82, 321.

47. Siegan, 266–67.

48. Siegan, 277 (all quotes).

49. Barnett, *Our Republican Constitution*, 52 (quote); Barnett, "Is the Constitution Libertarian?" 32 (quote); Barnett, *Restoring the Lost Constitution*, 354–57.

50. Barnett, *Restoring the Lost Constitution*, 11–52; Barnett, *Our Republican Constitution*, 20–26, 73–78.

51. Barnett, *Restoring the Lost Constitution*, 260, 261 (quotes).

52. For similar observations, see Weiner, *Political Constitution*, 99–115, 125–30. See also Steven Kelman, "'Public Choice' and Public Spirit," *Public Interest* 87 (Spring 1987): 80–94; and Farber and Frickey, *Law and Public Choice*, 42–47. Such criticism need not claim that libertarian public choice theorists were part of a "radical right" conspiracy to displace American constitutionalism, as Nancy MacLean would have it in *Democracy in Chains: The Deep History of the Radical Right's Stealth Plan for America* (New York: Viking, 2017). See the rejoinder by Michael C. Munger, "On the Origins and Goals of Public Choice: Constitutional Conspiracy?" *Independent Review* 22 (2018): 359–82.

53. See, generally, John A. Murley, "Congress and Straussian Constitutionalism," in Deutsch and Murley, *Leo Strauss, the Straussians, and the American Regime*, 331–50. Some figures treated in this section might best be described as Strauss-adjacent or Strauss-influenced, based on their intellectual lineage and general approach, as opposed to "Straussian," but for ease of expression I have not made mutatis mutandis adjustments in every instance.

54. Diamond, "Democracy and the Federalist," 60; Martin Diamond, "The Declaration and the Constitution: Liberty, Democracy, and the Founders" (1975), in *As Far as Republican Principles Will Admit*, 236. See also Zuckert, "Refinding the Founding," 242.

55. Edward J. Erler and Ken Masugi, *The Rediscovery of America: Essays by Harry V. Jaffa on the New Birth of Politics* (Lanham, MD: Rowman and Littlefield, 2019), 125–27, quote at 126; Harry V. Jaffa, "Calhoun versus Madison: The Transformation of the Thought of the Founding: A Bicentennial Celebration," paper presented at symposium "James Madison: Philosopher and Practitioner of Liberal Democracy," Library of Congress, March 16, 2001, www.loc.gov/loc/madison/jaffa-paper.html (quote). See also Kesler, "A New Birth of Freedom," 277; Murley, "Congress and Straussian Constitutionalism," 334; Zuckert, "Refinding the Founding," 249n17.

56. William F. Connelly Jr., *James Madison Rules America: The Constitutional Origins of Congressional Partisanship* (Lanham, MD: Rowman and Littlefield, 2010), 271 (quote), 37–47, 249–52, 254; William F. Connelly Jr., "Congress: Representation and Deliberation," in *The American Experiment: Essays on the Theory and Practice of Liberty*, ed. Peter Augustine Lawler and Robert Martin Schaefer (Lanham, MD: Rowman and Littlefield, 1994), 185–87. See also Murley, "Congress and Straussian Constitutionalism," 340.

57. Pangle, *Leo Strauss*, 118.

58. Joseph M. Bessette, *The Mild Voice of Reason: Deliberative Democracy and American National Government* (Chicago: University of Chicago Press, 1994), passim, quote at 5. The theme of deliberation is also treated with detail and insight in Connelly, *James Madison Rules America*, esp. 118, 158, 171–83. See also Murley, "Congress and Straussian Constitutionalism," 339–44.

59. Bessette, *Mild Voice of Reason*, 46, 36; Connelly, "Congress," 176; L. Peter Schultz, "Congress and the Separation of Powers Today: Practice in Search of a Theory," in *Separa-

tion of Powers and Good Government, ed. Bradford P. Wilson and Peter W. Schramm (Lanham, MD: Rowman and Littlefield, 1994), 187–89, 198; Connelly, *James Madison Rules America*, 16, 17.

60. Bessette, *Mild Voice of Reason*, 246.

61. Murley, "Congress and Straussian Constitutionalism," 340, 345 (quote).

62. Michael J. Malbin, *Unelected Representatives: Congressional Staff and the Future of Representative Government* (New York: Basic Books, 1980).

63. Jones and Marini, *Imperial Congress*; William F. Connelly Jr., John J. Pitney Jr., and Gary J. Schmitt, eds., *Is Congress Broken? The Virtues and Defects of Partisanship and Gridlock* (Washington, DC: Brookings Institution, 2017).

64. Gary J. Schmitt and Rebecca Burgess, "The Other End of Pennsylvania Avenue," in Connelly, Pitney, and Schmitt, *Is Congress Broken?* 129–50; Melanie M. Marlowe, "Reclaiming Institutional Relevance through Congressional Oversight," ibid., 107–27.

65. William F. Connelly Jr., John J. Pitney Jr., and Gary J. Schmitt, "Introduction," in Connelly, Pitney, and Schmitt, *Is Congress Broken?* 3; William F. Connelly Jr. and John J. Pitney Jr., "A Return to Madisonian Republicanism: Strengthening the Nation's Most Representative Institution," ibid., 229.